Routledge Revivals

Henry Stanford's Anthology

Henry Stanford's Anthology
An edition of Cambridge University Library Manuscript Dd. 5.75

Steven W. May

First published in 1988 by Garland Publishing, Inc.

This edition first published in 2019 by Routledge
2 Park Square, Milton Park, Abingdon, Oxon, OX14 4RN
and by Routledge
52 Vanderbilt Avenue, New York, NY 10017, USA

Routledge is an imprint of the Taylor & Francis Group, an informa business

© 1988 by Steven W. May

All rights reserved. No part of this book may be reprinted or reproduced or utilised in any form or by any electronic, mechanical, or other means, now known or hereafter invented, including photocopying and recording, or in any information storage or retrieval system, without permission in writing from the publishers.

Publisher's Note
The publisher has gone to great lengths to ensure the quality of this reprint but points out that some imperfections in the original copies may be apparent.

Disclaimer
The publisher has made every effort to trace copyright holders and welcomes correspondence from those they have been unable to contact.
A Library of Congress record exists under ISBN:

ISBN 13: 978-0-367-19890-9 (hbk)
ISBN 13: 978-0-367-19892-3 (pbk)
ISBN 13: 978-0-429-24392-9 (ebk)

GARLAND PUBLICATIONS IN AMERICAN AND ENGLISH LITERATURE

Editor
Stephen Orgel
Stanford University

GARLAND PUBLISHING, INC.

Henry Stanford's Anthology

An Edition of Cambridge
University Library Manuscript Dd. 5.75

Steven W. May

GARLAND PUBLISHING, INC.
NEW YORK & LONDON 1988

Copyright © 1988
Steven W. May
All Rights Reserved

Library of Congress Cataloging-in-Publication Data

May, Steven W.
Henry Stanford's anthology : an edition of Cambridge University Library manuscript Dd. 5.75 / Steven W. May.
p. cm.—(Garland publications in American and English literature)
Thesis (Ph. D.)—University of Chicago, 1968.
Bibliography: p.
ISBN 0-8240-6395-3
1. English literature—Early modern, 1500-1700.
2. Stanford, Henry—Manuscripts. 3. Manuscripts, English. I. Title. II. Series.
PR1125.M39   1988
820'.8'003—dc19   88-21422

Printed on acid-free, 250-year-life paper
Manufactured in the United States of America

TABLE OF CONTENTS

Volume I

	Page
ABBREVIATIONS	iii
INTRODUCTION	iv

    The Private World of Manuscript Literature
    The Compiler of Dd.5.75
    Stanford's Scribal Habits
        Accuracy
        Calligraphy and Accidentals
    Physical State of the Manuscript
        Provenance and Description
        Dates of Compilation
    Earlier Notices of the Manuscript
    Similar Manuscript Anthologies
    An Evaluation of Stanford's Anthology
        Authorship
        Dating
        Textual Improvement
        The Contribution of New Texts
        Conclusion
    Textual Apparatus

THE TEXT OF CAMBRIDGE MS Dd.5.75	1

Volume II

	Page
SIGLA	220
ABBREVIATED APPARATUS	224
NOTES	230
APPENDIXES	
I. INDEX OF FIRST LINES	382
II. INDEX OF AUTHORS	396
BIBLIOGRAPHY	398

ABBREVIATIONS

Frequently cited works in the Introduction and Notes are referred to with the following abbreviations:

Arber	Edward Arber, ed., *A Transcript of the Registers of the Company of Stationers of London* (5 vols.; London, 1875-1894).
CSPD	*Calendars of State Papers, Domestic Series* (various years and editors).
Fellowes	Edmund H. Fellowes, *English Madrigal Verse*, revised and enlarged by Frederick W. Sternfeld and David Greer (3rd ed.; Oxford, 1967).
Hebel and Hudson	J. William Hebel and Hoyt H. Hudson, eds., *Poetry of the English Renaissance* (New York, 1929).
Ringler	William A. Ringler, Jr., ed., *The Poems of Sir Philip Sidney* (Oxford, 1962).
Sandison	Helen Estabrook Sandison, ed., *The Poems of Sir Arthur Gorges* (Oxford, 1953).
STC	A. W. Pollard, *et al.*, *A Short-Title Catalogue of Books Printed in England, Scotland, and Ireland* (London, 1926).

INTRODUCTION

The Private World of Manuscript Literature

When Edward Bannister added a leaf to his personal manuscript collection of poetry, he recorded on its verso the circumstances of acquisition: "A Dyttye mad by S^r phillip sydnye gevene me Att pvttenye In svrrye Decembris x^o Ann^o 1584."[1] Similarly, Sir Stephen Powle, the compiler of Tanner MS 169, copies verses he had received from Sir Francis Davison in 1609, and from Nicholas Breton in 1617 (ff. 76^v, 173^v). And a copy of a poem in Chetham MS 8012 is entitled ". . . put into my Lad: Laitons pocket by S^r W: Rawleigh."[2] Such transactions were frequent throughout the sixteenth and seventeenth centuries, for despite the availability of printed books, an enormous amount of poetry and prose circulated from hand to hand in manuscript. In Tudor and Stuart times, members of the Inns of Court and the clergy, university students, courtiers, landed gentry, London merchants, in short, any gentleman with literary interests customarily kept a manuscript collection of works which appealed to him.

The varied contents of these anthologies might now and then include a transcript from a printed book, but they were usually derived from manuscript sources. Indeed, many connoisseurs among these anthologists would have nothing to do with printed works, an attitude which caused Michael Drayton to complain in the preface to his _Poly-Olbion_ that "In Publishing this Essay of my Poeme, there is this great disadvantage against me; that

---

[1] Ringler, p. 555; quoted from Additional MS 28253, f. 3.

[2] Agnes M. C. Latham, ed., _The Poems of Sir Walter Ralegh_, The Muses Library (London, 1951), p. 96.

it commeth out at this time, when Verses are wholly deduc't to Chambers, and nothing esteem'd in this lunatique Age, but what is kept in Cabinets, and must only passe by Transcription."[1] This attitude toward print was the collector's counterpart of a pose adopted by the well-bred Elizabethan poet, particularly the courtier, who did not seek or even permit publication of his verses, following instead Castiglione's advice: "let him take care to keep them under cover . . . and let him show them only to a friend who can be trusted."[2] As a result, contemporary print yields little or no verse by such widely recognized "courtly makers" of their day as Sir Edward Dyer, Sir Walter Ralegh, Edward deVere, Seventeenth Earl of Oxford, or Sir Arthur Gorges; nearly all their surviving works are preserved only in manuscript.

A certain amount of this private literature did nevertheless enter print, in the Tudor poetic anthologies and songbooks. The Paradise of Dainty Devices (first edition, 1576), for example, was based upon the private anthology of Richard Edwards, a former Master of the Children of the Chapel Royal. The "R. S." who superintended publication of The Phoenix Nest (1593), probably had access to a good collection of courtly verse, while the Englands Helicon and Poetical Rhapsody miscellanies were also largely derived from manuscript sources. The majority of such manuscripts, however, were private, and by tradition alienated from the vulgarity of print. Thus, printers did not usually gain access to the best collections of manuscript verse and they were seldom in a position to know who wrote a given poem. The great undercurrent of private manuscript literature emerges only partially and imperfectly in the printed anthologies.

---

[1] J. William Hebel, ed., Poly-Olbion, from the edition of 1613 (corrected edition; London, 1961), sig. *v.

[2] Baldesar Castiglione, The Book of the Courtier, trans. Charles S. Singleton, Anchor Books (New York, 1959), p. 70.

The study of these manuscripts is not justified, however, merely by their role as storehouses of courtly poetry which never reached print, for the whole range of private and elite literature is to be found in these anthologies, with courtly verse representing a prized but rather minor part of many collections. A Tudor gentleman's private manuscript might also contain censored religious and political satires, unprintable verse slanders of well known public figures, scripts of plays from the universities or Inns of Court, and specimens of the compiler's own poetry and correspondence. Along with lyric poetry, hand copies of poetic epitaphs, riddles, moral maxims, panegyrics and epigrams circulated widely. Prose speeches, by the Queen, members of Parliament, or such condemned favorites as Essex and Ralegh were very popular, as were sermons, decent and indecent jokes, and narrative accounts of almost any public ceremony: processions, burials and executions were among the most common. This enormous volume of privately transcribed works remains largely unstudied in the extant manuscripts, yet it represents a vast literary substratum with much to add to the corpus of Renaissance English literature, and much to reveal about the tastes and thinking of the age.

Just such a manuscript is Cambridge University Library MS Dd.5.75, an anthology of sixty-three folios begun no later than 1582 and completed by 1616.[1] Its more than 300 items in verse and prose, numbered consecutively in the following transcription, are entered in two major divisions of the manuscript: the first twenty folios constitute a "domestic" collection devoted to works by the compiler, his pupils, and members of the household he served. The remainder, a "public" section, contains works mainly from outside sources, from printed books as well as from manuscript copies of courtly verse.

---

[1] For the sake of clarity, all dates in the Introduction are given their New Style equivalents.

The substantive texts of Sidney, Gorges, Ralegh and Queen Elizabeth herself in this "public" section have been examined by modern editors, while those of Dyer, Breton, Spenser, and other anonymous poets, have not. Among its unique texts are a <u>blazon</u> in anapestic tetrameter and a lover's complaint in dactylic tetrameter, along with verses in the poulter's measure and fourteeners typical of the mid-century poets, balanced against satires of these metrical and rhetorical devices. The compiler added a prologue spoken "by ye players to ye Q." in 1599, and one of the three known poems of Ferdinando Stanley, Fifth Earl of Derby. The occasional and historical entries include a poem on the condemned traitor, William Parry (executed 2 March 1585), the Queen's speech to Parliament in 1576, a slander of Mary, Queen of Scots (in Latin Skeltonics), a copy of "Mar Mar-Martin," one of the last of the Marprelate tracts, and a libel against Edward Bashe, Elizabeth's Victualler of the Navy. Interspersed with these items are riddles translated from Straparola, a laudatory epitaph for the distinguished musician Thomas Tallis, a libelous epitaph against the Earl of Leicester, numerous epigrams and adages, a poem by Desportes, and superior texts of several already admired lyrics from Tudor songbooks. Dd.5.75 is both a representative manuscript collection and one with importantly unique characteristics and works. It deserves scholarly attention for the value of its substantive texts, for the heretofore unknown poetry it contains, and for its contribution to our understanding of Elizabethan tastes and attitudes.

The Compiler of Dd.5.75

The compiler of Dd.5.75 reveals his identity only in the "domestic" section of his anthology, which is mainly devoted to the juvenile works of William, later Fourth Baron, Paget (ff. 1-13), with a few verses written for "Robin Carey" on f. 14, and the poems of young George Berkeley on ff. 17-20.

From such content it seems reasonable to conclude that the most likely person to have saved these poems would be a tutor, one who had instructed these three unrelated youngsters in versification.

The only name in the manuscript which might reasonably be associated with such a person is the "H. Stanford" signed to Items 92 and 93, and abbreviated to "h. st." in Items 66, 84, and 85. Item 85, indeed, was printed among the commendatory verses in the 1637 edition of Philemon Holland's translation of Camden's Britannia (STC 4510), where it is subscribed, "Henry Stanford, M.A." A Henry Stanford received his M.A. from Trinity College, Oxford, 14 May 1575, and in 1586, officials of Elizabeth's government examined a "Henry Staunford," fourth son of Sir William Staunford, and tutor to the Lord Paget's son.[1] The Paget household tutor would have had a means of access to the Careys' service when young William Paget became the ward of George Carey in February, 1587, and this connection would explain Stanford's later acquaintance with both Carey's grandson, George Berkeley, and with Philemon Holland (see the notes to Item 85). Finally, in 1616, about three years after the last dated entry in Dd.5.75, a Henry Stanford was buried in St. Anne's Church, Blackfriars, an edifice adjacent to the Careys' principal lodging in London.[2] I think there is little reason to doubt that these are all notices of one man, Henry Stanford, who tutored William Paget, "Robin" Carey, and George Berkeley, transcribing their juvenilia along with at least five poems of his own into Dd.5.75, his personal manuscript anthology.[3]

---

[1] Joseph Foster, Alumni Oxoniensis, IV (London, 1892), 1407; CSPD, 1581-1590, ed. by Robert Lemon (London, 1865), CXCIII, 350, Articles 6-8.

[2] E. Stokes, ed., Index of Wills Proved in the Prerogative Court of Canterbury (The Index Library, Vol. V; London, 1912), p. 423. Stanford's will, 111 Cope, is preserved at Somerset House.

[3] I have not found a specimen of Stanford's handwriting to compare with that of Dd.5.75, and, presumably, an admirer of Stanford's or member

The Stanford (or Stamford), family had attained some prominence before Elizabeth's accession due to the talented efforts of Henry's father, Sir William Stanford (1509-1558). Educated at Oxford and Grey's Inn, Sir William was called to the bar in 1536, and elected to Parliament in 1541 and 1544. For his services to the crown during the reign of Edward VI he received the Degree of the Coif 19 May 1552, and retained his position as Serjeant of the Law under Queen Mary.[1] Stanford's Roman Catholicism and loyalty to the crown did not go unappreciated during Mary's reign. In February, 1554, she honored him by arranging for Princess Elizabeth to stop overnight at Stanford's home at Hadley, Middlesex, on her way to London for the execution of Lady Jane Grey;[2] and in 1555, Stanford was knighted personally by King Philip.

By his wife, Alice, daughter of John Palmer of Kentish Town, Middlesex, Sir William had a total of six sons and as many daughters--Henry, born with a twin sister, Margaret, was their fourth son. The year of Henry's birth can be approximated by reckoning backward from 23 October 1570, the date of his B.A. from Oxford.[3] Presumably, he matriculated in 1566 or 1567 at age fifteen or sixteen, and thus was born about 1550 or 1551. I have found no record of his occupation or whereabouts between 1575 and 1581, but by 1582 he had undoubtedly entered the Pagets' service and begun his manuscript anthology, into which he copied ten-year-old William Paget's poetic New Year's gifts for that year.

---

of his family could have compiled the manuscript. I have found no evidence, however, that Stanford, who died childless, had ever married, and it seems more logical that the tutor himself would have collected his own verse and that of his pupils.

[1] Edward Foss, Biographia Iuridica, A Biographical Dictionary of the Judges of England (Boston, 1870), p. 630.

[2] Frederick Charles Cass, "Notes on the Church and Parish of Monken Hadley," Transactions of the London and Middlesex Archaeological Society, IV (London, 1875), 273.

[3] Foster, IV, 1407.

The Paget household at this time apparently centered around Ann Preston Paget, William's grandmother, and widow of the first Lord Paget. As household tutor, Stanford no doubt spent most of his time either at Paget House in Fleet Street, London, or at West Drayton, Lady Ann's Middlesex residence. William's father, Thomas, Third Baron Paget, was as devout a recusant as the other members of his family, and constantly involved in pro-Catholic agitation in England, while his younger brother, Charles, had sought refuge on the continent as early as 1572 for his secret intrigues against Elizabeth's government.[1] Judging from the contents of Dd.5.75, Stanford did not come to the Pagets' attention for his Catholic or conspiratorial sympathies, but may have obtained his position with them through social or even family connections. The Stanford family was sufficiently prominent to mingle on at least the fringes of the Paget circle, and members of both families had no doubt encountered each other frequently at court and in London society. Moreover, Henry Stanford and William Paget shared a mutual uncle in Jerome Palmer, of Kentish Town, Middlesex, for Palmer had married William's aunt, Eleanor Paget, while his sister, Alice, was Henry's mother. Henry might well have been acquainted with the Pagets even before he went to Oxford, and afterward, would have been entirely eligible in social rank and education for the position of household tutor.

Unfortunately for Stanford, he began his service with the Pagets just as that family's fortunes were beginning a disastrous decline. In the spring of 1582, Thomas Paget arranged a separation from his wife, Nazareth, who died in April of the following year. With revelation of the Throckmorton Plot in November, 1583, Thomas, fearing a charge of complicity, fled in

---

[1] Joseph Gillow, A Literary and Biographical History . . . of the English Catholics (5 vols.; London, n.d.), V, 231.

secret to the continent where he joined his brother, Charles. As a result, the authorities began a lengthy investigation of the Pagets, all their relatives, and many of their servants--even the household tutor had been examined by September, 1586. The government concluded its investigation by attainting Thomas of treason in 1587, making his title and all his property forfeit to the crown. As a final blow, William's grandmother, the last firm support of the Paget family, died in early February, 1587, at which the Privy Council ordered the executors "of the late Lo. Paget" to deliver young William into the custody of George Carey "for the better maintenance and educacion of the said William Pagett."[1]

Stanford, who recorded young Paget's New Year's poetry each year from 1582-1587, had certainly remained with the family until its virtual dissolution upon Lady Paget's death. His exact whereabouts during the next few years is obscured by a nine year gap in the dated entries of his anthology, but I think it almost a certainty that the Carey establishment absorbed both William Paget and his tutor early in 1587.

The entries in Dd.5.75 immediately following Paget's works for 1587 are a series of poems written for "Robin Carey," son of Sir Edmund Carey, the brother of George Carey, second Lord Hunsdon. Furthermore, Item 167, which Stanford transcribed in 1588 or 1589 is given the partially illegible title: "Del. by master h. . . . to my lo Cham . . . be del. . . . to . . . maiestie." Apparently, Stanford was in rather familiar contact at this time with Henry Carey, first Lord Hunsdon, who held the post of Lord Chamberlain from 1585 until his death, 23 July 1596.[2] It is even likely, I think, that "master h."

---

[1] John Roche Dasent, ed., Acts of the Privy Council of England, New Series, XIV (London, 1897), 351-352.

[2] E. K. Chambers, The Elizabethan Stage, II (Oxford, 1923), 40.

is Stanford himself (a few letters after the 'h' are illegible), who felt that one of his own poems might be to the Queen's liking, and asked his employer, the Lord Chamberlain, to pass it along to her.

All three members of the family with whom Stanford was associated by the late 1580's, Sir Edmund, George Carey, and their father, the first Lord Hunsdon,[1] were military men, often away from home in the Queen's service. Sir Edmund's band of horse saw action in the Low Countries during the mid-1580's, while both George Carey and his father were largely responsible for defense of the borders.[2] Perhaps Stanford occasionally travelled with Henry Carey to Berwick, or with George Carey and his family to the Isle of Wight, where they were renowned for their generous hospitality.[3] By no later than New Year's, 1596, however, Stanford seems to have been serving in George Carey's household

---

[1] For the sake of convenience, I will refer to the first Lord Hunsdon as, simply, Henry Carey, his son, the second Lord Hunsdon, as George Carey, George Carey's wife as Elizabeth Spencer Carey, and their daughter as Elizabeth Carey Berkeley. Their relationships and connection with the Berkeleys is indicated by the genealogical chart below:

```
Henry Carey, first Baron
   Hunsdon (d. 1596)
   |
George Carey, second Baron ⊤ Elizabeth Spencer
   Hunsdon (d. 1603)       |
                   Elizabeth Carey ⊤ (1596) Thomas Berkeley
                   ┌───────────────┴───────────────┐
              George Berkeley              Theophila Berkeley
```

[2] For Sir Edmund's military activities, see The Calendar of the Manuscripts of the Most Hon. The Marquis of Salisbury, K. G., Preserved at Hatfield House, Hertfordshire (Publications of the Historical Manuscripts Commission, Part III; London, 1889), Items 606, 963, pp. 293, 458; and Dasent, XIV, 55-56. Henry Carey was Governor of Berwick and Warden of the East Marches, while Sir George served as Captain of the Isle of Wight.

[3] Ernest Albert Strathmann, "Lady Carey and Spenser," English Literary History, II (April, 1935), 33-56.

alone, for the New Year's poems he sent to members of the Carey family, beginning in that year, are addressed only to Lady Elizabeth Spencer Carey to her daughter, Elizabeth or to her grandaughter, Theophila Berkeley.

When he entered the Carey establishment, Stanford found himself in one of the richest and most powerful households in England. Their London headquarters centered in the fashionable Blackfriars conventual buildings, where Henry and George Carey had held leases from at least 1585.[1] Both father and son were long-standing members of the Privy Council and, respectively, first cousin and first cousin once removed to Queen Elizabeth. Indeed, the Queen no doubt accepted the Careys' hospitality on occasion, for John Chamberlain, writing of an impending marriage at Blackfriars in 1600, supposed rather matter-of-factly that "the Quene will vouchsafe her presence, and lie at the Lord Chamberlains or the Lord Cobhams."[2] When Henry Carey died in 1596, George Carey became the second Lord Hunsdon and continued his influential role in the government until his death, 9 November 1603. For Stanford, life in the prosperous Carey establishment must have been a far cry from the reclusive atmosphere and declining fortunes of the Paget household.

Between Stanford's New Year's gift of 1598 (Item 61), and that of 1610 (Item 66), there is a twelve year gap in the manuscript's dated entries, representing also a gap in our knowledge of his affairs during this time. I cannot point to definite entries in the professional section of Dd.5.75 after about 1602, and it is possible that Stanford spent some of this time as rector of Hansworth, a village in the neighborhood of Perry Hall, Staffordshire, the residence of his eldest brother, Robert Stanford. The only evidence for this,

---

[1] Albert Feuillerat, ed., Blackfriars Records, Part I (The Malone Society Collections, Vol. II; Oxford, 1913), pp. 123-124.

[2] Sarah Williams, ed., Letters Written by John Chamberlain During the Reign of Elizabeth (Camden Society Publications, Vol. XIX; London, 1861), pp. 146-147.

however, is the mention of a Henry Stanford there in 1604.[1] In 1610, Stanford was unquestionably in London addressing New Year's poetry to Elizabeth Spencer Carey (Item 66), and between 1611 and 1613 he instructed her grandson, George Berkeley (b. 1601), in the composition of similar verse New Year's gifts.

Stanford may have become a retainer of the Berkeleys when Elizabeth Carey Berkeley married Sir Thomas Berkeley, 19 February 1596, though far more likely, I believe, that he continued with her mother, perhaps as a secretary or in some such capacity, for between 1598 and 1613, Stanford records no poetic New Year's gifts of his own for young Elizabeth, while her mother receives three during this period. Thomas Berkeley, furthermore, was not inclined toward scholarly pursuits, and Elizabeth Carey Berkeley alone educated their daughter, Theophila.[2] John Smyth of Nibley, the Berkeleys' family retainer and biographer, mentions Dr. Philemon Holland and Henry Ashwood as George Berkeley's tutors, but makes no reference to Stanford in any capacity. Probably, young George came under Stanford's tutelage at those times when his family stayed with Elizabeth Spencer Carey at Blackfriars. They were certainly there during 1602-1603, and their visits no doubt became more frequent after 16 December 1609, when Sir Thomas' financial situation became ruinous and he signed a pact with Smyth agreeing to limit the size of his household and his expenses.[3] It is perhaps significant then, that the poems Stanford helped young George to write are all dated 1611 or after, and I suspect that the Berkeleys spent at least their Christmas holidays of 1611 through 1613 with Elizabeth Carey Berkeley's mother.

---

[1] Foster, II, 1407.

[2] John Smyth, *The Berkeley Manuscripts*, ed. Sir John Maclean (3 vols.; Gloucester, 1883), II, 400.

[3] *Ibid.*, p. 398.

I have found no evidence that Stanford ever married, and his family pedigree states that he died without issue.[1] He no doubt remained with the Careys at their Blackfriars residence until his death in 1616, for he was buried in St. Anne's Church of that ward.

It is clear from even this fragmented sketch of his life that Stanford was in touch with a number of sources which might have provided him with the materials he copied into Dd.5.75. Throughout his life, he may have been in close contact with his twin sister, Margaret, potentially a very likely source of courtly poetry, although Stanford does not mention a single member of his own family in his anthology. Margaret married Richard Astley, younger brother of John Astley, Master of Queen Elizabeth's Jewel House. Richard's post as a Gentleman of the Privy Chamber placed him in something of a confidential relationship with the Queen, and he and his wife would have had no difficulty acquiring manuscript poetry in circulation at court.

During his years with the Pagets, when Stanford apparently copied the poetry on ff. 25-29 of the "public" section of his anthology, his most important source may have been Sir Henry Lee, William Paget's uncle. Lee was a favored courtier and the Queen's personal champion at the yearly tilt held in honor of her accession. His own literary interests are evidenced by the pageants he arranged for the Queen's entertainment in 1572 and 1592.[2] Lee's wife, Lady Ann, spent at least part of her time during the early 1580's with her mother, Ann Paget, and Ann Lee's two epitaphs in Dd.5.75 (Items 18 and 19), suggest that Stanford was in touch with this side of the Paget family. If so, she or her husband may have supplied him with some of the works on ff. 25-29.

---

[1] Sir George John Armytage, ed., *Middlesex Pedigrees* (Publications of the Harleian Society, Vol. LXV; London, 1914), pp. 68-69.

[2] E. K. Chambers, *Sir Henry Lee* (Oxford, 1936), p. 46.

Through either the Pagets or the Careys, Stanford may have been in contact with Catherine Knyvet Carey, Lady Paget, the widow of Henry, Second Baron Paget (d. 1568). Catherine's second husband was Sir Edward Carey, Henry Carey's first cousin, yet, as William Paget's aunt, she perhaps received some of his poetic New Year's gifts in the early 1580's. She regularly exchanged New Year's gifts of her own with Queen Elizabeth, and seems to have been well acquainted with affairs at court. She was also distantly related to Sir Philip Sidney, who wrote to her in 1584 for permission to take a buck in the Careys' Park at Marybone.[1] Lady Catherine relayed her husband's consent to the gift of a doe 13 October 1584; perhaps Sir Philip in turn passed along some of his poetry to this branch of the Carey family, from whence it may eventually have reached Stanford. This connection is entirely speculative, of course, in the absence of any proof that Catherine kept in touch with her Paget in-laws or with other members of the Carey family.

By the late 1580's, however, Stanford definitely had access to the very highest courtly circles through Henry Carey. Whether or not Stanford wrote Items 166 and 167, he had access to verse which Carey, the Lord Chamberlain, apparently agreed to deliver to the Queen.[2] Here was a channel of communication that could work both ways, of course, and Stanford could not have asked for a better means of acquiring courtly poetry, a means, furthermore, which was extended in the person of George Carey. Both father and son held the post of Lord Chamberlain, "incomparably the most important figure at court in all matters concerned with entertainment,"[3] while the Careys' well known

---

[1] *Calendar of Salisbury Manuscripts*, Part III (London, 1889), p. 70.

[2] If Elizabeth did see these poems, she apparently did not save them, for they are not preserved among the British Museum's Royal MSS.

[3] Chambers, *The Elizabethan Stage*, I, 36.

-xviii-

literary interests made these men the logical recipients of any good verse circulating at court. These contacts adequately explain how even the most elite and exclusively circulated lyrics could have found their way into the anthology of a household tutor, Henry Stanford.

When Stanford entered the Carey household, moreover, he found himself in the midst of an important center for the advancement of arts and letters, courtly and otherwise. In addition to the hospitality they offered their peers, the Careys also doled out patronage to a number of writers and musicians, as seventeen contemporary dedications to George Carey, and seven more to his wife, amply testify.[1] Thomas Churchyard, the dean of Elizabethan poets, dedicated his Churchyard's Challenge (STC 5220), of 1593 to Elizabeth Spencer Carey, and his 1596 Pleasant Discourse of Court and Wars (STC 5249), to her husband. William Warner, who may for a time have held a post in the Carey household,[2] offered the first edition of Albion's England to Henry Carey, and the last four books to his son in 1597 (STC 25082). The most important prose writer to benefit from this patronage was Thomas Nashe, who dedicated Christ's Tears over Jerusalem to Elizabeth Spencer Carey in 1593, and The Terrors of the Night to her daughter in the following year. Most important of all, Edmund Spenser claimed kinship with Elizabeth Spencer Carey and reserved for her an entire dedicatory sonnet in The Faerie Queene--the only other woman thus honored was Sidney's sister, Mary, Countess of Pembroke. Elizabeth Spencer Carey did not deny relationship with Spenser and apparently rewarded his efforts, for in dedicating to her the "Muiopotmos" in his 1590 Complaints volume, he acknowledged "your great bounty to my self."[3]

---

[1] Franklin B. Williams, Jr., Index of Dedications and Commendatory Verses in English Books Before 1641 (London, 1962), p. 32.

[2] Strathmann, p. 45.

[3] R. E. Neil Dodge, The Complete Poetical Works of Spenser (Cambridge, 1908), p. 115.

Among musicians, John Dowland and Thomas Morley seem to have been the greatest recipients of Carey patronage. Dowland's <u>First Booke of Songes or Ayres</u> (<u>STC</u> 7091), was dedicated to George Carey in 1597, while in the same year, Morley offered him his <u>Canzonets or Little Short Aers</u> (<u>STC</u> 18126), followed in 1600 by the dedication of his <u>First Book of Ayres</u>.[1] The only obvious connection between Morley, Dowland, and Stanford is the Carey household, a connection which must have some bearing on the appearance of several lyrics in Dd.5.75, in Morley's <u>First Book of Ayres</u>, in Dowland's <u>First Booke of Songes or Ayres</u>, and practically nowhere else.[2] Apparently, the Carey residence was something of a clearing house for music and poetry, with some lyrics finding their way into these songbooks as well as into Stanford's private collection. Generally, the Carey household, with its important connections at court and reputation for artistic patronage, was an ideal place for Stanford to garner manuscript verse for addition to his private anthology.

Support of the drama is another and more famous aspect of the Careys' overall patronage of the arts. Their sponsorship of a company of actors probably resulted from their ties with Ferdinando Stanley, husband of Elizabeth Spencer Carey's sister, Alice, and patron of "Lord Strange's Men." The two families seem to have kept in touch with each other, which no doubt accounts for Stanford's copy of Item 165, a poem by "Ferd. Strange," and it is always possible that Lord Strange, later Fifth Earl of Derby, supplied Stanford with other courtly verse for his anthology. Upon Stanley's death in 1594, Henry Carey undertook the patronage of his company, thereafter known as the Lord Chamberlain's men, and his son continued to sponsor the company after his

---

[1] Not listed by the <u>STC</u>; ed. by Edmund H. Fellowes, <u>The English School of Lutenist Song Writers</u>, Vol. XVI (London, 1927).

[2] Items 99 and 188 appear only in Morley and Dd.5.75; Item 209 occurs in Dowland, Dd.5.75 and one other manuscript, Dyce 44, f. 9^v.

father's death in 1596. Shakespeare was apparently associated with this troupe by 1596, and while Stanford may thus have had access to some of his poetry, I cannot point to any of his known works in Dd.5.75. The verses from the players to the Queen in 1599 (Item 228), could hardly be Shakespeare's, although Stanford no doubt did obtain this unique text through his contact with George Carey, the Lord Chamberlain in 1599, and it is possible that other unique lyrics in Dd.5.75, derived from this same source, were taken from now lost plays.

As the contents of Dd.5.75 reveal much about the major events in Stanford's life, so they are even more useful in delineating his tastes, beliefs, and character. His Oxford M.A. posits a thorough grounding in Latin and in such standard university subjects of the day as rhetoric, logic and dialectic, theology and perhaps some Greek, but we must turn again to his private manuscript for a more complete view of Henry Stanford.

Many of the occasional and topical pieces in Dd.5.75 do not lend themselves to biographical interpretation because it is impossible to know whether the work reveals Stanford's opinion on a given subject or reflects only his literary taste. Did he, for instance, know of and dislike Edward Bashe, victim of a lengthy slander in Dd.5.75 (Items 212-213), or did he simply enjoy a rollicking-good libel for its own sake? Was he really opposed to the use of tobacco, or did he copy Item 255 because it was a clever riddle on the subject, and Item 298, for its humorous description of the perils of smoking? The literary nature of Stanford's collection makes biographical inference from such entries hazardous; as a rule, however, I think he would not have transcribed works which contradicted his opinions, though he might have copied a good satire or panegyric on a subject which did not concern him. I have tried to limit the following discussion to those items which I think do reflect extra-literary beliefs and attitudes.

Generally, the contents of Dd.5.75 show that Stanford was no cloistered pedant, but a man very much concerned with the issues of his day. The question of Elizabeth's marriage and the succession to the throne stood as the great domestic issue throughout most of her reign, and Item 220 is a direct verse appeal, urging her to marry for the sake of her people, if not for herself, while Item 112 records Elizabeth's speech to the Parliament of 1576, a cautiously worded promise that she will resolve the marriage problem to their satisfaction. But when the problem was unequivocally solved with the accession of King James, Stanford seems to have been displeased, to judge from Item 333: "he hath much nede of god his blessing wch kneles to a thistell."

Earlier, the accession of the Queen of Scots would have pleased him even less, apparently, for Item 214 is a vicious personal slander of Mary Stuart. Stanford's essential patriotism and loyalty to Elizabeth is amply reflected in Item 110, an attack on William Parry, convicted of plotting the Queen's assassination, and executed in March of 1585. It is ironic that Charles Paget, and to some extent Thomas as well, were promoting the intrigues of both the Queen of Scots and Parry while Stanford, a family servant, was copying out these libels.

From the Mar Mar-Martin tract (Items 183-187), we can infer that Stanford was a moderate in religion, neither defending the established Church nor siding with the reformers, but simply deploring the spectacle of such open, disruptive quarreling. The moral adages from the <u>Treatise of Moral Philosophy</u> (Items 147-164, 168-178), indicate not Stanford's particular religious beliefs, but his general desire for moral improvement through the study of morally edifying works, a characteristic Elizabethan interest. Similarly, the Nativity hymns which Stanford himself probably wrote (Items 281-283), indicate that he was a Christian without revealing specific denominational beliefs.

With so many of his countrymen, Henry shared an immense admiration for Sir Francis Drake, reflected in Items 166 and 167, along with a general dislike for the Earl of Leicester, object of a slanderous epitaph, Item 181. Assuming that Stanford influenced the style and content of his pupils' verse, Item 80's satiric characterizations of different nationalities may represent some of Stanford's own prejudices. The Italian is accused of lechery, the German, of drunkenness, the Englishman, of calling his swaggering, good fellowship. This sort of criticism and the numerous satires in Dd.5 75 seem to denote a touch of the malcontent in Stanford, fully expressed in Item 54, and more succinctly in Item 145: "ther is no good for to be don while we are lyving here/ Except we lie fawn flatter face cap knele duck crouch smile flere."

Stanford's purely literary tastes are thoroughly and unambiguously represented in Dd 5.75, where his opinion of literature is well summarized by his advice to Theophila Berkeley, "No Ornament can better fit a grace/ then mongst the muses for to haue a place" (Item 93:13-14). In accord with his genuine appreciation of literature, he filled the "public" section of his manuscript with works that appealed to him for their own sake, and not because they were written by a well-known author or popular courtier--he may not even have known who wrote the poetry he transcribed, or if he did, bothered to record the fact only twice (Items 109, 165). Stanford also alludes in Dd.5.75 to a number of identifiable printed books, thus providing some further means of evaluating his literary interests.

We know from the Paget juvenilia that by 1585 Stanford had read Turberville's <u>Epitaphes, Epigrams, Songes and Sonets</u> (first published in 1567), and that he approved of "Drab Age" metrics and copiousness, at least for teaching purposes, since the same techniques and devices recur in the poetry George Berkeley wrote under Stanford's direction. At the same time, however, and perhaps even before 1585, Stanford was also copying such novel stanzaic forms as Sidney's "Ring out your belles let mourning shewes be spred," and such metrical experiments as Item 111, a good, sensuous description of a woman couched in the unlikely rhythm of anapestic tetrameter couplets. The 1588 *Musica Transalpina* poems (Items 116-137), the first set of Italian madrigals translated into English, are further indication of Stanford's avant garde taste in lyric poetry, for aside from the works of Sidney and Spenser, little verse of equal merit was being written in English at the time.

    The books Stanford presented along with many of his New Year's verses between 1596 and 1613 were presumably ones which he had read and enjoyed himself, and they suggest that he kept in close touch with the current book market. During these years, he would have had little trouble in doing so since the hub of the English book trade was located in St. Paul's Churchyard, a scant block or two from the Carey's Blackfriars residence. In 1598, he apparently gave Elizabeth Carey Berkeley a copy of *The Queene of Nauarres Tales* (STC 17323), a series of "Nouels," short stories in prose first printed in English in 1597. The "frence historie" he had given her in 1596 was apparently *The Historie of France* (STC 11276), translated in 1595 from the French of Lancelot Voisin, Seigneur de la Poppelimière. He had read *The Faerie Queene* no later than 1611, for in that year he presented a copy to Elizabeth Spencer Carey along with verses of his own which refer in some detail to the characters and allegory of at least the first three books. Stanford speaks of "Bertas . . . sugred verse" in Item 93:5, a 1613 New Year's poem accompanying his gift, a copy of *La Semaine* no doubt, to Theophila Berkeley. And another poem addressed to Theophila in the same year by her brother, George, cites a passage from Chapman's *Epicede or funerall song on the Death of Henry Prince of Wales*, a work which Stanford probably had brought to his pupil's attention (Item 89:9-10).

In addition to Du Bartas, Poppelimière, and The Queen of Nauarres Tales, Stanford was exposed to several other works from French or Italian sources. Among the unique translations in Dd.5.75 are several riddles from a French version of The Nights of Straparola (Items 47-53), and a sonnet from Petrarch (Item 56). This work, and Stanford's own sonnets, ultimately based on Petrarch's "Pommi ove 'l sole occide i fiori et l'erba" (Items 284-289, 291-293), suggest that he may have known Italian, and he had certainly learned French by about 1590 when he copied out three French poems (Items 179, 180, and 182).

All of these continental works were transcribed after he had entered the Careys' service, and his interest in them probably resulted from his association with Elizabeth Spencer Carey and her daughter. As tutor or secretary, Stanford was apparently governed primarily by the women of the home, for his New Year's gifts were presented only to the ladies of the family. The multilingual literary interests of the Carey women seem to have affected Stanford's own tastes in reading, in the books he presented as gifts, and in the poetry he copied into Dd.5.75.

The chief value of Stanford's collection, of course, is found in the poetry he transcribed from manuscript sources, and here we find him exercising usually admirable taste. He enjoyed a wide range of Elizabethan love poetry, from Dyer's mournful examination of the lover's plight in "He that his mirth hath lost" (Item 99), to Sidney's clever "The fier to see my wrong for anger burnes" (Item 107), to Spenser's melodic "More fayr then most fair full of the lyving fyre" (Item 197). Least akin to modern tastes, no doubt, are the mid-century works Stanford copied, including several poems which also appeared in the Paradise of Dainty Devices, one from Tottel's Songs and Sonnets, and one by Thomas Churchyard (Item 215). Originally, most or all of these works were courtly, and circulated only in manuscript, and Stanford seems to have appreciated this style of poetry even after he had been exposed to the works of such "Golden Age" practitioners as Sidney and Spenser.

On the other hand, the verse he admired by these later Elizabethan poets represents some of their very finest output. Gorges' "The gentle season of the year" (Item 208) is probably his most skillfully worded lyric, his "I saw of late a lady wear a show," a clever bit of drollery, and even "A hapless man of late" (Item 204), is worth reading if only for the impact of its last line. Among Sidney's eleven works in Dd.5.75 is Item 195, perhaps the least trite, most tasteful description of a woman in Elizabethan poetry, and Item 196, a humorous satire of those worn out similes which were nonetheless revived to portray innumerable sonnet ladies, just as if Sidney had never shown their triteness. Ralegh's "Calling to mind" (Item 109), Breton's "Fair Phyllis" (Item 201), Queen Elizabeth's (?) "When I was fair and young and favor graced me" (Item 202), and the anonymous "What if thy mistress now will needs unconstant be" (Item 188), are a few of the better known works in Dd.5.75 which retain their appeal for the modern reader.

Although Stanford made entries in his anthology until at least 1613, his tastes seem to have stayed conservatively fixed on the poetic fashions of the 1580's. His love for riddle and satire apparently did lead him to appreciate, as reflected by Items 238, 242, 252-280, 294-306, the classically inspired satires and epigrams popularized by Hall, Davies, and Marston during the late 1590's; yet the simultaneous shift to the rhetorically simpler poetry of Jonson, Campion, and Donne, leaves no trace in Dd.5.75, and all of its lyrics could have been, or were written during the '80's.

For all his good taste in poetry, Stanford's own muse seldom managed to soar much beyond the copious inventions of the "Drab Age" poets, although he did pick up the English (Shakespearean) form of the sonnet during the mid-1590's. He wrote sonnets almost exclusively after 1596, and is even responsible, I think, for a tediously conceived "sonnet sequence" (Items 284-289, 291-293). Stanford probably wrote a good deal more verse than he copied into Dd.5.75, but I know of only one poem of his, Item 85, which ever entered print, and that posthumously among the commendatory verse in the 1637 edition of Camden's Britannia, translated by Philemon Holland (STC 4510).[1] The verse Stanford wrote was usually more meaningful than the often monotonous exercises he approved for Will Paget and George Berkeley, yet his lines are too frequently characterized by awkward inversion of syntax and the omission of words for the sake of meter: "as newyeares guift & pawn of mindfull mynd" (Item 92:2), for example, or, "This Holland hath at suite of learned dame" (Item 85:5). Stanford was surprisingly unsuccessful at bringing his own poetry up to the standard he admired in other writers.

To summarize, the Henry Stanford portrayed by the contents of Dd.5.75 is in many respects a "typical Elizabethan." He was patriotic, consciously desirous of his own moral improvement, and alert to the events and issues of his day. He was loyal to the Queen, unsympathetic with those who would upset the status quo, and yet not entirely satisfied with the status quo himself. But Stanford was not so typical in the variety of his literary interests, for he paid close attention to the current book market, taught English versification, and wrote poetry of his own. Fortunately, he was also interested in the private literature which circulated in manuscript, and devoted the largest part of his private anthology to works of this sort. He was better educated than most of his countrymen, without belonging to the class which wrote and disseminated the most elite manuscript works; yet his position in several

---

[1] Stanford may have been personally acquainted with Dr. Philemon Holland, who tutored George Berkeley, and undertook translation of the Britannia at the request of his mother, Elizabeth Carey Berkeley (see the notes to Item 85).

noble households put him firmly, if indirectly in touch with these circles. His more than twenty-five years of service with the Careys were especially important to his literary tastes and formation of the Dd.5.75 collection, for from this vantage point he could acquire some of the finest poetry of the age, while his own literary interests were directly stimulated by the richly cultural atmosphere of this household. The government's examination of Stanford in 1586 stands out as the most uncomfortably exciting event in what we know of his life; thereafter, he seems to have remained quietly employed as a family retainer, occupied with his own reading, writing and study, and filling in year by year the pages of his manuscript anthology.

Stanford's Scribal Habits

Accuracy

Stanford's anthology reveals in some detail his transcription habits and the extent to which he might be expected to deviate from his copy text. He no doubt added a few stanzas to Item 18, the epitaph on Ann Lee, and he may have changed a few words in the Marprelate tract, Items 183-187, but these are the only places where I have found signs that Stanford made additions or intentional changes in his copy. Instead, he seems to have followed his sources faithfully, leaving blanks in his own manuscript where he could not make out the reading (see Items 105:2-4, 112:53; and 195, after 1.33, for examples of this practice).

More important, Stanford copied from at least three identifiable printed books, and in these cases we can determine exactly the accuracy of his transcription. He took Items 116-137 from Nicholas Yong's _Musica Transalpina_, making twenty-four errors in a text of 1,420 words. Items 147-164, 168-178 are from the _Treatise of Moral Philosophy_, and while the exact edition cannot be determined, Stanford's maximum rate of error would be one word in fifty-four. Finally, a 435 word text, the six riddles from Bartholomew Young's translation of Montemayor's *Diana* appear as Items 229-234, with five variants from the printed text. Stanford's average rate of variance from these three sources is one word in sixty-six, or .015 per cent. The first two sets of transcriptions were made between late 1588 and the end of 1589, the third in 1599, so that some range in time as well as quantity of the texts copied is represented. He may not have been quite this accurate in all his copying, especially not from manuscript sources in a variety of hands; still, the printed books provide a valuable index to the accuracy we can expect to find in Dd.5.75 texts. On this basis, I have rejected the possible printed sources for Items 110, 183-187, 215, 217, 219, 221, 223, and 227 on grounds that Stanford's variance from them of more than one word in thirty did not represent a likely deviation from his proved accuracy as copyist.

Calligraphy and Accidentals of the Text

Most of Dd.5.75 is written in an ordinary and not very attractive secretary hand which shows a scattering of Italian forms for individual letters as early as 1582. The marginal note beside Item 61, "stilo Romano," shows that Stanford did pay attention to his handwriting, and the poem is, more or less, in the Italian style hand, termed Roman during the sixteenth century. The appearance of both a secretary and Italian hand in Dd.5.75 led me at first to believe that two or more persons had compiled the anthology. I am now convinced however, that all of the writing is Stanford's, for a specific comparison of individual secretary and Italic letters taken from folios of various dates, reveals an essentially uniform hand throughout the manuscript.

More and more Italian forms appeared in Stanford's writing as the years passed, but this trend is not striking enough to permit the dating of a folio from the handwriting alone. Even, as in Item 61, when Stanford considered his writing Italian, it is actually intermixed with secretary characters, and yet several lines in his Italian style are often distinguishable at a glance because the strokes are thinner and the script less cursive than his secretary. Stanford used the "stilo Romano" when writing a foreign language or English translation from a foreign tongue, as well as for miscellaneous works in English. Items 20, 29, 30, 31, 56-59, 61, 62, 66-94, 138-145, 166, 179-180, 182, 214, 229-234, 284-289, 291-293, and 335, are written in what I think Stanford intended to be his Italian hand. The best sustained examples of the Italic are unquestionably Items 179-180, and 182 (three poems in French), 214 and 335 (in Latin), and 229-234 (translations from Italian); to some extent, the other listings here are arbitrary.

Stanford's accidentals conform in general with standard Elizabethan habits. His spelling is more similar to modern practice than that of many of his contemporaries, although such anomalies as "aege," "hear" (hair), "freind," "bewtie," "veiw," "fruict," and "fier," crop up often, thought not consistently. Throughout Dd.5.75 Stanford used capitals rather sparingly, and it is often impossible to know if he intended capital or lower case 'w,' 'y,' 'v,' 'm,' and 'n.' In addition to the abbreviations listed in the textual apparatus, Stanford usually wrote "wth" and "w^{ch}" for "with" and "which," while a 'y' with superscript 'e,' 't,' or 'r,' stood for "the," "that," and "their," respectively. An ampersand generally replaces "and," and a macron over a letter or two indicates the omission of 'm' or 'n' in the vicinity, or an 'st' in Latin entries. Stanford did not make frequent or consistent use of punctuation, and his repertoire of marks was rather limited. Commas and periods occur often enough, and there are rare uses of parentheses and question marks, while either slashes or colons infrequently serve to separate lines of poetry written as one line (e.g. Items 54, 228-234).

Through calligraphy and accidentals, Stanford achieves neither a showpiece of good handwriting nor a model of consistent usage, but he does manage to keep his entries clear in meaning and, for the most part, legible.

Physical State of the Manuscript

Provenance and Description

Cambridge University Library MS Dd.5.75[1] consists of sixty-three folios measuring 14.5 by 20 cm., arranged in eight quarto gatherings with, originally, eight to twelve leaves apiece, though now reduced to the collation, 1^{12-1}, 2^{8-2}, $3\text{-}5^8$, 6^{8-2}, $7^{12-2(?)}$, 8^{8-2}. Four fly leaves before f. 1, and ff. 21-24, 52^v, $58\text{-}62^r$, are blank, while only the top third of the page, or less, is filled with writing on ff. 10^v, 11^r, 46^v, and 56^v. On full pages, Stanford wrote an average of forty-three lines across the shorter dimension of the leaf, with seldom fewer than thirty-eight, nor more than fifty lines to the page. The folios do not seem to have been cut down, except for ff. 17-24, which are one-half inch short at the bottom and somewhat trimmed along the outer margin. Elsewhere, the words Stanford squeezed to the very edge of the outer margin, and the leftover words he entered above or below the line (see, for example, ff. 4^r, 31^r, 41^v), indicate that the size of the folios has been altered very little since he filled them.

I have found no reference to Stanford's anthology between the date of his last entry in 1613, and 1856, when a brief description appeared in <u>A Catalogue of the Manuscripts Preserved in the Library of the University of Cambridge</u>, I (Cambridge, 1856), 284, Item 314. The Cambridge University Library has no record of its accession.

---

[1] I have personally seen neither Dd.5.75 nor any of the other manuscripts mentioned in this dissertation, but have examined only microfilm copies of them. The information used in the description of Dd.5.75 was kindly supplied to me by Professor William A. Ringler, Jr., after his first-hand study of the manuscript at Cambridge University Library.

The uniform size of the folios in Dd.5.75, and appearance of a single form of watermark throughout indicate that the manuscript was made up from blank sheets of paper before Stanford began writing in it. From the size of the leaves, I assume that it was constructed with sheets of "small folio," measuring twelve by sixteen inches, a common paper size in Elizabethan times,[1] while the quarto format of gatherings 3, 4, 5, and 6 suggests that the entire manuscript was probably produced by quarto folding. Upon rebinding the manuscript in 1956, Cambridge Library gave its collation as: four fly leaves, 1^{10}, 2^6, $3\text{-}5^8$, 6^6, 7^{12} (-1), 8^6, for a total of sixty-three folios. This formula can be clarified, I think, by noting which folios belong to each gathering:

Gathering	Folios
1	1-10
2	11-16
3	17-24
4	25-32
5	33-40
6	41-46
7	47-57
8	58-63

---

[1] Ronald B. McKerrow, *An Introduction to Bibliography for Literary Students* (Oxford, 1927), p. 103. In the discussion of format, I assume that Stanford, or whoever constructed the manuscript, formed gatherings of more than four leaves by folding the sheets two or more together, simply because this would be the easiest way to make such a volume. It would also be possible to fold each sheet in quarto separately, placing one inside the other to form gatherings of eight, twelve, or more leaves. For the problematic gatherings in Dd.5.75, neither method offers an explanation for the present state of the folios, while either method could explain the position of the watermarks in the gatherings which seem to be intact or can be reconstructed.

A sheet 12x16" produced a quarto gathering with leaves 6x8" when folded twice, joining the shorter edges of the sheet each time and creasing in the middle.

Obviously, if this collation is correct, some folios have been lost or rearranged, since the number of leaves in each gathering of a normal quarto must be divisible by four. An examination of the contents of the manuscript and the location of its watermarks resolves most of these inconsistencies and allows some partial reconstruction of the original volume. The continuity of a number of items on adjacent folios of Dd.5.75 indicates that the order of these leaves is unchanged from the time Stanford filled them. These leaves, and the evidence in each case, are listed below:

Folios	Evidence
4 and 5	carry-over poem
5 and 6	"
8 and 9	"
14 and 15	a series of entries from one source
19 and 20	carry-over poem
28 and 29	"
30 and 31	a series of entries from one source
33 and 34	carry-over poem
34 and 35	a series of entries from one source
37 and 38	catchword
39 and 40	carry-over poem
41 and 42	"
48 and 49	a series of numbered entries
49 and 50	carry-over poem
50 and 51	a series of numbered entries
51 and 52	carry-over poem
53 and 54	a homogenous "sonnet sequence"
55 and 56	a series of numbered entries

Accordingly, ff. 4-6, 8-9, 14-15, 19-20, 28-29, 30-31, 33-35, 37-38, 39-40, 41-42, 48-52, 53-54, and 55-56, should not be rearranged by any hypothetical reconstruction of the manuscript.

The paper used to make Dd.5.75 was apparently of standard workmanship, with a single watermark centered on one half of each sheet. With the sheets folded in quarto, these marks appear in the inner margin midway between the top and bottom of the page; approximately one half of the complete design of the watermark appears near the inner margins of two conjugate leaves. Professor Ringler found that the top portion of the watermark could be seen on ff. 3, 6, 14, 16, 21, 23, 29, 32, 36, 39, 41, 43, 50, 56, 59, and 60, the bottom half on ff. 5, 8, 11, 13, 18, 20, 25, 28, 34, 37, 44, 46, 49, 55, 61, and 62.

The positions of these marks suggest that at least five gatherings in Dd.5.75 are quartos in eights. Professor Ringler's examination of the manuscript showed that in gathering 3, ff. 17 and 24, 18 and 23, 19 and 22, 20 and 21, were conjugate. In addition, the top and bottom portions of a single watermark appear on the second and last of these pairs; these locations follow the pattern of a quarto gathering in eights. Similarly, the watermarks between ff. 25-32 and 33-40, indicate that these gatherings 4 and 5, are also in eights.

The sixth gathering, ff. 41-46, cannot be a complete quarto gathering since it has only six leaves. It seems probable, however, that this too was a gathering in eights from which two leaves were removed, for two stanzas of a three stanza poem at the top of f. 46^r are numbered "2," and "3." Presumably, Stanford copied the first stanza of this poem, which appears nowhere else in Dd.5.75, on a now missing leaf preceding f. 46. The watermarks for a complete gathering in eights occur on ff. 41 and 46, 43 and 44, so I assume that an entire, unwatermarked conjugate leaf was removed. No leaf can be missing between ff. 41 and 42, however, since the content of these folios is continuous. The only alternate position for a leaf conjugate with one originally before f. 46 is between ff. 42 and 43. Both the content and the format of a quarto in eights, then, suggest that a conjugate half-sheet was removed from gathering 6, one of its leaves from between ff. 45 and 46, the other, from between 42 and 43.

Much the same thing has happened, I think, with gathering 2, ff. 11-16. In this case, the unwatermarked conjugate leaves forming the first and last folios of the gathering, and falling originally between ff. 10 and 11, 16 and 17, are lost. Both the present set of watermarks in this gathering and the contents of its remaining leaves support this conclusion. Gatherings 2 through 6, then, were originally quartos in eights; their present condition can be represented by the formula, $2^{(8-2)}$, $3-5^{(8)}$, $6^{(8-2)}$.

To the first gathering, ff. 1-10, we must add f. 57, the only surviving leaf which remained with the manuscript among those which have been removed. Folio 57 was originally the first leaf of Dd.5.75, a fact which its contents indicate in two ways. First, William Paget's two New Year's poems on f. 57 (Items 306 and 307), are dated 1581, while his other poems of this date, Items 1-6, occupy the first three leaves of the anthology. Supposedly, then, the poems on f. 57 also belong with these three folios. Second, Item 307 is demonstrably the first part of Item 1, and from this we can determine exactly f. 57's original position. Stanford frequently counted the number of lines in young Paget's works and recorded the total at the end of each poem; thus Item 2, a poem of thirty-six lines, is subscribed "36," Item 3, with thirty-two lines, "32," and many of the other early works are similarly tallied. But Item 1, with only twenty-eight lines, is counted as "68" on f. 1, a total which is correct if added to the forty lines of Item 307. These two items, furthermore, join in this way to form one poem with as much continuity of meaning as is usually found in the Paget juvenilia. Thus, f. 57^r was the original f. 1^v, with the last portion of poem 307 continued onto the present f. 1^r and the total of sixty-eight lines registered at the end. After f. 57 was removed from its position as the first leaf of Dd.5.75, it was inserted between ff. 56 and 58 with its outer margin thrust into the binding, and in this way the recto and verso were interchanged.

With the addition of f. 57, a total of eleven leaves belongs to the first gathering, which probably consisted originally of twelve leaves. The watermarks on ff. 3 and 5, 6 and 8, however, will support only an octavo gathering in eights, for another complete watermark would appear somewhere if three sheets were folded twice in whatever manner to produce twelve leaves in quarto. Still, the gathering can be reconstructed on the assumption that two unwatermarked half-sheets were added to a normal quarto in eights. Folio 57, conjugate with a leaf falling originally between ff. 10 and 11, formed the first and last leaves of the gathering, while the second conjugate pair, now ff. 4 and 7, was inserted between the two full sheets in the gathering before the second fold had been made. This is the simplest explanation of the first gathering's present condition, albeit, a rather contrived way to produce a twelve leaf gathering. From the evidence available, however, I can arrive at no likelier explanation.

Without f. 57, gathering 7, ff. 47-56, is reduced to ten leaves, another impossible quarto gathering. Unfortunately, the watermarks again fail to support any hypothetical reconstruction. If this was originally a quarto in twelves which included ff. 58 and 59 as well, the top half of the watermark on f. 59 should match with its bottom half on f. 47; but no watermark appears on f. 47. Nor is there any way, if we assume that ff. 47-56 represent a fragmentary gathering in twelves, to remove two folios and leave the watermarks as they now appear on ff. 49, 50, 55 and 56. My attempts to reconstruct this gathering in a format of eights have been equally unsuccessful. It is possible, however, that ff. 49-56, as their watermarks indicate, form a normal quarto gathering in eights, before which an unwatermarked half sheet, now, ff. 47 and 48, was added. As with gathering 1, I do not feel that there is evidence for any satisfactory reconstruction of gathering 7; ironically, the contents of this gathering show that ff. 48-52, 53-54, and 55-56 were in their present order when Stanford transcribed them.

It is, of course, hazardous to attempt a reconstruction of gathering eight without an explanation for the present status of gathering seven; still I think it is at least possible that ff. 58-63 represent the remains of an original gathering in eights. A missing folio, 64, would have been the last one in the manuscript if this were the case, and the outer leaves are naturally the most likely to come loose or be torn from the binding. I suggest that this hypothetical f. 64 was conjugate with another missing folio which preceded f. 58, these two conjugate leaves forming the outermost cover of the gathering. These leaves were unwatermarked, as are ff. 58 and 63, while both watermarks of the two sheets used to make this gathering are found in normal positions on ff. 59 and 62, 60 and 61.

If the foregoing reconstruction of Dd.5.75 is correct, its original collation would have been: 1^{12}, $2\text{-}6^{8}$, $7^{(12?)}$, 8^{8}, for an original 72 folios, made from eighteen sheets of paper. If this was the original format, the present state of the manuscript would represent:

Gathering	Folios
1 (12-1?)	1-10 plus 57
2 (8o2)	11-16

Gathering	Folios
3 (8)	17-24
4 (8)	25-32
5 (8)	33-40
6 (8-2)	41-46
7 (12-2?)	47-56
8 (8-2)	58-63

Since my transcription of Dd.5.75 attempts to reproduce only what Stanford wrote in the manuscript, I have omitted all the later markings listed below. The foliation of my transcript follows the pencil notation of the original leaf for leaf, but since the manuscript's foliation is not Stanford's but probably a nineteenth century addition, I have not attempted to reproduce the position of these arabic numerals, which occur in the upper right-hand corner of the recto of each folio. The fly leaves at the beginning similarly, are numbered in sequence with Roman numerals. Besides this foliation, leaf 32^v is marked "32^v" in the upper left-hand corner, while the lower right-hand corners of ff. 10^r, 20^r, 34^r, 44^r and 54^r, are inscribed "10," "20," "30," "40," and "50," respectively. This foliation per ten leaves omitted blanks, so that after the blank folios 21-24, the notation deviates by four leaves from the actual number of folios in the manuscript.

The first leaf of the gatherings have been indicated by arabic numerals in the lower right-hand corners, "2" on 11^r, 3" on 17^r, "4" on 25^r, "5" on 33^r, "6" on 41^r, "7" on 47^r, and "8" on 58^r. The conjugate leaves which form the middle fold of each gathering are marked with small plus signs in the lower right-hand corners of the right-hand leaves, ff. iii^r, 6^r, 14^r, 21^r, 29^r, 37^r, 44^r, 53^r, and 61^r.

The other late markings in the manuscript are miscellaneous. A modern fly leaf just before f. i tells us that Dd.5.75 was formerly bound with Dd.5.76, and that the volume was rebound separately by Gray of Cambridge in 1956. On f. i^r, "75-76" is entered at the center of the page, on f. i^v, "Dd.5.75/76" at the top, and "F" in the center. Just below the last line on f. 1^r, "Dd-5-75" appears, and "63" is written in the lower right-hand corner of f. 63^r, followed by an indistinguishable mark, perhaps the initials of the foliator.

The list of folios still in their original order, the partial reconstruction of the manuscript's format, and its modern foliation, all indicate that Dd.5.75 was in very nearly this same physical condition when Stanford owned it, and that comparatively little has been lost or rearranged since Cambridge acquired it. If so, some modification of the two part structure I have claimed for the anthology is now in order, for the "domestic" works after f. 51, aside from those on f. 57, apparently are not out of place. Stanford, I think, planned to fill ff. 1-24 (and whatever leaves may be missing from this section besides f. 57), with poetry written by the youngsters under his supervision, along with other poetry related to his employment and other members of the households he served. The unfilled limits of this section are the four blanks, ff. 21-24. Folios 25-51 apparently mark the original boundaries of the "public" section, while Stanford began on f. 51^v a collection of his own poetry, represented by the three hymns, Items 281-283, and the "Place me" sonnets, Items 284-289, 291-293. This section was to run to f. 62, but instead, the "public" entries intruded beyond f. 51, and we find the series of numbered riddles and satires which begin on f. 48^r by-passing Stanford's works on ff. 51^v-54^v, and resuming again on f. 55^r. The fourth apparent section of Dd.5.75 now occupies ff. 62^v-63^v. This was Stanford's _enfer_, appropriately located at the very end of his collection, a place for short riddles, especially those which implied a bawdy answer, for a Latin account in questionable taste of certain hardships endured by schoolboys, and for similarly indecent materials. Thus, a more precise account of Stanford's organization of his anthology would note the "domestic" and "public" parts, followed by a section for the compiler's own works, and one for trivial or vulgar entries.

Dates of Compilation

The first section of the manuscript, ff. 1-20, along with the misplaced f. 57, contains ninety-five Items, entered in nearly sequential chronological order. Stanford dated in order the poems on the first thirteen folios from the year 1582 through 1587, while entries on f. 16 are dated 1596 and 1598 and on f. 16^v, 1610. The poems on ff. 17-20 seem to have been transcribed after 1613, for the dates here are somewhat jumbled between the years 1611 and 1613. This entire "domestic" section is of modest literary value, yet it proves that Stanford had begun his collection by New Year's, 1582, and that he added to its first portion chronologically, page by page, until at least the same date in 1613.

Apparently, Stanford also copied the Items in the "public" section, ff. 25-51, in the same chronological fashion. His habit of keeping up with recent books and his interest in current events are of much use in dating this section of the manuscript. He must have copied the <u>Musica Transalpina</u> lyrics on ff. 30^r-31^v after the songbook's publication, 1 October 1588, while the Marprelate tract copied on ff. 34-35 marks a last gasp in that controversy, in print by December, 1589, and probably entered in Dd.5.75 about the same time. Between these datable entries we have two poems on f. 32^v which apparently refer to Drake's Lisbon expedition and which were surely copied between the commencement of that venture in early 1589 and knowledge at home of its failure in June of the same year (see the notes to Items 166-167). We might expect the satiric epitaph on Leicester on f. 33^r to precede the Musica Transalpina works, since Leicester died 4 September 1588; but this was an unprintable work which could circulate only in manuscript, and it probably did not reach Stanford until mid or late 1589. Folios 30-33 then, contain a close-knit group of entries transcribed in the course of about one year, from the end of 1588 to late 1589, and we can confidently assign the works which precede or follow this grouping to dates before and after 1588-1589.

Items 95-115, the entries in the "public" section of the manuscript preceding f. 30, apparently were transcribed between 1580, at the earliest, and late 1588. Items 96 and 100-103, are from Sidney's Old Arcadia, which was finished in its earliest from by late 1580.[1] Item 110, the slander of William Parry on f. 27^v, could not have been written before Parry's arrest and conviction in February, 1585, and since Stanford's text does not seem to derive from the version printed in the 1587 edition of Holinshed's Chronicles, it may represent manuscript circulation of the work, probably copied while the event was still of topical interest, during 1585. Accordingly, Items 95-110 (ff. 25-27), appear to have been copied between c. 1580 and 1585, while Items 111-115 (ff. 27^v-29^v), probably represent Stanford's entries from 1585 through late 1588. The Items on ff. 32-33^v no doubt belong to 1589, and those in gathering five after the Marprelate tract, Items 188-208 (ff. 36-40), to the early 1590's.

The next readily datable Items in Dd.5.75 are on f. 46, the last leaf of the sixth gathering. Items 229-234, the six riddles from Young's translation of the Diana, were copied sometime after publication of that book late in 1598, and probably after February, 1599, since they are preceded by Item 228, a speech to "ye Q. by ye players 1598," presented at a 1599 Shrovetide

---

[1] Ringler, p. 365.

entertainment. Folios 36-46, then, seem to represent Stanford's entries for the years 1590-1599, and since gathering six originally held an extra two folios, Stanford could have filled a total of twelve leaves in that time.

It is possible, however, that the chronological sequence of entries is broken after gathering five, and that the entire sixth gathering may be out of place. I discuss the evidence for this in greater detail in a prefatory note to Items 212-234. Briefly, the topical slanders of Edward Bashe and Mary, Queen of Scots, the poem urging Queen Elizabeth to marry, and the mid-century style of Items 215-227, several of which were printed in the Paradise of Dainty Devices, argue for transcription in the early 80's instead of the early 90's. Still, there is no bibliographical evidence that any of the gatherings are out of place, and Items 228-234 on f. 46 were unquestionably transcribed in 1599, suggesting an uninterrupted chronological sequence of entries between ff. 36-46, dating between 1590 and 1599. In light of the conflicting evidence, however, I hesitate to assign dates of transcription in the sixth gathering (ff. 41-46), except to its last seven poems, Items 228-234.

Items 252-280, 295-306, are a series of riddles and satires numbered 1 through 40 which begin on f. 48, and which must have been taken from a single source. The date 1602 appearing in Item 271, and references to "Carnasions of Elizabeth" and "ye Queenes small shinking letters" in 279, suggest that these works were written and probably transcribed toward the very end of Elizabeth's reign. If so, the preceding entries in the seventh gathering, Items 235-251, may also have been copied during the first few years of the seventeenth century, or perhaps in the late 90's. Included in this group are several unique lyrics and epigrams, along with song IX from Astrophil and Stella (Item 237), a work which saw very little circulation among the manuscript anthologies.

The poems which interrupt the numbered series of Items appear to be Stanford's own works. The hymns, Items 281-283, are no doubt early works, for they are written in the thickly stroked secretary Stanford used primarily between 1582 and 1590, and the number of lines is recorded at the end of each poem, a practice he discontinued after about 1584. Items 284-293, the "Place me" sonnets, and a couplet written for George Berkeley (Item 290), are in Stanford's Italian hand, and were most likely copied sometime after 1590. The poem to young Berkeley was squeezed into a blank space at the bottom of f. 53^v and was no doubt copied after the sonnets--in any event, it could not have been written before George's birth in 1601.

Aside from Item 336, a sneer at King James' accession, Items in the last six leaves of the manuscript cannot be even approximately dated. Only ff. 62^v-63 contain writing (Items 309-339), probably entered at various times to form a commonplace section reserved primarily for indecent riddles and similar verse.

Fortunately, Stanford's method of entry seems to have been chronological within each of the first three sections of Dd.5.75; accordingly, the "public" section provides a dependable means of dating the most important literary texts in the manuscript, which occur on ff. 25-40. Perhaps none of these transcription dates come within several years of the date of composition, yet they do tell us when certain poems were circulating, and in some instances, push back the possible date of composition by several years.

Earlier Notices of the Manuscript

I list below in chronological order all the scholarly publications I have found concerning Dd.5.75, with the Items studied in each case, and the manner in which they were used:

Louise Brown Osborn, The Life, Letters, and Writings of John Hoskyns (London, 1937) (mentions Item 29).

Bernard Wagner, "New Poems by Sir Philip Sidney," PMLA, LIII (1938), 118-124 (collates with Item 208).

William A. Ringler, Jr., "Poems Attributed to Sir Philip Sidney," SP, XLVII (1950), 126-151 (mentions Item 208).

Agnes M. C. Latham, The Poems of Sir Walter Ralegh (Cambridge, Mass., 1951) (mentions Items 109, 193).

Helen Sandison, The Poems of Sir Arthur Gorges (Oxford, 1953) (collates with Items 192, 199, 204, 205, 208; reprints Item 193).

Ruth Hughey, The Arundel Harington Manuscript (2 vols.; Columbus, Ohio, 1960) (collates with Item 106).

Laurence Cummings, "John Finet's Miscellany" (unpublished dissertation, Washington University, 1960) (collates with Items 95, 96, 101, 107, 109, 113, 197, 198, 201, 202, 208, 212-213; mentions Item 216).

William A. Ringler, Jr., The Poems of Sir Philip Sidney (Oxford, 1962) (mentions Items 96, 100-195, 101, 102, 103, 106, 107, 194, 196, 200, 237).

Leicester Bradner, The Poems of Queen Elizabeth I (Providence, R. I., 1964) (collates with Item 202; reprints Item 222).

Laurence Cummings, "Spenser's Amoretti VIII: New Manuscript Versions," Studies in English Literature, IV (1964), 125-135 (reprints Item 197).

Similar Manuscript Anthologies

Although Dd.5.75 shares no more than fifteen poems with any one other collection, it has texts in common with at least sixty-three other manuscripts, not all of which are similar literary anthologies. Lyric poetry and private literature of all sorts was preserved in many different types of manuscripts, and while the richest collections are the purely literary ones, good poetry may show up in almost any context. The non-literary tenor of Egerton MS 2642, for example, is indicated by the lengthy title on its cover page: "The Booke of Heraldry/ and other things togither Withe the Order of Coronacons of Emperours, kinges, Princes dukes. Byshoppes, Earles, and other

Estates, withe the manner of their Buryalls and Enterrementes and of the fyrst re [unfinished]." The compiler actually set down all these things and a good deal more, including much Latin verse and some English poetry, notably, two copies of "The state of France" (Item 113), "The doubt of future foes," a poem by Queen Elizabeth, a copy of "The Scottishe Libell," and the Queen's oration at Oxford in 1592. Equally strange, a copy of the libel of Mary Stuart (Item 214), appears in a manuscript devoted mainly to heraldry, and courtly texts can be found in manuscript books dealing with naval matters, arms and seige equipment, interspersed with Latin tracts, and scrawled between copies of family letters. The full study of Tudor and Stuart private literature can not be confined to the purely literary collections.

For an understanding of the relative type of anthology Stanford produced, it will suffice to look, however, only at the more or less similar collections. Even here, there is great diversity in the compilers' tastes, the size and contents of the collections, and the period of compilation. The following descriptions include all the anthologies I have seen with four or more Dd.5.75 works.[1] The first six manuscripts here have also been discussed, with particular reference to their Sidney poems, by Ringler, pp. 552-561.

Foremost in similarity is the Harleian 7392 collection, sharing fifteen poems with Dd.5.75 (Items 95, 96, 99, 106, 107, 109, 113, 193, 196, 197, 202, 208, 216, 222, and 339). Bound in the same volume are two unrelated manuscripts, a collection of epigrams on ff. 1-10, and a body of Italian verse after f. 78, while the Elizabethan anthology falls between these two,

---

[1] I omit from this list the Bannatyne Manuscript, which contains Dd.5.75 items only because Stanford and George Bannatyne copied seven of the same poems from The Treatise of Moral Philosophy. The compilers' tastes were similar in this respect, but they were exposed to entirely different main streams of manuscript literature.

and might be more accurately designated, Harleian MS 7392(2). Apparently, the chief compiler of this manuscript was the antiquarian, St. Loe Knyveton; possibly the secretary hand which appears in the last ten folios of the collection is not his, but the majority of entries on ff. 11-68 are, to judge from his signatures on ff. 11 and 61. This collection seems to have been begun and completed during the 1580's, and compiled entirely of manuscript verse with great concentration on the poems of Dyer, Oxford, Ralegh and Sidney, with perhaps a few additions by the compiler's friends, Robert Allot and Humphrey Coningsby.

Knyveton's texts are seldom as accurate as Stanford's, but he preserved a much greater number of poems by the most famous poets of the age, and his frequent ascriptions, if not always accurate, are more helpful than Stanford's customary reticence.

Similar to Harleian 7392 is the Rawlinson Poetry 85 collection, with thirteen poems in common with Dd.5.75 (Items 95, 96, 101, 107, 109, 113, 197, 198, 201, 202, 208, 212-213, and 216). In his study of this manuscript, Laurence Cummings concluded that it was compiled between 1586 or 1587 and about 1590 by John Finet (1571-1641), both at court and during his enrollment at St. John's College, Cambridge.[1] This is probably the best known and longest used of the Elizabethan anthologies, for from among its 147 entries, scholars for over the past 150 years have taken their copy texts for poems attributed to Dyer, Ralegh, Oxford, Breton, and even, John Lyly. Finet's ascriptions are usually more reliable than Knyveton's, and his texts, generally in the middle range of accuracy between Harleian 7392 and Dd.5.75.

---

[1] Laurence Cummings, "John Finet's Miscellany" (unpublished doctoral dissertation, Washington University, 1960), p. 45. A xerox copy of this edition is available in the University of Chicago Library.

The Arundel Harington Manuscript is primarily a collection of early and pre-Elizabethan verse, but includes six poems in common with Dd.5.75 (Items 95, 96, 106, 107, 212-213, and 222). A family project, the anthology was organized by Sir John Harington of Stepney and Kelston (1520?-1582), and apparently completed by his son, Sir John of Kelston (1560-1612), the well known writer of epigrams and translator of Orlando Furioso.[1] Miss Hughey believes that the elder Harington filled in much of the volume early in Elizabeth's reign or before (p. 62), and that his son gradually filled in the blank leaves between his father's entries. In support of this theory, the Dd.5.75 texts in common with Arundel Harington, which we would expect to be later Elizabethan poems, all occupy the gaps between these older entries. Harington was quite a favorite at court and no doubt had access to the very finest courtly verse, although scribes other than the younger Harington apparently made entries in the manuscript, and three of the texts it shares with Dd.5.75 are not particularly good.

Additional MS 34064[2] contains five poems in common with Dd.5.75 (Items 100, 198, 200, 201, and 212-213), all found in the first forty folios of that manuscript which were probably transcribed in the mid-1590's. In the same section are eight Old Arcadia poems, copied from the edition of 1593 (Ringler, p. 555), extracts from poems also found in Spenser's Complaints volume of 1590, and good texts of a group of poems by Nicholas Breton. The compiler, perhaps the Roger Wright who signs his name on f. 1 with the date,

---

[1] Ruth Hughey, ed., The Arundel Harington Manuscript of Tudor Poetry (2 vols.; Columbus, Ohio, 1960), I, 27-28. Additional MS 28635 is a nineteenth century transcript of Arundel Harington. For my collations of works in this manuscript, I have depended entirely upon Miss Hughey's transcript.

[2] This manuscript is also described by P. M. Buck, Jr., "Add. MS. 34064 and Spenser's Ruins of Time and Mother Hubberd's Tale," MLN, XXII (1907), 41-46. Buck concludes that the excerpts from Complaints represent pre-publication manuscript circulation of the poems.

1596, seems to have enjoyed courtly lyrics without having as free access to them as did Finet, Harington, or even Stanford.

Harleian 6910 is a 194 folio collection of courtly and printed verse copied between 1596 and about 1601 by a professional scribe, probably in the service of a wealthy employer. In the resulting anthology, calligraphy seems to have taken some precedence over textual accuracy, to judge from the six poems in common with Dd.5.75 (Items 95, 109, 196, 198, 216, and 221), all of which contain obvious errors and deletions, without obscuring the fact that the scribe worked from generally sound texts. Spenser's Complaints poetry is copied in the first seventy-four folios, while Professor Ringler has also identified extracts from the Mirror for Magistrates and Chapman's Shadow of Night among the collection's 222 separate items of poetry. The important lyric verse begins on f. 139^v, and all six Dd.5.75 texts occur between ff. 142 and 168.

A professional scribe also may have copied Folger MS. 1.112, perhaps for Ann Cornwallis, a distant relative of Edward deVere, Seventeenth Earl of Oxford, who signs her name on f. 1^v.[1] Four of the twenty-six important poems in this collection are also found in Dd.5.75 (Items 109, 113, 202, and 216). The manuscript consists of only nineteen folios, interleaved with explanatory comments by its nineteenth century owner, Samuel Lysons. As Bond suggests, this is probably a collection of the early 1590's; if so, the taste in poetry is rather old fashioned, for the anthology is dominated by the verse of the early 80's, containing little that had not been written, in all probability, before 1590. Its four Dd.5.75 texts are also found in the Knyveton

---

[1] A transcription of seven non-professional poems by one John Bently in this manuscript, and some further examination of its contents has been printed by William H. Bond, "The Cornwallis-Lysons Manuscript and the Poems of John Bentley," in Joseph Quincy Adams Memorial Studies, ed. James G. McManaway, et al.(Washington, D.C., 1948), pp. 683-693.

and Finet collections, and its readings in each case agree with one or both of these manuscripts more than with Dd.5.75.

Egerton MS 3165, containing Sir Arthur Gorges' "Toyes and Vanities of his Youth," has six works in common with Dd.5.75 (Items 192, 193, 199, 204, 205, and 208).[1] A professional scribe copied the 112 poems in this manuscript, all but a few of which were written by Gorges, who revised and corrected the manuscript in his own hand. This is not, then, a collection gleaned from works circulating in manuscript, but an anthology for the most part of the poet's own works, and thus a very unusual find among sixteenth century manuscripts. A few of these poems found their way into the Knyveton and Finet collections, Item 205 appears in Additional MS 15117, and Items 193, 205, and 208 are found in contemporary print; with six poems, however, Dd.5.75 is the largest collection of Gorges' verse aside from the author's fair copy.

Miss Sandison argues that Stanford's texts are so good that they must have derived from the Egerton manuscript directly, a relationship I would concede only in the case of Item 199, and perhaps, 204. Stanford's extraordinary divergence from the Egerton texts in the remaining cases suggests, I think, that he received these items at several removes from the fair copy. Stanford's transcriptions were made during the early 1590's from texts lacking the corrections Gorges eventually added to his own collection. Miss Sandison points out Sir Arthur's contacts with William Paget and George Berkeley, yet neither one would explain Stanford's access to these poems at this time. I suspect that his position with the Careys must ultimately explain the appearance of Gorges' verse in Dd.5.75.

Among the seven manuscripts in this survey, only the Arundel Harington

---

[1] The manuscript has been edited by Helen Estabrook Sandison as *The Poems of Sir Arthur Gorges* (Oxford, 1953).

collection was definitely compiled over a longer span of years than Dd.5.75. Of the known compilers here, Stanford lacked the social standing of Harington and Finet, yet he managed to acquire nearly 100 unique items of literary merit in addition to many of the choicest courtly works in these and other anthologies. Items 199 and perhaps 204 show a probable direct relationship to the Egerton 3165 texts, but these are the only Dd.5.75 poems which relate more closely to other texts than in position on the same branch of the stemma. And in most cases, Stanford's texts appear to be direct offshoots from the author's original, without links of any sort to other copies.

In comparison with these seven manuscripts and with more than thirty other similar anthologies, Dd.5.75 has a large number of entries. Its 339 separate items compare with 324 in the Arundel Harington Manuscript, 222 in Harleian 6910, 147 in Rawlinson Poetry 85, and only 33 in the smallest of the 200-odd collections I have examined, Folger 1.112. Yet the number of Stanford's Items is misleading, for only 112, 195, 205, and 212-213 exceed 100 lines, while nearly a third of the Items in his professional section are adages and epigrams of from two to four lines each. Word for word, then, Dd.5.75 is actually a smaller collection than Arundel Harington or Harleian 6910, and closer in line count to such average size collections as Rawlinson Poetry 85 or Harleian 7392.

My general study of more than forty literary anthologies plus the collation of their Dd.5.75 texts produced several broad conclusions about Elizabethan manuscript circulation which helps put all these collections in some overall perspective. First, the lack of duplication among these anthologies indicates that an enormous quantity of private literature was available. The more than forty collectors who produced this fraction of the extant collections drew on essentially the same main stream of texts, but turned out quite individual manuscripts. Their one to fifteen works in common with Dd.5.75 are counterbalanced by another group of over 150 contemporary anthologies which duplicate none of Stanford's texts. The compilers' personal tastes, the period of compilation, and their means of access to the flow of manuscript literature naturally account for the specifics of such diversity, yet the diversity itself would have been impossible had there not been so many different works in circulation.

Second, where the anthologies do overlap, textual relationships among them are rarely demonstrable, indicating that relatively few of the original number of texts have been preserved or are now available for study. Not only did an immense number of works circulate, but the more popular ones were soon available in many different versions; the stemma of Item 113 (in the notes), represents the typically multiple lines of descent by which the text of a popular work might be transmitted. The nearly 200 anthologies I have examined probably constitute a meager percentage of all such collections, and doubtless many more of them are extant and awaiting discovery.

An Evaluation of Stanford's Anthology

The significance of the Dd.5 75 collection will not come into full focus until many similar manuscripts have been discovered and examined, although some specific as well as tentative evaluation is possible now, based upon what we already know. To help define the importance of Dd.5.75 I attempt to provide it with a context in the following discussion, limited by what we can expect to learn from equally close studies of other anthologies, and by what we have learned about manuscript literature from contemporary print, the miscellanies and songbooks.

Authorship

Our knowledge of the authorship as well as the texts of the courtly poets rests now on the evidence of early books, for the most part, yet the printer, traditionally excluded from the world of manuscript literature, frequently had no way of knowing who wrote the poems he printed. The ignorance could always be put to good use, of course, by ascribing the poetry to some well known poet, as Richard Jones did to an entire volume, Brittons bowre of Delights, 1591? (STC 3633). In 1592, Nicholas Breton protested that the book came out "altogether without my consent or knowledge, and many thinges of other mens mingled with a few of mine."[1] The miscellanies habitually subscribed individual poems with ambiguous initials, or simply left them unsigned, habits which detract from their value as a means of determining authorship.

A major difficulty in determining authorship in the manuscripts stems from the very nature of manuscript circulation, for the writer who passed along his verse in the traditional manner presumably would never sign his name to it. The same holds true for "outlaw" manuscript literature, which had to be anonymous to be safe. Thus, whoever received the author's copy might well be the last person to know his identity unless he transmitted the name with the poem as it continued to circulate. As a further complication, the names of certain prominent courtiers and public figures were likely to be attached to almost any stray bit of anonymous verse: Sir Walter Ralegh was always good for an ascription in some anthologies, Sidney was another favorite, and so was John Hoskins. As a result, the reputations of many poets no doubt rest in part on verse they did not write. Many of these problems in canon could be resolved through complete studies of the individual manuscripts involved. The overall

---

[1] Jean Robertson, ed., Nicholas Breton: Poems not Hitherto Reprinted (Liverpool, 1952), p. xxv.

accuracy of a manuscript's attributions should be established by comparing them with the definite canons, and the remaining specific cases, through a knowledge of the compiler's identity, the persons he associated with, his residence, and the subsequent likelihood that we would or would not know the work of a given poet. The manuscripts have the great advantage in questions of authorship of having been compiled frequently by those who were personally acquainted with the poets themselves, but we can not make use of this advantage until we are certain of these relationships.

Stanford's contribution to questions of authorship is rather limited, since he subscribed only two poems in the professional section of Dd.5.75; however, both subscriptions are significant. Item 109 is attributed to "W.R.," in agreement with the Harleian 7392 attribution to "RA" (Knyveton's usual abbreviation for Ralegh), and Puttenham's description of an excerpt from the poem in the Arte of English Poesie, "a most excellent dittie written by Sir Walter Raleigh."[1] These seem to be the earliest and most reliable testimonies to Ralegh's authorship, which is virtually certain in this case.

Stanford's second attribution points up the value of knowing something about the compiler of a manuscript. Given Stanford's employment in the Carey household, and the fact that Ferdinando Stanley, Lord Strange, was brother-in-law to George Carey and his wife, Elizabeth, Stanford's attribution of Item 165 to "Ferd. Strange," is undoubtedly reliable. If Stanford knew who wrote the other poems he copied, it is unfortunate that he did not give some indication of authorship, especially to his unique texts. He was more than likely in no position to know who wrote many of his entries, assuming that he received them primarily through his employers and not from the poets directly.

---

[1] George Puttenham, The Arte of English Poesie, ed. Gladys Willcock and Alice Walker (London, 1936), p. 201.

Dating

Composition dates of the better known Elizabethan poems have been largely determined from publication dates of whatever anthologies the verse appeared in, coupled with whatever was known of the poet's life. Here, the printers make an important contribution insofar as their books were either correctly dated, or their dates of publication can be determined very closely through reference to the Stationers' Register and study of bibliographic evidence. Yet printers were often the last to obtain such manuscript poetry as did reach print, and their dates seldom establish more than the last possible moment of composition. The Earl of Surrey, for example, had been dead for ten years before Tottel printed his poetry in 1557, and several versions of Sidney's Arcadia were complete by 1582,[1] and circulating in manuscript within the next few years, although the work did not reach print until 1590.

Manuscript compilers, on the other hand, were the first to obtain copies of such private works, but they did not often assign dates to their entries, while the manuscripts themselves, where they have been studied at all, are often assigned to no more definite limits than a certain decade. Obviously, dates of composition can be more accurately determined from the manuscripts, but only after establishing their dates of transcription. Again, this will usually require study of the entire collection, with attempts to date each work by reconstructing the physical condition of the volume where necessary and discovering the chronological order of its entries.

Fortunately, analysis of this evidence in Dd.5.75 provides fairly precise means for dating the transcription of Stanford's most important literary texts, entered in the "public" section of his anthology between ff. 25 and 40 (see pp. 39-42). The poems that can now be dated as a result of these findings

---

[1] Ringler, p. 370.

have in some cases never been so closely dated with an confidence. Item 95, Dyer's "He that his mirth hath lost," is the earliest work Stanford entered in the "public" section, transcribed no doubt between 1580 and 1585. Dyer's editor, Ralph Sargent, conjectures that most of Dyer's verse was written between 1560 and 1590(!), and that this poem was probably written while he was out of favor at court between 1572 and 1575.[1] The location of this work in Dd.5.75, however, provides the first real evidence that it was composed before c. 1585.

The seven Sidney poems before f. 27 (Items 96, 100, 101, 102, 103, 106, and 107), can be dated in other manuscripts before 1585, so that their position here merely shows that Stanford had access to these works during the first few years of their circulation. Item 109, Ralegh's "Calling to mynd," is entered on f. 27^r, and was probably copied in 1585, if not slightly before. In either case, the evidence of Dd.5.75 pushes back the composition date of this poem by a few years, for the only other certain dating is Puttenham's reference in 1589.

Between the Musica Transalpina lyrics of late 1588 and the Marprelate entries of late 1589 lies the unique poem by Ferdinando Stanley, evidence that his verse was circulating by at least 1589. This is the only definite dating of Stanley's work, since all other references to him as a poet are posthumous.

Items 188-208, the works in gathering five following the Marprelate tract, were unquestionably transcribed after 1589, and probably no more than a five-year span is represented in these folios. If this is a correct estimate, Item 188 came into Stanford's hands at least five years before Thomas Morley printed the only other known version in his First Book of Ayres, 1600, song 11.

---

[1] Ralph M. Sargent, At the Court of Queen Elizabeth, The Life and Lyrics of Sir Edward Dyer (London, 1935), p. 167.

Four more works by Sidney appear in this section (Items 194, 195, 196, and 200), along with five poems undisputably written by Gorges (Items 192, 199, 204, 205, and 208). Miss Sandison argues (p. xxxii) that these works were composed c. 1584, but their position in Dd.5.75 suggests only that they were circulating in unrevised form during the early 90's. In this same grouping, Item 201 by Breton appears at least five years before it first entered print in the 1600 England's Helicon. The version of Amoretti VIII here (Item 197), is probably the unrevised form which circulated in manuscript before Spenser added some final touches and published it in the Amoretti and Epithalamion of 1595.

Textual Improvement

Far more important than either authorship or dating, the known texts of much Elizabethan verse can be improved through a study of the manuscript sources. Again, the printer's exclusion from the most elite realms of manuscript circulation often kept him from getting the best texts. Thus, after extensive study and editing of the Tudor miscellanies, Hyder Rollins concluded that the Phoenix Nest of 1593 was "the most carefully printed miscellany . . . of the period. I think it evident that R. S. [the editor] not only followed copies derived from the authors themselves, but also read the proofs with care."[1] In the cases of two poems by Sir Arthur Gorges, however, we can compare the Phoenix Nest versions with those approved by the author: "Would I were changed into that golden shower" and "The gentle season of the year" (pp. 81 and 87 in Rollins' edition), also appear in Egerton MS 3165, Gorges' fair copy of his own works. In the first poem, the printed text contains nine substantive variants in its eighteen lines, and there are thirty-eight variants in the forty-two lines of the second. Even so, the Phoenix Nest texts are

---

[1] Hyder Rollins, ed., The Phoenix Nest (Cambridge, Mass., 1931), p. xxxi.

fairly good, as Gorges' editor admits[1]--but obviously, these texts and others in the printed anthologies, are not the best ones, and depend for correction on discovery and analysis of superior manuscript versions.

The compilers of such manuscripts often obtained very good texts, directly from the authors themselves in some instances, yet the process of manuscript transmission often detracts from this advantage. The Gorges manuscript is a rare exception, for in most cases, the modern editor must work from copies several or many times removed from the author's original. Such copies are almost always corrupt to some extent, for the secretary hand, in almost universal use throughout Elizabeth's reign, did not lend itself to accurate copying. It was characterized by almost indistinguishable forms for many letters and combinations of letters: 'c,' 'r,' and 't,' 'a,' 'o,' and 'e,' 'm,' 'n,' and 'u,' are either quite similar or virtually identical in many hands; 'f' and long 's' were frequently confused, or the swash 's' and descender could easily be taken for 'sl' or 'st.' The abbreviations for "with" and "which" (wth and w^{ch}) are interchangeable in most hands, and the common abbreviations for 'es' and 'us' endings could easily be mistaken for a single 'e' or 'y' or 'g,' or even, a meaningless flourish. The list could be infinitely extended with specific examples, but the point is that a manuscript poem which had been copied by one or two different hands usually picked up a good many more errors than a poem which had passed through two or three editions of print.

To demonstrate this, consider Rollins' complaint that with the 1559 third edition of Tottel's *Miscellany*, "degeneration of the text has been accelerated by careless printing and still more careless proof-reading";[2] yet

---

[1] Sandison, pp. 183, 201.

[2] Hyder Rollins, ed., *Tottel's Miscellany* (revised ed.; 2 vols.; Cambridge, Mass., 1966), II, 23.

the cumulative percentage of substantive variants through the 1559 edition averages about .006 in a random sample of pages, while a similarly distanced manuscript copy of Sidney's Astrophil and Stella with .013 per cent error is considered quite accurate.[1] As another example, the text of "Her face, her tongue, her wit" (Item 193), picked up only two very minor variant readings in the course of four editions of the Poetical Rhapsody (1602, 1608, 1611, 1612), while each of the six extant manuscript texts varies from any other by at least five words. In short, a text deteriorated more rapidly during manuscript transmission than through printed editions. Thus, editors of Elizabethan verse can expect to find rather average texts of those works which did enter print, and must hope that the better manuscript copies have survived or can be reconstructed.

The value of Dd.5.75 texts depends, of course, upon the quality of the materials copied, and the copyist's accuracy. Stanford did not have access to the best versions of every poem he added to his collection; his definite Breton poems, for example (Items 198, 201), are more corrupt than the texts in Additional MS 34064, and Item 201 is the most corrupt of three manuscript copies. The Dyce MS 44 version of Item 209 is slightly superior to Stanford's, and Harington's text of Item 112,[2] Queen Elizabeth's speech to Parliament, is better than either the Dd.5.75 or Tanner 169 versions. These are, however, the exceptions, and nearly all of them that are readily determinable, for Stanford seems to have had access to uniformly good texts. His copy of "The state of France," Item 113, is the best of nine manuscript texts I have collated with it. All eleven Sidney poems in Dd.5.75 are substantive, and four

---

[1] Ringler, p. 540.

[2] Printed from the family papers in the 1768 Nugae Antiquae; see the Notes to this Item.

of them (Items 194, 195, 196 and 200), superior to versions in the other manuscript anthologies. Stanford's texts of Items 99 and 188 are manifestly better than those printed in Morley's First Book of Ayres, Item 222 serves as copy text in Bradner's Poems of Queen Elizabeth I, and Item 216, Dyer's "I would yt were not as yt is," is the best of the two complete versions.

The Contribution of New Texts

The greatest value of the manuscript anthologies, of course, is their preservation of unique and unprinted works of genuine literary merit. These resources have been largely neglected by modern editors, who have been concerned for the most part with culling the manuscripts for individual works by known authors. The anonymous works, the satiric and suppressed works, the uniquely private world of literature here, remains to be read and appreciated.

I am not suggesting that new Faery Queenes and Shakespearean plays necessarily lie awaiting discovery in these unstudied manuscripts, but only that a good deal of valuable work from this golden age of English literature remains to be brought forth and enjoyed. The Gorges collection, Egerton 3165, is a dramatic case in point, for until its discovery in 1940, Sir Arthur's reputation as a lyric poet was largely hearsay, his canon uncertain, and less than a dozen of his poems known even as anonymous works. Miss Sandison's edition of the Gorges anthology revived a nearly forgotten courtly poet, bringing to light a number of pleasing but heretofore unknown poems.

Ferdinando Stanley is still a "lost poet," and several other Elizabethan poets exist more in reputation than in available, recognized works. Consider for example Henry Peacham's claim in The Compleat Gentleman (1625, STC 19502a, pp. 95-96), that "In the time of our late Queene Elizabeth . . . aboue others, who honoured Poesie with their pennes and practice (to omit her Maiestie, who had a singular gift herein) were Edward Earle of Oxford, the Lord Buckhurst, Henry Lord Paget; our Phoenix, the noble Sir Philip Sidney, M. Edward Dyer, M. Edmund Spencer, M. Samuel Daniel, with sundry others." Of these, only Sidney, Spenser and perhaps Daniel can be studied with any confidence that their major output is available. The canons of Oxford and Dyer are yet to be salvaged from the manuscripts; I do not know of any verse written by Buckhurst after Gorboduc, nor of a single line of poetry by Henry, Lord Paget. These and "sundry others" remain to be discovered and evaluated as poets. And beyond such specific quests lie the works which we may never be able to link with their authors, but which nevertheless deserve an audience.

In the following discussion of Dd.5.75's unique contents I will be concerned only with those texts which have evident literary value; the Biblical riddles (Items 309-317), and the bawdy ones between Items 318 and 330, 332 and 334 are not of exceptional interest. The unique works by Stanford and his pupils, primarily on ff. 1-20, 51^v-54, and 57, are of importance to our knowledge of the compiler and the circumstances of compiling Dd.5.75, without having great literary merit of their own.

Among the most interesting unique texts in Dd.5.75 are Items 252-280 and 294-306, a series of forty-two entries in verse and prose numbered 1 through 40 (4 and 23 appear twice, 17 is omitted, and Item 305 is not numbered). Stanford, similarly, had numbered several of the Musica Transalpina lyrics according to their order in the songbook, and I would not be surprised to find these riddles and satires showing up in some printed book, although their present unique status requires some consideration here.

If these works were printed, it is probable that the book was officially suppressed, for some of the satire treads on very dangerous ground. The attack on royal monopolies in Item 279, or the condemnation of the legal system in Item 299 might have escaped, but when we read:

> she y^t so many yeares refusd to wed, & boasted
> what virginitie was worthe
> Even she I say hath lost her maidenhead & daughters
> .3. to all ye world brought forthe
> W^ch Ile averre on Churche & on Churchesteple are bastar<u>des</u>
> bred right children of ye people
>
> (Item 275:10-12)

the apparent references to Elizabeth could hardly have been tolerated. Other attacks in this wide-ranging series are levelled at tobacco (Items 255, 298), spendthrift nobles (Item 253), and cutpurses (Item 251), along with epigrammatic portrayals of "Aetos" and "Ixion" (Items 276, 303), and a number of rather toothless riddles and jokes; erudite diction and snippets from foreign languages characterize the style throughout this grouping. Altogether, they reflect Stanford's taste for satire, libel, and riddles of all kinds.

Akin to these genres are the numerous moral adages, wise sayings, and genuine epigrams Stanford included in his anthology. The twenty-nine saws he transcribed from the <u>Treatise of Moral Philosophy</u> form the largest single grouping of this sort in Dd.5 75. From unknown sources Stanford copied Items 138-146, couplets on a variety of subjects, from cynical rejection of the world to child psychology. Items 238-251 are more typical of the epigrams which became popular during the mid and late 1590's--Item 238, indeed, is entitled "an epigram of an vntriftie gallant." This series of short works is diverse in content and may not have been taken from a single source or copied all at once. The dominant themes here are the importance of thrift and the means for living a pious life, plus one alliterative gem, "where will wantes wit welth worketh woe" (Item 250), and one truly humorous epigram, Item 242.

In the same general vein of moral didacticism, Item 114 is a thirty-six line harangue against the evil state of affairs in this world, beginning, "No faith nor frend nor suretie vnder sonne." A number of similar complaints crowd the pages of Tottel's <u>Miscellany</u>, the <u>Paradise of Dainty Devises</u>, and the works of the Turberville, Grimald, Googe school, in their more alliterative moods. The subscription, "Sarū" possibly refers to the tune of "Salisbury Plain," the recommended accompaniment for "Ye louing wormes come learne of me" in the <u>Handful of Pleasant Delites</u> (1584).[1]

The unique lyric poems in Dd.5.75 can be considered in two somewhat arbitrary groups, the representatives of the mid-century tradition, and the poetry of the "Golden Age." The most successful lyric in the first group is Item 97, a gracefully worded lover's complaint. Items 98, 203, 218, and 224-226 are melancholy laments, introspections and farewells in the <u>Paradise</u> fashion, set to the familiar poulter's and tetrameter couplets of the "Drab Age" syndrome. Somewhat more imaginative are Items 104 and 105, in which the lover expresses his mournful state by explaining its analogies with the surrounding landscape. All nine works in the older style are good enough examples of a tradition which, even as Stanford transcribed them, had been superseded by Spenser, Sidney and the later writers of Elizabethan poetry.

Among the unique texts of the second group are three technical experiments of interest not only because they are fairly successful poems, but because the second two seem to be very early examples of the break from the regular iambic foot and trite stanza forms which paralyzed mid-century poetry--a break which does not become noticeable in print until after the spread of Sidney's influence during the early 90's.

Item 94 is a purely experimental mixture of trochaic and iambic lines in three, five line stanzas. Internal rime occurs irregularly in the first three lines of each stanza, which range between seven and eight feet, while

---

[1] Hyder Rollins, ed., <u>A Handful of Pleasant Delights</u>, Dover Paperbacks (New York, 1965), p. 43.

the last two lines always form heroic couplets. The position of Item 94, at the very end of the "domestic" section of Dd.5.75, suggests that it may have been copied as late as 1613, and was therefore hardly an innovation.

Items 111 and 115 are more successful experiments. Composed before 1588, and perhaps as early as 1585 or 1586, they are undoubtedly avant garde for their day. Item 111, a concrete and sensual description of a woman, could have been the prototype for Sidney's "What tongue can her perfections tell" (Item 195)--but written not in iambic but in anapestic tetrameter couplets. Granted, Thomas Tusser, the "King of the Anapest," had used this meter extensively years before, but never for such lyric purposes. Stanford did not classify his entries by their form or meter, but it is interesting that this unusual work occurs on the same page with the Parry slander, a poem in trochaic hexameter couplets, and thus something of a metrical icebreaker in its own right.

Even more unusual is Item 115, a lover's expression of despair in dactylic tetrameter couplets, a form so exotic that not even Sidney is known to have tried it. The subject is nothing new, of course, but the form gives it new life and the last two lines are a fitting and unusually philosophical climax.

Of the remaining love lyrics, Item 165 is of interest as one of three known works by Ferdinando Stanley, and the only important unique text in Dd.5.75 which bears an attribution. Item 207, which compares a love triangle to a game of primero, provides an interesting contrast with Item 113, which compares French politics of the 80's to this same card game. Item 211 is an unusual portrayal of the tease, and Item 235, an uncommon reply from the woman's viewpoint to the hyperbolic promises of a lover; in this case, the woman suspects his real intentions and chastely declines his suit.

Of miscellaneous interest are Items 179 and 180, two French songs copied about 1589. Items 189 and 190 are apparently companion pieces, for in both, a man is chiding a woman for unnecessary quarreling. Item 206 is a Breton-esque pastoral not far removed in the manuscript from two of his known works (Items 198 and 201), although I would hesitate to say that it is his. Item 220, a Churchyardean plea for the Queen's marriage, is contrasted a few pages later with Item 228, the 1599 speech by the players to the Queen; the players wished her not a husband and children, but only eternal life. Their hope "that the babe wch now is yong/ & hathe yet no vse of tongue/ many a shrouetyde here may bow/ to y^t empresse I doe now," (11. 5-6), indicates that the play was given during the Shrovetide season, February 18-21, but the only known play acted during that period was Henry Chettle's Troy's Revenge, with the Tragedy of Polyphemus; unfortunately, the text is lost and there is no evidence that it was played before the Queen.[1]

To summarize, this survey of some eighty-three unique Items in Dd.5.75 previews the diverse materials we can expect to find among the unique texts in similar anthologies. Other versions, at least for some of these eighty-three works, will almost certainly turn up as other manuscript anthologies are examined; for the moment, however, they represent Dd.5.75's new contributions to Elizabethan literature.

Conclusion

Stanford's collection then, does contribute something of importance to each major category of information and material which, ideally, should derive from study of an Elizabethan manuscript anthology. It provides important, early testimony for Ralegh's authorship of "Calling to mind," and for Ferdinando Stanley's claim to Item 165; it establishes the latest possible

---

[1] Alfred Harbage, Annals of English Drama, revised by S. Schoenbaum (Philadelphia, 1964), pp. 68-69.

dates of composition for poems by Dyer, Breton and Ralegh, which are at the same time earlier than any other source could confirm; it provides substantive texts of works by Sidney, Gorges, Spenser, and Queen Elizabeth, among others, and contributes unique texts--lyrics, satires, epigrams, and riddles--diversely representative of sixteenth-century private literature.

For all this, Dd.5.75 is only one collection, and can reveal only a small portion of the great undercurrent of manuscript literature. The extent of the Dd.5.75 contribution, moreover, will not be precisely known until other such anthologies have been studied in equal detail. Perhaps the most intriguing unanswered questions in Stanford's anthology center upon the authorship of his anonymous and unique texts, for nearly any of the best poets of the age, including Shakespeare, could be represented in this group. It would also be interesting to know exactly how Stanford's transcriptions compare in accuracy with those of his fellow collectors, and how many of the works in Dd.5.75 are truly unique. Insofar as these questions can be answered, the answers will come through complete studies and evaluations of similar anthologies. This overall study will reveal the nature and importance of this whole body of manuscript material, introducing a new and important dimension to our understanding of Elizabethan literature.

Textual Apparatus

In the following transcription of Dd.5.75 I have attempted to reproduce accurately the format as well as the spelling and punctuation of the original. Thus the indentation of lines, rules between individual works or stanzas, and the location on the page of titles, signatures and catchwords follow the layout of the manuscript page as closely as possible. What could not be so conveniently indicated with the typewriter--brackets, flourishes, changes of ink or hand, blottings, smears, and the like--are described in transcriptional notes at the bottom of the page. Additional textual and collation notes for each item in Dd.5.75 will be found at the end of the transcription.

Page numbers of the present text are in arabic numerals, centered at the top of each page between hyphens. The items in Dd.5.75 have been numbered consecutively in arabic numerals, in brackets, centered above the first line of each separate work. Line numbers for each item are given in brackets, usually in the right margin, at five line intervals. Except for the prose passages, these line numbers indicate the number of lines in that work considered by itself, and are determined generally by rime scheme, regardless of how the lines were copied into Dd.5.75. Prose selections are numbered according to the number of lines they occupy on the manuscript page. Foliation is also indicated with brackets in the right margin, while collation markings, including the foliation added to the manuscript at some time after it left the hands of its compiler, are omitted from the transcription.

It was not possible to make a page-for-page transcription of the manuscript because its compiler averaged more than forty lines to the page, while barely twenty will fit the double spaced standard sheet.

Cross-outs or illegible words in the text are indicated by pointed brackets (< >), and any reconstruction of an indecipherable reading is italicized. Letters which do not have a distinctive capital form ('d,' 'm,' 'w,' and 'y,' for example), are transcribed as miniscules where the writer's intention appears uncertain. Long 's' has been normalized, but the contractions are retained throughout, except for the following forms which cannot be readily duplicated on a standard typewriter:

-lxvi-

ꝙ	expanded to	qu*od*
ẽ	"	*es*
ᷡ	"	*us*
ꝓ	"	*pro*
ꝑ	"	*per* or *pre*
ꝶ	"	*er*, *re*, or M*aster*
ꝗ (que)	represented by	q;

THE TEXT OF CAMBRIDGE UNIVERSITY LIBRARY

MANUSCRIPT Dd.5.75

[Item 1] [f. 1

My loue is pure & true, I never lerned to flatter
    nor never tyme or thing shall cause, yt for to moue or totter
Since then the case thus standes, & that no store I have
    of pedlars ware or parfumed gloves, wch me fr$\bar{o}$ shame might save
lest that I might now seme, more rude, then clounishe swayn   [5
yf that I nothing should present, wch so much bound remayn
In verses thes I gyue, my hart & willing mynd
W^{ch} for to dwell alwayes wth you yt fullie now I bynd
before that I do shrinke or fr$\bar{o}$ this promise swarve
the rockes shall swyme in toppes of seas & meat shall make m$\bar{e}$ starve   [10
Trent shall I say before, run over scowfill hill.
& mountes shall moue out of ther place & run the seas vntill
And monsters vncouthe strange, shall joyn in league of loue
before that any worldly thing do cause my mynd to moue
for tripping stag shall chuse, the tigre for his make   [15
And doue the Eagle for his fear, as then shall not forsake
nor seelie shepe the paw, of lion feirce shall fear
And clyming goat in salt sea⟨s⟩ foames, to swym then we shall hear
befor that I forget, what dutie that I owe
    or cease wth wordes or thoughtes or deedes, yt alwayes
                forth to shooe   [20
Receaue for newyeres gift, this shew of loving mynd
    & in all dutie & good will, me slacke you shall not fynd
I pray almightie god, wch rules the golden sphear
---

to graunt to you all happines, & many a merye year.

And that when you shall passe, out of this vaile of payn [25

you may wth him in cristall skyes alwayes in pleasure raigne.

   Your little sonne Will Paget dothe

    thes verses to you send

  wch in good will gives place to none

   & thus he makes an end.

    68

     [Item 2]   [f. 1^v]

1581.   A newyeres gift

A gloue I do present, in signe of mindfull mynd

 god graunt yt may thie fingers fit, & hand in no place bynd

no parfume I them gaue, for that wer folie great

thie handes alreadie are parfumed, more sweete thē violet

the yealow golden bend, wch thē doth compasse round   [5

dothe shew the golden precious giftes, in wch thou dost abound

thie beutie golden is, & yealow golden hear

& giftes wch thou in mynd possessest, most golden are & rare

thie modest courteous speache, & gentle haviour mild

 are worthie of eternall fame, yf I be not beguiled.   [10

the fear & loue of god, wch in thie brest doth raigne

 do make the seeme a heavenlie wight, or erthly goddesse playn

If that thou lyved haddest, in ancient tyme of yore

Item 1] No carry-over lines in the MS.

when that to superstition men, were given more & more
    they would haue the advaun'st, aboue the starrie skie   [15
  & caused this fame by trumpet shrill, throughout the world to flie.
The youthfull colours w^{ch}, my gloue in riband beares
do shew the green & flowring glie, of thie yong tender yeres
the workmanship wch makes, thē s⟨e⟩me bothe fine & feat
is for to shew the curious shape, of all thie partes most neat   [20
& eke the glittering glee, of mynd wth virtues frought
wch dothe excell the Indian pearle, & thing_es_ of greatest weight
Receaue therfore this gloue, wch frend to the dothe gyue
  & kinsman alwayes to cōmand, as long as he shall lyue
God graunt that thou mayest lyue, full many & merie a year   [25
& that of gloves I may bestow, on the full many a payr
god graunt the for to haue, the sōm of thie desire
& send the such a fere as thou, in mynd dost most require
wch will the serue & loue, & seeke to please thie mynd
no otherwise then Gracchus did, to his Cornel' him bynd   [30
or as that Plaute' was, to Horestill' his wife
whom he more loved as the effect did shoo, thē his own pr_o_per life
And that of pretie Impes, thou mayst bring forth great store
wch the in face resemble may & eke in vertuous lore
& that when thou hast lyved old Nestors aeged yeares   [35
    thou mayst receaved be in joy, wher never greif appeares.
                36

              [Item 3]   [f. 2

   1581.   A new yeares gift
The face they say a picture is, of mynd wch lurkes wthin

If that be true then mynd of thin, no doubt is most devyne.
thie pure & clear complexion, wch staynes the lilie whight
dothe shew the purenes of thie mynd, & glorious virtues bright
thie roseall & carnation cheekes, wch precious stones do passe [5
do shew thy modest maidens mynd, wch never stayned was
thie cherefull looke & cristall ey, wch twinkleth as a starre.
dothe shew thy wit wch dothe excell, thie sex in most thinges farre
thy heavenlie hear in colour like, to glittering files of gold
doth shew that mynd of thine is fraught, wth treasures more vntold [10
thie pretie mouthe wch sendeth out, thy breath perfumed & sweete
dothe shew thie fear & loue to god, wch ar for the most meete
If then thou art in outward shew, most fair, for to behold
the virtues of thie mynd no doubt, do passe the purest gold
for basest thinges are left abroad, & Iewels of great price [15
ar locked vp in secret place, of them wch would seme wise
since then thy giftes wch ar abroad, most rare & precious ar
no doubt thou keepest in mynd locket vp, y wch thes passeth farre.
for he wch the hathe made, most careful is & wise

   wherfore this greatest treasures he, hath hidden frō our eyes [20
Al hail thou pearles paragon, god send the happie chaunce
& many new yeares for to see, & fame of thyn t'advaunce
& loving husband wch may hold, the (wch shalt be his wif)
more dear as thou wilt wel deserue, then his own propre life
God send the little pretie babes, wch the may mother call [25

And worldlie ioyes as many as, ther droppes of rayn do fall
when little kid starres they do sette, vnder the Atlantick seas
Or when that boistrous sothern wyndes, to send Ioue yt doth please
And when that thou hast run the race, of long & happie dayes
   for to enioy a place wth him wch heavenly scepter swaise   [30
      On wch a favrer is, of rare good giftes of thine
         hath ventred his good wil to shew, in rude & ragged rime.
   32.

[Item 4]   [f. 2ᵛ

Althoughe thou art not sprong of princes as I hear
   yet sure thie bewtie doth deserue a prince to be thie fere
   what face more worthie is to wear the golden crown
   what countenance a royale court more better may becom
   the roses do not match thie pretie lippes most sweete   [5

                                 whight
nor yet the snow thie necke doth passe althoughe yt be most
⟨be most whight⟩
   The violet<u>es</u> do yeue place to shining hear of thine.
   and twinckling starres to thie clear eyes ther glorie do resign
   how iust proportion both, thie browes betwene the̅ beares.   [10
   what modestie can ther be more then in thie cheekes appeares

                 cherry
                 comlie
   An equall mixture is of white & ⟨purple⟩ red
   for nether haue they to much bloud nor yet are pale as lead
   thie pretie fingers passe Auroraes though most pure
14 thie streight & stately corps excelles Dianaes I am sure.   [15
   thou dost surpasse thie sexe.

   Item 4: 8] 'The' is written over the crossed out line 7, and
'violet<u>es</u>,' entered just below 7.

[Item 5]

The marigold all flowers doth passe in glittering glorious hew
    And eke in sweete & pleasaunt smell yt giveth place to few
althoughe the crimson roses fair & gilliflowers most braue
    do vaunt & bost in orient hue, yet no such sweete they haue
This flower wth phe<u>bus</u> glorious beames doth turn in evry place   [5
    from whence yt takes such pleasaunt light ẙ none can yt disgrace
yf that my iudgment curraunt were & that my hest might stand
    this flower should be preferred before all other in this land
let other men place their delight in violet<u>es</u> purple blew
    in pances or in rosmary or others fresh of hue   [10
yet none shall wyn my hart but this wch doth surpasse thē all
                  beames
as farre as phe<u>bus</u> lamp surmountes a little candle small
yf that this flower in presence be yt doth m̄y ey so please
    that I the ioifull sight therof for no on thing would lease
the fragraunt swetnes doth delight so much my sence & mynd   [15
    that I me thinkes all pleasures ther & worldly ioyes do fynd
O pereles flower of princely hue all good I wish to the
    And that wth heat of sonne nor frost thou never parched be
    that
but this pleasaunt colours fresh for ever thou mayest kepe
and that for thie decay or harme we haue no cause to wepe   [20
    yf for my self now I should wish the greatest & best good hap
22. yt should be this the for to haue my sweete flower in my lap.

[Item 6]   [f. 3

so fair a creature never I, wth eyes of myne haue sene
    nor so bedect wth bewtie braue she semes to be a quene.
to golden glittering ve(nu)s she in bewtie may compare

in wit Minerva she doth match & other giftes most rare.
Even as a golden glittering star, in moist & darksom night [5
    doth draw mens eyes yt to behold & therin to delight
even so the heavenly passing hew of this sweete bonni bell
    doth charme mens eyes & th̄ constrayn, on her fair face to dwell.
What ever that she dothe or turnes her heavenly face
                                makes   haue
    streight steppes behind her comlines, & yeues yt a good grace [10
In worthie face of hers such maiestie doth shine
    that yt amazeth ech mans mynd, & makes th̄ for to pine
he wch doth go about to yeld to the dew praise
    is as absurd as though he should powre water in the seas
or as yf that he should on Cycill men bestow [15
    great store of corn since in their soil most plentie ther doth grow
  as
or ⟨yf⟩ yf to the wooddes sōm fuel he would lend
    ch
  w   do to vs at all assayes aboundaunce therof send.

                    [Item 7]

                question

fayr Ccourteous Dame I the besech this question to vnfold
    and tell to me what knight he is wch the in armes doth hold.
and what are yonder yonkers thre, wch hither com apace
wch do resemble the somwhat in countenance & face.

    Item 6:11] Between 'hers' and 'such,' two or three letters have been crossed out.

    Item 6:11-12] Bracketed along the right margin.

Answere

The first good syr my vncle is, on fathers syde doubtles [5
    the second on my mothers syde my vncle is no les
    the third is on my bodie born myn own & naturall child
    & all are sonnes vnto this knight or els he is beguild.

    & all ⟨be⟩ are born in wedlocke true w^{th}out all breach of law
    no swarving from the cōmon course the breadth of hear or straw. [10

resolution

suppose that Benet for his wife a ⟨lustie⟩ braue. widow hathe wonne
    wch by a former husband had on Williā to her sonne
    & he on her begat also a lustie gallaunt boye
    wch cleped was Antonio his mothers only ioye
    & when that fates this former wife from Benet had bereft [15
    an other widow then he toke wch had a daughter left
    by husband wch before she had men Catheryne her did call.
    of this same widow he begat a sonne wch clept was paul.
    now eldest sonne of former wife wch Williā had to name
    did match himself wth Catheryn a fair & comly Dame [20
    & of her this same williā a daughter did beget
    wch frauncesse hight & maried was to him wch called was Benet
    of frauncesse Benet did beget a boy wch Robert hight
    wch proved in course of tyme to be a braue & ⟨noble knight⟩ worthie wight
    The aeged knight wch did imbrace the fair & comly dame [25
    Syr Benet hight his ladie fair dame frauncesse had to name
Antonio vncle is doubtles to her by fathers side

-10-

& Paul by mother vncle is this case is clearly tried
to haue a sonne wch Robert hight is fallen vnto her lot
& all these thre in wedlocke are of Benet right begot [30
wthout all filthy stayn or spotte of Incest as I weene
wch once my resolution skanned most playnly may be seene.

[Item 8] [f. 3^v]

for to vnfold these riddles darke my skyll is veray small
they may more riper wittes then myn, wth hardnes sone appall
I never was acquaynted wth old Œdipus his skyll
nor yet of springes of Helicon haue dronke throughout my fill.
for to obey your honours hest this rash attempt I gaue [5
& for my rudenes humbly I good madam pardon craue
at all tymes redy prest I am your will for to obey
as far as little power of myn may reatch by any way
wch thing er I forget the day shall chaunged be to night
the sea shall burn the fier shall freese the sonne shall
       leese his light [10
your riddle I haue aymed at as wittes of myn would reatch
yf I haue missed I hope the truth you madam will me teach
your little scoller in this art I greatly long to be
  yf you can teach me to vnfold so straunge a mysterie,
  but least that over rude & bold your ladiship me deeme [15

Item 7] A diagram of the riddle has been drawn in the right margin, extending from the title line to line 9:

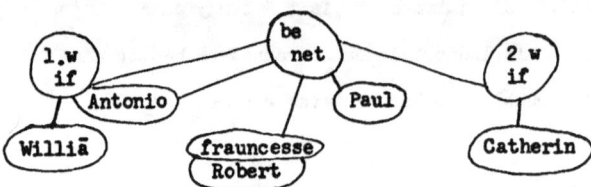

or that the rules of modestie t'haue passed I might seeme
In humble sort I take my leaue, god gard & keepe you aye
& send to you as many ioyes as flowers ther are in maye
or fleting fishes in the Temes or starres in welkyn clear
or chirping birdes on pleasaunt trees or minutes in a year [20
& that when you haue lyved in ioye thrice Nestors aeged day⟨s⟩
you may a place possesse in heaven, wher never joy decayes
  your little nephew thoughe as yet
    power
  his ⟨force⟩ & might be small
  in good will to your ladiship
  gives place to none at all.
24

[Item 9]

On brother by my fathers side, I haue, the truth to show
 an other by my mother side my brother is also
The third is of my body born, & lawfully begotte
& all be sonnes to husband myn wthout all maner spotte
of filthie crime or Incest vile as playnly I can proue [5
althoughe to you at first yt may som admiration moue.

[Item 10]

Syr on is my brother by my fathers syde the truth to show
 the other by my mothers side is my brother also
the third is my own sonne lawfully begotte
& alle sonnes to my husband that sleepes on my lap [5
wthout hurt of lignage in any degree

Item 8] No carry-over lines in the MS.

shew me by reason how this may be.

[Item 11]

1582. A new yeres gift

In sign that phebus now: his course & race hath ronne
& proofe that Ioifull Ianus hath: an other year begonne
As Herault of my hart least that I seme vnkynd
          to you.
these verses rude & harsh, as newyeres gift I send
for what? shall other men? ther frendes wth giftes present
Shall Tib & Thom & Colin Clout: by giftes shew how they ar bent
        ⟨ ⟩ good will make no show.
And I like lumpish swayn: ceasse ⟨my good will to show⟩
to you my dear & loving Aunt. to. whom so much I ow
nay then I might be thought: t'haue suckt som tigres teat
& in the desert savage woodes: t' haue had my dwelling seat
      good will ⟨shown⟩
for yf that ⟨loue bestowed:⟩ require like loue agayn
     borne me most entier good will   playn
to haue ⟨loved me most entierly well:⟩ you haue showed by profes most
yf band of kynred do: a faithfull hart require
   nede no more
I ⟨ther nedes no more⟩ you are know to be the sister to my syre
  courte⟨sie⟩ s   deserue
yf ⟨benefites⟩ bestowed ⟨require⟩ a gratfull mynd
you haue don ynough to linke me fast & ever for to bynd
yf long acquayntaunce breede: loue wch is like to last
                  life   passed
wth you the halfe of all my ⟨tyme⟩ I thinke now I haue ⟨placed⟩ .
  Sith then so many knottes: me faste to you haue tied

-13-

            forget in legue of loue & dutie
     Shall I ⟨be found in league of loue vnwilling⟩ for to byde   [20

nay ⟨first⟩ first all natures workes shall topsie turvie turne

the fier shall freese, the earth shall sinke, the brinishe seas shall burne

    the ryvers shall retore. into ther springes agayn

    and heaven & all shall be resolved into old Chaos playn.

& therfore this new yere: to shew my myndfull mynd   [25

   I wish that you all pleasures may: & wished ioyes now fynd.

more then ther are tenne fold: bright starres in welkyn clear

   or names or kyndes of thinges in th' world: or minutes in a year

more then ther colours are or flowres, wch decke the grounde

more then of golden girles ther may, in any place be founde   [30

more then ther fishes swime, or birdes in ayr do flie

                         fowles
more then ther fethers are of ⟨birdes⟩ or shippes at anchore lie

more then ther are in heaven of sayntes & happie wightes

more then ther tormentes are in hell: or store of develish spirites

                                 &   bathed in
And that when you haue lived: long tyme ⟨in ioye⟩ & blisse   [35

to lyue in heaven eternally, you never fayl nor misse

               to shew his loving mynd

               your nephew hath begonne

         wch shall continew fast & firm   38.

               till lunaes date be donne.

                 38.

              [Item 12]

1582.

by newyeres gift to seperate, you twayn wch so are knit

-14-

    In bloud in mynd in all respectes, I thinke yt farre vnfit
by bloud & birth you sisters are in mynd most loving frendes
    In bewtie rare such paragons, as seldom nature sendes
    In wit in favour & good grace, sure of som phœnix kynd   [5
    I thinke such two could scarse be found, fro͞m Orcades to Ind
    your heavenly hew most perfect i⟨s⟩, your features passing fyn
I ⟨thinke⟩
for to adorn your face ye haue stolen fro͞ Cupid both his eyen
no marvell now yf that to him no sight at all be left
since you his eyes as twinckling starres fro͞ him haue guite bereft   [10
                         ye
In modest gentle haviour myld of all you bear bel
In courtesie & virtue rare, your sexe you do excell
your parentes happie are no doubt wch haue such daughters twayn
    I thinke when you cam to this world som͞ golden starres did raign
your kinsmen happie are by you, & I among the rest   [15
but happiest he whom ye shall deme, meete to be loved best
yf that my fancie I may speake & seeke to fordge no lie
his happines except for kyn I surely should envye.
  bothe
you I now salute & do, fro͞ god all goodnes craue
yt greves me that for golden maydes, no golden giftes I haue   [20
What then? wher welth & giftes do want, shall frendship bear no price
then farewell virtue & good mynd yf all in money li⟨es⟩.
but what? is this enough to say, y^t I you both haue loved?
    In truth he is but a lumpish swayn wch therto is not moved
but this much I may truly say I loue ye passing well   [25
& will do still as long as life, in ly͞mes of myn shall dwell

———————

bothe in my tender childish yeares, when first I did begin.

& when the dounish mossie hear doth crepe vppon my chyn.

& also in more stayed aege, when youthly trickes are fled

& when that hore & sylver heares haue covered my hed [30

yf I be found at any tyme fro̅ this mynd for to stray

I pray the Goddes I gyven be to lions feirce a pray

or that the birdes of Caucasus my ly̅mes in peices tear

Or that I drenched be in seas & never more appeare.

or els by Diomedes stedes I be devourd & rent [35

& stigian Curre my ghost in hell forever may torment

God graunt you both to lyue in ioye, full many & mery a yere

& shortly each of you to haue a wished loving fere

ye debtoars are vnto vs all till you so̅m childre̅ bring

& by that meanes do seke to encrease the nu̅ber of our kyn [40

me thinkes yt would my hart reioice to see placed in y̌ lap

so̅m little Impes whom I might feed, wth sweete & sugred pap

wth whom I dallie might & sport these tedious wynter nightes [f. 5

yf they be like ther mothers sure, they must be pretie sprightes.

And after long expense of yeares & blessed happie dayes [45

    ye primerose maydes may rest, wth him, wch heavenly scepter swayes

your Cosyn to you chained & tied, as far as in him lies

or els I wish the   Eagles may, pec & pull out his eyes.

    1582.   48.

[Item 13]

when men to catche the fleting fish, shall angle in the ayre

 & in the sea wth houndes shall hunt, the swift & fearfull hare
when boistrous club of Hercules, a tender babe shall vse
& frogges the muddie moorish groundes t'enhabite shall refuse
when fish shall quight forget to cut wth finnes the sylver streames [5
 & duskish candle shall appear more bright, then phebus beames
when lumpish asse wth winges as bird shall skale the lofty skyes
& Nightingales in sylver tunes gyue place to chattring pies
when that th' vnweldie Camel shall a lustie galiard daunce
 & sadled Oxe wth man on backe as palfrey braue shall praunce [10
when learned Pallas must be taught of grosse & filthy sow
& men wth yoked foxes shall begin ther land to plow
when selie Asse shalbe content for meat hard bones to gnaw
& greedie dogges shall fill ther paunche, wth hey & eke wth straw
when glittering starres shall wanting be in skies wch are most pure [15
& Emeraud in brightest day shall seeme a stone obscure
when men wth hatchetes open dores & keyes do cleaue y̅^r ⟨th⟩ logges
& hunt the hare wth Oxen slow as yf yt were wth dogges.
Dear Grandame then & not before will I be found vnkynd
both nature & your benefites, therto me fully bynd [20
As long as life in lymes shall lodge & breath my longes ⟨&⟩ shall. blow
To satisfie your mynd & will my care I will bestow
both tymes & yeares do flete & passe & all thinges els decay
 but day by day my loue to you yt self shall more bewray
It is an vse this day to frendes som newyeres gift to send [25
wch custom though I greatly like & highly do comend

yet for no custome I ⟨do⟩ ^now^ write nor yet my skyll to show

but for a pawn & pledge of zeal & dutie wch I ow

 In stede of capons Turkeys & fat swannes wch now are sent

 fro̅ frend to frend in token of good frendship wch is ment   [30

 In stede of gold & Orient pearle & other costly ware.

 I forced am to wish you well in wordes both rude & bare

 not Cresus bagges haue I in store nor Cofers fraught wth gold

  nor costly robes nor Curious sylkes wch derely must be sold.

1582   [f. 5ᵛ

but mynd wth dutie as full fraught althoughe I say yt my self   [35

 as ever merchauntes cofers were wth store of worldly pelf

wch thing that yt to you might be more fully now displayed

I wish into my brest your eyes might be by art conveighed

y' would marvel I am sure to see, in roome so streight to lie

such heapes of loue & dutie both as their you might espie.   [40

fro̅ bottom therfore of my hart & wth vnfayned ⟨mynd⟩ loue

I wishe you madame this new year, all ioy & good may proue

And as the pleasaunt cherefull sonne, wch fro̅ vs far was gon

hath turned his chariot & beginnes vs now to look vppon

& wth his golden heavenly beames doth make all creatures glad   [45

wch by his absence were before as yt were wth sorow clad

& as the sonne of god did chuse, this drousie drouping tyme

when as into this world he cam̅ to raunsom̅ vs from crime.

to shew to vs & signifie that as the year begonne

as then to grow more temperate b'approching of the sonne   [50

So this same sonne of righteousnes by lightening of our mynd would chase away all mystes & cloudes, wch yt before did blynd

& eke restore the golden world, by virtue of his might

wher golden virtue should prevayl & put all syn to flight

So Madame now the deadest tyme of wynter being past [55

I wish all comfort & all ioye most fullie you may tast

that having spent your aeged dayes in blessed happie sort

you may at last arryue vnto the haven & eke the port

of everlasting blessednes for ay ther to enioye

more ⟨blessed⟩ happie state then I can tell wth out greif or annoy [60

your little sonne for ever prest & to your service bent

or els I wish the savage beastes his corps in peices rent.

62

[Item 14]   [f. 6

anno. 1582.

A little map may represent the earth & eke the skies

A little picture may expresse mars bignes & his sise

A little counter standeth for somtymes an hundred pound

A little sphere or globe shewes forth the world in cōpasse round

 Even so somtymes a little gift shewes what the mynd entend<u>es</u> [5

 As well as gold & precious pearl wch India to vs sendes

 my gift is small I do confesse yet such as now I haue

 wch yf yt serue t'expresse my mynd, tis all y^t I doe craue

 wch is that I not only wish a pleasaunt happie year

 but long continuance of all ioye to you & eke your fere [10

 that when that ye shall linked be in Himeneus bandes

ye may the fruictes of frendship reap wch passe both goodes & landes

& comfort haue of little Impes, wch myndes in loue fast ties

& after golden happie dayes, may scale the cristall skyes

dame nature she hath made your fere & fortune you my frend [15

I loue ye both & will do still till death my dayes shall end

        16 anno 1583.   Calendis Ianuarij

[Item 15]

In tyme the vnruly Steere is made to draw the heavy plow

    & necke of his to croked yooke in tyme is taught to bow

In tyme the horse of stomacke stoute vnto the bridle yeldes

    & quietly in champing mouth the girding bit he feeles

In tyme the lion feirce is tamed, his angrie moode is gon [5

wch erst did make those for to quake, wch him did looke vppon

The Elephant in tyme dothe learn his maister to obay

& thinkes his service for to be but as a sport & play

Tyme makes the grapes to swell wth iuice, & so doth fill the skyn

that they are like to burst wth wyn wch is contayned w^thin [10

Tyme bringes the corn sowed in the ground vnto a ripened stalke

& makes the sowre & bitter fruites an other tast to take

Tyme weares the share of forrowing plow, & flintes consumeth quight

the diamond most hard & strong can not resist his might

Tyme doth asswage & mollifie the feirce & angrie mynd [15

Tyme easeth greif & comfort gyues, to pensiue men I fynd

Long tyme therfore is wont to make, all worldly thinges to chaunge

But yet my loue & mynd to you, yt cannot make to raunge

for sooner shall I quight forget the name to me assignd

    then that the loue wch you me bear can slipp out of my mynd [20

   & sowle of myn shall leave my corpse & wander forth abroad

      before that I vnmyndfull be of courtesies bestowed
This newyeres tyde because I want som̄ gift to shew my mynd
la madame here I gyue my self & fully do me bynd

      to serue at all assayes & tymes, in such sort as I can   [25
yf I may stand you in any stede, vse me as twere your man
your welfare I do wish & will I dare say no man more

      my prayer is to god on highe, therof to send you store

                              worldly
god ease your greif & graunt you may all comfort tast
& after fading brittle ioyes, haue those wch ever last.   [30
Although my mynd be out of tune not apt in verse t'endight   [f. 6^v

      yet dutie forced me thus much. in ragged ryme to wright.

          32.   anno. 1583.   Calendis Ianuarij

[Item 16]

myn Alderleivest lady deere whom nature hath decreed

      to be the autour of my life & succour in my neede
And perfect loue & kyndnes born, haue made my greatest frend

      to whom the part of parent<u>es</u> now crosse fortune hath assignd
fayn would I this new year in verse, som̄ shew of dutie make   [5

      but that my crazed wittes refuse therin ther paynes to take
And senses dulled wth greif & care admitte no sport nor game

      a verse requiers a quiet mynd my witt<u>es</u> are out of frame
Alas how can I tune my verse or sing a cherefull song

         that
      synce my deerest cheifest frend I misse now all to long   [10

the staffe of my estate & life, the comfort of my woes
the patrone of my studie and, my rampier from my foes
the guider of my muse & verse, the ground of all my ioye.
whose presence was my comfort &, his absence myn annoye
but sith that present tyme requiers sõm token of good will [15
and that no other gift I haue then practise of my quill
althoughe my muse being cloyed wth cares, all pleasure doth debar
& that her musicke is out of tune, & notes do fowly iarre
yet dutie now doth her constrayn a while to lay asyde
her pensiue thoughtes & you to wish a happie new yeres tyde [20
God graunt y' a mery year & tyme, god graunt y'a happie aege.
and when his will & pleasure is your sorrowes to asswage
he wch no power & might doth want vs frõ our graue to rayse
to cure our greifes & ease our payn no doubt hath many wayes
God send you ioye & comfort of your impes & children all [25
& that ther childres children to twice Grandã you may call
God graunt you for to lyue to see the little pretie mayd
wch now in cradle wrapt in bandes, as prisoner is layd
In mariage well bestowed & linckt to bring a pretie boye
wch may his mothers comfort be & eke to you a ioye [30
and that when natures doome is com to wch all subiect are
from wch no force nor engyn can vs kepe or els debarre
replent wth comfort every wae, your own may close your eyes
& ghost of yours most cherefully may skale the cristall skyes
for me I swere no dutie shall be wanting on my part [35

    vntill that grisly death wth dart shall peirce my tender hart
vntill that water wanting be in clear & cristall streames

& heavens & skyes shall be bereft of golden phebus beames
vntill that earth shall cease to breede the strong & sturdie oke
& little Pigme shall wthstand the force of Hercles stroke [40
for want of new yeres giftes of wch god knowes I haue no store
dere Grandame here my⟨n⟩ mynd & hart I gyue what will you more
42:

[Item 17] [f. 7

anno 1583 Calendis Ianuarij
A paper I do send as Herault of my hart
   I would the half of my conceipt to you yt could impart
but greif hath so appald my carefull pensyue hed
   that I as lumpish am to write, as yf I were of lead
yf that I curraunt were, & mynd were free frō care [5
no better theme would I desire, then thie perfections rare
nor muse then should I nede my wittes for to enspire
A hevenlier creature then thy self I never would desire
but sith that nether tyme nor leysure me dothe serue
to paynt thy virtues in such sort as they do well deserue [10
I the salute & wish as many happie dayes
as ther be sandes vppon the shore or eges wch fishes layes
or flowres in pleasaunt spring or stalkes of corn wch grow
in sōmer tyme or Autumne fruictes or winter flakes of snow.
And when thou maried art wch tyme is near I guesse   tristiū 4°.
                                                                                           248.
thou mayst all comfort feel & tast & wished ioyes possesse.
And loving husband haue wth children of his name

   Item 17] "tristiū 4°/248." is enclosed with rules.

wch by resemblaunce of ther face may shew frō whence they cā

for me I never can forget of the to thinke

although of drousie Lethe floud I were compeld to drinke [20

The ryvers shall retyre into ther springes agayn.

   & phebus backe into the East shall dryue his golden wayn

the earth bedect wth starres the heaven cut wth the plow

the water fire shall yeld & from, the fier shall water flow

all thinges to natures hest shall arsie versie turn [25

nor any part of all the world his right course forth shall runne

The doves shall leave to haunt the toppes of stately bowres

the beastes ther caves the shepe ther grasse, didopper raynie showres

before that I do leaue to beare to you that mynd

that ever loving Cosyn yet in kinsman true did fynd [30

not only this new yere I wish to the good hap

but all that ever any had wch sate in fortunes lap.

Adeiu my most beloved for I must goe my wayes

yf I may stand the in any stede, vse me at all assayes.

       34:

                [Item 18]   [f. 7^v

      epigramā sepulchr⟨u⟩m dn̄ae Lee incisū

I. yf passing by this place thou doe desire

   to know what corps here shrind in marble lie

   the som̄ of that wch now thou dost require

   this sclender verse shall sone to the descrie

   Item 18] The title is written in Stanford's Italian hand.

E. entombed here dothe rest a worthie dame [5

 extract & born of noble house & bloud

  her
 ⟨whose⟩ syre lord paget hight of worthie fame

 whose virtues cannot sinke in Lethe floud

T. two brethern had she Barons of this Realme.

her feere a knight wch Henry Lee was cald
 ⟨a knight her feere syr Henry Lee he hight⟩ [10

  to whom she bare thre Imps wch had to name

        sone by death appald
 Ihon Harry Mary ⟨slayn by fortunes spight⟩

       her for to
F. first two being yong wch causd ⟨ther parent*es*⟩ mone

 the third in flower & prime of all her yeares.

    do rest ⟨w^th⟩ vnder
 all thre ⟨enclosed lie⟩ in this marble stone [15

 by wch the fickelnes of worldly ioyes appear⟨*es*⟩

H. I nead not here blase forth this ladies praise

 she lyved to die & died to lyue agayn.

 her helping hand was prest at all assayes

 for in her brest the fear of god did raign [20

 her modest life I ned not

 here to show

  nor other gift*es* in wch she

   did abound

 those can report w^ch

   somtymes her did know

 before that death her w^th

---

  his dart did wound.

   good frend
W. ⟨Wherfore⟩ sticke not to strew wth crimson flowres   [25

  this marble stone wherin her cindres rest

  for certes her ghost lyues wth the heavenly powers

  & guerdon hath of virtuous life possest.

   24.

     [Item 19]

The Virtuous lady Lee Sr Henry Lee his wife

 vnder this stone doth lie interred bereft of erthly life

 whose body though yt be by mortall fate possest

 her ghost no doubt ascended is into the place of rest

 three children in her life she had & held most dere   Lilly [5

 wch having ronne ther race do rest wth her ther mother here

 Attending for the daye when as the elect shall rise

 & lyue wth god & all his sayntes in ioye that never dies.

     [Item 20

A Grayhound must be hedded like a snake

necked like a drake. brested as a lion

sided as a maiden footed as a Cat   [5

Tayled as a rat. eared as an ape

then is he well Ishapt

 Item 18:21-25] These lines are entered in the right margin opposite lines 17-20, which are completely enclosed by rules.

  Item 19] "Lilly" is to the right of a bracket enclosing lines 1-8.

  Item 20] The ends of the lines are enclosed with a bracket.

[Item 21]

Anno 1584 calendis Ianuarij

The earth no worse a monster bredes
    then is a thankles man
this saying of the wise dothe make
    me fear because I can
devise no meanes to shew my mynd
    as dutie would require
my will is prest & ready bent
    but styll I sticke ithe mire
for wher that force & strenghe doth want
    ther will is but a thrall   [5
my mynd is bent to play his part
    but power I'aue none at all
yf that the goddes king Cræ<u>sus</u> welthe
    or Cras<u>sus</u> had me sent
I might haue shewed by golden giftes
    how that my will were bent
yf that the strenghe of Hercules
    to me by lot befell
A champion then you should me haue
    your enymies to quell   [10
yf in the court wth prince in grace
    and favour that I were
as servaunt then you might me vse
    (your) sui your suites for to preferre
yf golden gift<u>es</u> of learned lore
    and wisdom<u>es</u> skyll I had

As counseillour I might you serue
    though I be but a lad
yf flowing vayn of eloquence
    in me ther did a bound   [15
I might at least in word$\underline{es}$ my mynd
    & your desert$\underline{es}$ forth sound
but since these rare & precious gift$\underline{es}$
    beyond my forces goe
I am compeld this new yeres tyde
    to imitate the crow
wch did salute the emperour
    withe Chaire kesar once
Loe madame here like stuffe you see
    proceding from my skonce.   [20
but thoughe that word$\underline{es}$ be rude & playn   [f. 8^v
    yet good will is not skant
as long as life in li$\overline{m}$es shall lodge
    therof shalbe no want
And therfore now this newyeres tyde
    as little crow I craue
of god that you such happines
    as you would wish might haue
And yf that any clowd$\underline{es}$ of care
    your sense & mynd oppresse   [25
by present comfort & good hap

    Item 21:19] "Chaire kesar" is printed in Stanford's Italian hand.

    all greif may quigt surcease
beleue me madame as that peace
    dothe bloudye warres ensue
and after mistie darkesom night
    Syr phe$\underline{bus}$ beames renew
So after irksom pensiue greifes
    great ioye receaue we shall
for wisemen say our life is mixt
    wth honie & wth gall   [30
No daye we see so moist & wet
    wth sothern watry showres
as that the rayn withouten ceasse
    continually down powres
nor any feild so barrayn is ⟨that ther⟩
    that ther may not be found
amid the thistles & the weed$\underline{es}$
    so$\overline{m}$ holsom herb othe ground
nor fortune hath for any on ⟨pilles⟩
    pill$\underline{es}$ of such bitter tast   [35
but that so$\overline{m}$ ease & comfort bothe
    doth alwayes co$\overline{m}$ at last
yf ў abilitie would serue
    for me to helpe herin
you might be sure I would yt racke
    vnto the highest pinne
Nor this wch now I say & vow,   [f. 9
    proced$\underline{es}$ from childish mynd

But from affection to the whiche

    your benefittes me bynd   [40

As long as Thracians fight wth dartes

    & Scythes shall vse ther bowes

⟨as long as hilles shall bring forth okes⟩

    ⟨& Ister overfrose⟩

& Ganges shalbe parched wth heat

    & Ister overfrose

as long as hilles shall bring forth okes

    & grasse in medowes grow

as long as Temes wth cristall streames

    his banckes shall overflow

you shall me fynd in dutie & ⟨goodwill⟩

    ⟨to none to yeld⟩
    good will to none to yeld   [45

I shall reioice to doe you good

    as on wch winnes a feild

God graunt you in this world to haue

    what hart can best desire

and afterward to heavenly ioyes

    & blisse you may aspire

Accept of this roughe filed verse

    wch nether poetes skyll

Nor Muses Learned lore hathe framd

    but only mere good wyll

finis quod fyrkyns the Ierkin maker in S^{t}. Martyns

[Item 22]

anno 1584 calendis Ianuarij

Sweete Cosin though I want som gift fit for this tyme & tyde
  I would not haue you thinke that I from courtesie am wyde
  for wher that power doth want they say, good will supplies the place
  wer loue aboundes ther want can not our meaning good disgrace
  and therfore thoughe for many giftes wch I receaved haue   [5
  I can not like on you bestow as courtesie would craue
  yet that wch in my power doth rest, I still will myndful be
  & when I may most willing to requight as you shall see
  I'the mean tyme now for giftes of yours loe paper here you see
  wch I haue wild as messenger to tell this tale fro̅ me   [10
  that I not only this new year do wish to you good hap
  but all that ever any had wch sate in fortunes lap
  & that this happie state may last, till death the doe supplant
  being able for to help this frendes, & no mans ayd to want
  that husband maye the promise keepe made when he did the wed   [15
  and that no iarre betwixt you fall when ye are ⟨layd⟩ coucht in bed
  that kynred may the lovingly wch such good will imbrace
  as Pollux Castor did of yore, wch no tyme can deface
  & that this little mopsie maydes maye so in likenes grow
  that to be thine by face & deedes eache creature maye them know   [20
  and by ther mariage once agayne thou mayst a mother be
  and in this youth a Grandame eke ther childrens child to see
  and that this fruictfull bellie w^{ch}, these pretie girles doth yeld

may bring vs store of lustie boyes, to fyght wth spear & sheild
The somer & the winter dayes shall com both to on tune [25
& Christmas nightes shall post awaye as fast as t,were in Iune
braue Babilon her smouldring heat & pontus cold shall lose
& marigold shall sweeter be then fragraunt damaske rose
before that I wilbe vnkynd or any waye will start
from loue wch bothe by nature and, I owe by thie desart [30
Adeiu farewell & lyue thie tyme, & loue thie frendes agayn
and after old Sibillas aege, a crown in heaven obtayne

[Item 23] [f. 10

  Gulielmi Pagetti versiculi quos ^ex suo cerebro depromptos Aviae
  officii & aij testificandi causa obtulit Calendis Ianuarij anno dm̄i
  1584. annos natus 12 dies 14.

Sith that the sonne his yearly course hath brought vnto an end
 & now beginnes his cherefull light vnto vs for to lend
 and since the costome hathe endurd from th'old Heroes tyme
 each man to frend should send such gift as might most fittest seeme
 deere Grandame dutie me constraynes my mynd to you to show [5
 more fraught wth loue then ever was Olimpus highe wth snow
 I wish to you as many ioyes as cornes com to your mill
 or ^bussing bees by heapes & thronges, flocke out of Hibla hill
 As many as ther leaues do fall from trees in Autumne cold
 or sandes wch lie in Libian sea wch are not to be told [10

———

Item 23:8] The caret is in the MS.

-32-

As many as ther fishes swymͤ in roughe Atlanticke seas
or starr__es__ in heaven or fowles in lakes or kyd__es__ in pastures playes
for me as dutie dothe require & natures hest__es__ me bynd
I never will at any tyme be found to be vnkynd
As long as beares shall haunt the hill__es__ & fish loue pleasant lakes [15
or greshoppers shall feede of dew or bees ther hony makes
As long as starres in heaven shall rolle or gras in medowes grow
Or trees in hill__es__ shall stedfast stand, or wynd__es__ wth tempest__es__ blow
so long me ready you shall fynd your hest__es__ for to obay
& also prest to please your will in those thing__es__ wch I may   [20
Wherfore synce every on this daye wth gift__es__ ther frend ⟨present__es__⟩
                                         present__es__
Loe here a paper as a pawn of my good will I send
and also this new year to you, I wish such happie lucke
as dothe the flattering nurse to child, wch of her teat doth sucke
bothe in this world redresse of greif & comfort every wayes   [25
& afterward to raign wth him wch heavenly scepter swayes.

& when that you shall called be out of this world of woe
to blisse wch everlasting is I wish y̌ you may goe.

⟨i⟩

[Item 24]   [f. 10^v]
anno 1585. calendis Ianuarij.

when turtle shall haue many a make

& aspen leaves shall cease to shake

Item 23:27] "called" is written over an original "cald."

There is an indecipherable small smear beside the "i" at the bottom
of f. 10; both figures were blotted onto the bottom of f. 9^v when the
page was turned.

when dog & hare together play
& when the starres appear by day
when tree on craggie stones shall grow [5
& waters leaue to ebbe & flow
when yvye leaves shall loose ther hew
& liers shalbe counted true
when Egypt land shall freese wth yse
& fooles shalbe accompted wise [10
when fidlers passe musitions skyll
& ravenous wolves shall haue ther fill
when haukes shall dread the little bird
& men of owles shalbe afeard.
when sune no more on erth shall shyne [15
& fleming cease to loue good wyne
till that tyme me to be vnkynd
deere grandame you shall never fynd.
but you shall see me as I ⟨thou⟩ ought
most dutifull in word & thought [20
god send to you a good new yere
& all you frendes whom you hold deere
that god to you suche hap may lend
as he dothe to his servantes send.
I mean great stoar of blisse & ioye [25
wth out all care or els anoye.
even as the waves in seas do flow
or stalkes of corn in harvest grow

& when these wavering ioyes do moue
you may remayn wth god aboue. [30

[Item 25] [f. 11

anno 1585 calendis Ianuarij

In yong & tender aege in youthfull year*es*
   in aeged dayes when snow white hear*es* appear*es*
in luckie state when fortune hap doth lend
& when she frownes & miserie doth send
by day when that the glittering sun doth glide [5
by night when that the golden mone dothe slyde
In su̅mer when that every bush is grene
in winter when great tempest*es* are most seene
& when in helthfull state my li̅mes shall rest
& when wth sicknes I shalbe opprest. [10
in happie dayes when cruell warr*es* do cease
in blustering stormes when men flie ioyfull peace
in surging seas & in the sinking sand
in safer coast when I shalbe on land
in all this chaunge of fortune & of state [15
In dutie & good will Ile not be late
nor ever I this promise will forget
till cruell death my vitall breath shall let
good Aunt this new year this to you I send
desiring god you store of ioyes to lend [20
as many as ther starr*es* in heaven do slyde
when golden phebe his chariot gi̅n*es* to hide

-35-

& when this vale of miserie is past

you maye then skale the loftie skies at last

[Item 26]   [f. 11^v]

anno 1585 calendis Ianuarij

In greene & ⟨lu⟩ childish aege in lustie yeares

in latter tyme when sylver heares appeares

whilest that a batchiler you do me see

whilest that to wife fast yoked I shalbe

yf fortune smile on me wth cheerfull face   [5

or yf she lowre & put me to disgrace.

whilest that in countrie soyl I stay at home

or els in forreyn landes abroad do rome

whither in peace or quiet rest I lyue

or els by martiall feates do praise atcheue   [10

whither on land wth wife at home I stay

or else in ventrous sort do sulke the sea.

by daye when phebus glorious beames appear

by night when foggie mistes do clowde the ayr

In sommer when the cherefull dayes vs please   [15

by winter when that stormes do tosse the seas

when that in happie health I doe remayn

or else by force of sicknes pyne in payn

in mirth in greife what chaunce so ever fall

good aunt I am yours my faith shall never quail.   [20

this new yeres day as token of my hart

this my conceipt to you I do impart.

wishing to you as many happie dayes

as motes are seene in golden phebus rayes.

or chirping birdes on sprayes in pleasaunt spring [25

wth pretie tunes melodiously do sing.

& when from hence at last your sowle shall flie

yt may in cherefull sort streict perce the skye

---

   finis quod firkins

[Item 27]   [f. 12

   anno 1585 calendis Ianuarij

when turtle shall forsake his make

 & aspen leaf shall leaue to quake

 when hound & hare shall gin to play

 & starres be sene to shine by day

 when swelling seas shall leaue to flow   [5

 & corne on stony rocke shall grow

 when grasse shall leaue to grow on ground

 & stones no wher in stretes be found.

 when laurell leaves shall loose ther hew

 & frendes no where found to be true   [10

 when Etna flames shall freese to yse

 & Cat shall leaue to kyll the mise

 when fooles do passe wise men in skyll

 & Iacke no more shall loue his gill

 when foxe of geese shall stand in dread   [15

 & men of pigmees be afeard

 Item 26] There is a double flourish after the signature, "firkins."

when flattery shalbe of no price

nor men addicted vnto vice.

when fortune proves a constant dame

& boyes forget ther cristmas game [20

Till then me never you shall fynd

dere Grandame any waye vnkynd

but as I ought so you shall see

obedient alwayes me to be

I hope this paper as a band [25

of this my promise now may stand

wch I this newyeres tyde pr<u>e</u>sent

not meaning ever to relent

to you I wishe a prosperous year

& those whom you do hold most dear [30

that you & they such hap may haue

as men of god are wont to craue

I mean such store of ioye & ⟨blisse⟩ glee

as leaves in Autumne fall from tree

or dropp<u>es</u> of rayn in winter showre [35

or flakes of snow fall in an howre

& when the fading ioyes we misse

we may attayn to heavenly blisse.

---

    finis qu<u>od</u> firkins

[Item 28]

1585 carmen sepulchro Thomae Tallis in re musica peritissimi incisū

    Item 28] The title is predominantly written in Stanford's Italian hand.

Entombed her doth lie a worthie wight

    who long tyme did in musicke bear the bell

his name to say yt Thomas Tallis hight.

    In modest virtuous life he did excell

And servd long tyme in chapple wth great praise.   [5

    fowr soveraignes raignes a thing not often seen

    I mean king Henry & prince Edwardes dayes

    In tyme of Marie & our gratious Quene.

He maried was thoughe children he had none

& lyvd in loue & liking thirtie yeares   [10

wth loyall spouse whose name yclypt was Ione

who here entombd him companie now beares

As he had lyvd so also did he die

in patient quiet sort (o happie man)

to god full oft for mercie did he crie.   [15

wherfore he lyves let death do what he can.

He died the year fiue hundred eightie fyue

    on thousend and synce Christ tooke mortall weede.

    his fame no doubt for musicke skyll shall lyue

    thoughe sisters three haue cut his fatall thred.   [20

        Decembris Die

        [Item 29]

here lies he who was born, & cried

liued threscore winter, fell sicke & died

[Item 30] [f. 13

anno. 1586. in Auspiciū novi anni Aviæ suae officii ⟨car⟩
ergo Gulielmi Pagetti carmen.

Læticia afficior mihi ter gratissima mater
    quod morbū expuleris læticia afficior
Læticia afficior Iam quod salva Calendas
    videris & læta es læticia afficior
Læticia afficior spes quod te vivere diu nobis   [5
    promittatq; diu læticia afficior.
Læticia afficior animo quod accipis æquo
    vulnera fortunæ læticia afficior
Læticia afficior domus est tua libera luctu
    quodq; vacet lachrymis læticia afficior   [10
Læticia afficior quod nullā fata tulerunt
    hoc anno ex nobis læticia afficior
Læticia afficior quod me quoq; pergis amore
    quod fers in oculis læticia afficior
Læticia afficior contingant si tibi læta   [15
    si nihil adversi læticia afficior.
Læticia afficior si primitias studiorū
    omen vt accipias læticia afficior
Læticia afficior vivas si tempore longo.
    si fero repetas sidera lætus ero.   [20

Item 29 is within a ruled rectangle.

Item 30 is written in Stanford's Italian hand.

[Item 31]

⟨Aviae⟩
Amitae chariss in auspiciū
novi anni Guliel. Pag.
carmen dimetrū
maximus olim
Ille orientis
qui iure certo
venit habenas
Gessit & vna   [5
persica sceptra
fronte sereno
accipit vndam.
Quā sibi pauper
obtulit olim.   [10
Amita chara
exiguum istud
munus amico
Accipe vultu
sperne nec ista   [15
Carmina quamvis
Ingenio ⟨limata⟩ li-
⟨nec⟩ mata nec arte.
minima magnos
edere ⟨solent⟩ possunt   [20
semina faetus.
―――――

    Item 31 is written in Stanford's Italian hand. Lines 1-39 are entered in the right margin of f. 13 beside Items 30 and 32, and separated from them by a vertical line; lines 40-71 are in the right margin of f. 13^v, separated from the text of Item 32 by a vertical line.

maxima quercus
virga fuit &
fluvius ingens
exiguus fons [25
& vitulus quem
horreo taurū.
Sic pueroru͞
capita primo
edere possunt [30
nil nisi nugas '
Attamen edunt '
tempore fructus,
vberiores
nunc ego divos [35
supplice voto
obsecro vitā
vt tibi longā
attribuant vt
Nestoris annos [f. 13ᵛ
degere possis [41
sine querela.
ac tua vota
quod cupierunt
tangere possint. [45
comprescor atq;
hic novus annus

sit tibi faustus.
dū iuga montis
porcus amabit [50
piscis & vndas
poscet amicas
poscet & αἴγας
nuda mirica
rosq; cicadas. [55
nulla valebunt
flumina λήθης
pellere nostro
pectore fixū
Amitae amorem. [60
dii tibi ⟨fo⟩ donent
corpore sano
vivere semper
dii tibi faxint
omnia fausta [65
cūq; vocarint
te tua fata
& tibi mortis
venerit hora
scandere possis [70
sidera coeli

[Item 32] [f. 13

The same in english

my Grandame dere I do reioice
    that you recovered are
of former sicknes wch from vs
    all comfort did debarre
I do reioice that you are com   [5
    to see this newyeres daye
wch that to you yt lucky proue
    I will not cease to pray
I do reioice that now thers hope
    that all the worst is past   [10
and sicknes once being chaced away
    you may som comfort tast
I doe reioice to see that you   [f. 13^v
    wth patience armed are
dame fortunes blowes & cruel iares   [15
    in good sort for to bear
I do reioice that house of yours
    from suche mishap is free
as should yt cause wth teares & playnt<u>es</u>
    replenished to be   [20
I do reioice that all this year
    wch now is past & gon
No on by death miscaried hath
    for whom we might make mone
I do reioice that you me loue   [25
    as you haue don before

And styll continew me to bear
    affection more & more
I shall reioice to see all thing<u>es</u>
    concurre to make you glad   [30
yf no mishap amiddest do chaunce
    to cause you to be sad
I shall reioice yf these first fruict<u>es</u>
    of barrayn childish brayn
for pawn of loue you do accept   [35
    as is my meaning playn.
I shall reioice yf that you lyue
    long tyme in happy wise
And late yt be before you scale
    ye golden cristall skies   [40
God shield you from mishap & harme
    & send you for to haue
As many happie newyeres as
    your mynd shall list to craue.

                                        [Item 33]   [f. 14

    of an a.b.c.
This a.b.c. you do read
    but little do prevail
vnles y^t you take heede
    well whipt shalbe your tail.

[Item 34]

of a torn globe

This globe to vs you see

    the world doth represent

but yt I know not how

    is pitifullie rent

[Item 35]

of the Chimney

This chimney to this chamber is

    more worth then gold

for we this winter lacking yt

    oft tymes should be a cold

[Item 36]

of ye bed.

This bed may well be cald

    ye place of quiet rest

for Robin Carey wthout care

    roostes ther as bird in nest

[Item 37]

of ye glasse

This glasse the outward shapes

    of creatures doth display

I would the affections of ye mynd

    to vs yt could bewray

[Item 38]

of ye fiershovell.

A fiershovell doth ⟨belong⟩

  belong to vulcans art
& therfore yt fr̄o chimney doth
  but seldom tymes depart.

         [Item 39]

As newyeares gift this booke I send
  & wishe to the such happe
As those are wont to haue wch sitte
  in Ladie fortunes lappe.

         [Item 40]

  of ovid<u>es</u> metamorphosis.
This booke good matter doth
  in yt contain I know
I would the half therof to you
  I able were to show.

         [Item 41]

  of a rushe taken to make a knot
This rushe I take in hand
  to make a true loves knot
althoughe true meaning & good loue
  is seldom seene god wot

         [Item 42]

  of ye table
A table for a chamber is
  nedefull at every cast
yt serves vs for to write theron
———

  & eke to bleak our fast

        [Item 43]

   of the window

This window dothe to vs

  the north directly show

& throughe the same y^e blustring blast<u>es</u>

  of Boreas often Blow.

        [Item 44]

   of a brushe

This brushe dothe serue to kepe

our garment<u>es</u> net & clean

see that $\overset{u}{y}$ kepe thie soule also

  from sin & eke from stayn.

        [Item 45]

In sign of this new year

  & myndfull mynd of myn

I send these prayers & do vow

  to pray for the & thyne

        [Item 46]

long tyme mans becke for to obey

  hath tought y^e lions fierce

long tyme hath caused y^e water soft

  hard marble stones to pierce

  Items 33-39 are entered in order on the left side of f. 14, Items 40-46, on the right side. Item 39 is set off with rules above and below, and bracketed along the right margin.

The year doth ripen grapes y^t grow [5
    vppon ye sonny banck<u>es</u>
The year dothe bring ye star<u>es</u> about
    in order & in rankes

[Item 47] [f. 14^v

  2. noctis:⟨ ⟩ Ænigmata ex francisco Strapparola. le pot.
I am ashamed my name to tell.
  to feele & see I'm nothing feat
  great mouth but no red lipp<u>es</u> nor teeth
  all black about & neere ye seat
  suche heat wth in somtyme I tast [5
  that frothe & fome I fourth do cast
  of som̄ base wenche thinke me to be
  sithe each on seekes to fishe in me.

[Item 48]

    .1. noctis. ⟨<u>2</u>⟩
At supper three companions sate
  eache on wth meat full fraught will be.
  In com̄es a waiter wth a plate
  in wch three pigeons I did see
  eache on doth eat on of those three [5
  & yet remayning two ther be.

[Item 49]

    .2. noctis .4.   l'ame im̄ortelle.
A goodlie thing in vs ther lies

wch speakes & feeles heares sees & goes
hathe senses none & yet is wise
no head no tongue no hand no toes
wth vs yt roustes & eache thing sees [5
yt loues & beares vs (good) great good will
yt lyves & never life can leese
yt once is born & dureth still.

[Item 50]

.2. noctis. 3. La belle & Blanche seruiette
I am a thing both fair & smooth
of white also I haue no lacke
ye mother & the daughter doth
me whip & yet I cloth their back
my mother mother is of all [5
I do no man or thing refuse
& yet when old men do me call
they seeke wth blowes me to abuse.   2. noctis.2. vn home q̄ produit le fou
                                         du pierre & du fusil.

[Item 51]

On lyving wth two dead hath made on lyue
    from whom an other dead hath gotten life
    by meanes of wch ye lyving first contriveth.
    to talke wth th' dead as twere wth him y^t livethe
        2. noctis. 1

[Item 52]

My Ihon I would thou shouldest me gyue

    the thing wch yet thou haddest never   a child

    nor never shalt thoughe y^t thou lyue   a husband

    a thousand year & seeke yt ever   milke

    but yf thou louest me as thou saist

    then gyue yt me for sure thou maist.

[Item 53]

  .1. noctis.1.   La febre seiche.

Enclosd betwene two walles I first was born

& after that my self brought fourth a child

as big (a wretch) as is som grain of corn

who me devourd as Canniball thates wild.

ah wretched froward fortune that I haue

a mother not alowed to lyue as slaue.

[Item 54]

    1. noctis. 2.

In every place of old & yong: so many vse amisse ther tongue

    that in this world its hard to know: into what place a man may goe

what er I do I am sure to haue: [5] som sluit or gibe of everie knaue

---

Items 47-53] The titles and answers to the riddles are written predominantly in Stanford's Italian hand. Items 47, 51, 52, and 53 are bracketed along the right margin. The answers to Item 52 are entered to the right of the bracket, and are themselves bracketed on the right. The title and answer to Item 51 is written opposite lines 7 and 8 of Item 50, but separated from them by a vertical line.

yf m̄aster man or lord thou be frō their vild tongue thou art not fre

yf well apparayld thou do goe: in outward port & makest som show   [10

to say these felowes will not spare that thou wth kinges sekest to compare

but yf thie coates be old & bald: then rogue of them thou shalt be cald

yf fair thou art & freshe of hew: [15] a leachors name thou canst not eschew

as wencher but they will the mocke: nor sticke to call the a swell smocke

yf weak yf grosse or swart of face, thou art wth sliutes theil

                the disgrace   [20

yf once thou chaunce a wife to gayn theyl say thou shalt haue

                michel pain

& voice in all the town wilbe that she is maister vnto the

yf riche thou art they will say plain [25] that thou art but a

                covetouse swayn

yf poore thou art & in distresse into the house thou must not presse

but stand w^thout like simple mate: & pine in wretched wofull state   [30

yf lernd thou art & seekest not here: a port & state ith world to bear

theyl call the sot & simple beast: because thou wilt not be a preist

yf preist thou art they say likwise: [35] the world doth swarme w^th

                such fleshflies

of modest haviour yf thou be both mild & good in each degree

thou shalt be cald of everie bodie a folishe sot & senseles noddie   [40

yf thou be youthfull fresh & gay & spend thie tyme in sport & play

theyl say this bedlem youth wilbe on day hanged on a gallow tree

yf thou with woemen chaunce to walke [45] or wth them of som secret talk

---

    Item 54] No carry-over lines in the MS.

-52-

they will diffame the bie & bie & say wth them thou meanest to lie
yf thou so chast & modest seeme: that men may the an angel deeme   [50
ye vulgar sort will swear by god: this gentle youth hath nere   [f. 15^v
                                 a codde
& whatsoever that thou be great small of highe or low degree
preist lay man, bad or verie good:[55] base born or comen of noble bloud
fowle fair riche poore thou shalt be sure reproches vile still to endure
& therfore tis a wisemans part not for to take such thinges at hart   [60
nor greatlie speaches suche to mynd: but to comitte them to ye wynd.

                                 finis.

                               [Item 55]

     we of these .2. children are the 2. mothers
        & vnto our husbandes they be brothers
    our husbandes be fathers to these childrē two
    vncles to each other they be also.
    now take hede & make no outrage   [5
    for these childrē be born in trew mariage

     Item 54] There is a double flourish to the left of "finis."

    The following diagram is entered to the left of Item 55, which is completely enclosed with rules:

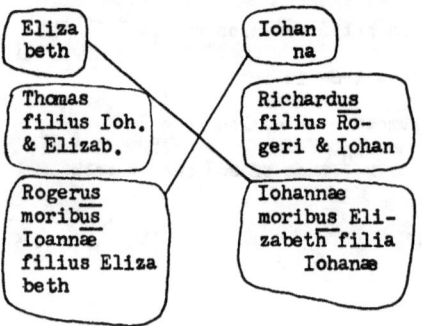

[Item 56]

Petrar sonet 19.

To purchase peace at those fayre eyes of thyne.
A thousand tymes o thou my sweetest foe
⟨to purchase peace at those fair eyes of thyne⟩
I gaue my hart but thou wth mynd dyvyne
vouchsafedst not to bend thy lookes so low.
yet yt to haue yf other dame aspire   [5
she hopes in vayn & is deceaued quight
for I do skorn what fitt__es__ not thy desire
and can not ioy in any other wight
now yf I dryue yt from me & you skorn
in this exile yt comfort for to gyue   [10
            serue an
to be alone or ⟨folow⟩ others ⟨call⟩ turne.
yt cannot but must cease to ioy & lyue
thinke what remorse ought both our mynd__es__ to moue
but cheifly yours since you yt did so loue

[Item 57]

The first is my vncle of my fathers side doubtles.
The second of my mothers w^thout any misse.
The third myne own sonne born by right
And all be sonnes vnto this knight
And all born in true mariage.   [5
   w^thout defiling of lignage.

   Item 56:14]There is a flourish to the right of "loue."

-54-

[Item 58] [f. 16

To m^rs Elizabeth Carey sending poppellimer his frence
historie for a newyeres gift .1595.

Goe booke as token to my mistris deere
 tell her from me I wishe her all such good
 for ay not only for this now new yeare
 that erst had any who in fauour stood
And yf she daign to looke in thie recordes [5
 & looke she will for lettres she doth loue
 tell her the famous dedes of noble lordes
 suche as her Impes are like in tyme to proue
And for her swain somtymes thy maister say
 he wilbe hers as long as life shall last [10
 & for her happie state will alwayes pray
 till deathe his spirites & vitall powres shall wast
  Loe this is all saue that I wishe that she
  only vouchsaufe for to accept of the.

[Item 59]

In sign y^t thou art fair & matcheles wth out peere
 I send this fayrie quene & wishe ye a new happie yeare
And all suche earthly ioyes as hart can wishe or craue
 and after long expense of yeres a seate in heauen to haue

[Item 60]

because ye nightes are long & nouelles tyme deceaue

Items 59 and 60 are bracketed along the right margin.

for newyeares gift this day these tales of me receaue

y̌e autour was a quene of witte & bewtie rare

except y̌e giftes of fortune thou wth her maist well compare.

[Item 61]

Loe here in signe of seruice wch is due

    and of the loue & dutie wch I beare [you above I]

    this little book & verse I send to you   An° 1597

    as token small in this beginning yeare.   stilo Romano

By wch I wishe your Ladiship such hap   [5

    wth golden dayes of all ease & content

    as erst had any lull'd in fortunes lap.

    or that ther ⟨dayes⟩ in ioifullst wise haue spent [tyme above dayes]

And that you liue as many happie dayes   [10

    as whilom did the prophetesse of Cume

    to see your Impes y̌e Barclays name to raise

    & fair Theophile a grandame to become

        ffor me althoughe of Lethe I should drincke

        yet never can I leaue of you to thinck.

[Item 62]

A Crabtre face y̌e felow had his stature great & tall

    his forces were accordingly men vulcans sonne him call

Cacus into his caues had drawen his oxen by the tayles

[Item 63]

deere nephew pallas put not on this dismall armour braue

    Item 61 is bracketed along the right margin, with "An° 1597/
stilo Romano" to the right of this bracket.

yet put yt on, for sure thy deathe a great revenge shall haue

[Item 64] [f. 16ᵛ]

By on thing som̄ men famous are, & names & titles haue

of golden chain from enmy tane, or crow wᶜʰ help them gaue.

O noble pompey of thie dedes the measure is thy name

but he in fame muche greater is who the in feild orecame

Aboue the fabies never yet did any title bear [5

these noble men for ther desertes, the greatest called were

[Item 65]

This fauour streight was tane away, for wᶜʰ eche matrone deere

    resoluethe to her vnkynd man, no children more to beare

    and that she might not issue yeld wᵗʰ secrete punche or blow

    she rashely beates the burden out, wᶜʰ in her corps did grow

of wiues this cruell fact the lordes, did reprehend full sore [5

but yet ther former honour did again to them restore

[Item 66]

To the lady Hunsdon 1609 homer giuen

Thrice honourd dame yf I a gift estem'd

    of valew rich, as token this new yeare

    of zeale, should send I might perhaps bee dem'd

    to Athens owles or pottes to same to beare

A little mappe the world doth represent   H. St [5

    Items 64 and 66 are bracketed along the right margin; "H. St" is
entered to the right of bracket beside Item 66.

  & counter may stand for an hundred pound

  a little gift may shew good meaning ment

  as well as what in India may be found

In stede of pearle or riche peruuian oare.

  for new yeares gift I send a little booke   [10

  of proffit & delight therin is store

  yf that your honour deign therin to looke

    As duty bindes, my wishes still shall craue

    that you long life & comfortes all may haue

     [Item 67]

"to pray I will not cease

"& all contentes increase

"my wishes shalbe still

"& haue of ioys your fill.

     [Item 68]

   To ye the lady Hunsdon. 1612. Brittaines Troy sent

A newyeares gift receaue thrice honourd dame

  this booke as pledge of duty wch I ow

  my mynde you wishethe all the good it can

  although meanes want to make therof a show

This booke may yeld both proffit & delight   [5

  when you doe seeke to passe the tedious tyme

  yf you pervse it in som winter night

  you may old Troiane tales here reade in rime

  Item 67 is inserted in the right margin, lines 1 and 2 to the right of the bracket and opposite lines 13 and 14 of Item 66; lines 3 and 4 are below the rule separating Items 66 and 68. Line 4 is underlined.

And eke the storie since the worldes creation
    of heathen & our famous Christian kinges [10
    of ancient Brittons & ther life & fashion
    whose fame & honour through ye world now ringes
    And since we are new Brittons made in dede
    it will delight old Brittons actes to rede.

[Item 69] [f. 17

George Bercley 1611

In stede of gift a stamering verse I send to shew my loue
& pray to god your ladiship all happie happes may proue
The best grac't giftes not from the chest but from ye minde proceede
& loue of loue & kindenes is, of kindnes the true mede
nor doe I thinke to cancell debt but debtour stil do rest [5
to pay my skore would not suffice I thinke Ioues golden chest
Liue long dere Grandam & inioy health wealth & happie state
& cloyd wth yeares mount vp to heauen & be an angels mate
these orphan wishes he doth send who is to you by kynde
a granchilde but a slaue & son in dutie hart & mynde. [10

[Item 70]

George to Sr Iohn Millesant 1610

My knight as many happie happes I wishe the this new yeare
as golden starres in frostie night in welkin doe appeare
as crimson deinty kernels be in appels to be founde
wch trees that planted are do yelde in riche Iberian grounde
as france giues grapes, as ripened cornes
appeare in Draiton feild [5

when from the lion phebus skippes, to see Astrea mild
or Honicombes on Hybla hill, & oliues syvill sendes
as deinty pepins kentishe soil, to cheapside market yeldes
accept these wishes as a gift & loue me yf you please
and I to loue & wishe you well do vow never to cease.   [10

[Item 71]
George to master Orwell 1611

Last newyeares day my rugged rime orwell did the salute
Thefore I cannot wth out blame, this newyeares day be mute
thou still remainest the same vnchang'd, & wishest well I trow
therfore I still ye like good will & loue to the do ow
the boares shall leaue to haunt the hils & fishe ye riuers blew   [5
the bees shall leue to feede on thyme & grashoppers on dew
the aery Alpes of lancashire, Pendle & Pennigent
shall first moue from ther place before, my loue shall ere relent
Liue many newyeares in content, inioy all wished ease
Loue suche as honest loue deserue & me Iames if you please   [10

[Item 72]
George to mrs Egerton 1610

my Egerton this paper I you send
& wishe you all good happes as faithfull freind
long life & husband comfort you to giue
and Impes in whom your memorie may liue

[Item 73]   [f. 17v
George Berckley to mrs margaret Edgerton 1611.

My Egerton receaue my verse & me excuse I pray

that I to the no golden gift do send this newyeares day

my thoughtes are all of gold, my wishes golden are

But suttons golden purse I want to make th'effectes appeare

It is not pelf that arguethe loue nor giftes can it supplie [5

    The will wth god & men dothe scuse the purses penury

    all haile my girle long liue & loue, first god & then thy frend

    And doubt not to assure thie self, of my loue without end

---

[Item 74]

George Berkley to Ann fitche. 1610

My fitche I wishe the store of heauenly grace

and husband to supplie thie Robins place

my loue to the shall last til sun run East

as Erst he did when he did shun Thiestes feast

[Item 75]

George to the same 1611.

My Nan althoughe I haue scarse tyme, allotted to indight

yet loue & long acquaintance makes me somwhat for to write

all hail therfore I send to the & wishe the well to fare

y^t thou maist many newyeares liue, wthout all carke & care

& comfort haue of little mall who the a Grandame make [5

& eke a louing fere obtain late husbandes place to take

I will not leaue to loue the still for changeling I am none

my wordes & deedes I the assure will still agree in on

[Item 76]

George to his Grandame 1610.

                                    towres
The doues shall leaue to haunt the stately bowres
and duckes shall not delight in raynie showres
wild beastes shall leaue ther dennes & sheepe to graze
& Titan shall not shine wth golden rayes
before that loue deer Grandame from me part   [5
wch I you ow by dutie & desert
This newyeares tyde because no other gift I fynde
    a paper I you send as herault of my mynde
God send you all content & many a happie yeare
    & when this life shall fade to sit in heauenly quire   [10

[Item 77]   [f. 18

George Bercklay to his sister 1610

Sybyllas tyme I wishe you sister deere
    that you may see full many & merrie a yeare
    my loue to you shall alway last
        thoughe I of Lethe brooke should taste.

[Item 78]

George Berckley to his mother 1610

Deere mother I you wishe a merry yeare
    & after death to sit in heauenly quire
    my loue from you shall neuer flit
    till Atropos my life thred slitt

[Item 79]

George Berckley to his Grandfather 1610.

Thrice honourd lord the prop & cheifest stay

  of my poore state & of my tender yeares
my duty biddes me this same newyeares day
  to shew my mynde & to congratulate
An asse did speake as scripture⟨s⟩ dothe vs show   [5
  king Crasus son born dumb being mou'd did speake
   Augustus was saluted by a crow
  No meruail then yf that I silence breake
   All hail deere Grandsire & long liue in ioy
    yf I deserue then count me still your boy   [10

[Item 80]
George Bercklay to Sr Iohn millesant 1611

Last newyeares day I wish'd the well & now doe wishe againe
my knight & vow thie faithfull freind for ay still to remaine
As long as fine Italian shall loue a flattring punke
the spaniard shalbe vanting proud, the Germain beastly drunke
As long as Switzers fight wth pikes, & frenchmen wth long speares   [5
And Pygmees shall assault the cranes & moscouites white beares
As long as courtly dames shall were braue gownes wth hanging sleiu^s
& faire yong wenches shalbe proud, & borderers be theues
as long as Greekes Carouse & lie, & Turkes will Cristians hate
as long as moores perfidious proue & pettifoggers prate   [10
as long as faithles Iewes shalbe to other nations thrall
& Englishmen y^r swaggering good felowship shall call
I will the loue & thou vppon, this newyeares gift I send

Loue me againe as I doe ⟨y⟩ the & so I make an end.

[Item 81]

.1612. to Sr Iohn millesant

Sir Iohn I the salute, & wishe the this new yeare
   such hap as euery kindest freind doth wishe vnto his pere
   let Clotho draw the thred of thy liues line at length
   To bleake or curtall it let not sad Atropos haue strength
   Let fortune the in wealth & credite make to flow   [5
   And Iuno on the Deiope for comforter bestow

                            that thou maist
These fortunes I now wishe ⟨as comforter best⟩ still inioy
As long as Thames shall bath the banckes of our new famous Troy
Thrice I haue wisht you well in sclender riming vaine
I loue you & yf that you please, you may loue me again   [10

[Item 82]

George to his Grandmother 1612.

        ipi
Thrice Phebus in the Goate hath taken vp his Inn
                  in rime
   since I my my duty to expresse, ⟨deer Grandam⟩ did first begin
And since dere Grandam you are pleased my papers to receaue
I see no reason whie that I this custom now should leaue
I ancient is & laudable, my duty & your loue   [5
the same that erst, my silence might I feare ingratefull proue
yf on begin to build a howse & maketh not an end
Each on will mocke & ieast at him that vainly so doth spend
Who so in learning spendes his tyme & leaueth at the best
what er he thinke the better sort will deme him but a beast   [10

who striueth in a maistery to get the highest place
yf he in middest do faint & quaile he getteth but disgrace
So I yf now this newyeares tyde should cease you to salute
To'th wise vnnurtured seriph frog I might be calld thus mute
Daign therfore deerest dame again, my rime for to pervse [15
and cherefully this tribute take of my poore stam̄ering muse
I wishe you all the good I can Imagin in my mynd
And vow that you most dutifull for euer me shall fynde
Before that I vnmindfull be of promisse now thus made
The earth shall sinke, the sea shall flame & heauen shall retrograde [20
God grant you long to liue in health in wealth & honour flow
That many yeares my rimes I may as newyeares giftes bestow

[Item 83]

My fitche I the salute I know thou dost me loue
this newyeares day I wishe thou maist all comfortes proue
maist liue in health long tyme, of thy 4. Impes haue ioy
a louing husband haue & also a new boy
maist florish still as long as thou liuest on the ground [5
and shortly maist be payd thy due a thousand pound
That little mall may grow to be a prety wenche
That she may learn to sow and also to speake frenche
Twice I haue wisht the well and still wilbe thy freind
farewell & loue thy mall, & so I make an Ende [10

George to
m^{rs} fithe
1612.

The title of Item 83 in the right margin is separated from the text by a bracket.

-65-

[Item 84] [f. 19

h. st. to ye lady Hunsdon 1610. faery quene

hauing no other gift right noble dame

    to testifie my mynde this booke I send

    the autour when he liu'd did beare your name

& for to honour ladies this he penn'd

    here may you reade in sugred verse set out [5

    the praises of Belphebe worthie Quene

& faery landes adventures all about

    wth other exploites worthie to be seene

here Georges holines may vs direct

    to Conquer all the monstrous shapes of sin [10

& Guions temperance make vs suspect

the sugred baites of pleasures wanton ginnes

    Daign it to reade & reape such fruictes it beares

    I still will wishe you long & happie yeares.

[Item 85]

h. st. to D. Hollandes translation of Cambdens Brittain

What Cambden wrote for proffit & delight

    of Brittishe Isles of blessinges wch haue store

    in latian language for each learned sprite

    to reape such fruictes as passe peruuian oare

This Holland hath at suite of learned dame [5

    with paines transfused into our vulgar speache

    his care of comon good deserues that fame

    wch vnto late posterity shall ⟨reache⟩ stretche

Wherfore all worthie wightes wch doe take pleasure
    to ⟨f⟩ know the stories of ther countrie ⟨deere⟩ sweete   [10
    ought kindly to accept this so greate treasure
    & yeld such thanckes to th' autour as is meete.
    I like his pen & iudgement eke no lesse
    for making choise of such a patronesse

[Item 86]

God send you all content & to bring forth a boy
W^ch other self, to me may be, to you a lasting ioy
or else som prety girle to picture you in face
in gentle nature or in wit or som part of your grace
& after long expense of many happie yeares   [5
as quirister for to be placed among the heavenly quires

[Item 87]   [f. 19^v

George to his mother 1612

Most louing mother this new year let me my duty shew
    ffor cancell I cannot the bandes of due debt wch I ow
you bred me first wth in your wombe & brought me forth wth pain
Since fostred me wth busie care & kept me from my bane
By tutours paines you haue me taught, & made that I now rellish   [5
Castalian springes & Helicon wch virtuous myndes embellish
And still you loade me wth your loue, & kindnes every way
O that I once might able be these debtes of myne to pay
But God_es_ & parent_es_ benefites transcend so to the eye
That doe what ere I can I see I must ingratefull die   [10

That loue descendes & not ascendes I scarsely can beleue
To be found bacward in my loue, it would my hart muche grieue
me thinkes at your comaund I could like Atlas heauen vpreare
And cherefully like Hercules inioyned labours beare
God send you long & happy dayes & now this yeare beginnes   [15
to clere your mynde of booteles cares as snakes do doff $\overline{y}^r$ skinnes
ffor sure as rust doth mettall marre, & moath y^e garment eate
So greife & care as canker doe the life & marrow fret
Accept my ruff & rugged rime & me your blessing giue
but for to loue & honour you I would not wishe to liue   [20

[Item 88]

George to his sister 1612

Dere sister I this newyeares tyde do wishe to you such hap
As flattring nurse to tender childe when she feedes him wth pap
A healthfull able body and a virtuous mynde & true
And coffers wch are stuft wth store of riches of peru
And husband you a mother make of many a pretty boy   [5
who may procure ther countries good & eeke ther parentes ioy
long life & many a happy day & when ⟨death⟩ stoppes your breath
(aege)
Your patience faith & virtue may still triumph ouer death
These wishes I do send to you as heraults of my hart
I vow to loue you & therfrom my mynd shall neuer start   [10

[Item 89]

George again to his sister

Sweete sister you are riche, in golden g⟨ifts⟩ of grace

---

in bewty also you are riche & lineaments of face

in birth & kinred riche, in wit & learning rare

O would to god I worthy were, wth you ther to compare

In flowre of youth you are, riche in tall & goodly stature [5

In temperance & modesty & gentlenes of nature

It grieues me for to see you riche in so great store

of other thinges but state of health, this tyme to be so poore

modern phisitions say as Chapman doth relate

The agew from Hungarie cam wch gaue our prince ye mate [10

Let that be as it may yf I my mind may tell

I thinke these pale diseases cam from vgly pit of hell

And thither they return, yf patient<u>es</u> will vse glee [f. 20

ffor Diet: Quiet: merry mynde doth make them hence to flee

procure for to be strong & loue me as before [15

And I a brother kynd wilbe both now & euer more

[Item 90]

George to m^{rs} Caue his mother wayting woman

my Caue I wishe the this new yeare suche fortune & suche hap

As they doe vse to proue wch sit in lady fortunes lap

long life & store of worldly wealth, & husband the to loue

of whom thou maist haue store of brattes, & ioyes of wedlock proue

Thie name I trow a sentence is & willes the to take hede [5

Ile descant of yt by thy leaue, for it may profite brede

do you be not made I say wth flattring speaches drunke

ffor fawning smiling speache hath made, an honest wenche a punke

---

Take hede thou be not led wth gaine for Couetise is a vice
and gold of honest wenche hath made full oft a Cockatrice   [10
Take hede thou be not arrogant, for that will the disgrace
A prowd & haughty cariage marrs full oft a pleasing face
Take hede of Anger it becomes, feirce beastes & vgly creatures
more then thy milde & gentle sex, wch hath so goodly features
But I surcease for see thy name, doth yeald to large a theame   [15
my only purpose was to tell how muche I the esteme
liue happie I will the regard & wishe the as my freinde
Doe thou the like yf so thou please, & thus I make an ende

[Item 91]

To his sisters Gentlewoman m^rs powel.

my powel I this newyeares tyde doe wishe to the good hap
for old acquaintance I the knew when I did feede on pap
I knew the fore I did begin to sow my wildest oates
I knew the when I romed about like wenche in my long coates
I knew the when vneath I could out of my bed arise   [5
I knew the when a bunting boy, I hunted after flies
Seuen yeares I trow I haue the known since that I first began
when I looke back I meruail muche I am not yet a man
But man or boy I am to the on wch doth wishe the well
And mynde so to contnew still, this newyeares day farewell   [10

[Item 92]

H. stanford to th lady Berklay 1612.

My deerest dame this history I send

-70-

  as newyeares guift & pawn of mindfull mynd
  yf you in reading daign som howres to spend
  a world of pleasing pr_o_ffet you shall fynde
A story is a treasury of witt   [5
  and truly call'd the register of fame
  no reading can your ladiship more fit
  whose virtues haue procured so good a name
I wish you all good fortunes suitable
  to the rare worth of your most sincere brest   [10
  long life & comfort_es_ never mutable
  and this new yeare & euer to be blest
Althoughe the gowte dishable ioyntes and handes
My mynde is yours in more, then Gordian bandes

       [Item 93]   [f. 20^v

  H. stanford to m^{rs} Theophila Berkelay 1612
for newyeares guift accept this little booke
  fayre Nymphe although it make no show of price
  no doubt I make you daign ther on to looke
  for you in wit wth mother sympathize
Here Bertas doth in sugred verse indight   [5
  the rarest workes of god_es_ creation
  his verse & language surely will delight
  and proffit yeld wth virtuous contentation
As I from cradle you haue wished well
  so do I now & will continew euer   [10

  Item 92 is bracketed along the right margin.

procede in virtue wherin you excell

 and in your studies feare not to perseuer

No Ornament can better fit a grace

 then mongst the muses for to haue a place

[Item 94]

Anonymus

nethor life nor death affordes ease to my troubled mynd

 for I liue wthout my light, O what a greif is liuing blind

and dy I should for death would ease my moanes pytying my

   greiuous groanes

but when he sees thine Image in my hart

he flies & dares not peirce yt wth his dart   [5

what art hou whom death doth feare death suche a terrour deemid.

what art thou who makest life sowre, life such a blessed

   sweete estemed?

wert thou humaine thou couldst not but relent, to see my discontent

wert thou a god & sainct thou pity must

for all ye goddes & sainctes are pytifull & iust   [10

Pitty then O pitty me, so wilt thou proue diuine

take me for thy votary, Ile offer dayly at thie shrine

myne eyes the lamp, my loue shalbe the flame, my vowes shall

   prayers frame

& to appease thie rage & ease my smart

Item 94] No carry-over lines in the MS.

vppon thine alter will I sacrifice, my hart. [15

[Item 95] [f. 25

bewayling his exile he singeth thus

He that his mirthe hathe lost whose comfort is dismayd
  whose hope in vayne whose faithe in skorn whose trust is all betrayed
  yf he haue held them dear & can not ceasse to moan
  Com let him take a place by me he shall not rew alone
  but yf the smallest sweete be mixt wth all his sower [5
  yf in the day the monethe ye year he feele on lightning hower
  then rest he wth himself he is no mate for me
  whose fear is fallen whose succour, death must be voyd, whose helpe his
  yet not the wished deathe wch hath not playnt nor lacke
  wch making free the better part is only natures wracke [10
  Oh noe that were to well my death is of the mynd
  wch alwayes yeldes extremest pangues but keepes the worst behind
  As on wch lyves in show but ⟨out⟩ in wardly dothe die
  whose knowledge is a bloudie feild wher all help slayn dothe lie
  whose hart the alter is whose spirit a sacrifice [15
  vnto the powers whom to appease no sorow may suffise
  my fancies are like thornes on wch I goe by night
  myn argumentes are as an host whom force hath put to flight
my sent ye passions spie my thoughtes like ruins old
  of famous Carthage or the towne wch Synon bought & sold [20
  wch still before myn eyes my mortall fall dothe lay

    Item 95:12] The 's' of "yeldes" has been written over an original
'st' of "yeldest."

-73-

whom loue & fortune once advanced but now haue cast awaye

oh thoughtes no thoughtes but woundes somtyme the seates of ioye

somtyme the seates of quiet rest but now of all anoye

I sow^d the soile of peace my blisse was in the spring   [25

& day by day I eat the fruict wch my lyves tree doth bring

To nettles now my Corne, my feild is turned to flint

wher sitting in the Cypresse shade I eat ^reap the hyacinthe

The peace the rest the life wch I enjoyed of yore

Cam to my lotte that by my losse my smart might sting the more   [30

So to vnhappie men the best fares ^me for the worst

oh tyme ohe place o wordes most dear, ⟨both then & now accurst⟩ ^sweet then but now accurst

In (was) standes my delight in (is) & (shall) my woe

my horrour fastened in the (yea) my hope hanges in the noe

I looke for no relief, reliefe would com to late   [35

To late I fynd I fynd to well somtyme stood my estate

behold suche is the end what pleasure here is sure

ohe nothing els but care & playnt dothe to the word^1 endure

forsaken first am I then vtterlie forgotten

& they that were cam to my faith of my reward haue gotten   [40

o loue wher is the sawce ^then that makes thie tormentes sweete

what is the cause that many thinke ther death throughe the but meete

The statly chast disdayn the secret thankfulnes

Item 95:39] This line was apparently squeezed in after lines 38 and 40 had been copied.

   the grace reserued the comon light that shines in worthines
oh that yt wer not so or⟨that⟩ I ^{yt}could excuse   [25
   or that the wrathe of Ielousie my iudgement did abuse   [46
oh frail inconstaunt kynd, a life to trust to wemen
         lo
   no wemen aungels be & yet my maystres is a woman
yet hate I but the fault & not the faultie on
nor can I rid frō me the bond in wch I lie alone   [50
Alone I lie whose like in loue was never yet
the prince the poore the yong the old the fond or full of witte
here styll remayn must I by death by wrong by shame
I cannot blott out of my brest what loue wrought in her name
I cannot sett at naught wch I haue held so dear   [55
I cannot make yt seme so farre wch is in deed so neere
me yet I mean henceforth y^{s} straunge will to professe
as on that could betray suche trothe to build on ficklenes
for yt shall never faile that my faithe bore in hand
I gaue my word my word gaue me, bothe word & gift shall stand   [60
Sithe then yt must be this & this is all to yll
I yeld me captiue to my curse my hard fate to fulfill
the solitarie wood my citie shall becom
the darkest denne shalbe my lodge wherin I rest or runne
of eben blacke my boord the wormes my feast shallbe   [65
wher wth my bodie shalbe fed till they doe feede on me
    of Niobie
my wyne merobie my bed a craggie rocke

   Item 95:64] The 'd' of "lodge" was formed from an original 'g.'

the serpentes hisse my harmonie the scriching owle my clocke
my exercise nought els but raging agonies
my bookes of spightfull fortunes foiles & drery traiedies [70
my walke the pathe of playntes my prospect into hell
wher Sisiphus that wretched wight in endlesse payn dothe dwell
And yet althoughe I seeme to vse the poetes stile
to figure forthe my ruthfull plight my fall & my exile
yet is my greife not fained wherin I sterue & pyne [75
who feeles his most shall fynd yt least, yf his compare wth myne
my songe, yf any aske whose greivous case is suche
die er thou lette his name be knowen his folie shoes to muche

        to
but best is the hide & never com̄ to light
for on thie deathe may none but I thie accent sound aright [80

[Item 96] [f. 26

Locke vp sweete liddes the threasures of my hart
   preserue those beames, this age his only light
   to her sweete sence som̄ ease (sweete sleap) impart
   her sence to weake to bear her spirites might
   And while o sleape thou closest vp her sight [5
   her sight wher loue did forge his fairest dart
   O harbour all her partes in easfull plight
   let no strange dreame make her fair bodie start
   but yet o dreame yf thou wilt not depart
   in this fair subiect from thie com̄on right [10
   but wilt thie self in such a seat delight

then take my shape & say vnto her spright

    kise her from me & say vnto her spirite

till her eyes shine I lyue in darkest night.

[Item 97]

                                         spring &
The palme ere yt by force doth. faynt doth sprought ⟨& spring⟩ aloft

    the sonne retaynes his brightnes still, though yt be clouded oft

Then is this peice of passing price wch natures art begon

    whose virtues like the palme do spring & bewtie like the sonne

thou pretie bird wch bringest vs newse of the most pleasaunt spring [5

    & wth sweete & mournfull tunes dost cause the wooddes to ring

wch dost our weried myndes refreshe wth thye delightfull sound

    O nightingall com tune my song, & help to cure my wounde

[Item 98]

I alwayes would yet haue no will

    my would I want my will I haue

I fynd my fancie forced still

    the more I lacke the lesse I craue

Thus I wthstand my own consent   [5

    compeld by force & yet content.

[Item 99]

Com sorow com̄ sitte down & mourn wth me

    ha⟨n⟩g down thie head vppon thie balefull brest

that god & man & all the world may see

our hevy hartes doe lie at little rest

enfold thyn armes & wring thie wretched handes   [5

to shew the state wherin poore sorow standes

Crye not outright for that is childrens guise
but let thie teares fall trickling down thie face
& weepe so long vntill thie blubbred eyes
do shew in somne the depthe of thie disgrace [10
o shake thie head but not a word but mume
the heart once dead the tongue is stroken dume
And let our fare be dishes of despite
   to breake our hartes & not our fastes wth all
& let vs suppe wth sorowes soppes at night [15
   a dish for death to make an end wthall
thus let vs lyue till heavens may rue to see
the dolefull doome ordayned for the & me.

[Item 100]

What tongue can her perfections tell in whose each part all pennes

     may dwell

       [Item 101] [f. 26^v

like those sicke folke in whom straunge humours flow

can tast no sweete the sowre ⟨thing*es*⟩ only please

              dothe

so to my mynd while passions dayly grow

   whose fiery chaynes vppon my fredom seaze

Ioyes straungers seeme I cannot byde ther show [5

   nor brooke ought els but well acquaynted woe

   greife tastes me best, payne is my rest & ease

   sicke to the death still loving my disease

Item 100 is written as one line in the MS.

[Item 102]

how is my sonne whose beames are shining bright
    becom the cause of my darke ougly night
or how doe I captyved in this darke plight
bewayle the case & in the cause delight
my mangled mynd huge horrours still doe fright   [5
wth sense possest & claymed by reasons right
      ixt
betwene wch two in me I haue this fight
where whoe so wynnes I put my self to flight.

[Item 103]

Sweete roote saye thou the roote of my desire
    was virtue clad in constant loves attyre

[Item 104]

they that describe the world thre famous lakes do note
the on wher in all thinges do sinke the other wher they flote
a third of nobler kynd but not lesse straunge is found
    wherin all sensyue thinges are saved the sensles ever drownd.
my lesse world hath the like by meanes of hope & feare   [5
      taketh
    feare strikethe down all pleasing thoughtes, hope all aloft
              doth bear
but then the honre due wch comon is to none
    doth iudge my hart but doth preserue but what she likes alone.
Amongest the isles that bear the name of fortunate

    Item 104] No carry-over lines in the MS.

ther is a tre or at the least yt hath byn seene of late [10
about whose toppe a clowde continually doth stand
that dewes the leaves & of the droppes he drinkes y^t owes the land
vnto the tre my mynd vnto the clowd my care
& to the dew that ever falls my playnt I do compare

[Item 105]

Olympus head is raised aboue the reache of wynd
wher they that cōm   the ayr to percing fynd
yet may the so prepare that then yf they
they see the lampes of simple fier
this hill shapes forth her mynd, all passions set be wynd [5
wthin whose heightes who seekes his place, to trie his lacke
doth tend
but who by virtues guyd dothe that degre attayn
shall ther enioy such heavenly giftes as els to hope were vayne

[Item 106]   [f. 27

ring out your belles let mourning shewes be spred, for loue is dead
all loue is dead infected wth plaugue of depe disdayn
worthe as nought worth reiected, [5] & faith fair scorn doth gayn
from so vngratfull fancie frō such a femall franzie
from them that vse men thus good lord delyver vs. [10
wepe neighbours wepe do you not hear yt sayd that loue is dead
his death bed peacockes follie, his wynding sheete is shame
his will false seming holie, [15] his sole executour blame
frō so vngr

Items 105 and 106] No carry-over lines in the MS.

let dirdge be song & trentalls rightly red for loue is dead
    Syr wrong his tombe ordayneth, my mistres marble heart   [20
    his epitaphe contayneth her eyes were once his dart from so vngrat
    Alas I lie rage hath this errour bred loue is not dead
    loue is not dead but sleapeth [25] in her vnmatched mynd
    wher she his counsel kepeth till dew desert she fynd
                                       who loue can
    therfore frō so vild fancie to call such wit a franzie [30]
                temper thus
                good lord delyver vs

[Item 107]

    the fier to see my wrong for anger burnes
    the air in rain for my affliction weepes
    the sea to ebbe for greif his flowing turnes
    the earth wth pitie dull the centre kepes
    fame is wth wonder blazed [5] tyme runnes awaye for sorow
    place standeth still amazed/ to see my night of evils w^{ch}
                hath no morow
    alas alonly she no pitie takes to know my miseries but chast & cruell [10
    my fall her glorie makes/ yet still her eyes gyue to my flames
                ther fuell
fire burn me quite till sence of burning leaue me
    ayr let me draw no more thie breath in anguish
    earth take this earth in wch my spirit<u>es</u> languish   [15
    fame saye I was not born/ tyme hast my dying howre
        place see my graue vptorn/ fire, ayr, sea earth, tyme, place
                you
              shew your powre

    Item 107] No carry-over lines in the MS.

alas frō all ther helpes I am exiled/ [20] for hers am I & death
     feares her displeasure
fye death thou art beguild/ though I am hers she makes of me
     no theasure

[Item 108]

I pray the booke when I am gon
to tell thie mistres here was on
that would be very well content
to be at her comaundement.

[Item 109]

1. Calling to mynd myn eye went long about   W. R.
 to cause my hart for to forsake my brest
 All in a rage I thought to pull yt out
 by whose devise I lyved in such vnrest
 what could he saye then to regayn my grace?   [5
 forsothe that yt had sene his mistres face

2 An other tyme I cald vnto my mynd
 It was my hart that all my woe had wrought
 for that to loue his fort he had resignd
 when on suche warres my fancie never thought   [10
 what could he saye when I would haue him slayn?
 that he was yours & had forgon me clean

3 At last when bothe my eye & heart
  excused them selves as guiltles of myn yll

 Item 109 is bracketed along the right margin, with the
initials "W. R." to the right of this bracket.

I found my self the cause of all my smart [15
    and told my self my self now slaye I will
but when I saw my self to you was true
    I loved my self because my self loved you.

            [Item 110] [f. 27^v

Williā Parrie was ap Harrie by his name
from the Alehouse to the gallowes grew his fame
gotten westward on a bastard was he thought
wherbie on way kyn to Conwey hath he sought
wth Incest like a best he begon [5
mother maried daughter carried him a sonne
muche he borowed wch he sorowed to repaye
Hare his good bought wth bloud as they saye
Yet for payment had arraignment of his debtour
she that gaue him life to saue him hangd a better [10
Parrie his pardon thought no guerdon for his worth
wherfore he sought that he mought travell firth
wch obtayned he remayned as before
& wth wastnes shewed his basenes more & more
he did enter to adventer even her death [15
by whose favour he did ever draw his breath
It was pitie on so wittie mall content
voyd of reason should to treason so be bent
but his giftes were but shiftes voyd of grace
& his braverie was but knaverie bold & base [20

Wales did beare him fraunce did swere him to the pope
Venice wrought him london brought him to the rope.

[Item 111]

of force I must prayse her I like her so well
for favour & bewtie she beareth the bell
No helene nor Creside can once stayn her face
    yea Venus she passeth for bewtie & grace
Ech gift that dame nature had power to bestow   [5
    she gaue to my lady I certaynly know
The heavens were helpfull the starres did her paynt
    she might all the aungeles for bewtie attaynt
& this is her personage most fyn to behold
    her hear is so yealow as glistering gold   [10
her eyes are of cristall her nose white as mylke
    her cheekes are of roses her skyn soft as silke
her lippes are of Corall her teeth are of pearl
    her tongue is of sugar ah delicate girle
her breth is of amber or sinamone sweete   [15
      it
    her speach is of musicke to lull on a sleep
    her chin hath a dimple to wyn a kinges hart
    her only farre visage all ioyes would impart
    her necke yt hath whitnes much brighter then snow
who would not his liking of her ther bestow   [20
her feet & her fingers in forme do excell
    In all other members I know yt right well

her vaynes are of azure & then I tell all
her delicate bodie is tender & small
wch whoso embraceth of this he may vaunt [25
a more fairer creature the godes could not graunt
then who so not liketh is much for to blame
for nature on like her agayn could not frame.

[Item 112] [f. 28

oratio Elizabethæ reginæ habitu in regni conventu convocato
ad diē 15 Martij anno 1575

        sacred
Do I see godes most holie   word & text of holie writ drawen to so
diverse senses being/ never so precisely taught & shall I ⟨sh p⟩
hope
that my speache can passe forth through so many eares/ wthout
mistaking wher so many ripe & divers wittes do ofter bend themselues
to conster/ then attayn the perfect vnderstanding. If any looke
for eloquence I shall deceaue y^r/ hope. yf som thinke I can match
ther gift wch spake before they hold an open heresie/ [5] I can
not satisfie ther longing thirst y^t watch for these delightes
vnles I should afford thē/ what my self had never yet in my possession.
If I should say the sweetest tongue or/ eloquentest speach y^t ever was
in man were able to expresse y^t restles care/ wch I haue ever bent
to govern for the greatest wealth I should wrong myn/ entent &
greatly bate the merit of myn own endevour. I can not attribute
this/ [10] hap & good successe to my devise, wthout detracting

    Item 111] Lines 26-28 are written in the right margin parallel to the length of the folio and separated from the rest of the text by a jagged vertical line.

much from the dyvyn providence./ nor chalenge to my own comendation
what is only dew to his eternall glorie./ my sexe permites yt not
or yf yt might be in this kynd, yet fynd I no empeach-/ment whie to
persons of more base estate the like proportion should not be allotted/
on speciall favour yet I must confesse. I haue iust cause to vaunt
of that: wheras/ [15] varietie & loue of chaunge, is ever so rife in
servantes to ther masters, in children/ to ther parentes & in private
frendes on to an other, as y^t thoughe for on year or perhapes/for
two they can content themselves to hold ther course vpright yet
after by mistrust or/ doubt of worse they are dissevered & in tyme
waxe werie of ther wonted liking yet/ still I fynd y^t assured zeal
amongest my faithfull subiectes to my speciall comfort/ [20] w^{ch}
was first declared to my great encouragement. Can a prince wch of
necessitie/ must discontent a nūber to delight & please a few
continew so long tyme w^{th}out great/ offence muche mislike or comon
grudge? or happes yt oft y^t princes actions ar concea-/ved in so
good part & favourably interpreted. no no my lordes how great my
fortune/ is in this respect I twere ingrate yf I should not acknowledge
And as for those/ [25] rare & speciall benefites wch many yeares
haue followed & accompanied my happie/ raigne I attribute to god
alone the prince of rule & count my self no better then his/
handmayd rather brought vp in a scole to byde the ferula then traded
in a kingdom/ to support the scepter ⟨of policie⟩ yf policie had byn
preferred before truthe/ would I trow you even at the first
beginning of my raign, haue turned vpside/ [30] down so great

affaires or entered into tossing of the greatest waves & billowes
of/ the world: that might if I had sought myn ease haue harboured
& cast anchore in/ more seming securitie. It can not be denied but
worldly wisdom rather bad me/ linke my self in league & fast
alliaunce wth great princes to purchase frendes on/ every syde by
worldly meanes & ther repose the trust of myn assured strenghe/
[35] wher force could never want to gyue assistaunce. Was I to
seke y^t to mannes/ outward iudgement this must nedes be thought the
safest course? no I can never/ graunt my self so simple as not to
see what all mens eyes discovered. But all/ these meanes of leagues
alliaunces & forrayn strengthes I quite forsoke & gaue my/ self to
seke for truth wth out respect, reposing myn assured staye in godes
most mightye/ [40] grace wth full assurance./ thus I began, thus I
procead & thus I hope to end./ These 17 yeares god hath bothe
prospered & protected you wth good successe/ vnder my direction,
& I nothing doubt but the same maynteyning hand will/ guyde you [f. 28^v]
still & bring you to the ripenes of perfection. Consider w^th
your selves/ the bitter stormes & troubles of your neighbours,
the true cause wherof I will not attri-/ [45] bute to princes god
forbyd I should since these misfortunes may procead as well from/
sinnes among the people. for want of plagues declare not alwayes
want of guilt/ but rather proue godes mercie I know beside y^t
private persons may fynd rather/ fault then mend a princes state,
& for my part I graunt my self to guiltie to/ encrease the burden
or mislike of anye Let all men therfore bear ther private/ [50]

Item 112:41] The slash after "assurance" is in the MS.

faultes, myn own haue weight enoughe for me to answer for. The
best waye I/ suppose for you & me were by humble prayers to
require of god that not in/ wening but in perfect weight, in being,
not in seming, we may wish ye best & furdir/ yt wth our abilitie.
   not the finest wit the   iudgement y^t can rake most/
deaply or take vp captiouse eares wth pleasing tales hath greater
care to giud you/ [55] to the safest state or would be gladder to
establish you where men ought to ⟨assure⟩ thinke / themselves most sure
& happie then she y^t speakes these wordes. And touching/ daungers
cheifly feared, first to rehearse my meaning lately vnfolded to
you/ by the lord keper, yt shall not be nedefull (thoughe I must
confesse myn own/ mislike so much to striue agaynst the matter,
as yf I wear a milkemayd wth a pail/ [60] on myne arme wherbye my
private persen might be little set by, I would not/ forsake y^t
single state to match my self wth the greatest Monarch. Not y^t
I con/ demne the doble knot or iudge amisse of such as forced by
necessitie can not/ dispose themselves to an other life, but wish
y^t none were dryven to chaunge/ saue such as can not kepe honest
lymites) yet for your behoufe ther is no/ [65] waye so difficile
that may touch my private, wch I could not well content my/ self
to take, & in this case as willingly to spoil my self quite of my
self as/ yf I should put of mȳ vpper garment when yt wearies me
yf the present/ state might not therbye be encombred. I speake
not this for my behoufe I/ know I am but mortall, wch good lesson
m^{aster} speaker in his third division of/ [70] a virtuous princes
properties required me wth reason to remember & so ther/ whilest

prepare my self to welcom death whensoever yt shall please almightie/ god to send yt as yf others would endevour to performe the like yt could not be so/ bitter vnto many as yt hath byn counted. Myn experience teacheth me to be no/ fonder of these vayn delight<u>es</u> then reason would, nor furder to delight in thing<u>es</u>/ [75] vncertayn then may seme convenient. but let good heed be taken least in reaching/ to far after future good, you perrill not the present or begin to quarrell & fal⟨l⟩/ by dispute together by the eares before yt be decided who shall wear my crown./ I will not denie but I might be thought the indifferentist iudge in this respect/ that shall not be at all when these thing<u>es</u> be fulfilled, wch none beside my self can speak/ [80] in all this companie. Misdeme not of my word<u>es</u> as though I sought what hereto/ fore to others hath byn graunted. I entend yt not. My braynes be to thine to carrie/ so toughe

⟨grosse⟩ a matter, althoughe I trust god will not in such hast cut of my dayes/ but that according to your own desert & my desire I may provyde som̄ good waye/ for your securitie. And thus as on wch yeldeth you more thankes both for your/ [85] zeal vnto my self & service in this parlament then my tongue can vtter I recom-/ mend you to the assured gard & best keping of the almightie who will preserue/ you safe I trust in all felicitie & wish wthall y^t each [f. 29 of you had tasted som̄ droppes/ of Lethes floud to deface & Cancell these my speaches out of your remembraunce.

    Dixj.

———————

[Item 113]

The state of fraunce as now yt standes
   is like primiero at fower handes
wher som do vie & som do hold
   & best assurd may proue to bold

The king was rashe wthout regard   [5
   & being flush would nedes discard
but first he past yt to the Guise
   & he of nought streight wayes yt vies

Navarre was next & would not out
   for of his cardes he had no doubt   [10
The Cardinall fayntly held the vie
   & watcht advantage for to spie

for to goe out his frendes him bides
   but Cardinals hattes make busie heddes
all restes were vp & all were in   [15
   whilst philip wrought that Guise might wyn.

Quene mother stoode behind his backe
   & tought him how to make his packe
the king who all the cardes did know
   sayes what goe lesse before you shew.   [20

He proferd daliaunce for to make
   to saue himself & Guises stake
& we that saw them & ther play
   did leaue them ther & cam awaye.

[Item 114]

nō ē fides super terrā.

No faith nor frend nor suertie vnder sonne
   no trust no trueth nor playnnes men may fynd
   fyne hedes by sleight beyond playn wittes doth run
   all natures babes do dayly grow vnkynd
   The sonne somtymes doth wish the father dead   [5
   in brethren oft is traitrous trechery found
   old frendes fall out & takes me toyes in head
   the myndes of men are ficle & vnsound
   nere kynred iarres & kyndnes shoes far of
   true earnest loue is made a ieast & scoffe   [10
   Sad mischeif shewes a mizzie muffted face
   leud life can cast a shadow on fowle fact
   the killing hand can mortall foe embrace
   in conning brayn is pryvie paltrie pact
   no promisse kept smooth wordes proue nought but wynd   [15
   the craftie foxe can knitte & then vntwynd
    The tongue but talkes to serue the alone   [f. 29^v
   the wit but workes how welth may com by wiles
   the warme good will growes cold as marble stone
   the fleering cheere bewrayes the world wth smiles   [20
   the humble port but harbours hollow hart
   the lonely lookes bides gorgon byte the bayt
   the kissing handes can play the Iudas part
   the mild regard is mixt wth meere deceipt
   the fawning cur for crumes crepes close in lap   [25
   the hongrie mouth gapes wyde for others foode

the flecing fist can fynly follow hap
the murthring mynd can shew a pleasaunt moode
& so the rest of all our paynted trade
are somer snakes that sittes in secret shade [30
whose vizars faire but hides the vipers sting
semes clear & clean proves fowle & false wthin
a broken staffe a feeble flattring thing
puft vp wth breath wth flesh. & fayntie skyn
the cloke & ⟨case⟩ cace of all the craft on earth [35
from cradell caught & brought to world by birthe

     Sarū.

    [Item 115]

Weried wth thoughtes of troubled anguishe
toild wth despair, despair of obtayning
forst for to yeld, not hoping I languishe
yelding I fynd no comfort remayning
 what resteth then wretch to ease y^e of greife [5
 death onlie must be thie happie reliefe
Dye then in silence blase not thie follie
 blame not the wight y^t all worth excedeth
 blasphemis blemishe the blame not ye holie.
 hevens face in the woundes of her sayntes bledeth [10
  Creatures on earth were born to admire.
   to wonder to honour but not to desire.

[Item 116]

So gratious is thie sweete self so fair so framed.
  that who so sees the wth out an hart inflamed
  either he lyues not, or loves delight he knowes not

[Item 117]

These y^t be certain signes of my tormenting
  no sighes be they nor any sighe so showethe
  those haue their truce sometimes these no relenting
  not so exhales the heat that in me glowethe
fierce loue y^t burnes my hart makes all this venting
  while wth his winges the raging fier he blowethe
Loue say wth what devise thou canst for ever
keepe yt in flames & yet consume yt never

[Item 118]

The fair Diana never more revived
  her lovers hart y^t spied her in ye fountain
While she her naked lims in water dyved
  then me the countrie wenche set by ye mountain
washing a vaile to clothe ye lockes refined
that on fair Laura's head ye gold resemble.
wch made me quake althoughe ye sonne then shined
& everie ioynt wth loving frost to tremble

[Item 119]

Ioy so delightes my hart & so relieves me
when I behold the face of my beloved

that any hard mischaunce or pang y^t greeves me
is quite exiled & presently removed
& yf I might to perfite vp my pleasure   [5
bestow myn eyes where I repose my treasure
for a crown & a kingdom sure possessed
I would not chaunge my state so sweete & blessed.

[Item 120]

false loue now shoote & spare not
false loue now doe thie worst I care not
& to dispatche me vse all thin art & craft to catche me
for youthe amisse bestowed I now repent me
& for my faultes I languishe ⟨wch brought me⟩   [5
wch brought me nothing else but greif & anguishe
& now at last haue vowed at libertie to lyue
    synce to assaile me
    both thie bow & thie brand nought dothe availe the
    for from ye good nor ill, comfort nor sorow   [10
    I will not hope nor fear now nor to morow.

[Item 121]   [f. 30^v

O Greife yf yet my greif be not beleved.
  crie wth thie voice outstretched
  that her dispightfull heart & eares disdaigning
  may hear my iust complaining.
& when thou hast her told my state most wretched   [5

tell her that thoughe my hart be thus tormented
I could be well contented
yf she that now dothe greeue me
had but the least desire once to relieue me.

[Item 122]

As in the night we see the sparkes revived
& quite extinct so sone as day appeareth
so when I am of my sweete sonne deprived
new feares approche & ioy my hart forbeareth
but not so soone she is agayn arryved   [5
as fear retireth & present hope me cheareth
O sacred light o turn agayn to blesse me
& dryue away this fear that doth oppresse me.

[Item 123]

In vain he seekes for bewtie y^t excelleth
that hath not seene her eyes wher loue soiourneth
how sweetly here & ther the same she turnethe
he knowes not how loue healeth & how he quellethe.
that knowes not how she sighes & sweete beguilethe.   [5
& how she sweetly speakes & sweetly smilethe.

[Item 124]

What meanethe loue to nest him
   in the fair eyes wth louely grace & heavenly sprite enspired
   of my mistres delightfull.

-95-

Envious dames confesse & be not spightfull
ah fooles do you not mynd yt [5
that loue hath sought & never yet could fynd yt.
from sun arising till wher he goes to rest him
a braver place then in her eyes to nest him.

[Item 125]

Sweet loue when hope was flowring.
wth fruict<u>es</u> of recompence for my deserving
rest was the price of all my faithfull serving
O spitefull death accursed, o life most cruel
the first by wrong doth pain me [5
& all my hope hath turned to lamenting
the last agaynst my will here dothe detain me
fain would I fynd my Iuel but death to spite me more
yet wth a mild relenting me think<u>es</u> wthin my hart he place
she holdeth
& what my torment is plainly beholdethe [10

[Item 126] [f. 31

Ladie that hand of plentie that gaue vnto the needfull
did steale my hart vnheedfull
sweet theafe of loue so dayntie y^t rob when you are gyving.
but you do gyue so surely y^t you may rob & steale ye more securely
that my poore hart be eased you doe yt not to ioye [5
but still by freshe assault<u>es</u> quite to destroye me.

———

Item 125:9] The line is not a carry-over in the MS.

[Item 127]

Who will ascend to heaven & ther obtain me
   my wites forlorn & sillie sence decayed
for since I tooke my woond y^t sore dothe pain me
from your fair eyes my spirites are all dismaied.
not of so great a losse I doe complain me   [5
yf yt encrease not but in som boundes be staied
but yf I still grow worse I shalbe lotted
to wander throughe the world fond & assotted.

[Item 128]

Ladie your looke so gentle so to my hart deepe sinketh
   that of no other nor of my self yt thinkethe
Whie then do you constrain me Curel t
to lyue in plaint in pain & sadnes
when on sweet word may gayn me   [5
peace to my thoughtes & everlasting gladnes

[Item 129]

from what part of the heaven, frō what example brought
was the mould whence nature hathe deryved
that sweete face full of bewtie in wch she stryved.
to proue in earthe her power aboue was ample.
nor sylvan quene adored, y^t so daintie fyne lockes in ayr displaed [5
nor hart dyvine wth so great virtue stored, yet by her lookes
                                                  ed.
                       my life is all betray

Item 129:6] The line is not a carry-over in the MS.

[Item 130]

In everie place I fynd my greife & anguish
   saue wher I see those beames y^t me haue burned
   & eke myn eyes to floudes of teares haue turned
   thus in extremest pangues eache howre I languish
O me O me my shining star so sweete & sacred   [5
   cause of all comfort of this world the Iuell
   for want of the my life I haue in hatred.
   was never greif so great nor death so cruell

[Item 131]

When shall I cease lamenting, when shall my playntes & moning
   to tunes of ioye be turned, good loue leaue thie tormenting.
   to long thie flames wthin my hart haue burned.
O graunt alas wth quicknes
   som little comfort after so long a sicknes.   [5

[Item 132]   [f. 31^v

.23.
I saw my ladie weeping & loue did languish
   & of ther plaint ensued shuche rare consenting
   that never yet was heard more sweete lamenting.
   made all of tender pitie & mournfull anguishe.
the floodes forsaking their delightfull swelling   [5
   staied to attend their plaint, the wyndes enraged
   to quiet calme asswaged their wonted storming & every blast rebelling

[Item 133]

24 like as from heaven the dew full softly showring
   doth fall & so refresh both feildes & closes
   filling the parched flowres wth sap & savour
   so while she bathd the violetes & the roses
   vppon her louely cheekes so freshly flowring   [5
   the spring renewed his force wth her sweete favour.

[Item 134]

28 Sleepe Sleepe myn only Iuel
   much more thou didst delight me
   then my belou'd to cruell
   that hid her face to spite me.
   thou bringest her home full nie me   [5
   while she so fast did flie me.
   by thie meanes I behold those eyes so shining
   long tyme absented
   that looke so mild appeased
   thus is my greife declining   [10
   thou in thie dreames dost make desire well pleased
   Slepe yf thou be like death as thou art fained
   a happie life by suche a deathe were gained

[Item 135]

30 Sound out my voice wth pleasaunt tunes recording
   the new delight that loue to me inspirethe

pleasd & content wth that my mynd desirethe

thanked be loue so heavenly ioyes affording

she y^t my playntes wth rigour long reiected [5

bynding her golden tresses

in recompence of all my distresses

Sayd wth a sighe thie greife hath me infected.

[Item 136]

31 liquide & watrie pearles loue wept full kyndly

to quenche my hart inflamed but he alas vnfrendly

so great a fier had framed, as were enoughe to burn me

w^thout recomfort & to ashes turn me

[Item 137]

32 The nightingale so pleasent & so gay

in greenewood groves delightes to make his dwelling

in feildes to flie chaunting his roundelay.

at libertie agaynst agaynst the case rebelling

but my poore hart wth sorowes overflowing [5

throughe bondage vile binding my freedom short

no pleasure takes in these his sportes excelling.

nor of his song receaveth no comfort

[Item 138] [f. 32

3. Comaund a child to eat a pear he will not eat a bitte

comaund him not to eat the pere, the child will long for yt.

[Item 139]

5. plucke vp your heart leaue all to me trie what a frend can do
in heat or cold I am your own, to ride or els to goe.

[Item 140]

5. by threatnim̄ges or by flatterie by smooth talke get thou all
as Esopēs foxe allured the daw to let his breakfast fall

[Item 141]

Laertes sonne what so I say must be or els not be
for great Apollo hath bestowed a pro⟨p⟩phetēs gift on me

[Item 142]

yf davus do but talke amisse a coxcomb & a bell
such badges might beseme somtyme the maister very well

[Item 143]

The roister weares not alwayes plumes nor yet ye devill a tayl
yf every foole did were a bell ther would be iolie sayl

[Item 144]

he brake vp howse put mise to grasse himself fed nothing fine
wth colewartēs & such carters cates oft would the caitife dyne.

[Item 145]

ther is no good for to be don while we are lyving here
Except we lie fawn flatter face cap knele duck crouch smile flere

[Item 146]

Asperius nihil ē humili cōsurgit in altū

a Lewder wretche ther lyves not vnder skye, then clown y^t climes

               fr̄o base estate to hie.

[Item 147]

  what thing a man in tender age hath most in vre

  the same to death alwayes to kepe he shalbe sure   euripides

  therfore in age who greatly longeth good fruit to mow

  in youth he must applie himself good seede to sow.

[Item 148]

As long as a tonne or vessell may last: of the first licour yt

               kepeth the tast.   hora

& youth being seasoned in virtuous labour: will ever after

               therof kepe the savour   ce.

[Item 149]

he that at ons instance an other will defame: will also at an others

               to ye last do ye same

for none are so daungerous & doubtfull to trust: as those y^t are

               readiest to obey every lust   herme(s)

[Item 150]

& hundred tongues & mouthes as many: althoughe I had wth eloquence highe

& thoughe my voice all yron were: In strenghe yet could I not

               declare   virgil

ye vices of men nor yet can tell: [5] what paynes therfore they

               suffer in hell   Ænedis

    Items 146, 148-150] No carry-over lines in the MS.

    Items 147-150 are bracketed on the right with the names of the philosophers to the right of these brackets.

[Item 151]

for covetous people to die yt is best: for the longer they lyue
               the lesse is ther rest
for life thē leadeth ther substance to double: wher death thē   sen
              dischargeth frō endles troble

[Item 152]

A nice wife & a backe dore oft maketh a ritch man poore.

[Item 153]

yt were better for a woman to be barreyn: then to bring forth a
              vile wicked carrayn.

[Item 154]

by ordring the tongue is a triall most true: to know yf a man
              his lustes can subdue.
for he that can not rule his tongue as him list: hath mutch lesse
              power other lustes to resist

[Item 155]

by fortunes good fortune who cōmeth in favour: by fortunes misfortune
              may catch a displeasure

[Item 156]

ye more that a man hath of abundaunce: so much the lesse hath he
              of assurance

[Item 157]

he is nether rich happie nor wise that is a bondman to his own avarice.

    Items 151, and 153-156 have no carry-over lines in the MS.

    Items 151, 154, and 155 are bracketed on the right, and "sen"
in Item 151 is to the right of the bracket.

[Item 158]

he is not wise wch knowing he must hence: in worldly　　　pytha
　　　　　　　　　buildinges makethe great expence.
but he that buildeth for the world to come: is wise expend　goras
　　　　　　　　　he never so great a sume

[Item 159]

of bodylie imprisonmentes sicknes is the cheif: but the gail　hermes
　　　　　　　　　of ye soul is sorow & greif

[Item 160]

prayer to god is the only mean: to preserue a man frō a wicked　socrates.
　　　　　　　　　queane

[Item 161]

he that to wrathe & anger is thrall: over his witte hath no　socr.
　　　　　　　　　power at all

[Item 162]

be merie & glad honest & virtuous for that suffiseth to anger　herēs
　　　　　　　　　the envious

[Item 163]

the frendes whō profit & lucre encrease. when substance fayleth
　　　　　　　　　therw^th all will cease
but frendes that are coupled wth heart & wth loue: nether fear nor
　　　　　　　　　fortune nor force may remoue

[Item 164]

yf that in virtue thou take any paynes: the payn departeth but
　　　　　　　　　virtue remaynes.

　　Items 158-163 have no carry-over lines in the MS.

　　Items 158-162 are bracketed on the right, with the names of the philosophers to the right of these brackets.

but y<u>f</u> thou haue pleasure to do that is ill the pleasure abateth
> but ill tarieth still.
>> [Item 165]   [f. 32ᵛ]

A restless life by losse of that I loue
> I doe endure whose torment none can tell.
A graved soul as well these lines may proue
> desyring death but spend<u>es</u> not half so well.
>> A mazed mynd wherin affection dies   [5
>> A wounded hart that still for mercie cries

A wofull man in prison bound by greefe
> Ransackt by loue condemned by disdayn
A wayting death yet fyndes no suche relief
> but nedes must lyue to linger out in pain   [10
>>> none
>> whose terrour but I my selfe cā shew.
>> that do the terrour best of any know

Let this suffise to gyue the world a gesse.
> of my estate of whence & what I am
And let these lines to my last loue expresse.   [15
> when first & how for what these torment<u>es</u> cam.
And if that this moue not in the relent
> then kill the heart wch conquered dies contēt.
>> ferd. Strange.

    Item 164] No carry-over lines in the MS.
    Item 165] There is a double flourish after the signature.

[Item 166]

Draco maximus & fidelis cū potentissimo suo brachio æmulos suos proditores exterminabit/ terrā superbiæ conculcabit Gallia etiā comprimet. multa regna inviset, tota vita sua vi⟨c⟩/ toriosus erit & tandē cū rege quasi Cedar venecabitur.   Merlin

[Item 167]

The faithfull drake most great of might his traiterous   Del. by
                     foes shall quell

And wth his arme them put to flight frō out ther $\overline{\text{aster}}$ h.
                     countries soil

the land of pride he shall destroy [5] & vnderfoote   to my lo
                     yt tread

the coastes of fraunce he shall anoy & bring yt in   Cham
                     his dread.

he visite shall full many a land victorious shall   be del. to
                     he be   [10

and wth a king be honoured then even as the Cedar tree.   maiestie

---

[Item 168]   [f. 33

to fayn to flatter to glose to lie: require colours & word<u>es</u>
                     fair & slie.

but the vtterance of truth is so simple & playn: y^t it   plato.
                     nedeth no studie to fordge or to fayn

    Item 167] The explanatory phrase in the right margin is separated from the text by a bracket.

    Item 168 is bracketed on the right, with "plato." to the right of this bracket; there are no carry-over lines in the MS.

[Item 169]

to strike an other yf that thou pretend thinke yf he　　　Pythag.

　　　　　　　　　　　stroke the thou wouldest ye defend

[Item 170]

to beastes much hurt hapneth because they be dūme: but much more to

　　　　　　　　　mē by speach hath com

[Item 171]

he that of all men wilbe a correctour shall of the most part　socr

　　　　　　　win hate for his labour.

[Item 172]

for serpentes never so deadly do sting　　pyth

as when they bite wth out any hissing.

[Item 173]

wisdom in bookes wth the booke will rotte

but written in mynd will never be forgot.

[Item 174]

a frend is not knowen but in necessitie　　anach.

for in tyme of welth each man semeth frendly

[Item 175]

what ever yt chaunce y^e of any to hear　　socrates.

thyn eye not consenting beleue not thin ear

for the ear is a subiect full oft layd awrye

but the eye is a true iudge y^t in nothing will lie

　　Items 169-171] No carry-over lines in the MS. Items 169, 170, 172, 174 and 175 are bracketed along the right margin, with the names of the philosophers to the right of these brackets.

　　Item 173 is entered in the right half of the page opposite Item 172.

[Item 176]

althoughe for a while this vice thou maye hyde: yet canst y^n not

alwayes kepe yt vnspide

for truthe ye true daughter of god & of tyme: hath sworn to detect

all sin vice & crime.

[Item 177]

Almes distributed vnto the indigent　　　　　　　socra
is like a medicine gyven to ye impotēt　　　　　tes.
but to ye vnnedye a man to make his dole.
is like ye ministring of plaisters to ye whole.

[Item 178]

better yt is for a man to be mute　　　　　　　py
thē wth the ignorant much to dispute

[Item 179]

---

vraiement vous estes importun allez vous derriez avoir honte
mais estes de la vostre main tant vous avez celle la prœmpte   laisses cela
Que est ce que voulez taster [5] en colieu vous ne avez que faire
Voulez vous point vous arrester, ma foy l'appelleray ma mere   laisses cela
ma Joy vous estes importun, vous me avez tout decoiffée　　　　　　　[10
S'il venoit maintenant quelque vn, me voila fort bien atiffé . lasses cela
Ha par mon dieu vous me blesses, penses vous que ie soy si forte
A l'ayde au meurtre c'est assez, [15] helas ma mere ie suis

morte.　　　　　　　　　　　laisses cela.

Item 176] No carry-over lines in the MS.

Item 178 is entered on the right half of the page opposite Item 177. Both poems are bracketed on the right, with the philosophers' names to the right of the bracket.

Item 179] No carry-over lines in the MS.

Laisses cela he bien, he bien, puis que ce est faict ie l'veiux bien.

[Item 180]

pastereau ie vous aime bien, mais pour tant ie n'en fera rien

Car on dit qu' en cueillant la fleur, la rosier pendroit sa   viue l'amour
valeur

Ony bien qui la voulait rauir, [5] on l'emporter pour s'en seruir

    mais belle mon contentement, est de vous baiser   viue l'amour
seulement

Ie crains que soubs ceste raison soit cache quelque trahison   [10

Car au iourd' huy tous les bergers sont trompeurs   viue l'amour
menteurs & legers

[Item 181]

Here lies interred to make wormes meate

    little Robin that was so greate

Not Robin Goodfelow nor Robin Hoode

but Robin that neuer was born for good

A monster sent from angers fate   [5

to spoile the countrie & the state

his life was full of divilishe endes

Traines for his foes trickes for his freindes

I care not nor I can not tell

Whither he be gon to heauen or hell   [10

But surely here they haue earthed the foxe

    Item 180:1] The apostrophe of "n'en" strikes out an original 'e.'

    Item 180:2] The apostrophe of "qu'en" strikes out an original 'e.'

    Item 181 is bracketed along the right margin.

that lothsomly stancke & died of the poxe.

[Item 182]   [f. 33ᵛ

Adeiu poloign adeiu terres desertes
    tous iours de neiges ou de glaces couvertes
A deiu pais de vn eternal adeiu
    ton air tes moeurs m'ont si fort sceu displaire
quil fouldra bien que tout me soit contraire   [5
Si iamais plus ie retourne en ce lieu

Adieu maisons d'admirable structure
poisles adieu qui dans vostre enclosture
mil animaulx pesle mesle enlaces
filles garsons veaulx & boeufs tout ensemble   [10
tant regrete par les siecles passes.

Quoi qu'on me dit de voz moeurs inciviles
de vos habites de vos meschants villes
de vos esprites pleins de legerete
Sarmates ⟨legeres⟩ fiers. ie ne voulois rien croire   [15
ne pensois que vous peussies tant boire
leussay ie creu sans y avoir este

Barbare peuple arrogant & volage
vanteur causeur n'ayant rien que langauge
qui iour & nuict dans vn poisle enferme   [20

pour tout plaisir se ioue avec vn verre
ronfle en la table & s'en dort contre terre
puis come Mars veult estre revere

Ce ne sont pas vos grandes lances croiseez
vos peulx de loups voz armes desguiseez [25
ou maint plumage & maint aesle s'estend
vos bras charnus vos traictes redoubtables
lourdes polonois qui vous font indomptables
le pauurete seulement vous defend.

Si vostre terre estoit bien cultiuee [30
que l'air fut doux quelle fut abbreuuee
de clairs ruisseux riche en bons cites
en marchandize en profondes riuieres
quelle eut des vins des portes & des minieres
vous ne series si long temps Indomptes. [35
Les Ottomans dont l'ame est si hardie [f. 34
aiment mieulx Cypre ou la belle Candie
que vos desertes presque touse iours glaces
& l'allemand qui les guerres demande
vous desdaignant court la terre flamonde [40
ou ses labeurs sont mieux recompenses.

Noeuf mois entiers pour complaire a mon maistre
le grand henry que le ciel a fait naistre

comme vn bel astre aulx humains flamboyant
pour ce desert Iay la france laissee [45
y consumant ma pauure ame blesse
sans nul comfort sinon quen le voiant

face le ciel que ce valereux prince
soit bient tost roy de quelq; autre province
riche de gens de citez & d avoir. [50
que quelque iour lempire parvienne
& que Iamais ici Ie ne revienne
bien que mon coeur soit bruslant de debvoir

[Item 183]

Mar Martin. Mar Marmartin

I know not whie a fruictles ryme in print
may not as well wth modestie be toucht
As truthles prose sith neither hath his stynt
And eithers doinges cannot be avoucht
    Then yf both ryme & prose impugn the troth [5
        how like you him likes nether of the both.
Our prelates Martin saithe want skyll & reason
    Our Martinistes Mar Martin termeth asses
    Eache on an other dothe accuse of treason
    he passeth best that by the gallowes passeth. [10
      Traitour no traitour heers such traitour stryving
        that Romishe traitours here are set athryving.
Whilst England falles a Martining & marring [f. 34^v
    Religion feares an vtter overthrow

    Whilst we at home amongest our selves are iarring   [15
    those seedes take roote wch forrey seedmen sow
      If this be true as true yt is for certain
        Wo worth Martin marprelate & mar martin

[Item 184]

On whitson even last at night
  I dreaming saw a pretie sight
  three monsters in a halter tide
  & on before who seemd their guid
  this formost lookt & lookt agayn   [5
  as thoughe he had not all his train
  wth that I askt the gaping man
  his name, my name is Lucian
  this is a Iesuit quoth he
  these martin & marre martin be   [10
  I seeke but now for machievell
  and then we would be gon to hell.

[Item 185]

Two bookes vppon a table lay
  for wch two youngers went to play
  they drew a die, & this did make
  who threw the most should both bookes take
  he that had martin ⟨threw⟩ flang the first   [5
  An asse that was, wch is the worst
  Mar martins maister in the hast
  hopt then to hit a better cast

And yet as cunning as he was
he could not fling aboue an asse [10
Together by the eares they goe
wch of the asses got the throw
The first vppon vppon his asse would stand
he wonne y^t by the elder hand
Tushe quoth the second that no matter [15
myn was an asse thoughe myn were latter
& turning backe he spake to me
who all this while their sport did see.
Ist not a wonder say of loue
that none of vs should fling aboue [20
No syr quod I yt were a wonder
If either of you had flong vnder

[Item 186]   [f. 35

What sonnes? What fathers? sonnes & fathers fighting?
    alas our welfare, alas our health
what moates? what beames? & both displaied in writing?
    alas the Churche, alas the comon welth

What at this tyme, what vnder suche a Queene [5
    Alas that still our fruict should so be greene
What? wanton calues? what? lost our former loue
    alas our pride alas our mutabilitie

What Christes at oddes? what? serpentes nere a doue

-114-

    alas our rage alas our inhumilitie [10]
What? bitter tauntes? what? lies in stead of preaching?
    alas our heat, alas our neade of teaching.

bear gratious Soveraign, Europes matcheles mirrhour
    bear noble lord<u>es</u> renowned counsail gevers
bear cleargie men for yours ill all ye error [15]
    bear comon people comonlight beleevers.
        bear ioyntlie on an others weaknes so
        that thoughe we wither yet ye Churche may grow

          [Item 187]

yf all be true that lawyers say
the second blow doth make the fray
mar martins fault can be no lesse
then martins was that brake ye peace.
    Martin Mar Martin, Barrow, Brown [5
      all help to pull religion down.
          [Item 188] [f. 35^v

What yf thie mystresse now will need<u>es</u> vnconstant be
    must thou be then so false in loue as she
    no no such falshod flie for women faithles be

my Mystresse frownes & swears that now I loue her not

    Item 187] There is a triple flourish below the last line.

    Item 188] At some time after the poem had been copied, ink was spilled and blotted across most of the first nine lines. Several drops seem also to have been blotted on f. 36 toward the top of the page.

th⟨   ⟩s that wch my despair begot [5
⟨   ⟩since she all faith forgot

She blames my⟨   ⟩& causeleßly accusethe me
I may not l⟨et⟩ my eyes report what they do see
my thought_es restraynd must die⟨ ⟩yet she will go free.

yf she do chaunge yt must not be inconstancie [10
for whie she doth professe to take such libertie
her self she will vntie & yet fast bound am I

yf she doth please at once to favour more then on
And I agrieved in humble sort do make my mone
I speake as to a stone where sence of loue is none [15

But now let loue in tyme redresse all these my wrong_es
& let my loue receaue that due to yt belong_es
else thus I frame my song_es for chaunge my mystris long_es

wch yf she do my hart som other wher shall dwell
for loving not to be beloved it is a hell [20
synce this my hap befell I bid my loue farewell

[Item 189]

Of fairest mother more then fairest child
& purest witte of fathers subtill brain

Item 189 is bracketed along the right margin.

-116-

I cannot cease to muse whie on so mild
should picke a quarrell on a ground so vain
& force a frowning out of that same face [5
wch nothing else but frowning can disgrace

[Item 190]

Content is turnd to malcontent I see
& your not pleasd vnto displeasd I fear
wthout a cause I thinke I know in me
who yet the brunt of all your anger bear
& dare not once to com a gayn in sight [5
least wth your angrie look you kyll me quite

[Item 191] [f. 36

A syllie Ihon surprisd wth Ioy for Ioy had made Ihon sillie
  Ioy to enioye his loved Ione Ione white as any lillie
ò god I loue alas I loue a loue that failes me never
I loue a loue y^t loues my loue & loue will me forever
our life is loue ⟨our⟩ loue is blisse god grant we do so ever [5
we can not mend we may do worse god grant yt be so never
the mone is fair & so am I but blessed be an other
but fairer Sun yet fairest she wch can make blessed other
her hear as fair as fairest gold wch kinges in crownes do wear
for fayr & fairest is that gold that like is to her hear [10
who is fair tis Ione who is clear tis Ione, tis Ione surmountes
    the skye

  Item 191:11]Written as one line in the MS.

who is kynd tis Ione but who doth loue o god tis Ione & I
that I loue hir my glorie is that she loues me my treasure
that I loue her & she loues me my mirth & heavenly pleasure.

[Item 192]

I saw of late a lady were show: y^t was as white as any driven snow
her soft sylk hose was of carnashin hew: & this she wore because
      ye world should know
She did desyre a Virgins step to tread: [5] this wth these colours
      she her fancies fed
The garter wch did strayn her tender knee: by speciall grace myn
      eyes likewise did see
but more then that o greif I might not vew: wherof the colour [10
      was a watchet blew
And labour lost that garter meaning was: to such as sought aboue
      the same to passe
yet som̄ perhaps will deeme this but a Iest: & say wth all she
      never meant no suche
but you your self fayr mistris knowes yt best: [15] y^t I ye truthe
      in colours two did touche
but yf your watched garters ment not so: y^t fault Ile mend yf I
      the truthe may know.

[Item 193]

your face your tongue your witte

 Item 192] No carry-over lines in the MS.

so fayr	so sweete	so sharpe	
first moud	then drew	then knit	
my eyes	myn eares	my⟨n⟩ hart	
myn eyes	myne eares	my hart	[5
thus moued	thus drawn	thus knitte	
dwelles in	hanges on	yeldes to	
your face	your tongue	your wit	
your face	your tongue	your wit	
wth light	wth sound	wth art	[10
doth blind	doth chain	doth wilte	
myn eyes	myn ear	my hart	
myn eyes	myne eares	my hart	
dothe see	dothe hear	doth like	
nought but	nought as	nought like	[15
your face	your tongue	your wit	
your face	your tongue	your wit	
is face	is tongue	is wit	
of graces.3.	of muses.9.	of Ioues own brayn	
of graces.3.	of muses 9	of Ioues own brayn	[20
I looke	I harke	I hope	
som grace	sweete wordes	trew loue	
to haue	to hear	to gayn.	

Item 193] Lines 17-23 are written opposite lines 1-7 on the right half of the page, and separated from the rest of the text by a vertical rule.

[Item 194]

Sweete gloue the witnes of my secret blisse
wch hiding didest preserue that bewties light
that opened further my seal of comfort is
be thou my starre in this my darkest night
now y^t myn eyes his cherefull sun doth misse [5
wch dazeling still doth still mayntain this sight

Be thou sweete gloue the anker of my mynd
    till my frayl barque his haven agayn do fynd

Sweete gloue the sweete despoiles of sweetest hand
fayr hand the fairest pledge of fairer hart [10
trew hart whose truth doth yeld to trewest band
cheif band I say wch tiest my cheifest part
my cheifest part wherin do cheifly stand
those secret ioyes wch heaven do impart
vnite in on my state thus still to saue [15
you haue my thankes let me your cōfort haue.

[Item 195]

What tongue can her perfections tell: in whose ech part all pens
    may dwell
her haires fyn thredes of finest gold: in curled knottes mans
    thoughtes to hold

    Item 194:14] "do" has been written over an original "to."
    Item 195] No carry-over lines in the MS.

but that her forhead sayes in me [5] no whiter beawtie you may see
whiter in dede more white then snow: wch on cold winters face doth grow.

that doth present those even browes: whose equall lines ther   [10
angles bowes

like to the mone when after change: her horned head abrode doth range
and arches be to the heavenly lid<u>des</u>: whose wink each bold attempt
forbid<u>des</u>

for black star<u>res</u> those spheares contain: [15] the matcheles praise
even praise doth stayn

no lamp whose light by art is got: no sun wch shines & seeth not
can liken then wthout all peer: saue on as much as other cleere.   [20
wch only thus vnhappie be: because them selves they cannot see.
her cheekes wth kyndly claret spred: Aurora like new out of bed
or like the fresh quenapple side: [25] blushing at sight of
phoebus pride

her nose her chin pure yvorie weares: no purer then the <u>pretie</u> eares
So that therin appeares som blood: like wyne & milk y^t mingled stood   [30
on whose in circle<u>tes</u> yf you gaze: your eyes may tread a lovers maze
but wth such turnes the voice to stray:
the tippes no Iewels nede to wear: the tip is Iewel of the ear   [35
but who those ruddie lip<u>pes</u> can misse: wch blessd still themselves
do kisse

Rubies cherries & roses new in worth in tast in perfit hew
wch never part but that they show: [40] of precious pearles a
double row

---

the second swetly fenced ward: her heavenly dewd tongue to gard.
whence never word in vain did flow: far vnder this stately doth grow [45
the handle of this pleasant worke the necke in wch straunge

     graces lurke

suche be I thinke the sumptuous towers: wch still doth make in

     princes bowres

So good assay invites the eyes: [50] a little downward to espie
the louely clusters of her brestes of venus babe ye wanton nestes
like pomels (clere) rownd of marble clere: wher azurd vaynes well [f. 37
     mixt appear [55
wth deerest toppes of porphyrie: betwixt these two away doth lie
a way more worthie beawties fame: then y^t wch beares milken name
this leades vnto the Ioyous feild, [60] wch only still doth

     lillies yeld

but lillies such whose natyue smell, the Indians odours doth excell
wast it is called for yt doth wast mens lyves vntill yt be embrast [65
Ther may on see & yet not see her ribbes in white well armed be
more white then Neptunes fomy face: when strugling rockes he

     would embrace

In these delightes the wandring thought: [70] might of each side

     astray be brought

but that her navill doth vnite in curious circle busie sight
a dayntie seal of virgin waxe, where nothing but impression lackes [75
her bellie ther glad sight doth fill iustly entitled Cupides hill
A hill most fitte for such a maister: a spotles myn of alablaster

like alablaster fayr & slike [80] & supple soft satten like
in that sweet seat the boy doth sport loth I must leaue his
      cheife resort
for suche an vse the world hath gotten: the best thing must be   [85
      forgotten
yet never shall my song omitt: those thighes for ovides songes
      more fit
wch flanked wth two sugred flankes lift vp ther statly swelling banckes
that Albion cliftes in whitenes passe: [90] wth hauñches smooth as
      looking glasse
but bow all knees now of her knees: my tongue doth tell what
      fancies sees
the knottes of Ioy the Iemñes of loue: whose motion makes all graces moue [95
whose bought incaued doth yeld such sight: like conning painter
      shadowing white
the gartring place wth childlike sign: shewes easy print in mettall
      fyne
but ther agayn the flesh doth rise [100] in her braue calves like
      cristall skyes
whose Atlas is a smallest small: more white then whitest bone of
      whale
therof steales out that round clean foote: this noble Ceders   [105
      precious roote
in shew & sent pale violetes: whose step on earth all bewties settes
but backe vnto her backe my muse: wher ledaes Swan her fethers mewse

a long whose ridge such bones are met: [110] like confectes round
     in marche pain set
her shoulders be like two white doues: pearching wthin square
     royall roomes
wch leaded are wth sylver skyn: passing the hate sport Ermelin [115
and thence those armes derived are: the phoenix winges be not so rare
for faultles lengthe & stainles hew: ah woe is me my woes renew.
now course doth lead me to her hand: [120] of my first loue the
     fatall band
wher whitnes doth for ever sit nature her self enameld yt
for ther wth strange compact doth lye: warme snow moist pearl [125
     soft yvory.
ther fall those saphir coloured brookes: wch conduit like curious
     crookes
Sweet Ilandes make in that sweete land: as for the fingers of y^t hand
the bloudy shaftes of Cupides warre [130] wth Ametistes they hedded are
thus had ech part his beawties part: but how the graces do impart
to all her limes a speciall grace: becoming every tyme & place [135
wch doth even bewtie bewtifie & most bewitche the wretched eye
how all this is but a fair In of fairer guest wch dwelles wthin
of whose hie praise & perfit blisse: [140] goodnes ye pen heaven
     paper is
the inke imoltall fame doth lend: as I began so must I end

no tongue can her perfections tell in whose eche part all pennes [145
    may dwell

        finis

[Item 196]   [f. 37ᵛ]

what length of verse can serue braue mopsas good to show
whose virtues strange & bewties suche no man may thē iknow
1 thus shrewdly burdned then how can my muse escape
the godes must help & precious thinges must serue to shew her shape

Like great god Saturn fair & like fair venus chast   [5
2 as smoothe as pan, a Iuno mild, like goddesse Iris fast
wth Cupid she foresees, & goes god vulcans pace
and for a tast of all these giftes she borowes momus grace

her forhead Iacint like her cheekes of opall hew
her twinckling eyes bedect wth pearl, her lippes of saphyre blew   [10
⟨her lippes of saphire blew⟩
3 her hair pure trappall stone her mouthe o heavenly wyde
her skyn like burnisht gold, her handes sylver vntried
As for those partes vnknowen wch hidden sure are best
    happie are those wch will beleue & never seeke the rest.

        finis.

[Item 197]

More fayr then most fair full of the lyving fyre

   Item 196] All three stanzas are bracketed on the left, with the stanza number to the left of each bracket.

kyndled aboue the highe creatour neer

not eyes but ioyes wth whom all ⟨thoughtes⟩ conspire [powers above thoughtes; "n" above "not"]

that to the world nought els be counted deer

Throughe your deer beames doth not the blinded guest [5

shoote forth his dartes to bare affections wound

but angels com to lead frail myndes to rest

in chast desires on heavenly bewtye bound.

you rule my thoughtes you fashion me w^thin

you stay my tongue & moue my hart to speake [10

you calme the stormes y^t passion dothe begin

strong throughe your looke but through your bewties weake

Loue is not knowen wher your loue shineth never

blessed are they wch may behold you ever..

[Item 198]

Sitting late wth sorow sleping: where hart bleedes & eyes are

weeping

I might see from heaven descending beawtie mourn for loues ending

wher wth handes most rufully wringing [5] she entombd him w^th

this singing

muses all leaue of endighting: poetes now gyue over wrighting

---

Item 198] No carry-over lines in the MS.

Nimphes com tear your tender heares. sheapheardes all cō   [10
        shed your teares

Cupid now is but a warling: death hath wounded venus darling

Cursed death & all to cruell hast thou stoln myn only Iewell
do the heavenly fates so spight me: [15] y^t on earth shall nought
        delight me
but of such a Ioy bereaue me as no loue of life should leaue me.

                                         So my

                  [Item 199]   [f. 38

how durst a seelie painter vndertake
to represent my mystris louely chere
when all the heavens wth on assent did make
y^t peice divyne to stand wthout a peere
how could he well wth clere vnblemisht sight   [5
take perfect veiw of her fair percing eyes
or of her cheekes the colour paint aright
vermillion like as when the sun doth rise
what liked gold could he wth pensil vse
to portrait out her amber crisped hair   [10
what liniamentes of favour might he chuse
to forme a face y^t yeldes both hope & fear
her port her grace & shape to draw aright
let loue himself imploy his cheifest art

    Item 198] The catchword below line 18 refers to tne continuation
of this poem at the bottom of f. 38, wnere it is also numbered as
Item 198 although it follows Item 200.

yet not in tables nor in colours slight [15
but in the depthe of my most loyall hart.

[Item 200]

transformed in shew but more transformed in mynd
I cease to stryue wth doble conquest foild
for wo is me my powers all I fynd
wth outward force & inward treason spoild
for from wthout cam to myn eyes the blow [5
wherto myn inward thoughtes did fayntly yeld
but these conspird poore reasons overthrow
false in myself thus I haue lost ye feild

And thus myn eyes are placed still in on sight
& thus my thoughtes can thinke but on thing still [10
thus reason to his seruants gives his right
thus is my power transformed to your will
⟨what mervail then I take a⟩
  what mervail then I take a womans hew
  since what I see thinke know is all but you.

[Item 198]

So my flocke then leaue your feeding all your life now lies a [20
     bleeding

 Item 200:11] The contracted form of "seruants" is simply a
curved line over the letters "sunts."

 Item 198 is here continued from f. 37^v, pp. 125-126.

while my sheapheard did attend you wolf nor tiger could offend you
but now he is dead & gon: I shall loose you every on.

Muses all com shew your powers.[25] earth gyue o⟨v⟩er bringing flowers
never trees now bear more fruict: let all singing birdes be mute
& loue no more be spoken for the hart of loue is broken.   [30

Therw^th all as in a cloud she did all her singing shrowd
wher swete phillis gaue such groanes: as did peirce the very stones
that the earth wth sorowes shaked [35] & poore Coridon then awaked.

[Item 201]   [f. 38^v]

fayer philis is the sheapheardes quene, was never quene so fair
                    as she
  & Coridon her only swayn was never such a swayn as he
Swete phillis hath the fairest face that ever yet did eye behold
& Coridon the constantest faith y^t ever yet kept lames in fold
fair phillis hath the finest wit y^t ever yet the world did breed   [5
& Coridon the trewest hart y^t ever yet ware sheapheardes weede
Sweete phillis is the only sweete that ever yet y^e ⟨y⟩ earth
                    did yeld
  & Coridon the kyndest swayn y^t ever yet did keepe the feild
Sphilomita is phillis breed thoughe Coridon be he y^t caught her
& Coridon did hear her sing thoughe phillida be she y^t taught her   [10
the little lames are phillis loues yet Coridon is he y^t feedes them

---

    Item 198:26] The second letter of "o⟨v⟩er" is heavily overwritten,
but 'v' seems to have been the final intention.

    Item 201] No carry-over lines in the MS.

the gardens sweete are phillis groundes yet Coridon is he y^t
        weedes them.
poore Coridon doth keepe the feildes thoughe phillida be she
        y^t soowes them
& phillida doth make the meades but Coridon is he y^t mowes them.
since then that phillis only is the only sheapheard & only quene [15
& Coridon her only swayn that only hath a sheapheard byn
thoughe phillis kepe her bowre of state, shall Coridon consume
        away
no Shepheard go worke out this weeke & sonday shalbe holiday

[Item 202]

when I was fayr & yong & favour graced me
of many was I sought vnto there mystris for to be
but I did scorn them all & said to them therfore
go, go, goe seeke som other where importune me no more
but there fair venus sonne, y^t braue victorious boy [5
said what thou scornfull dame, sith y^t thou art so coy
I will so wound this hart, y^t thou shallt leaue therfore
go go go seke som other where importune me no more
but then I felt straightway a chaunge wth in my brest
the day vnquiet was the night, I could not rest [10
for I did sore repent that I had said before
go go go seeke som other whear importune me no more

[Item 203]

I muse what iealousie did the moue: my proferd kyndnes to forsake
   that causeles fear will cause lesse loue & nedeles care will
      careles make
for to be trusted makes on true [5] & falshood is suspicion due

In seeking that thou wouldest not fynd thou maist fynd that thou
      wouldest not seeke
and by mistrust makes her vnkynd whom trust hath tried true &   [10
      meeke
for fear of faith makes faith to fear, a sharp edged toole
      no iest will bear

Loue me thou maist but for the best, & cast me of but on the shoar
   vexe me thou maist but for my rest, [15] & barre my ioyes to
      breede me more
doe only in this thie good moode that thou wilt proue for
      ever good.

[Item 204]   [f. 39

A haples man of late whom loue had plunged in feares
   his hart of fier his tongue of playntes his eyes all full of teares
distempered in his mynd in record of his wrong
vnto his lute wth heavie tunes thus plained in his song
Witnes wth me ye heavens wherto my sowle doth seeke   [5
yf hell can more torment my ghost then dread of her dislike

Item 203] No carry-over lines in the MS.

witnes wth me my thought<u>es</u> for you best know the same,

yf ever you haue found repose but in her worthie name

witnes wth me myn eyes when you did ever see

the sight that so muche as herself hath bred content to me [10

Witnes wth me myn eares yf any melodie

hath so much power as her sweete voice my greif to remedie

witnes wth me my tongue so slow to plead my case

yf thou haue ever spared speach to gyue her glorie grace

witnes wth me my hand that hast subscribd alone [15

to her & to none else alyue, more yours then myn own

and yee my trew desires accuse me yf you may

hath ever any straunge delight seduced my faith away

and thou my constant happ whom hope hath so disdained

thou canst aledge in truth for me that thou hast firme remaind [20

and thou my vanquist hart subdued wth my good will

wth droppes of blood thou canst describe ye cares y^t doth the kyll

and thou my lothed life by the yt shall appear

that she doth wound the faithfull frend that loued her most dear

and thou vnhappie world wherin I lyue so long [25

shalt rue on me & her condemn, that dothe her servant wrong

thus don he brake the string<u>es</u> & threw the lute on ground

as on vnmeete in such disgrace to ioy in musick<u>es</u> sound

and discontent he lyves & vowes so to remain

till she vouchsaufe wth her fair hand to tune his lute agayn. [30

[Item 205]

between a sheapheard & a heardman an eglogue.

Com gentle heardman sit wth me & tune thie pipe by myn
here vnderneth this willow tree to sheild the frō sun shine
where I haue made my somers bowre, [5] for profe of phoebus beames
& dect yt vp wth many a flower sweet seated by the streames
for daphne euer once a day these flowring banckes doth walke   [10
and in her bosome beares away the pride of many a stalke
but leaues the humble hart behind that would her garlandes dight
& she swete sowle the more vnkynd [15] to set true loue so light
yet thoughe that others bear the bell as in her fauours blest
her sheapheard loued her as well as these whom she loues best   [20

H

Alas poore pastour now I fynd thie loue lodged so hie
that of thie flocke thou hast no mynd but feedest a wāton ey
yf daintie daphnes lookes besot, [25] thie doting hartes desire
be sure that far beyond thie lot this liking dothe aspire
to loue so sweete a Nimph as she & looke for loue agayn.   [30
is fortune fitting highe degree not for a sheapheardes swayn.
for she of lordly laddes is coid & sought of great estates
her favous scorn to be enioyed [35] of vs poore lowly mates
I read the therfore now be wise goe wth me to our walk
wher louely lasses be not nice ther like & choose thie mate   [40
wher ar nor gold nor pearles to veiw nor pride of silken sight
but peticotes of scarlat hue that vailes the skyn snow white

there truest turtlels byn to get [45] for loue & little cost
there sweete desire is paid his debt & labour seldom lost

S.

No heardman no thou liest to lowd our trade so vile to hold [50]
my weed as great a hart doth shrowd as his thates clad in gold
and take for troth that Ile the tell this song fair daphne singes
that Cupid wilbe served as well [55] of sheapheardes as of kinges
for proof wherof old bookes record that venus quene of loue
would set a syde her warlike lord & youthfull pastours proue [60]
how paris was as well beloued a simple sheapheard boy
as after when that he was proued, king priams sonne of Troye
and therfore haue we better hope, [65] as had these laddes of yore
our courages takes as large scope, althoughe their happes were more
and for thou shalt not deme I Iest nor bear a mynd more base [70]
no meaner hope shall haunt my brest then deerest daphnaes grace
my mynd no others thoughtes retaines myn eyes nought else admires
my hart no other passions straines [75] nor other hap desires
my muse of nothing else entreates, my pipe nought else doth sound
my veines no other fier heates such faith in sheapheardes found [80]

H:

A sheapheard then I see wth greif thie Care is past all cure [f. 40
no remedie for thie relief but patiently t'endure
thie wonted libertie is fled [85] fond fancies breed thie bane
thie sense of follie brought a bed, thie witte is in the wayn
I can but sorow for thie sake since loue lulles the asleepe [90

& till out of this dreame thou wake god sheild this straying sheepe
this haples flocke may rue & curse, these proud desires of thyne
whose wretched plight from bad to worse, [95] this careles ey wil pyne
and even as they this self likewise wth them shalt wear & waste
to see the spring before thin eyes thou thirsting canst not tast [100]
Content the therfore wth conceipt whilst others gayn the grace
& thinke this fortune at the height to loue but daphnes face
for thoughe this truth deserved well [105] reward aboue the rest
this hap shalbe but marke to tell how other men are blest
So gentle sheapeheard farewell now be warned by my reede [110]
for I see written in this brow, this hart for loue doth bleede
yet longer wth the would I stay yf ought might do the good
but nothing can the heat delay [115] wher loue enflames the blood

         S.

Then heardman since it is my lot & my good liking suche
stryue not to loose the faithfull knot that thinkes no paines to muche [120]
for what content$\bar{es}$ my daphne best I never will despise
so she but wish my sowle good rest when death shall close myn eyes
Adieu good heardman once agayn [125] for now the day is fled
so might these cares poore sheapheard$\bar{es}$ swayn flie frō this
       carefull head.

[Item 206]

when I was a little swain keping shepe vppon a plain

  Item 205:125] "Adieu" is written in Italian characters.

  Item 205:128] The line is not a carry-over in the MS.

playing on an oaten pipe in y^e tyme y^t nuttes were ripe

by chaunce I saw a bonny lasse [5] lightly tripping on ye grasse

weghing scarse a daisey down, in a short vnlaced gown

wearing on a tawdry lace, platted hear in carelesse grace [10

she was fair & louely brown, she had no peere in all ye town

                                                                         she

down she stowpt to gather flowres, stowping down surprisd my powres

every stalke her sweete hand brake [15] coldnes to my hart yt strake

when her handes had flowres plentie in her lap she did them emptie

then I wisht I were a flowre, to haue place in such a bowre [20

but alas she was so wight, she sylent shrunke out of my sight

since y^t that tyme I never slept, I never laught but ever wept

but & my maister me misvse, [25] my service then she shall refuse

for I had rather be in her bowers then be lord of many towres

but yf yt please her me to call, farewell shepehooke lambes & all

---

                       [Item 207]   [f. 40^v

Are dreames but toyes to tosse in idle brayn or do they shadow

                    truthes in senseles slepe

the thinges we dreame I graunt ar often vayn, & yet in thē the

                    hiddē sense is deepe

As yester night to me can witnes bear [5] who dreampt a ioy &

                  yet a truthe I fear

my thought I played at y^t entising game, wch like to loue no losse

                  can loathsom make

Item 207] No carry-over lines in the MS.

where restes are set by them that vse the same, & as in loue stocke
       ventred for a stake   [10
& that wch most of all resembleth loue fayr showes do fail when
       contraries do proue
yet did fayr shewes my ryval force & me vppon our suit of hartes
       our restes to set
I 39 was in hart & he wth little hartes [15] in number .3. had met
but see the lucke when either pluckt his game, an ase of hart to
       either of vs cam
what this doth mean my syllie hart can tell, ye hartes were false
       & in ye hartes ye ase   [20
no suyt no card could fit my hand so well, as y^t on hart y^t
       bare a doble face
I must not way y^t ase of hartes a rushe y^t makes me S S. & other flushe

---

[Item 208]

The gentle season of ye year hath made the blooming braunche appear
& bewtified the landes wth flowers, the ayre doth savour wth delight
the heavens do smile to see the sight [5] but yet myn eyes augment
       their showres
the medowes mantled all wth greene, the trembling leaues haue clothed
       treen
the birdes wth fethers new do sing but I poore sowle whom wrong doth
       wracke   [10
attyre my self in mourning blacke whose leaues doth fall amiddest
       the spring.

  Item 208] No carry-over lines in the MS. Centered above the first line is a letter (or letters) indecipherable.

And as we see the scarlet rose, in this sweete prime his bud disclose
whose hue is wth the sonne reuiued, [15] so in this Aprill of myn aege
my lyuely colour doth aswage, because my sonnshine is depriued
my hart that wonted was of yore light as the wind to raunge & sore [20]
in every place wher bewtie springes, now ever hovers over you
even as the bird that taken new & flutters but wth clipped winges.
when all men are bent to sport, [25] then pensiue I alone resort
into som solitarie place as doth the dolefull turtle doue
who having lost her faithfull loue, sittes mourning on som withered [30]
stalke
therto myself do I recompt how farre my woes my ioyes surmount
how loue requitethe me wth hate how all my pleasures end in pain
how hap doth doth shew my hope but vayn, [35] how fortune frownes
vppon my state
And in this moode charged wth dispair, wth vapourd sighes I dime
the ayre
and to the goddes make this request that by the ending of my life [40]
I may haue truce wth this straunge strife & bring my sowle to better

---

[Item 209]   [f. 41

Now o now I nedes must ⟨pyrt⟩ part: parting thoughe I absent mourn
absence can no ioy impart: ioye once fled can not return
while I lyue I nedes must loue: [5] loue lyues not when hope is gon.
now at last dispair dothe proue. loue devided loveth none.
sad dispair doth dryue me hence, this dispair vnkyndnes sendes [10

yf that parting be offence yt is she wch then offendes
Absent thoughe her sight I leaue: sight wher in my ioyes do lye
 till that death doth sence bereaue [15] never shall affection dye
deere frō the when I am gon gon all all my ioyes at once
 I loued the & the alone in whose loue I ioyed once   [20
dere yf I do not return loue & I shall die togither
for me never absent mourn, whom you might haue ioyed ever
part I must althoughe I die, [25] die I doe to part frō you.
him dispair doth cause to die, who both lyued & died trew.

[Item 210]

I saw a spider draw her thred to whom I sayd wth in my thought
 like to thie worke such is my spede, as thou dost now so haue
   I wrought
 as thou in vain dost draw this line [5] euen so for nought I
   frame my suit
thie labour lost & so is myne.

[Item 211]

she that doth go to euerie faire nothing at all ther for to buy
 & to all feasting doth repair delighting in strange companie.
 & hauntes the court in eache office [5] wth open ear to every tale
 & takes all giftes that proffred is shewing her self as to ye sayl
 I speake to you that knoweth loue what do you thinke that she
    will proue   [10

 Items 210-211] No carry-over lines in the MS.
 Item 211 is bracketed along the right margin.

[Item 212]

I know not how yt comes to passe, but sure it is not as yt was
my penne is sette on ryming now & yf you aske me whie or how?
forsoothe my witte is growen so rashe, [5] that I must bourd wth
  m<u>aister</u> Bashe
& thoughe I leap beyond my lashe, & play the knaue a little crashe
yt is but rime & reuell dashe, for whie my libertie is large.   [10
I am not bound by any charge, to call a spade a spavavade
nor yet to count a curtall Iade to be a genette bred in Spain.
my witte is dull, my speach is plain, [15] for I must call a knaue
  a knaue.
& thoughe he thinke I rayle & raue, yet when I speake of such a slaue
Let him be sure I will not spare to rune a little out of square.   [20
But would you know wch Bashe I mean, for els all were not worth
  a beane
It is not Bashe the Millars man, nor Bashe the Brewar of ye Swanne
nor Bashe the butcher thoughe he be [25] as butcherlye a knaue as he
but this is bashe the new made squier of Stansted town in Hartford
  shire
duke of all beefe named for the nones & marquise of the marowbones   [30
Count of Calues hed<u>des</u> by like degree, Baron of oxe Iawes so
  mought I the
& viconte Neatestongues this ⟨h⟩ is he, but shall I spend a little
  tyme
To blase his name in riding rime, [35] then will I doe the best I can

---

Item 212] No carry-over lines in the MS.

to paint you forth a proper man, first for his birth & Countrie crown

this Bashe was born in worcester town,

perhaps you take my wordes as skornes [40] but ther his sier made

shoinghornes

of truth that his mercerie to proue his sonnes antiquitie

as for his youthe he spent yt well not wher his father wont to dwell [45

but wandring both farre & nere in many a town & many a shire

to take the vantage of his hap till at the last he caught a clap

In Beuer castle by the vale [50] as some men say marke well my tale   [f. 41^v

nether for better nor for worse but euen for cutting of a purse

well let that passe his hap was good to skape that skowring by

the roode   [55

from thence he skapt but wotte you what y^t countrie after was

to hotte

& then he cam to london walles, wher after sondry clyming falles

he fell of consanguinitie [60] & linked in affinitie

wth Bawdes & Brothels whores & knaues Cutthroate merchantes &

banquerowt slaues

       priuie promoters & purueyours
Clippers coiners & couriers, ⟨pollers takers & pl pilferers⟩   [65

 pollers takers & pilferers
⟨bribers & false extorcioners⟩ Bribers & false extorcioners

that at lengthe he scrapt suche mucke & grew so riche wth

Cuckoldes lucke

as now he ⟨he⟩ gan for to disdaign, [70] the name of purveiour

was to plain

yet ere he let his office slip he gaue poore Elliot such a trip
  that he was fain to cracke two point__es__ for nought but hemp
     could hold such iointe__s__   [75

well Elliot once was purveiour, & Bashe became a noble squire
his walles at Stansted were to low & vp in hast now must they goe
much like the tower of Babilon [80] wch fell to fowle confusion
& so will they at last I hope for thoughe mast Bashe did skape
    y^e rope

& now be stowt as Turke, or Pope: yet yf you gyue me leaue to grope [85
within the lyning of his cope ther of his howse this must hitte
that either fier will perishe yt vel raptor alter habebit
& whie for sothe because yt is [90] varijs constructa rapinis
be as be may this is no banning a knaues   is scarse worth the
    skanning

for yf yt were ⟨then I⟩ would ⟨I⟩ would you tell y^t he vsed his
    talent well   [95

and neuer hid yt vnder ground, whie should he to on stocke be bound?
no I dare lay you twentie pound, ther was no harlot to be found
but he durst broache her barrell low, [100] what not his brothers
    wife I trow?

beshrew me Syr yf I say so, but let y^t passe amongest ye rest
vox populi vox dei est, yea muche good do yt him let him take her   [105
he bought his hornes euen of ye maker, his Dad could make him
    hornes good chep

& therfore since the colt could leap, god knoweth but little might
    he doe

Item 212:84] "as" is written over an original ampersand.

to plucke on his own brothers shoe. [110] wth a shooing horn
or two.
and be his brother not vnkynd, but of an honest thanckfull mynd
he might do well on of these twain, to send him home his hornes
again [115
or els to lend ⟨the⟩ him som as good in token of ther brotherhood
for thoughe he once might spare them well while he was yong & bare
the bell
yet now forsooth I can you tell [120] that he hathe worke enoughe
at home
he nedeth not abrode to rome, he hath a yong wife hathe he caught her.
yea out of doubt s^r for he bought her, I will not say how long he
sought her [125
nor that she was a wise mans daughter, nor y^t yt was a wise mans
part
but sure poore wenche yt pincht her hart, wherof the lord sone
send her ease
for trulie yf yt might her please [130] I could assure her now & than
a pretie morsell of a man, y^t should be toothsom neate & good
better then Neatstongues by the roode, alas alas yt fretes my bloud [135
for she was as I heare men say delyuered this other day [f. 42
of a knaues child both fair & fatte, wch was good lucke but wotte
you what?
how muche the better had yt byn, [140] yf she had byn delyuered clean
both of ye knaue himself & all, ohe that had byn a festyuall

for then som Lustie reveller might haue byn glad to marie her   [145
and so double Almes deedes as first to carue her at her nedes
& next to set a broache the tonne of pound<u>es</u> & pence so lewdly wonne
but synce I haue this gear begonne, [150] I will assay & not to
misse
to tell you playnly what he is, first for his shape he doth appeare
muche like a tonne of doble bere, & he that well doth marke his nose [155
thoughe yt be red as any rose, yet sure he playnly will suppose
that Bashe loueth double beare full well, A question also haue I
heard
whither his filthie fewtered beard [160] were fitter for to serue
a dissard.
or for a masker wth a visard, & then this question dothe arise
whither the twinckling of his eyes, be all for ale or ought for
Sleape   [165
and when he smileth like a shepe, what faith & trothe he meanes
to kepe
now som again will put this dout whither his turkey coloured snowt
be bigger then his mouthe about, [170] loe thus they deale wth
the lowt
but I doe know & dare avow, that he is wasted like a cowe
made like a bull of brest & brow & somwhat snowted like a sow   [175
eyed like a ferret when he winkes, mouthed like a paddocke when
he drinkes
breathed like a polcat when he stinkes & may not such a man as this

thinke himself worthie to kisse [180] a Chancellours child wher
she doth pisse
yes trulie & so he shall wth lips nose wth tongue & all
but of his shape a little more or els I should offend him sore [185
sette him on foote he goeth than reeling & rowling as a swan
seate him on horsbacke out of doubt & he sittes like a demie lout
or yf I not forget the fowle [190] a toad vppon a washing stole
and hang hym vp, for yt is best, & hang he east or hang he west
vppon his shoulders wilbe fixed a plain sign of the Sarazins head [195
his tongue, his tongue alas, alas, I had forgotten by the Masse
som say yt is a Neatstongue right, thicke full & fat in lustie plight
som other saye yt is so fyne [200] like to the taber of a Swyne
som by a Calues tongue takes most kepe, & som say likest to a shepe
& yf I should rightly say yt is a knaues tongue euery way [205
to prate & to Clatter, to lie & to flatter
to rayle & to sclaunder, to sneke like a gander
to fill vppe my letter [210] to checke wth ye better
I thinke from Denmarke into Inde a fowler tongue can no man fynd
now synce the case so plain doth stand, that he is thus at euery hand [215
me thinkes yt would be better skand whie & wherfore he giues the
griffin
Comming so latly from the kytchin, o syr you are deceaued muche
the beast he beares is nothing suche, [220] for when ye Heraultes
did espie.
his walles at Stansted climbe so highe & playnly might perceaue therbie [f. 42^v
that Bashe would haue armes in hast, they thought they should be
trimly plast [225

they then appointed him a thing muche like a griffin by the wing
but gryping talantes hath yt none & in the mouthe a marowbone
wch som men take for a broken speare. [230] now tell me did you euer heare
of suche a strange deformed beast, yet Bashe himself that foolishe beast
could neuer espie this misterie, but tooke yt for great dignitie [235]
now sure & by myne honestie, ye herauldes vsed him handsomlie
yet plain dealing is alwayes best he should haue gon among the rest
& armes he should haue none of me [240] yf I were herald as they be
but yf I should for charitie bestow som armes vppon a knaue
behold these armes then should he haue
partie par panche durtie & draffe [245] vppon his cheiffe a sacke of chaffe
betwene three purses to stynt strife a cheuron like a cutting knife
all counterchanged like a cope & brauely broidred wth a rope [250]
supported as yt comes to passe both by an oxe & by an asse.
a shooing horn might be his crest because his Dad did bread that beast
Set on a wrethe of oken bowe, [255] least yf the whoreson heauie cow
should straine the halter by his stresse, this withe might be in readines
& on his helme this may be borne, a pretie thimble made of horn [260]
& on a thumbe yet must nedes stand a sharp knife & a Nymble hand

mantled mangie & lined wth lice, thus should he beare by my devise
as for his word he should applie, [265] oues boues pecora campi.
for a knaue he was born & so he will die.
& now mast Bashe I tell you trew me thinkes highe tyme I bid adieu
to suche a stable squire as you, [270] but yet before I goe my way
this thing to you I must nedes say that yf I die this present day
I ame not in your debt on word, no not the valew of a turd. [275
not a turd yes sure yt is my debt, I trow I did not vse yt yet
see how a man may sone forget, whie then yt were a small request
to tell what turd might like you best, [280] a childes turd or a

mans turd

the deuils turd or his daumes turd, take wch turd you list to chuse
& so you doe no turd refuse, but vse yt gently as a frend [285
turd in your teeth & thers an end   To ye Reader
───

[Item 213]

My masters you that read my rime I pray you take yt for no crime
thoughe I vse some brauerie, for therin surely haue I sought
to keepe decorū as I ought, [5] my maister Chawcer tought me once
a pretie lesson for ye nonce, y^t yf a man would paint a pike
wth asses eares yt were not like & yf I haue writ slouenly [10
Bashe is a slouen certainly, yf bawdy wordes be my offence
his bawdie dedes be my defence, Il fauourdly yf writ I haue
whie Bashe is an ill fauaured knaue [15
─────────

Item 212] The rule beneath the last line of the poem slants
sharply upward to separate "To ye Reader" from line 286.

& this is Brauishe rime say I, & yf yt be not say I lie.

[Item 214] [f. 43

In mariam scotiæ Reginā advlterā, veneficā & viricidā Dutam
patricij Buocsargensis Rithmus satyricus.

O Maria scota meretrix o vndiq; nota. impura illota veneri deditissima
tota
quae stimulis mota [5] mersos trahis ad tua vota vinoq; perpota
futuis vt rancida gota
Reproba regina magis salax quam messalina [10] altera faustina
semper recubans resupina
pellex palatina temeras coniugia bina: moribus lupina [15] vere
es tu regni ruina.
belle incepisti puellula quando fuisti Inguine pruristi pr_o_cax
viros appetisti [20
hinc excussisti pudorem & aperisti seram tuæ cistae quā
claudere nõ potuisti
quid praeter egisti tu in francia quando fuisti [25] Anteq^g
nupsisti cū Cardinale coijsti
marito & tristi tu cornua multa dedisti contra & ius christi [30
vitrico temet subiecisti
nec minus presisti postq̄ in patriā redijsti nonne tuo mystae
Dauidi succubuisti

mortis
vnde viro tristi [35] causā vindictae dedisti, sic huic & isti ⟨causa⟩
tu causa fuisti

Item 214] No carry-over lines in the MS.

no me viro est scitū te propinase aconitū [40] & blande accitū
somne iugulase sopitū

nec more protritū moechū duxisti maritū regis insignitū [45] cæde
scelerisq; peritū.

Corde & crudeli siccine sponso & patrueli sub specie zeli nes
fila pessimae telae   [50

Asperior feli plus ferrea cuspide teli, Iuro deū coeli quod
nequior es Iezabeli

At principatus [55] moecho est pro munere datus huic scotie status
tumultibus est cruciatus

miles & armatus iugi in statione Locatus [60] vsque quo fugatus
est Bothwell dux sceleratus

præter & haec ista fortis es vsq; papista pro triplici crista   [65
gladiatrix Antagonista

Tunc & lanista feriens vt arcubalista, subdola vt sophista
fascinatrix ac Atheista.   [70

Crimina ob predicta misera es prorsus derelicta & q^{ia} nō ficta
iusto iudicio victa.

Carcere es constricta [75] regni corona relicta, sic digne afflicta
merita vt saxis fores icta

Sic permansisti captiua carcere tristi [80] cū te gessisti
contentū cū cruce christi

falsa & finxisti custodi & imposuisti vnde evasisti [85] & ad
Anglos te recepisti

Ast tibi nunc rari quod amici sunt tibi chari desine mirari
facile referā tibi quare   [90
nō sunt ignari quod ipsis imperitare molita es clare ius regni
& anticipare.
Itaq; cū tota [95] sis intus & auucula nota Demoni devota tā
sapiens qā idiota
Vt sis amota cupiunt per omnia vota, [100] sic fortuna bella
reflectit væ tibi scota

[Item 215]

draw home betyme ere youth take leaue & aege vppon the growes. 1.
& do not thou thie self deceaue wth hope of worldly showes
whose pomp doth nought but feede thine eyes wth that thou canst
not haue
& carrieth the like clowd in skies to that should be thie slaue.
he courtes somwhile, that cart doth driue er many yeares run out 2 [5
& they that most for fortune stryue do lyue in greatest doubt.
A thriftles sonne enioyes ther store & ther wth serues his lust
when those that sore haue swet therfore are troden in ye dust   3
what proffit bringes the weried bones of vnknowen sightes abrode.
yt weres but feete vppon ye stones & dothe the conscience lode   [10
Ten thousand yeares heaped vp in head & all therin hast past   4
& marke eche thing is donne & sayd & weighe the same at last
& thou shalt see yt breakes but braines & bredes muche greif
in brest

Item 215] No carry-over lines in the MS. The numbers in the right
margin are separated from the text by a bracket.

then travail nedes must lose his paines when home must be
                                            thie rest   5
then hart desires the eye doth craue a sight of all thinges donne [15
    when proofe therof a man shall haue what hathe our trauail
                                      wonne
wherfore thou pilgrim to & fro trusse vp thie toyes in hast
for tyme & all thinges els I know wth the will weare & wast

                                [Item 216]   [f. 43^v

.1. I would yt were not as yt is or that I card not yea or noe
1   I would I thought yt not amisse or that amisse might blameles goe
    I wishe yt were yet should I not [5] I might be glad yet could
                                  I not
2   would god desire knew the meane or that the meane desire knew
.2. I would I could my fancie weane from these swete thoughtes
                                y^t do ensew   [10
only to wishe is least of all a badge wher bie we know the thrall.
3. O happie man that dost aspire to that wch thou maist semely craue
     twise happie for thie hartes desire [15] may ioyn wth hope
                            good hap to haue
but woe is me vnhappie man whom hope nor hap acquite yt can.
4.   my life in hope is life wth feare & still my sore presentes
                            his face   [20
my fate yf hap the palme did beare vnto my hap would be
                              disgrace

    Item 216] No carry-over lines in the MS. The "1" to the left of lines 3 and 4, and ".2." to the left of lines 9 and 10, have been partially erased.

as diamant in wood were set or Irus ragges wth golden fret

5. behold my tired shoulders beare [25] desires weary baiting winges
& at my heeles a clog I weare tied on wth self disdaigning stringes.
my wing to get at gate doth hast my clog doth sinke me down as
fast [30

6 Suche is our plight lo this we stand, we rise to fall that climb
to highe.
the youthe that fled king Minos land may teache ye wise more
low to flie.
what gaind his poynt so neare the sonne [35] he blames the sea
his name hath wonne.

7. yet Icarus more happie was by present death his cares to end
then I who lyue in whom alas ten thousand deathes ther pangues
do spend [40
now loue now feare now playnt now spight, long sorow mixt w^th
short delight

8 The scarre & fellon of my smart prometheus I am in dede
vppon whose ever lyuing hart [45] the greedie gripe doth tire
& feede.
& yet no wrong for whie we craue the thing that godes themselues
would haue.

9. But ⟨the⟩ let them moan & waile ther case that of vild choise
them selues would blame [50
let them lament ther faltes disgrace whose base desires worke
the same
who hath advanced his hart on hie must be content to pine & die.

[Item 217]

1. Alas when shall I ioy when shall my wofull hart
   cast forth this foolish toy y^t breedeth all my smart
   a thousand tymes & more [5] I haue attempted sore
   to rid this restles woe that rageth more & more.
2. but when remembrance past had laid dead coles togither. [10
   old loue renewes his blast wch cause my ioyes to wither
   then sodenly a sparke startes out of my desire
   & leapes into my hart [15] setting the coales on fire.
3. Then reason runnes about seeking forgetfull water
   to quence & cleane put out the cause of all this matter. [20
   & saith dead fleshe must nedes be cut out wth ye core
   for wethered rotten weedes can heale no greivous sore.
4. but than euen sodenly [25] the feruent heat doth slake/ shake.
   & extreme cold draweth me that makes my body quake
   alas who can endure to suffer all this pain [30
   since she that should me cure most cruell death hath slain.
5. well well I say no more let dead care for ye dead

Item 217 is bracketed along the right margin. To the right of the bracket, opposite lines 1 and 2 are the following lines:

the dolefull bell y^t

systers larūs ringes

The rule below these lines is connected by a vertical rule along the left margin to the rule below Item 216.

that woe is me therfore [35] I must attempt to lead

an other kynd of life then hitherto I haue

or else this pain & strife will bring me to my graue [40

[Item 218] [f. 44

.1. farewell since I must want of force, that thou canst not forgoe

    the pleasant presence of thie soght that did delight me soe

    farewell & so farewell I say as I would wishe to fare

    liue free from greif from iealous dread from sorow pain & woe

.2. farewell & in thie midwelfare, suppose the to behold [5

    thie absent frend whose present greife thou keepest still

             in hold

    farewell & let not thie well fare to blotte him out of mynd

    whom greife forbiddethe to forget his only & true frende.

[Item 219]

.1. In choise of frendes what chance had I to choose on of

             sirenes kynd

    whose harpe whose pipe whose melodie could feed myne eyes

             & make me blind

    whose pleasant voyce mad me forget that in great trust was

             great disceit.

.2. In trust I see is treason found & man to man disceitfull is

    and wheras fortune doth abound of flatterors ther doth

             not misse [5

    Items 218-219] No carry-over lines in the MS. Both poems are
bracketed along the right margin.

      whose painted speache & outward show as frendes do seme but
                         be not soe

.3. would I haue thought in the to be the nature of the crocodil
    wch yf a man asleepe may see wth bloodie thirst desires to kyll
    & then wth teares a while can weepe ye death of him that<u>es</u>
                         slain a sleepe

.4. Oh fauell false thou traitour born what mischeife more mightest
                         thou deuise   [10
    then this dere frend to haue in skorn & him to wound in
                         sondrie wise
    yet still a frend pretendst to be & art not so by proofe I see.

[Item 220]

.1. whiles depe conceipt renowned quene present<u>es</u> vnto my mynd
    this statly race & birth sprong forth from passing princely kynd
    three titles doe I note in the & twain I see do fail
    the want wherof wth me alas doth Brittain land bewail

.2. A daughter to a mightie king the heauens do the alow   [5
    a princes sister & a neipce, the world & we advow
    but princes wife nor mother yet thou wilt vouchsafe to be
    thoughe euery name of euery wight is wished vnto the.

.3. O let such glittering glorie peirce this pure vnspotted brest
    that this renown may be preferd aboue the starres to rest   [10
    but yf this constant virgins mynd such passing prayse forsake
    yet at the least regard the plaint this pensiue people make.

    Item 220 is bracketed along the right margin.

[Item 221]

1. how can y^t tree but wast & wither quight y^t hath not somtymes
        comfort of ye sunne.
   how can y^t flower but fade & sone decay y^t alwayes is w^th
        darke clowdes ouerrunne
   Is this a life nay death you may yt call [5] y^t feeles eache
        pain & knowes no ioy at all
2. my gredie will that seekes the goodly gain, my luckles lot
        doth alwayes take in worth
   my mazed mynd that dredes my suit in vain my pitious plaint
        doth help for to set forth   [10
   so that betwene two waues of raging seas I driue my dayes in
        trouble & disease.
3. my wofull eyes doe take ther cheif delight to fede ther fill
        vppon ye pleasant maze
   my hidden harmes that grow in me by sight [15] wth pining paines
        do driue me frō ye gaze
   and to my hap I reape none other hier but burn my self & I to
        blow the fier.

[Item 222]   [f. 44^v]

1. now leaue & let me rest, dame pleasure be content
   go chuse among the best my doting dayes be spent

Item 221] No carry-over lines in the MS.

Item 222 is bracketed along the right margin.

    by sundrie signes I see [5] thy proffres are but vain
    & wisdom warneth me that pleasure asketh pain
    & nature that doth know how tyme her steps doth trie   [10
    giues place to painfull woe & biddes me learn to die

2. Synce all fair earthly thinges sone ripe will sone be rot
    & all that pleasant springes [15] sone withered sone forgot
    & youth that yeldes men ioyes y^t wanton lust desires
    in aege repentes the toyes y^t reckles youth requires   [20
    all wch delightes I leaue to suche as folie trains
    by pleasures to deceaue till they do feele the pains.

3. And from vain pleasures past [25] I flie & fain would know
    the happie life at last wherto I hope to goe
    for wordes or wise reportes ne yet examples gon   [30
    gan bridle youthfull sportes till aege cam stealing on
    the pleasant courtly games, that I do pleasure in
    my elder yeares now shames [35] suche follie to begin

4. And all the fancies strange that fond delight brought forthe
    I do intend to change & count them nothing worthe
              processe worn
    for I by prooffes ⟨am taught⟩ am taught to know ye skyll
    what might haue byn forborn in my yong reacheles will.
    by wch good proofe I fleete [45] from will to witte again.
    in hope to set my feete in suretie to remain

[Item 223]

1. wth painted speache I list not proue my conning for to trie
   nor yet will vse my pen to fill wth guilefull flatterie
   but pen in hand & hart in breast shall faithfull promis make
   to loue you best & serue you most euen for your virtues sake.
2. And since dame nature hathe you deckt wth giftes aboue the rest [5
   let not disdain a harbour fynd wthin your noble breast
   for loue hath lent her law alike to men of eache degree
   so that the begger wth the prince shall loue as well as hee
3. I am no prince I must confesse nor yet of princes line
   nor yet a brutishe begger born that feedes among the swine [10
   the fruict shall trie of tree at last the blossomes good or noe
   then doe not Iudge of me the worst till you haue tried me so
4. As I deserue so thou reward I make you iudge of all
   yf I be false in word or dede let lightning thunder fall
   & furies fell wth frantique fittes bereaue & stop my breathe [15
   even for example to the rest yf I shall breake my faithe.

[Item 224] [f. 45

1. when pallas lost the price & Iuno toke offence
   at paris in the vale of Ide for venus highe defence
.2. whose gift he most preferd assignd to be ther Iudge
   refusing wisdom & renown to be but venus drudge.
3. Loue lead his iudgement thout a hastie iudge & blind [5
   whose ruyn for his fair reward the Troians felt I finde.

Items 223 and 224 are bracketed along the right margin.

4. by many a bloudie whore that bought the rape full dere
     of wretched menelaus wife till all betrayed they weare
.5. Lo thus was least the loue that rose of light desire
     a right reward to quenche the flame that follie set on fire   [10
.6. but Mauger enuye now that pines at others Ioye
                              & bredes
     by sad suspect that demes awrie ther own annoy.
7. Can no loue be deuoyd of fowle repentant lust
     shall on advltrous rage approue, th'vnspotted loue vniust
8. Can faithfull frendship framd of faith & fast goodwill   [15
     with on consent of Iudgementes like be neuer vsed but ill
9   The goddes forbid suche losse that malice should haue might
     t'vntie the trothes of meaning chast & virtues put to flight
10. Let venom tongues infect wth poison of disdain
     & Cankred hate enforce you naught your frendship to refrain   [20
11. know Craft but not beguile & somtime shun your wishe
     for oft we see the intising bait betray th'vncraftie fishe.
12. Eake wepe not at your wronges to cause your foes to smile
     of other faultes to make your harmes & so your self beguile
13. Let Iealousie goe prie let lying sclaunder passe   [25
     a conscience pure devoid of guile is worth a wall of brasse
14. for yf that deedes & thoughtes bothe chast & vndefild
     & virtue be no sure defence then seeke none other shilde.

[Item 225]

1. The glore great of blisfull ⟨state⟩ fate the sugred roote of
                         gladsom fruict

Item 225] No carry-over lines in the MS.

is constant mynd reposed in state of due desire to loiall suite

the Ioy the blisse that beares the fame [5] that virtue is

wch knittes the same.

.2. the prince of all the state the life by knot therof enioyes

her right

the husband sured of his wife the maister free from seruantes

spight [10

for constancie in loiall mynd the knot must be that all may bynd

3. The stable frend that wenes him thrall to daintie choise of

highe desire

throughe constant faithe performeth all [15] y^t bond of virtue

can require

for constant will in loialtie a fruict is still of highe degree.

4. A watchfull gard in tyme of rest a saufe defence in ioy or smart [20

a gladsom frend a welcom guest, is constant mynd in loiall hart

for whie the same in verie sight buildes vp the frame of all

mens right

.5 this virtue great of rarest price, [25] this steadie rule of

all dothe bynd

performes such fruict by due devise as answers well to noble mynd

then for my part shall praised be the constant hart in loialtie. [30

[Item 226]   [f. 45^v

1. Right dreadfull is the talke what thing & pain is hell, ⟨&

wher yt is w⟩

Item 226] No carry-over lines in the MS.

    & wher yt is who will discusse he nedes advise him well

       wth god<u>es</u> booke I deale not but poetrie rehearse

       to ease my hart & harme no wight me list to frame a verse.

2 And yf som enuious wight shall aske what dothe me moue   [5

       to treate of hell & not of blisse that angels hold aboue

       wth weeping eyen exprest the cause of my blacke write

       the paines I fynd the ioyes I misse & yet are both in sight

.3. for yf nought els be hell saue place all voyd of blisse

       on earthe althoughe I seeme to be in hell my being is   [10

       wher Tātalus the king & others bide ther woe

       aboue or vnder wher yt is that where I do not know

4. but sure of this am I alas to sure of yt ⟨no paines⟩

       no paines I read in hell hath byn that comes not in my fit

       the cold & freshe liquour that from the rocke distild   [15

       the place where ruthfull tantall bode vnto his breastes

                        were fild

.5. when drery thirst him prickes & pine most deadlie foe

       to vse these present remedies then bothe they fled him fro

       this Tantalus am I wch ay behold my blisse.

       wch as most nighe yet farthest of what hell is worse then this   [20

6 for loe huge furies three assaultes me on everie side

       as sclaunder enuy & Iealousie that beares me tyme & tyde

       ohe slaunder woe worthe the whose venome is so strong

to kyll the quicke & harme the dead whom graue hath hidden long

7. Envie leaue of to freat to make of loue debate [25
 yf I haue hap & thou no harme what cause is this of hate.
 & Iealousie go sleape pine not without cause whie
 not Argus wth his hundred eyes can louing thoughtes descrie.

8 Twise hate is forced loue & Iealousie folkes fain
 enflameth more not quencheth loue thoughe he would burst
    in twain [30
 these are my endles pangues my pain encreaseth so
 to strong to byde to long to tell yet hope is not my foe

9. Thou hope hold vp thie charge let not dispair prevail
 oh wretched wight what hap haue I yf hope & fortune faile.
 yf hope & fortune fayle yet this I sweare & say [35
 that I throughe loue & loue throughe me shall never haue decay.

    [Item 227] [f. 46

2 Thus while I held the eele but by the tayle
 I had som hope yet neuer wanted fear
 of double dread that man can never fail
 that will presume to take the wolf by the eare.
 I snatche for fleashe muche like to Esoppes dog [5
 I sought for fishe & alwayes caught a frog

3. Thus did I long bite on the foming bit
 wch found me play enoughe vnto my pain
 thus while I loued I neuer wanted fitte

-162-

  that lyued by losse & sought none other gain.   [10

  but whie should I mislike wth fortunes fetters

  since that the like hath hapt vnto my betters.

[Item 228]

to ye Q. by ye players 1598.

As the diall hand tells ore/ ye same howers yt had before

  still beginning in ye ending/ circuler account still lending

So most mightie Q. we pray/ like ye diall day by day

  you may lead ye seasons on/ making new when old are gon.

that the babe wch now is yong/ & hathe yet no vse of tongue [5

  many a shrouetyde here may bow/ to y^t empresse I doe now

that the children of these lordes/ sitting at your counsell bourdes

  may be graue & aeged seene/ of her y^t was ther father Quene

once I wishe this wishe again/ heauen subscribe yt wth amen.

[Item 229]

A riddle

nere to a sheapheard did a dam sell sit as leane as withered

         sticke by scorching flame   a bag-
       mi⟨ght⟩
her body as full of eyes as could be in yt a tongue she had

         but could not moue the same   pipe or

  Item 228] The slashes are in the MS.

  Item 229] No carry-over lines in the MS. The poem is bracketed along the right margin, with the answer to the riddle to the right of this bracket.

her wynd she drew aboue & eke beneathe but frō on part she
  never yet did change   flute
A wofull sheapheard came to kisse her b(re)ath, then made she
  plaintes̄ most sorowfull & strange
the more the sheapheard put his mouthe vnto her mouthe in stopping
  yt she cried amayn.   [5
opening her eyes & shutting them again see now what this dumb
  sheapherdess could doe.
that when her mouthe he did but touche or kisse he waxeth dumb
  but she still speaking is
  [Item 230]

2

I saw a hill vppon a day lift vp aboue ye aire wch watered wth
  bloud alway
& tilled wth great care/ herbers brought forth of mickle
  worth   house ⟨ ing ⟩ 5
pulling a handfull frō that ridge & towching but the same
  wch leauing nere vnto a bridge   a Rebecke
dothe cause muche sport & game, a thing scarse of beleefe   [10
  lamēting wthout greife
  [Item 231]

.3.

What bird is that so light her place that never changethe she flies
  by day & night

Items 230-231] No carry-over lines in the MS. The poems are
bracketed along the right margin with the answers to the riddles to
the right of the brackets.

-164-

in all y̅ world she rangethe, ouer ye sea at once she flies   [5
                    mounting aboue ye loftie skies   ones
she is never sene by eyes & who dothe seeke to showe her hath
                    byn accounted wise   thought
    yet sometymes we do know her [10] only the walles by
                    veiwing well
    of her close house where she dothe dwell
                    [Item 232]

                    4
Tell me what maister he may be/ whose maister is his man/ bound
                    like a senseles foole is he/
    wittie yt nothing can/ vnlearned yet he dothe abound/ [5] in
                    learning graue & most pro̅found
when y^t I take him by the hand althoughe I heare him not, his meani̅g
                    yet I vnderstand though him I haue
forgot/ [10] so wise is he thoughe wordes nor motions showing yet
                    thousand thinges he tells me worth
ye knowing   a booke
                    [Item 233]   [f. 46^v]

                    5.
Shew me a horse of such a kynd that in ye strangest fashion, dothe
                    never eate but of y̅ wind
doth take his sustentation/ winged before & winged behind [5] strang
                    thinges he doth & wondros deedes

   Items 232-233] No carry-over lines in the MS.; the slashes appear
in the MS.

& when he runnes his race vppon his brest wth hast he spedes his
                    reines wth merveilous grace
come from his sides that never bledes [10] & in his course he dothe
                    not fail yf rightly he doth wag
his tayle.   A ship.
                    [Item 234]
                6
Tell ⟨m⟩e good sirs what bird is y^t that flies .3. cubites highe &
                    yet doth never rise
                    doth
wth more then 30 feet ⟨that⟩ mount & fall wth winges y^t haue no
                    plumes nor pennes at all
beating the air yt neither eates nor drinkes [5] yt neither cries nor
                    singes nor speakes nor thinkes
Approching nere vnto her cruell deathe she woundes & killes vs w^th
                    the stones she throwes
A frend to those that spend ther deerest breathes in spoiles &
                    theftes in mortall woundes & blowes   [10
Wher in she takes her pleasure & her fill hiding ye men in waues
                    that she doth kill
                    a galley.
                    [Item 235]   [f. 47

you loue you say & loue for loue you craue
& loue for loue by due desart you haue
yet somwhat more than loue you wishe in hart
—————

    Item 234] No carry-over lines in the MS.

wch more me thinkes doth lessen your desart
when more then loue for only loue you claime   [5
you gyue the loue wch you pretend a maime
vnfained loue doth nought but loue regard
& for ytself doth thinke ytself reward
yf ought com else yt is for yt esteemd
not yt for ought that may be only demed   [10
vnles my loue be somwhat worse then your
I see no cause whie I should graunt you more
& yet y^t more wch you so much require
makes me suspect a more then fond desire
for yf your loue were good as yt would seeme   [15
yt would in me nothing but good esteme
those other thinges wch your affection moue
are toyes of lust & not the ioyes of loue.
wherfore good sir let loue for loue suffice
I am no marke for those imodest eyes   [20
that only looke on that they only see
& make of myne more then they make of me
I bear a hart thoughe loving to my frend
yet free from loue that hath an evill end

[Item 236]

A wretch I lyue yet haue the world at will
the sweete I tast yet bitter feedes me most

great is my greif yet haue I ioy my fill
full firm I stand yet staggering like am tost
tormented aye my pleasant ease not small [5
exceding hope yet deepe dispair wthall

My death I craue & would not willing dy
   I seeke for peace & bloudy warres embrace
   content I lyue a mangled martyr I
   more quiet none yet run a restles race [10
   my secretes known yet speach to none I vse
   ne thoughtes offend yet never voyd of muze

In Ise I burn in scorching heat I freese
in darkest nightes I see, in sunshine blind
in weale & woe like ioyes to me arise [15
in life I mourn to die no will I fynd
wth fancies fraught a thoughtles head I bear
And thus wth thwartes my lingring life I wear
my loue I flie my hate I folow fast [f. 47^v
my self I pine & please an others eyes [20
I dy the death & lyue agayn at last
my breathing spirite in others breste yt lies
of such my good, my ill my ioy my care
example take yee lovers & beware

[Item 237]

Go my flock go get you hence
seeke som̄ better place of feeding
wher we may fynd som̄ defence
frō these stormes in my brest breeding
& showres frō myn eyes proceding [5

Leaue a wretch in whom all woe
can abyde to kepe no measure
merry flocke such a on forgoe
vnto whom mirth is displeasure
only ritch in sorowes treasure [10

Yet alas before ye goe
hear your maisters wofull stay
wch to stones I else would showe
sorow only then hath glorie
when itz excellently sorie [15

Stella fairest sheapheardesse
feircest but yet fairest ever
stella whō o heavens do blisse
thoughe agaynst me she persever
thoughe I blisse inherite never [20

Stella hath refused me

Item 237 is entered in the right half of f. 47 opposite Items 235 and 236, and separated from them by a wavy vertical line. The last stanzas of Items 236 and 237 are carried over to f. 47ᵛ, where they are likewise entered on the left and right halves of the page respectively, and separated by a wavy vertical line.

stella who more loue hath proved
in this caitife hart to be
then in good ewes can be moved
vnto lambkins best beloved [25

Stella hath refused me
Astrophill who so well served
in this pleasant spring must see
whilst in pride flowres are preserved
himself only winter sterved [30

whie alas then doth she swear
that she lovethe me so dearly
knowing in my brest I bear
coales of fier y^t burn so clerely
& yet leaues me haplesse merely [35

Is this loue forsooth I trow
yf I saw my good dog greived
& a help for him did know
my loue will not be beleved
but by me he were relieved [40

No she hates me wellaway
fayning loue somwhat to please me
knowing yf she should display

all her hate death sone would seise me
& of hideous tormentes ease me [45
then adieu deere flocke adieu [f. 47ᵛ
yet alas yf in your straying
heavenly stella meete wᵗʰ you
tell her in your piteouse blaying
her poore slaves vniust decaying [50

[Item 238]

an epigram of an vntriftie gallant

As gallant as you see this youth to praunce in plumes of pride
   he is in middest of all his gooddes yᵗ cannot be denied
   denied yes sure & redenied for he muche rather is
   in middest of others gooddes or else in marchantes bookes for this

[Item 239]

great wealth great health & holie mynd: by early rising thou shalt fynd.

[Item 240]

who spares to toyle & spares not how to spend
all bare in care his nedy life doth end.

[Item 241]

yf yᵗ a beard doth make men wise how may yt com to passe
   but that a bearded goat may be as wise as plato was.

   Item 237] There is a double flourish beneath the last line.

[Item 242]

this glasse deceaves the gellia for yf this glasse were plain
yf once thou lookedst therin, then thou wouldst nere looke
ther agayn.

[Item 243]

thou lookest in glasse to see this self, & yet this self art blynd
for whie this glasse shewes outward glasse but not this inward mynd
thin inward mynd as outward shape yf ẏ yt did vnfold
this mynd more fowle then face is fair I fear thou shouldest behold.

[Item 244]

three thinges are in the world wch more the vemin vile offend
a froward mate, a naughtie wife a false & fayned frend.

[Item 245]

he worthiest is who all thinges knowes him self of self behest
& wittily such thinges receaves wch alwayes are the best
he also is right good wch heares an others warning right
& thinges devisd to put in vre is glad wth all his might
but to whom his wisdom nether gyveth sound advise   [5
& yet he doth induce his mynd true counsell to despise
  he is vnto the world a hate
  & thriftles to each worldly state.

Item 242:2] The line is not a carry-over in the MS.
Items 244 and 245 are enclosed on the right by a single bracket.

[Item 246]

In morning rising thinke thou hast thie life a lease thie breath a blast

at night laid down account to haue, thie sleap thie death thy bed thie graue

---

[Item 247]

me thinke̲s y^t bewtie hath but small avail: thoughe many of ther bewtie be so proud

for those whom Cupide̲s flattering flam̄es assayl, of thē the fowlest are for fair alowed

& those wch lovers trades do vain esteme, [5] the fairest ẙ be to them do fowlest seeme.

[Item 248]

thou nedest not greatly recke my frend what roabes thie corps array

for whie the wisdom of the mynd is not in garmente̲s gay

by base attyre is basenes seene by fyne is pride exprest

vse decent tyre that semes thie state for sure ye mean is best

---

[Item 249]

yf so thou wilt be wise obserue these sixe I gyue the then.

what thing thou speakest, & whear, of whom, for what cause, how & when.

Items 246-247] No carry-over lines in the MS.

Item 249 is bracketed along the right margin.

-173-

[Item 250]

where will wantes wit

welth worketh woe.
_____

[Item 251]

hard is the choise

where y^e best is to bad.

[Item 252]   [f. 48

    1.

Are woemen craftie are they so? only they? I faithe sir no

    But those are laddes of perfect crafte that in on hand take

        blade & haft

And buckler to vppon the thum, [5] & then wher so er the knaues

        becom̄

At meeting on the holie dayes, at sermons tiltinges, tourneys

        playes   Cutpur-

They cosen lawyer lasse & preist, clergie & lay by them

        are fleeste   ses. [10

They catche the bodie & the skin, that law & loue could

        never win.

And then the ambitious whorsons clime, promotion in ther

        latter tyme

_____

    Items 250 and 251 are entered to the right of the bracket beside Items 244 and 245.

    Item 252 is bracketed along the right margin, with "Cutpur-/ses." to the right of this bracket; there are no carry-over lines in the MS.

About som citie or good town, [15] sone ther are vp & soner down.

[Item 253]

2.

A vico'nt came vp to this towne, wth twentie in a liverie

   The liuerie laddes were sone sent down, my lord staied at his

       leacherie

A countrie clown came to this town [5] wth twentie in a liuery

   he left them here he himself went down to looke vnto his

       husbandrie

My Lordes fair crew went down in blew to keepe ther gutt<u>es</u>

       in quiet   [10

   the clownes red coates, gaue pence & groates & paid well for

       ther diet

[Item 254]

.3.

A sillie fowle was Barbarossa taken from his dame

   A headles witles simple thing as nature well could frame

   or either you or I could thinke or any man can name

   But since that he from prison came & finely got awaye   A Cock

   he ever hath a hacster byn ther passethe him no day   [5

   but battailing he is or at the least in battail raye

    Item 253 is bracketed along the right margin. There are no carry-over lines in the MS.

    Item 254 is bracketed along the right margin, with "A Cock" to the right of the bracket.

To tournementes he is ever prest yf any somons ring

he is spurred & booted like a knight & crowned like a king.

And talkes of newes & monishementes this is a mervailous thing

Is he a prophete Babarosse well then & so am I. [10

   Let him looke well vnto his throate & I will tell you whie.

   pro salute peccatorū Barbarosse must die.

[Item 255]

.4.   Tabacco

A foole or a phisition I know not whither his penner hath &

          inckhorn all in on

kept in an eeles skin or in a case of leather & made of clay

          converted to a stone

his Cotton is of darke decaied greene/ [5] his matter all wthin

          his nose is pend

and in the strangest guise y^{t} may be seene he drawes his incke

          out of a Candels end.

herewth his missiues round about he sendes ⟨he wringes his necke

                         des⟩

          & giueth to his fren⟩   [10

till breath & beard & all the house do stin

he wringes his necke & giueth to his freindes

hold Galantes here & to Galerus drinke

   Item 255] "Tabacco" in the title is written in Italian
characters. The poem is bracketed along the right margin and there
are no carry-over lines in the MS.

[Item 256]

4.

Mack Mackrell in may & Iune ye woemen sing wth cherefull tune

    But after whie leaue they this song maquerel lasteth all y^e

        yeare long

It sendes men in quicke wherries to hell [5] a plague take

        all suche maquerel

[Item 257]

.5.

Shad shad an other cries, she had or els the storie lies

    she had but yt would not be kept she lost yt but she never wept

    or changed wth her lustie louer [5] a thing wch nothing can

        recouer

[Item 258]   [f. 48^v]

6

Then co$\bar{m}$es a third blest might she be giue eare I pray y^u what

        sing<u>es</u> she

Turn vpps, Now fie on this y^e Oni<u>us</u> trade, the ses supines are

        all on turnvppes made.

[Item 259]

7.

Cardanus & Pontanus bothe wth plinie doe in on agree

    Items 256-258] No carry-over lines in the MS.

    Items 256 and 257 are bracketed along the right margin.

That a woeman were she nere so loath may to a man transformed be
And this for truthe I will you shew [5] yf that I lie then let
me burn
I had fiue Auntes all in a row they every on to men did turn

[Item 260]

.8.

To two freindes every day ye daintie dame she goes　　A Close stole
her secretes every way to them she doth disclose　　A glasse.
The on delightes her eye [5] the other offendes her nose
Now tell me by & bie, freind, what two freindes are those

[Item 261]

.9.

Mary Bloomer hath ye properties of an honest wife. She is not
exceding/ gorgious in attire, not aromaticall not perfumed not
supra modū bewtifull/ but full of iuice swete wholsom, fat & very
fertile, more ouer a good leache or/ phisition wch is an excellent
qualitie in a woman. But her cheif honour/ is the excellent loue
she bearethe to her noble Lord so greate & perfect & yf [5] he
be but out of sight she is out of countenance. And goe he wher
he list or/ loue he whom he list . she still is readie to receaue
his return wth her/ best & cherfullest face never looking meryly
when he is gon

　　Item 259] Lines 5 and 6 are written as one line in the MS.

　　Item 260 is bracketed along the right margin with the answers
to the riddle to the right of the bracket.

[Item 262]

10.

Let your many officers your tongue well advise
In his behauiour to be warie & wise
& looke well to your officers whilst you are yong
kepe them from corruption wth an honest tongue
you haue eight Gelasinoi iollie laughing fooles   [5
Tomici som call them, they are right cutting tooles
take heede least they & ther felowes cut your purse
leaving you & themselues not better but the worse
next to Gelasinoi, two in either ⟨order⟩ border
Cynodontes follow of ye Cynickes order   [10
The highest two of fowr toward your windowes grow
ware how you stire them lest y^r light<u>es</u> you overthrow
youre millers should be twentie myne are not so many
a yonger then I perhaps hath skantly any
The flouddes of som̄ mens braines to send down suche defluccion   [15
that millers dwell in paines & com vnto destruction

[Item 263]

.11

how can you make a thing of weight lighter by adding weightie

thing<u>es</u> to yt

    Item 262 is bracketed along the right margin.

    Item 263] No carry-over lines in the MS.

muse you at this tis a comon sleight, fooles somtimes better then
wisemen doe yt.

[Item 264]

12.

Whie dothe the syluer smithe like a sot, put out his hornes they
are nothing worthe
Are they his eyes? yf yf they be not I mervaile whie he puts them
forthe
Whie dothe he spend his mettail so, [5] the slavering foole is at
greate cost
he guildeth all wher he dothe goe yet no man desires to be his host
he will to ye highest roomes exalt himself he is no mate for me   [10
he fedes on sallettes & loues no salt, his complexion cannot
wholsom be

[Item 265]

13.

A thatcht howse & a showre of raine when sol to southacre was run
  An vnsene guest did intertaine & they togither had a sonne
vnto his sire he was not like
⟨he took his physnomie & frame⟩[5] he toke his phisnomie & his frame
by accident & yf you seeke his substance it was from his dame
        still.
All his life long he‸did sucke his father held him to the teate   [10

Item 264] No carry-over lines in the MS.

Item 265:9] The caret is in the MS.

And had the weather brought him lucke ye vrchin might haue
     waxed greate
But still methought it lookt to fall, alas it was but even a
     crust
It fell indede so shall we doe all, [15] in weather or world
     let no man trust

     [Item 266]
    14.
Ther is somtyme a serpent to be sene I see not whie I may not well
     so call her
y^t is in somer mantled most in greene a dragon leeke but she is som
     what taller
In winter all her strengthe goeth to her head, [5] & ẙ^t kept warme,
    w^{th}in ye ground abideth
she makes no shew but even as she were deade, a wonder tis to see
     how life she hideth
before mid may she wakes as from a sleepe, & makes as yf she stode
     vppon her legges   [10
yet all y^t she can doe is but to crepe & worcke increase by
     knottes of many egges
wch egges fond men do gather for ẙ^r foison & wth y^r handes or heeles
     they all to tear thē
but in y^r heades ye yolkes do worke suche poison, [15] ẙ^t handes, heles,
        them
     head can all but hardly bear

Items 265-266] No carry-over lines in the MS.

[Item 267]

15.

In the 7th yeare of this quenes raign an old Cutler or hornes maker cam out/ of the north & fell here in loue wth a strumpet wch kept the southe part of/ london. they called her comonly Tamasin. This Cutler had a pestilent vnsauery/ breathe. & often tymes he left a drie salt vppon every thing he kissed. poore/ Herbagreene could not in a moneth shake of an agew wch she got by being/ [5] acquainted wth him a weeke. Tamasin therfore vtterly refused to haue/ any familiaritie or comorance wth him, pretending somtyme that she/ was to goe to her husband to Quinboroughe, somtyme y^{t} it was terme/ & her old customers must first & cheifly be regarded. well thought/ the Cutler I will pay you your fifpence for this geere yet er yt be/ [10] long. Shall every western pug be serued in his turn & an old northern/ lad be cleane shut out of dores? he had read in a loue storie y̌ perseus/ had never byn born had Iupiter not won Danae by torning himself/ into gold: wch mettall because it was daintie wth my Cutler, the/ fine Chymicall slaue makes no more ado, but transformes himself/ [15] into a showre of white money, and was as freely admitted by his/ daintie dame as ever she admitted any since her name was Tamasin. He/ layd her on ye lippes & bare bellie, till she swelled againe: & sodainly resuming/ his old shape & occupation leaving her in her bed he shut her vp

[f. 49^{v}]

ther in a neiw/ peice of armour   A brestplate so cunningly close
& finely made, that all ye Cutlers/ [20] of London might throw
ther cappes at yt for ever being able to make the/ like. Tamasin
being thus made ye Cutlers prisoner, her lustie companions/ were
all kept from her & ther was muche wamenting. Multitudes of men/
& woemen came to see this strange indurance, and many wch perhappes
had/ deserued to be walled vp themselues reioisingly insulted on
this drabbes/ [25] miserie. But after 12. or 13. dayes the cheife
Iustice of Gaole delyvery/ that inlargethe more prisoners in a
yeare, then ther be theues in wales/ or true men in England,
looking out wth compassion Tamasin was left/ to her wonted libertie,
& by infusion of suche matter as that wherof it/ was made the
strange armour wch I haue told you of was cleane dissol-/ [30] ued
rivers grew rewmatique & Owse bridge was caried awaye.

[Item 268]

16.

A Di(a)mond is a good fair stone, a Saphire so & not muche vnleeke

Lordes haue good stones many a on, & ladies for stones will not

be to seeke

But this to say Ile make no bones [5] none are so good as Tom

Milners stones

[Item 269]

.18.

If farting be naught els but aires reverberation

Item 268] No carry-over lines in the MS.

follis is a farter the cheife of any nation
for be the weather fowle or be ye weather fair
she dothe none other thing but reverberate ye ayre
she takes breathe at her bome & lets goe at her nose [5
And yf it frely com frely awaye it goes.

[Item 270]
19.

Behold a ladie fair al couered in her hair
    except yt were behind wher nothing you could fynd
    had vnderneathe he heele [5] a little turning wheele
    And on her feete a pair of winges to cut ye ayre
    She of a kynd intent vnto her servant bent   [10
    as yf she would him blisse for ever wth a kisse
    And he been so bold fast on her hair to hold.
    kindly to entertaine [15] her in her loving vaine
    vnto his darrein end she would haue byn his frend
    he had ye world had seene for ever happie byn   [20
But oh she came in hast, & she was gon & past   [f. 50
    before ye pore man saw what made her to him draw
    he snatched at her bomme, [25] neere wch he could not come
    but foole was left to crie o what a foole am I
    Som say vppon this toye the ladie was a boy   [30
    but boies are not afraid starke naked to be staied.
    A boy he wilbe bold, vnles it be far cold

    naked as well as clad [35] to play ye wanton lad.
But seldom shall you fynd a woman of y^t mind
    all listed she to playe y^t will all naked staye   [40
vnto so rare a sight by day or candle light
before ye day of dome I never looke to come
A woman at a tide [45] may chance to make a slide
in womanly behauiour to shew a man a favour
yet then she will be bent to couer her intent   [50
& bashfully com forthe els is it nothing worthe
And when she shewes him grace to giue him tyme & place
yf that he let it passe [55] men say he is an asse.

[Item 271]

20.

In the yeare of our lord twice fiftie half a thousand ten hundred
& two a/ popes sonne w^thout ever drawing sword shall make all
or most part/ of Cristendom subiect vnto him. Millain shall
hold out against him/ a certaine but no long space. He shall come
into England greatly/ welcomed of many and not a few of our
bishops prelates Clergie/ [5] men & suche as are in autoritie
shall ad heare vnto him. he shall/ stand vppon old orders &
ceremonies restraine mariages & pretend/ good to ye comon welthe.
But because many of the richer sort as of/ ye poorer shalbe
excedingly evill intreated by him he shalbe hated & after/
extraordinarie praying preaching & fasting not w^thout death

of many/ [10] Innocentes & effusion of muche bloud vppon ẙe
Earthe he shalbe/ overthrowen & chased away. And som more like
dogges then true/ englishemen, wch fawned & semed as thoughe
they would licke his/ trencher, shall shew by the terrour w^ch
they find in ẙe likres of his/ steppes when he is gon how
muche they misliked hym whilst he/ [15] was here.

[Item 272]

21.   birdes. Conies.

A freind did to Erasmus write I meane to sup wth you to night
make preparation very small flies & pismeares let that be all
w^thout good doble Hamboroughe beere [5] suche simple cates
make single cheere

[Item 273]   [f. 50^v]

22.

No miracle no oracle no beaste no birde no man
No Sybille witche no sorcerer what devill is it than
that in his garmentes stiffe & cold as any tanned leather
by somer harvest winter spring shrinkes not at any weather
See see, having no feete he goes & going still he standes   [5
casting accomptes of precious thinges & yet he hathe no handes
well might he be the issue of some conning monke or frier
this spartan speaking w^thout a mouthe a southsayer & a lier.

Item 272] Lines 5 and 6 are written as one line in the MS.

[Item 274]

23.

Robyn Hoode in grenewood stode & leaned him to a tre he fell backward in/ a greene cowsheard & all to berayd was he. Men take this for a sillie/ peice of poetrie or at the best hand that it importethe no more but y^t Robin/ Hoode was on wch refused to stand rectus in curia, hiding himself in a wood/ or forest to scape a capias. But the truthe is that our old Bardi of Englād/ [5 wch were no les wise & wittie then Orpheus, pindare, & Hesiode, Homer/ or any of them all: gaue vs here to vnderstand that vulcan (whom all/ aeges haue acknowleged to be lame) could stand no longer then he had som staffe, tree or wood to leane vnto & by way of vaticination warned vs to/ spare our timber in carestia annona, to feede vulcan on turves, turdes &/ [10] so forthe. I speake not this to derogate any thing from vulcans celsitude/ whom I haue presently in ye middest of my depest speculations for/ good cause in greate veneration. And in veritie amongst all ye mocke/ Iupiters I see not two y^t may paragonner this criple, in similitude to his / sire. In whose quarrell he overthrew the college of giantes, o what a/ [15] world of creatures hathe he begotten. this legittimate son of Iupiter/ & Iuno & that not many out of many, as the bastard of Latona dothe/ but infinites out of on & that suche a on as phoebus & saturn to can/ scarsely

---

Item 274:10] The 's' of "spare" is badly smeared or written over another letter.

make any thing on. you will say perhaps that this forgeror/
makethe nothing but small birdes? hathe he not made falcons
sakers/ [20] Eagles, suche as pray not on lambes mallardes & quailes,
but on men/ townes & castles, he hathe made thonder & lightning,
yea he hath made a/ sonne & moone, & will stand on tiptoes somtyme
on ye top of a candle to/ laughe at fooles in their studies &
counting how ser admiring his creatures/ I grant he can doe no
thing wthout his Cyclopides, but what would you haue/ [25] on to
doe y^t ever since his cradle hath byn lame? will you see y^e
Iouitatem/ of this Iolly Mulciber? Behold well his .2. greate
commissioners of/ multiplicamini, wch being as second parentes in
many of his productions/ like father & mother, agent & patient doe
not wthstanding in procreation of any/thing impart nothing of y^r
own substance. Tell me who they be how long/ [30] they haue byn
& wch of them is tempore prior & eris mihi magnus/ Apollo.

[Item 275]   [f. 51

23.

She y^t was thought so full wth wisdom fraught, y^t all ye world might
go to her to scole

& he y^t at no tyme by her was taught, is taken yet by som but halfe
a foole

She y^t taught princes how ther states to weld [5] & y^r imbassadours
what to doe & say

Item 275] No carry-over lines in the MS.

she y^t for sober & devout was held & clerckes & preistes taught
> how to preache & pray

she y^t so many yeares refusd to wed, & boasted what virginitie
> was worthe [10

Even she I say hath lost her maidenhead & daughters .3. to all
> ye world brought forthe

W^ch Ile averre on Churche & on Churchesteple are bastardes bred
> right children of ye peo- ple.

[Item 276]

24.

Aetos is a cruel bloudie king he holdes his subiectes mervelously
> in awe

And whom he listeth, he dothe to ruin bring, w^thout inquest or
> any forme of law

what all endure is easie to be born, [5] (the Ottomans do vse
> y^r subiectes so)

the greatest kinges to die must take no skorn, subiectes must die
> thoughe 20. kinges say noe

& by my conning in philosophie, althoughe I haue no skill in
> magique arte [10

of Aetos deathe I here will prophecie, y̆^t famin at ye last shall
> kill his hart

Item 276] No carry-over lines in the MS.

his nose shall so inclose his mouthe in de⟨d⟩e, y̆ᵗ he shall not

know him self to feede.

[Item 277]

25.

Calisto was taken vp to heauen & placed in those bright starres

seaven

  The skies garland & fairest crown, from Europaes eyes never

going down.

Calisto from heaven descended down [5] to weald a scepter weare

a crown

And rule yᵉ Realme yᵗ once was seaven, holden imedia'tly of god

in heaven

Calisto shine out Chast child of heaven Europe doth glorie in   [10

thie crown   119

Ioue make this yeares seventene tymes seuen & throw thine enymes

headlong down

[Item 278]

26.

Couldst thou not frier Bacon make a brazen head to speake

  Alas good frier now in good soothe this invention was but weake

The Necromancers now adayes more cunning & more fine

    Item 277 is bracketed along the right margin, with "119" to the right of this bracket; there are no carry-over lines in the MS.

Can put a familiare in a box & guid him wth a line
wch having nether fleshe nor bone, nor tongue nor head nor face [5
can crie & speake bothe soft & loud & clere a doubtfull case
And yf we marke him well he giues vs cristian counsell to
your life saith he runes fast away take good hede what you doe.

[Item 279]

27.

Calamus pontificis men say it growes in Rome
    And yt hath powr to sweepe vp gold as it were wth a broome
    But we haue flowres in England here, wch doe subdue yt quight
    The Calamus pontificis against them hath no might
    Carnasions of Elizabeth her subiectes many saue them [5
    against the fowle Epilepsie & happie are they that haue them
    Doe you not know what flowers I meane ye Queenes small
              shinking letters
    They set fooles forward now & then sixe miles before ther betters.

[Item 280]

28

Ther is a thing is granted free to ye king of france & vnto me
I haue as muche therof as he and as good for ought y^t I can see
few zelanders in any degree [5] shall haue yt to yeare so good as wee

---

   Item 279:7] Written as one line in the MS.

[Item 281]

Let all reioce & sing for birth of Iesus Christ,
    wch do inhabite from the west vnto the farthest East
the maker of the world of servant toke the shape
that flesh by flesh he might redeme & vs to mercie take
Into his mothers wombe from heaven doth cō such grace   [5
that she vnknowing doth conceaue a child of heavenly race
the caban of her brest wch was most chast & pure
is made the mansion seat of god wch cam our woundes to cure
vntouched of any man remayning still a mayd
by word of god she did conceaue a sonne wch made her glad   [10
a virgin⟨ ⟩ forth him bringes
  ⟨& brought a bed of him⟩ whom Gabriel did forshoe
& Ihon enclosed in mothers wombe by leaping semed to know
he was content to lie in crib full many a night
& to be fed wth milke he wch gyves food to every wight
the Aungels carols sing the powers in heaven reioice   [15
this sheapheard to the sheapherdes is revealed by heavenly voice
O lord wch as this day of virgyn pure was born
in bethlem vs for to redeme, wch were wth synnes forlorn
to the be glorie ay and, all praise for evermore
wth holie ghost & father thyn, wch mercie hath in store.   [20

[Item 282]

He wch of heavenly father was before all worldes yborn
 surnamed alpha & Omeg the hope of vs forlorn
the fountayn & the only spring & eke the end also
 of all thinges wch haue byn or ar or may herafter grow
  as long as sonne shall gyue his light   [5
  or phebe vse to shyne by night.
O golden birthe of pereles babe, a mayd a mother is
 & being inspired by holy ghost to vs salvation gyves
this sacred imp frō mothers wombe as this day shewes his face
 wch is to be our saviour by his mercie & his grace [10
⟨as lo⟩   as long as sonne shall gyue his light
  or phebe vse to shine by night.
Let heavenly powers wth ioy now sing & Angels all reioyce
& Cherubs wth the seraphims godes prayse extol wth voice
let no tongue now be tied or still but all wth on accord [15
sing Caroals & most ioiful songes, to this our gracious lord
  as long as sonne shall gyue his light
  or phebe vse to shine by night
for lo. he wch in former tymes the prophetes had fortold
 & sacred holy men by faith did as wth eyes behold [20
 he wch was promised long before doth now cōm down fro' skyes
 his praises now let creatures all send forth wth ioiful cries

-193-

as long as sonne shall gyue his light

or phebe vse to shine by night

26 [f. 52

Let grey & sylver heared syres let little wanton boyes

let yonkers all wch geven ar to much to worldly toyes

let wyves & maydes & little girles wth on accord now sing

& wth ther cherful ioiful noyse make places all to ring

As long as sonne shall ⟨shine by night⟩ gyue his light

& phebe vse to shine by night. [30

To the o Christ wth father thine & wth the holy ghost

be hymnes & songes & lasting praise o wch of ⟨m⟩ight art most

Al honour strengh & victorie, & thankes for evermore

be vnto the o lord of might of mercie wch hast store

As long as sonne shall gyue his light [35

or phebe vse to shine by night.

[Item 283]

O lord ⟨   &   fr   p   was   ⟩

In ⟨   ⟩

Let heaven & earth reioice & Christians Carolles sing

this day of virgin pure was born our saviour & our king

Sing we all wth on voice o golden glorious day [5

In wch our Saviour Christ was born wch cā our debtes to pay

---

Item 283] The first line was corrected in several places and then apparently crossed out, along with the second line.

O happie glorious day thrice welcom we may sing

   in wch of virgin pure was born our Saviour & our king

Thrice welcom happie day in wch vs to redeeme

   was born of sacred virgin pure the glorious king of heaven.   [10

what greater ioy to vs could be then birth of Iesus Christ

   for ⟨whose⟩ wch all Christians may reioce wch dwell frō

              west to East

he tooke the shape of mortall man vs all for to redeeme

   & from the devils slavery vs for to raunsom clene

This golden boy in Crib did lie, a bed ful hard & cold.   [15

   & in poore ragged simple cloutes he wrapped was & rolled

the heavenly angels frō aboue melodious songes do sing

   & creatures all make ioy & myrth at birth of this ther king

Dame phebe she more bright her beames vppon the earth doth send

   & golden glittering starres ther light more cherefully do lend   [20

the seelie sheapheardes wch ther shepe abroad did keepe that night

   did hear such heavenly Carolles as before did never wight

the Indian kinges wch cam frō far to this babe presentes bring

   & him do reverence & adore as ther most sovereyn king.

   Item 283] There is a stanza break between lines 6 and 7.

   Item 283:12] Written as one line in the MS.

   Item 283:24] "sovereyn" appears to be written over an original reading, "heave."

O heavenly lord wch of all thinges art Alpha & Omeg   [25

    graunt vs this short & brittle life in virtue so to lead

that when that thou shalt com as iudge, in ⟨heaven⟩ cl o des / wth aungels thine

    through mercie thine we may be found devoyd of ⟨mortall⟩ deadly. crime.

          20.

       [Item 284]   [f. 53

Place me i th' town wch name toke from hartes horn

    or wher wth nutshales Dennis shaued his beard

    where Hierosme learnedst cristian erst was born

    wher Giptian kinges ye piramides vp reard

Where Syrene drownd gaue name to idle town   [5

    ⟨wher Aristotle did himself once drown⟩

    wher famous Austin somtimes bishop was

    wher Aristotle did himself once drown

    wher Midas got ye eares of foolishe Asse

where Ambrose kept from Churche Theodose ye greate

    where Iuliet & Rome strangely died   [10

    wher Christian emperour first did place his seate

    wher oynious Cattes & dogges were deified

      Ile be to ye vntill my life shall end

      as true as These to peritho his frend.

       [Item 285]

Place me where pawle shooke viper frō his hand

    where Diomede ^his Iades wth fleshe did feede

⟨where perill had of phalaris his mede⟩
 wher of ẙ sun ẙ greate Colosse did stand
 wher perill had of phalaris his mede
Wher king Busiris Thrase did sacrifice   [5
 wher hipsiphile did serue her lord as page
 where Scythes on strangers vse to tirannize
 where Scylla & Charibdis vse to rage
Wher Mares conceaue wth breathe of western wynd
 where Gerion & Antœus hercles tamed   [10
 wher Nausica Vlisses drencht did find
 wher polypheme of Galatee complaind.
  yet still to ẙ Ile constant be & kynd
  as erst faire hero did Leander fynd.

[Item 286]

Place me ith' town wch was ẙ ey of Greece
 or wher Achilles vsd to make his race
 wher Iason shipt to fetche ẙ golden fleece
 where girles did wrastle . leape & run at base
Wher ovide plaind as wretchedst man aliue   [5
 whence hercules did fetche ẙ dog of hell
 wher Salomon a thousand quenes did swiue
 or Cinique Diogene at first did dwell.
Where persian treasure was laid vp in store

where pegase hoofe to town a name did giue [10
wher blind men built a citie fair of yore
wher Priam did wth his fiftie children lyue
    yet constant still to ye I mind to proue
    as erst Theagene to his fairest loue.

[Item 287]   [f. 53^v

place me ith' town wch ay enquird for newse
    or where y^t riuers run wth gold thats yellow
    wher venus first set vp an open stewse
    wher Ioue in shape of Bull for loue did bellow
Wher Perseus freed Andromeda ye faire [5
    wher Antioche wth mothers loue did burn.
    where Artemisia built a tomb most rare
    wher marble Image did to woman turn.
Let me be set on top of ye Rames head
    or where Augustus Cesar went to scole [10
    where Antonie wth Cleopatra fled
    where xerxes did wth vine & sloa play th' foole.
    yet me doubt not thou still shalt find as kynd.
    as ever did Euridice Orpheus find.

[Item 288]

Place me where .I. did sleape 300 yeares
    or wher was born ye conquerour of ye East

where Biblis mournd & turned was to teares

wher Hercles set ye farthest boundes of West

Where king Decebalus somtyme did raign [5

where Lucrece made of her chast mind a show

where th'emperour maxinimus tooke his bane

or wher ye sea seven tymes doth ebbe & flow.

Where died virginia wth her fathers knife

where maidens sonnes did build ye feastfull citie [10

paris stale king. menelaus wife
where Massiniss sent poison to his wife

where phillis hangd herself ye more ye pitie

yet still in me thou shalt not misse to find

a true & loving constant Damons mynd.

[Item 289]

Place me in Iapan Zeilan Barbarie

in Chatay China or in Arabie

in Inde Calecute persie or in Armeine.

in Lawrence Isle melinde or Guinee.

Place me where parrates prate in Cube or Nubie. [5

in Iaue sumatra Natolie or els in surie

in Caribane new france Quivire or Russie

Item 289] In the right margin opposite lines 6 and 7 are two markings, one an apparent testing of the quill, the other, the letters "fo," which are repeated beneath and to the right of Item 290 at the bottom of the page.

in spagnnole Iamaic, Baccalaos Chile.

Place me in florida estotilant or els Amazonie:

    in mainconge in Brasile or in Natolie   [10

    in Boriquen s^t Thomas Azores or Canarie

                               virginia.
in Cape verd Isles, molocques or Abissini

    No proteus nor vertuma̅s will I proue

        but true in frendship as ye turtle doue.

[Item 290]

        of George Barckelay.

Whilst nature doubted wch to make a boy or damsell fair

    almost thou had'st byn made a wenche o boy of bewty rare

[Item 291]   [f. 94

Place me on Tuarus Athos Carpathus

    on hiperborean or Biphean hill<u>es</u>

    on haemus Atlas Aetna Caucasus

    on Alaun, sevo, peuce Budinus.

In Numidie mauritania or marmarica   [5

    wher Dido raignd in Chios or Trinacria

    in Melite Zacinthe mitilene or Corcyra

    in Carpathe Trapesonde or els bythinia.

Item 290 is bracketed along the right margin.

Middes hamaxobij getes, hippophagi

    pterophori scythes or Agathyrsi   [10

    In Illiric Dace Epire or Attica.

    In hircin woodes, Noric, paunony or Moesia

        Not like to Metra or Battus will I be

        but ay performe what I haue said to the

[Item 292]

Place me in Europe Afric Asia

    In ye vnknown land or else Americ fair

    In maine in Island or peninsula

    on Isthmus Cape or promontorie bare

On Ocean Midland persique or Red sea   [5

    on Caspian Gulf or else wthin som streight

    wher Arctique circle sees Callisto gay

    or where ye Equator paiseth day & night

Wher sun betwene ye tropickes still doth roll

    wher's parallele or circle of ye none   [10

    where ye Antarctique viewes ye sothern pole

    wher's ye cold ye temperate or hot zone

        No distance place or tyme can alter me

        but that sweete girle I still must thinke on the

[Item 293]

Place me in England scotland or hibernia.

    In spain in france in Almain or sarmatia

In Denmarcke Norway suedland or moscouia

In hungarie Waluch moldaw or Tartaria.

In sclavonie in seruia or Lituania [5

In pelopennesi macedon Thrace Grecia.

In Crete in sicile Corsique or Sardinia.

In Lesbos Lemnos Zante or Taurcia.

Place me in Orcades hebudes or Islandia

In Lapland friseland Grunland or Biarmia. [10

In Brittain Thyle Cimbric or scandia

In Gades, Euboea ⟨Gades⟩ or braue Italia.

Not all this change from the shall make me shrinke

Althoughe were I of Lethe constraind to drinke.

[Item 294]   [f. 55

Riddle. 29.

Holbourn is quasi holie bourn because it leades ye way

vnto ye holie bowres of these that beare in Iustice sway

for I may confidently speake ⟨ ⟩ I a Bractor were

A troope of holie preistes are they wch lawes administer

or Holborn may be holie bourn when pilgrims going astray [5

Invoiaged to ye holie crosse are rectified that way

No force no harme to saue a sowle, what skils ye bodies losse

yf secrete theues went all this way, it were a holie crosse.

Item 293] Beneath the rule under line 10 are seven or more letters; 'fo,' and two 'f's' are distinguishable.

[Item 295]

.30.

The horrour y^t all or most men find in her vglie shape & companie
giueth/ to suspect, but her life & demeanour doe necessaryly
conclude that pipistrello/ can be no other then a very witche.
The biting of her teeth hath caused/ madnes & by only towching
of her neighbours egges they are made forever/ vnable to be
chickens. Her vse is when countrie people are at rest/ [5] wthout
putting on a smocke or any garment more then a wide sleued cassocke/
or hairie mantle to rig in ye aire⟨ ⟩nd having not so muche as
on/ feather to flie wth she not only dares to mount steeple heighthe,
but she/ will also make as yf she would fathom a steple & take it
in her armes/ & by leaning her elbowes to y^e on side of yt, she
will cling fast vnto it/ [10] learning her yong toward impes to
doe ye like. who when by sucking of/ her brestes they are come
to som vigour, she will carrie them somtymes/ .2. at once in y^e
ayre as safely & as fast as any ladies in a coache/ drawn wth
4. horses can harrie vp & down highe Holbourn. yf/ this be not
a witche Ione was no pope nor Merlin any prophete/ [15

[Item 296]

.31.

And when I haue beheld ye market all day I return at night to my
Cabin./ & my Concubines complaining on while wth heraclitus that
men are all/ guiltie of vsing false weightes & bie & by laughing

wth Democritus/ to see how merely the old pedler piping on y^e
little boies toe cariethe his/ pack about & serueth in ther turnes
all those y^t are hable to bring ther/ [5] measure wth them. for
ther is but vna mensura pro totū regnū, on measure/ of breade wine
ale by ye lrē. & of every thing else by extension of magna/ charta.
By this measure is ye world kept in traffique. for wiues for/
husbandes, for freindes for counsaile, for audience, for office
for function/ & charge & for every thing./   [10

[Item 297]

    32.

A man, not a man seing not seing
   killed wth a stone not a stone being
   A bird not a bird fleing not flying

[Item 298]   [f. 55^v

    33.

Imitating sir Iohn that was beyond sea born
   of whose birthe & bare arse no honest man takes skorn
   being once at Malden amidest⟨ ⟩iollie presse
   of gallant men & woemen y^t genlenes professe
   seing them in scuppettes supping vp of smoke   [5
   shewed y^t in that Cookerie he longed to haue a stroake

   Item 297 is bracketed along the right margin.

he looked round abowt east west north & south

still more & more he wisht the spigot in his mouthe

he fell to it at last & tooke so sound a draught

that had a horse perceaved it a horse must nedes haue laught. [10

But yet ther had not past the mountenance of an howre

before his chere was chang'd he looked very sowre

he thought he had bin poisoned misliking muche his physique

he keckt & coughed like to on y^t long had had ye tissicke

At lengthe the powre retentiue, that dothe ye nerfe restraine [15

of rednosed goodman spi⟨nc⟩ter decayed so amaine

That eyes & noses to of all y^t were in place

di⟨d⟩ by his Symptomes find s^r Iohn in heavie case

had he byn trussed round wth many silken pointes

he had byn fowlie oyl'd in many of his ioyntes [20

Car il se couchia that is the very truthe

he made a Cacophonia for example to y^e yowthe.

[Item 299]

34.

An ignorant is worse then an affectionate iudge & on irreligious
worse then/ them both. I should aske did I not see how foolishe
& vnhallowed people be/ whither amongest vs ther is found,
sapiens ne vnus quidē $\overset{i}{q}$ $\overset{t}{p}$ iudicare & sed/ frater cū fratre
litigat idq; sub infidelibus. I haue seene men in suite for
ther/ gooddes before suche iudges as in dede might well haue

-205-

byn holden for forme/ [5] & appearance steadie & setled, by
nature voide of affections partialitie &/ from briberie as clere
as the Iudge whose tribunall was couered wth his/ fathers skin.
But because they had of themselues no skill & they wch directed
thē/ no honestie bothe to geather being infidi, after many false
oathes by verdit of/ a great grand Iurie the law leaned vntowardly
on ye ton side & either som/ [10] bodie lied or no bodie muche
gained by the suyte./

[Item 300]

35.

good fortune makes good bloud I will not cleane deny it
but sildom is iudgement good till stormes doe find & trie yt
youthe is freshe & iollie [5] but easie it is to shame it
it is so full of follie vntill som tempest tame it
when in a mead I see ye gamballes of a calfe   [10
  good faithe it freates not me I would not be his halfe.

[Item 301]   [f. 56

36.

when on y^r helmes captaines did horsetailes weare
  then was it y^t contention first began
wch of the two preheminence should beare
  the souldiour valiant or ye learned man
This might not be determined wth blowes   [5

Item 299:11] The slash at the end of this line is in the MS.

for scollers so had byn in wofull case

Doctours had so gon down highe god it knowes

   lawyers would not haue dar'd to shew y^r face

Bothe fell to wordes to make y^r titles clere

   souldiour & clerke confusedly clapt it on [10

But order wanting nothing ther could appeare

   that made to th'issue either pro or con.

The Iudge that stode on incest point<u>es</u> of lawes

   affirmed plaine vnlesse that they would write

Ther pleading<u>es</u> all & therof every clause [15

   he knew not how to giue his sentence right

Parchement & inke was fetcht into ye place

   stoutly stoode vp then bothe these worthie men

They had not pleaded thus a little space

   But y^t ye garland was giuen vnto ye pen [20

Swoundes q̊the ye souldiour is it com to that

   his horstayle turnd to a feather in his hat

[Item 302]

37.

The valiantst prancke is not to hack & kill ye wisest war is not

         wth horse & shot

   Item 302] No carry-over lines in the MS.

The largest libertie is not vntamed will, nor gretest conquest wth
    blowes & bloudshed got
kingdomes to win is not for every elfe, [5] let evrie on seeke
    conquest of himselfe.

[Item 303]

38

---

permission pages let a gibbihorse passe, Ixion a proud fastidious asse
that might by his lookes som potentate be, lord what a wardrop of clothes
    hathe he
he thinkes he could put a world to scole, [5] but more is more wise
    & proues him a foole
More saithe of vanities none is so wide from soundnes of wisdom
    as pecocklike pride
he saithe they are fooles y^t reckon yt sping, before either Cuckoe
    or nightingale sing   [10
he saith it is wisdome to kepe thie self warme, a flie for they
    brauerie yf it doe ye harme
Stormes are not past thoughe swallow sing prime, florishe not Ixion
    before this tyme

[Item 304]

39

To homer once this bone a sawcie seaman gaue.
 we tooke them that are gon ye vncaught still we haue

Item 303] No carry-over lines in the MS.

Homer could not discusse [5] how this thing might betide
   But being set nō plus, wth skorne & sorrow died
from Anglers lord kepe me wch death haue in y^r question   [10
   And from all riddles y^t be so dangerous in disgestion

[Item 305]

The feoffees were but vlpian ye goose ye sheepe ye lamb ye bee
   they haue ye state of every man in all this sublunaritie

[Item 306]   [f. 56^v

40.

Ware & wades mill are worth all london. And the greatest citie in england/ next London is westminster. The sainges are so & so is soothe. yet I say not y^t/ wares mill wth westminster or london. hath any proportion of likenes or/ possibilitie of comparison. True it is y^t townes & cities are more comēded/ by iust harmonie & equall distribution of lawes then by ether salubritie of/ [5] ayre, comoditie of seate aboundance of wealthe or splendour of armes. A⟨n⟩d wades mill hath a representation of a well ordred comon wealthe./ But alas yf you looke neerely ther is not so muche as a painted Image/ or cut out embleame of any such matter, for those thinges wch really or/ simbolically might be ye arche supporters of a state are at wadesmill/ [10] bought & sold for money. wch is a greate strobeligo or solecisme in go-/vernment.

[Item 307]

1581.   A newyeres gift

The tyme is ronne about & Phebus golden sphere
   by revolution iust beginnethe I hope a happie year
And Ianus doble faced dothe now put vs in mynd
   of tyme that is past & for to wishe good successe to our frend
And all bothe riche & poore prepare giftes to present   [5
   to thos to whom in hart they ar & goodwill frendly bent
The countrie farme he, his hennes & capons sendes
   And maides & wyves suche giftes provides as fortun to the lendes
The citisens wch haue of worldly welthe no lacke
   provyde for to present ther frendes wth wares of pedlars packe   [10
The little wanton boy & pretie Mopsie Mayd
   present som comfites or som toye to make ther parentes glad
The court now swymes in sylke & Monsieur playes his part
   And lordes of fraunce & English dames do stryue to shew y^r art
Who shall to frend present, the thing of greatest price   [15
   or may by gallant gift advance, himself in bravest wise
Ther brodered purses flie, wth store of pelf well fraught
   & plate of silver & of gold, & Velvetes derely bought
The Indian precious pearl & Iewels passing brave
   are ther presented for to shew, what mynd the givers haue   [20
W^{ch} thing when I do thinke, yt makes my hart full sad

that I for you my Grandam dear, no gift can get (though bad)
fo⟨r⟩ thoughe I be a boy, in yeres & wit a child
yet none in dutie doth me passe, yf I be not beguiled
The countrie farmers giftes, are sent for privye gayne [25
that they therbie ther landlordes grace, & favour may retayn
the wafers wch are sent, of wyves & maydes to frendes
are ⟨t⟩ rather thinges of course & vse, then signes of loving myndes
the Citisen hathe lerned, to flatter & speake fair
his newyeres giftes are but a bait, to vtter well his ware [30
Althoughe the little child, wth no dissembling is clad
yet for to bear a great good will, his yong wittes are to bad
The court the place is thought, wher flatterie cheif doth raign
I dare say som̄ would wish ther giftes, might brede to frendes y^r bane
but I my ladie dear, & Grandham most beloved [35
  do bear to you suche great good will as seldō hath byn p<u>ro</u>ved
I thinke yf Homer lyved, wth streames of golden speache
  he could not to my loving mynd, wth all his witt now reache
Nor Tullie wth his ⟨witt⟩ skill. & lerned sugred worke
could half expresse the dutie w^ch, wth in my mynd doth lurke [40

       [Item 308]   [f. 57^v

1581.   a new yeres gift   g
If Momus wish had taken place, that to eche mortall mynd,
  A dore or window had byn made, therbie his thoughtes to fynd

    Item 308] To the right of the 'g' in the title line are two or three indistinguishable characters, perhaps an ill-formed 'P. gt.'

Good Madā then you should haue seene, the mynd wch I you bear
more fraught wth loue then Cresus bagges, wth worldly pelf ere were.
But sithe ther can no suche like way, be found or els assignd [5
   for to conveighe the eyes into, the caban of the mynd
I must contented be in wordes, to shew my loving hart
wch so is setled in good will, that yt shall never start
As long as either I my self, shall able be to know
or that wth bellowes of my longes, my vitall breathe shall blow. [10
As dutie therfore doth me bynd, in this beginning year
I wishe vnto your ladiship all ioye & happie chear
Suche as the flattering nurse doth wish, when babe she holdes in lap
and feedes her little tender impe, wth sweete & sugred pappe.
God graunt you may in yeres outlyue, the old & aeged Greeke [15
And eke obtayn at fortunes handes, the thinges that you most seeke
I wishe to you as many ioyes, as leaves frō trees do fall
when frostie winter ginnes to bite, & nippes the roote & all
As many pleasures do I wish as birdes to vs repair
frō frostie Scythian land when cold, dothe make thē seeke warme ayr [20
As many contentations as, be waves in Africke sea
when roughe Orion hides himself, & lettes the wyndes thē play
As many sportes as stalkes of corne, be parched in the sonne
In fruictfull fieldes of Licie land, or wher that Herme dothe run.
And that when you haue traced the pathe, of this vnquiet lif [25
   You may in joyes for aye remayn, wher i⟨s⟩ no worldly strife

Accept of thes rude verses w^{ch}

yong wilkin doth you send

As messengers of his good will

& so he makes an end

28.

[Item 309] [f. 62^v]

My wife like Niobe is turnd to stone my name is fortunes chance,   Lot
now tell yt me for knowen yt is in England & in fraunce

[Item 310]

2. The noblest clown did wed, of all ye fairest dame
they parentes never had/ tell yf thou canst ther name ⟨Noe⟩ Adam & Eva.

[Item 311]

                                                        largest
.3. What pilot ever wth his ship did sail on greatest seas   Noe.
& nighest to ye skies was born wth monstrous swelling waues

[Item 312]

4. Whose deathe bemond before he died was 90. yeares & horee   Iosephe.
& who was told by dreame that he a famous prince should be

[Item 313]

5. What woer ever bare ye bell in throwing in a sling   david
& won vnto his wife therbie ye daughter of a king   convay .

    Items 309, 310, and 313 are individually bracketed on the right,
while Items 311 and 312 are enclosed with a single bracket on the right.
The answers to the riddles fall to the right of these brackets.

[Item 314]

6 who ever did most of on kin from libick land ⟨transport⟩   Moses.

  to fruictfull Asia & them led ⟨this h⟩ most ⟨woundrus⟩ sort
                                     ye   vns⟨ tte⟩ waye

[Item 315]

Tell wher yt was ye cat would see ye little mise all dede   holofernes.

& for ye same by them did leese his life & eke his head

[Item 316]

Tell me what ladie by .2. lordes was brought to greife & blame   Susanna.

& clered by the names of trees her ennymies put to shame.

[Item 317]

What Pilot ever wth his ship throughe deepest seas did flie

  & caried was by surges strange most nere vnto ye skie.

[Item 318]   [f. 63

     A pastie of red dere cold. & a loaf of bread of a day old.

                 & a runt of ye first hea⟨r⟩

a pintle of 21 year . written wth a holie nunnes hand . is the best

              thing in all ye land.

[Item 319]

Nature hath shewed her self to me vnkynd

she nether gaue me legges nor armes nor but on ey to see   a

   Items 314-316, and 319 are bracketed along the right margin, with
the answers to the riddles to the right of the brackets.

   Item 318] No carry-over lines in the MS.

yet many a depe wound haue I made & left my tent behind me.   nedle
& loue to be wth maidens kynd goe seeke & you shall fynd me

[Item 320]

Nature a niggard of her giftes hathe shewed herself to me
she nether gaue me armes nor legges & but on eye to see   nedle
yet many a depe wound haue I made & left my tent behind me
among woemen kynd I loue to be goe seeke & you shall fynd me

[Item 321]

I saw a wonder wondrous was the sight ye name therof is nedeles
to recite
her eye was in her foote, hart in her head, mouthe had she none
but by ye eye was fed
she clothed her self an hundred tymes a day: [5] 100 tymes she cast
her clothes away   a
she daunct alday vppon a syluer hill, skipping frō thence, thither
returning still   ned⟨le⟩
I question askt on did this answer bring. yt was a woman or a
womans thing.

[Item 322]

A certain man bespake a thing wch when ye owner home did bring
                                                              a a dead mans
he y^t bespake yt would not vse yt & he y^t made yt did refuse yt
                                                                  coffen.

   Items 320-322 are bracketed along the right margin, with the
answers entered to the right of the brackets.

   Item 321] No carry-over lines in the MS.

& he yt had yt did not knowe [5] whither he had yt yea or noe

[Item 323]

5 Theues came to my house & wrapt me all in woe   a fishe. water net

  my house leapt out at ye windowes & left me⟨ ⟩wth my foe

[Item 324]

6 It was my chance of late to see 4. frendes all ioined in amitie

                   count
  I cald them frendes & ⟨   ⟩ them soe because they never a

                  sonder goe   Millesailes

  among these 4. a strife begon [5] wch should eche other

                  ouerrun

  A long swift course they fetche about & ended where they first

                  set out

  & yet ye race being trulie run not on of ye other an inche

                  had wonne   [10

[Item 325]

7. The goodwife went to ye market & stombled at a roote

  ye bignes of her arme ye lengthe of her foote.

  she tooke yt in her hand & put yt to her thighe.

  & cald yt lambkin wth on ey.

    Items 323-325 are bracketed along the right margin; the answers to the riddles are entered to the right of these brackets.

    Item 324] No carry-over lines in the MS.

[Item 326]

8. The goodwife hathe in store a handfull & more

      beside ye hair   a brushe

  & ever & anone. she takes yt in her hand & put<u>es</u> yt

     to her geere.   [5

althoughe yt be bad it makes her hart glad yet aege

     makes yt were

[Item 327]

9. I haue a thing yt standethe stiffe in ye end yt hath a cliffe. a pen.

  & yeldethe moisture in such sort as makes ye fairest

    lady sport

[Item 328]   [f. 63^v]

  Anigmata.

Ther was a ladie leaned her backe to a wall

   he tokte vppe peticote smocke & all

   he laid her legg vppon his knee

   yt was a⟨s⟩ white, as white might bee   A shooe.

he tooke a thing that stiffe did stand   [5

   & hunched her & punched her & made great game

O god<u>es</u> bodie sayd she fie for shame

   yet he would not leaue her so

   Items 326 and 327 are bracketed along the right margin, with the answers to the riddles to the right of the brackets. There are no carry-over lines in the MS.

    did
but he would ease her & please her befor he would goe
      [Item 329]

Two stones hathe yt or els yt is wrong
 wth a bald hed & a tag somwhat long   A clocke
& in the ⟨ ⟩ night when wymen lie awake
 into ther conscience they doe yt take
      [Item 330]

I haue a hole aboue my knee
 & pricked yt was & pricked shalbe   sheathe
& yet it is not sore
& yet yt shalbe pricked more
      [Item 331]

  a
I haue thing & roughe yt is
 & in the middest a hole ther is   a gloue
ther cam a yong man wth his gin
& thrust yt even a handfull in
      [Item 332]

backe bent smocke rent
 slipperie yt was & in yt went

thrust in stiffe standing
           a tost
 it comes out lithe & dropping
Stife standnging roughe handling
 betwene a womans legges in a mornīg

-218-

[Item 333]

ther is a thing as I suppose

wch hath a face but never a nose   a peache

hath a mouth but no toth therin

hath a beard but never a chin

[Item 334]

Cut wth a a com hunt

to cocke. tread. to thred pearles

[Item 335]

ludimagister qui quicquid p⟨u⟩er egisset in nates euis se ide̅
velle expeniminaret/ tande̅ cū eū lances et discos lingente̅ ce⟨ ⟩
velle se etiā eius nates lingere/ exclamavit ide̅ de osculo./
Adæisceus qui muliere̅ se osculari velle dixisset cū aut rideret
aut suspiraret emisso/ crepitu iussus est etiā podice̅ besiare, q°
suspiriū esset/[5] moribundus testametū conscripsit, his verbis vt
multū Cerevisiū daretur paulutu/ prius, tande̅ illud de pane delendū
inssit, euis quoq; loco poni Cerevisiā ⟨tū⟩/ mulieres ex ossibus
fabricatæ, huic congregatæ, instar ossiū tumultuantur./ fati
doctrinā concionater quis re ipsa elusit, nō cū secū tucetī, et
lapidi/ in sui detulisset vtrimq; deinde quanto potuit impetu in
auditores conie/ [10] coniecturā, huic capieas/

 Item 333 is enclosed in a small ruled rectangle opposite Item 331;
" a peache" is to the right of the rectangle.

 Item 335:1] The caret is in the MS. 11] The slash at the end of
the line is in the MS.

[Item 336]

he hath much nede of god his blessing wch kneles to a thistell. sro sapio

[Item 337]

In absence cheif to rest. in presence second best

bent to content yf you so will chuse: but either playn dealing or

flatly refuse.

[Item 338]

syr Ihon hunt, cut my punt, hunt my cut, cut my punt.

[Item 339]

as wemen haue faces to set mens hartes on fire

so wemen haue places to quench ther hot desire

Item 337] Lines 3 and 4 are written as one line in the MS.

SIGLA

* In the Notes, asterisks are used in the collations to indicate that all the texts being collated against Dd.5.75 agree in the reading which immediately precedes the asterisk.

31   Rawlinson Poetry MS 31

64   Additional MS 34064

76   Paradise of Dainty Devices, edition of 1576 (ed. Rollins), STC 7516

78   Paradise of Dainty Devices, edition of 1578 (ed. Rollins), STC 7517

90   Sidney's Arcadia, 1590, STC 22539, 22539a

93   Sidney's Arcadia, 1593, STC 22540

98   Sidney's Arcadia, 1598, STC 22541

1575 Baldwin's Treatise of Moral Philosophy, 1575, STC 1260

1579 Baldwin's Treatise of Moral Philosophy, 1579, STC 1260a

1581 Desportes' Les Premieres Oevvres (Paris, 1581)

1583 Desportes' Les Oevvres De Philippes De Portes (Lyons, 1583)

1584 Baldwin's Treatise of Moral Philosophy, 1584, STC 1261

1587 Baldwin's Treatise of Moral Philosophy, 1587, STC 1262

1591 Desportes' Les Oevvres De Philippes De Portes (Antwerp, 1591)

A   Ashmole MS 781

A17 Additional MS 15117

A38 Ashmole MS 38

Ad   Additional MS 15227

-221-

AH	The Arundel Harington Manuscript (ed. Hughey)
Am	Spenser's Amoretti and Epithalamion, 1595, STC 23076
As	Huntington MS HM 162
B	William Barley's A New Booke of Tabliture, 1596, STC 1433
Ba	Additional MS 28253
Bn	The Bannatyne Manuscript (ed. The Hunterian Club)
Bo	Bodleian è Museo MS 37
C	Folger MS 1.112 (Anne Cornwallis' manuscript)
Ch	Chetham MS 8012 (ed. Grosart)
Cl	Folger MS 4009.03
Cm	Cambridge University Library MS Kk.1.5
Co	Egerton MS 2642
D	Brittons Bowre of Delights, 1597, STC 3634
Da	Additional MS 41204
Do	John Dowland's First Booke of Songes or Ayres, 1597, STC 7091
Dy	Dyce MS 44
E	Egerton MS 3165 (Sir Arthur Gorges' manuscript)
EH	England's Helicon, 1600, 1614 (ed. Rollins), STC 3191, 3192
F	Folger MS 452.4
F1	Folger MS 2073.4
Fn	Rawlinson Poetry MS 85 (John Finet's manuscript)
Fo	Folger MS 1.28
G	Gorgious Gallery of Gallant Inventions, 1578 (ed. Rollins), STC 20402
H	Harley MS 6910
H37	Harley MS 3787

H73	Harley MS 7371
HD	*A Help to Discourse*, 1619, STC 1547
Ho	Wye Plantation, Maryland, Arthur A. Houghton, Jr. MS (described by Ringler, pp. 540-541)
Ht	Huntington MS 198
Je	Oxford University, Jesus College MS 150
Kn	Harley MS 7392 (2) (St. Loe Knyveton's manuscript)
L	Lansdowne MS 740
Le	Additional MS 41498
M	Marsh's Library, Dublin MS 183
MM	*Marre Mar-Martin*, 1589 (?), STC 17462
Mo	Thomas Morley's *First Book of Airs*, 1610 (not listed by the STC; ed. Fellowes)
MT	*Musica Transalpina*, 1588, STC 26094
NA	*Nugae Antiquae*, 1769
PDD	*Paradise of Dainty Devices*, all editions, 1576-1606 (ed. Rollins), STC 7516-7524
Ph	Additional MS 38892
Pm	Pierpont Morgan Library, "Rulers of England" Collection, Queen Elizabeth, Vol. I, Folio Sheet MS
PN	*Phoenix Nest*, 1593 (ed. Rollins), STC 21516
PR	*Poetical Rhapsody*, 1602-1621 (ed. Rollins), STC 6373-6376
Qu	Oxford University, Queen's College MS 301
R	Rawlinson Poetry MS 153
R17	Rawlinson Poetry MS 117
Ra	Rawlinson Poetry MS 172
S	Stowe MS 932

Sl   Sloane MS 1446

So   Sloane MS 1489

St   Cambridge University, St. John's College MS I.7

T   Tanner MS 306

Tn   Tanner MS 169

ABBREVIATED APPARATUS

Item	Contemporary Texts	Notes and Collations
1-17	none	pp. 231-238
18	Lady Ann Lee's monument, Aylesbury Church, Buckinghamshire	pp. 239-240
19	none	p. 240
20	STC 3308-3313, 12412; the prints bear no demonstrable relation to the longer Dd.5.75 text.	pp. 240-241
21-27	none	pp. 231-238
28	Thomas Tallis' epitaph, Church of St. Alphege, Greenwich, as transcribed by John Strype in his continuation of Stowe's Survey of London	pp. 241-243
29	A38, Ad, Ch, So, STC 4521	pp. 243-244
30-32	none	pp. 231-238
33-45	none	pp. 244-245
46	none	p. 245
47-54	none (Riddles Englished from a French translation of Straparola's Le Piacevoli Notti)	pp. 245-247
55	none	p. 247
56	none (anonymous translation of Petrarch's Rime 21)	pp. 247-249
57	none	p. 249
58-61	none	pp. 249, 254-256

Item	Contemporary Texts	Notes and Collations
62-65	none	pp. 249, 256
66-67	none	pp. 249, 256
68	none	pp. 249, 257
69-83	none	pp. 249-254
84	none	pp. 249, 257
85	STC 4510; a commendatory sonnet attributed to Henry Stanford, having only three verbal variants from the Dd.5.75 text.	pp. 249, 257-259
86	none	pp. 249, 259-260
87-88	none	pp. 249-254
89	none	pp. 249, 260
90-92	none	pp. 249-254
93	none	pp. 249, 261
94	none	pp. 261-262
95	A, AH, Fn, H, Ht, Kn, M, T; attributed to Sir edward Dyer by Fn, Kn, and T, a claim further substantiated by the pun in line 78.	pp. 262-269
96	93, 98, AH, As, Bo, Cl, Da, Fn, H, Kn, Le, Ph, Qu, St (Sidney)	pp. 269-276
97-98	none	p. 276
99	Kn, Mo	pp. 276-277
100	(see Item 195)	pp. 269-276
101	93, 98, As, Da, Fn, Je, Qu, St (Sidney)	pp. 269-276
102	93, 98, As, Da, Ph, Qu, St (Sidney)	pp. 269-276
103	93, 98, As, Da, Ph, Qu, St (Sidney)	pp. 269-276
104-105	none	p. 278

Item	Contemporary Texts	Notes and Collations
106	98, AH, Ba, EH, Kn, St (Sidney)	pp. 269-276
107	90, 93, 98, AH, Cl, Cm, Fn, St, STC 3631, 11338	pp. 269-276
108	none	p. 278
109	31, A, Ad, C, F, Fn, Fo, H, Kn, PN, R, S, Harley MS 4064, Rawlinson Poetry MS 84, Rosenbach MS 192 (Ralegh)	pp. 278-281
110	STC 13569	pp. 282-284
111	none	p. 284
112	NA, Tn, Additional MSS 32379, 33271, Harley MSS 787, 4808	pp. 284-290
113	C, Co, Fn, H37, Kn, M, Pm, Tn, Ellesmere MS described by Grierson, Poems of John Donne, II, xcix.	pp. 291-296
114-115	none	p. 296
116-137	copied from MT	pp. 296-299
138-146	none	pp. 299-300
147-164	Bn (Items 160-162 only), Ho (Items 157, 164 only), Sloane MS 2497 (Item 151 only); Bn was copied from the 1567 edition of Baldwin's Treatise of Moral Philosophy, STC 1259, while Stanford copied from this or a later edition of the same work.	pp. 300-303
165	none (Stanford attributes this poem to "ferd. Strange," i.e., Ferdinando Stanley, fifth Earl of Derby).	pp. 304-305
166-167	none	pp. 305-307
168-178	(A continuation of the series begun with Items 147-164). Bn (Items 168-169, 177-178 only), Ho (Items 175-176 only); Bn was copied from the 1567 edition of Baldwin's Treatise of Moral Philosophy, STC 1259, while Stanford copied from this or a later edition of the same work.	pp. 300-303

Item	Contemporary Texts	Notes and Collations
179-180	none	p. 307
181	Dy	pp. 307-308
182	1581, 1583, 1591	pp. 308-310
183-187	MM	pp. 311-313
188	Mo	pp. 313-315
189-190	none	p. 315
191	F (first two lines only)	pp. 315-318
192	E (Gorges)	pp. 316, 318-319
193	Ad, B, E, Kn, PN, PR, R17, Additional MS 22118	pp. 316, 319-321
194	As, Da, Ph, Qu, St (Sidney)	pp. 269-276
195	The complete text of Item 100; 64, 90, 93, 98, As, Cm, Da, F, Je, Ph, Qu, St, Additional MS 27406, Egerton MS 2421, Sloane MS 1925, STC 378-180 (Sidney)	pp. 269-276
196	90, 93, 98, As, Cm, Da, H, Kn, Ph, Qu, St, Additional MS 22118, STC 378-380 (Sidney)	pp. 269-276
197	Am, Fn, Kn, Sl (Spenser)	pp. 321-324
198	64, H, Fn (subscribed "La: R." in H, "Britton," in Fn)	pp. 324-326
199	E (Gorges)	pp. 316, 326
200	64, 90, 93, 98, As, Cm, Da, Je, Ph, Qu, St (Sidney)	pp. 269-276
201	64, EH, Fn (ascribed to "Britton" in Fn, and to "N. Breton" by a cancel slip in EH)	pp. 327-329
202	C, Fl, Fn, Kn (attributed to "l: of oxforde" in C, to "ELY" in Kn, and to "Elysabethe regina" by Fn)	pp. 329-332
203	none	p. 332

Item	Contemporary Texts	Notes and Collations
204	E (Gorges)	pp. 316, 332-333
205	A17, E, PR (Gorges)	pp. 316, 333-336
206-207	none	p. 336
208	E, Fn, Kn, PN (Gorges)	pp. 316, 337-338
209	Do, Dy	pp. 338-341
210-211	none	p. 341
212-213	64, AH, Fn, L, and the Rosenbach MS described by Tannenbaum, PMLA, XLV, 821.	pp. 341, 344-359
214	H73	pp. 341, 360-362
215	STC 5250 (Churchyard)	pp. 341, 362-363
216	C, H, Fn, Kn (ascribed to Dyer in C, Fn, and Kn; last two lines quoted by Sir John Harington, STC 746	pp. 341, 363-366
217	Appeared first in the second edition of Tottel's Miscellany, 1557, STC 13861; reprinted in all later editions.	pp. 341, 366-367
218	none	pp. 341, 367
219	PDD (attributed to "W. H." [William Hunnis?])	pp. 341, 368
220	none	pp. 341, 369
221	PDD (A combination of two poems from the Paradise, one ascribed to Lord Vaux, the other, to Jasper Heywood; Vaux's poem also appears in B and H, Heywood's, in G)	pp. 341, 369-370
222	AH, Kn	pp. 341, 370-372
223	PDD (attributed to William Hunnis)	pp. 341, 372
224-226	none	pp. 341, 372
227	76 (ascribed to Richard Hill)	pp. 341, 373
228	none	pp. 341, 373
229-234	Copied from STC 18044	pp. 341, 374-375

Item	Contemporary Texts	Notes and Collations
235-236	none	p. 375
237	98, Do, EH, University of Edinburgh MS De.5.96 (Sidney)	p. 375
238-251	none	p. 375
252-280	none	p. 375
281-283	none	p. 375
284-293	none	pp. 375-377
294-296	none	p. 377
297	HD (Stanford's text varies widely from the print)	pp. 377-378
298-306	none	p. 378
307-308	none	pp. 378, 231
309-317	none	p. 378
318-320	none	p. 379
321	Rawlinson Poetry MS 212	p. 379
322	HD, Ra, S1	pp. 379-380
323-338	none	p. 380
339	Kn	p. 380

NOTES

A Prefatory Note to Items 1-94, 307-308

These entries occupy ff. 1-20 and f. 57, and thus comprise the first twenty-one leaves of Dd.5.75 in its original state, since f. 57 originally preceded f. 1. Stanford devoted this, his "domestic" section to works by himself, his pupils, and, perhaps, other members of the households in which he served. He apparently intended for this section to continue through f. 24, but completed only these twenty-one leaves, for ff. 21-24 are blank.

Items 1-17, 21-27, 30-32, 307-308

While household tutor to the Pagets, Stanford seems to have entered in his anthology Items 1-32 complete, and 307-308, although the following notes are concerned only with the poems written by William Paget, later fourth Baron Paget, under Stanford's direction. This group consists of the New Year's gifts dated 1581-1586 (Items 1-6, 11-17, 21-27, 30-32, and 307-308), and the riddles and their answers, Items 7-10.[1] By modern reckoning, the transcription

---

[1] Items 307 and 308, on f. 57, are considered here because both are entitled as New Year's gifts for 1582. Folio 57, moreover, was originally the first leaf in the manuscript. Its date suggests that it must belong with the only other works assigned to 1582, Items 1-10 on ff. 1-3, while Stanford's habit of recording the number of lines in his pupil's works exactly determines its original position in Dd. 5.75. Stanford wrote "36" at the end of Item 2, for example, a poem of thirty-six lines, and similar tallies appear after Items 3, 4, 5, 12, 15, and 16, among others. But the "68" after Item 1 does not fit this twenty-eight line poem, although when added to the forty lines of Item 307, the total is correct. Items 307 and 1, then, are one poem, beginning on f. 57^r and ending on f. 1^r; in addition to the evidence of Stanford's "68," both Items are written in poulter's measure and the content of 307:40 ties in gracefully enough with

of these poems occurred between New Year's, 1582, and the same date in 1587, for it was the common Elizabethan practise to exchange New Year's gifts on or about the first of January, but to delay changing the number of the year until March twenty-fifth. Thus, Stanford's dates throughout must be increased by one to agree with the Gregorian calendar, and to avoid confusion, dates in this note are given only their modern equivalent.

Young Paget apparently wrote all of these poems between the ages of nine and fourteen years, albeit not without generous assistance from Stanford.[1] Each poem was written for a specific member of William's family, and while a pair of gloves was presented along with Item 2, the poems themselves apparently served as the gift in all other cases. As a group, these New Year's gifts reflect the declining fortunes of the Paget family between 1582 and 1587, and especially, the personal misfortunes young William endured as a result.

His parents, Thomas, third Baron Paget, and Nazareth Newton Paget, had arranged a separation early in 1582, through no less an

---

1:1. Both Items, furthermore, must have been entered on adjacent pages; thus, Item 307 on f. 57^r must have appeared originally as poem 2 on the verso of the first leaf of the manuscript. Item 308 was originally the first poem of the collection (unless other folios are missing), but recto and verso were interchanged when the folio became detached and was thrust outer edge first into its present position in Dd.5.75.

[1] The title of Item 23 records that Paget was twelve years, fourteen days old on 1 January 1585. Echoes of the Paget juvenilia in Stanford's own verses and in those which George Berkeley composed under his direction, testify to the importance of Stanford's influence on his pupils' work (cf. Paget's poem 14:1-7 with Stanford's greeting to Lady Hunsdon, Item 66:5-9, similar repetitions in Stanford's later verses, Items 84, 85, and 92, and the rhetoric of Berkeley's poems 70, 71, and 88, with Paget's in Items 11, 23, and 27).

intermediary than Lord Treasurer Burghley himself.[1] Nazareth died 16 April 1583, and Thomas, fearing a charge of complicity upon exposure of the Throckmorton plot, fled to the continent in late November of the same year. His flight, unfortunately, left those at home to bear the full burden of a long-lasting official investigation into the family loyalty, which ultimately resulted in William Paget's transfer to the wardship of Sir George Carey, 27 February 1587.[2] By 20 December 1583, Thomas' mother, Ann Preston Paget, was subjected to so thorough an examination as "'left not so much as the very planks'" of her Fleet Street residence unsearched. The homes of Thomas' sisters, Etheldreda Allen and Griselda Waldegrave, underwent the same ransacking during the next few years, family servants, including Stanford, were "examined" at length by the authorities, and Thomas himself was finally attainted of high treason in 1587.[3]

William Paget's attempts to comfort members of his family through his New Year's poems during these years show that he was fully aware of the difficulties which beset them in his father's absence. His own unhappiness, expectedly, is most fully expressed in the poetic gifts of 1584 (Items 16 and 17), just after Thomas' flight, while references in 1585 to "irksom pensiue greifes" (Item 21:28), and "redresse of greif & comfort every wayes" (Item 23:25), mark his concern for the

---

[1] John Strype, *Annals of the Reformation* (4 vols.; London, 1820-1840), III, Part I, 88.

[2] John Roche Dasent, ed., *Acts of the Privy Council of England*, XIV (London, 1897), 352.

[3] Robert Lemon, ed., *Calendar of State Papers, Domestic Series, Elizabeth, 1581-1590*, CLXIV (London, 1865), 138, Article 47; Sophie Crawford Lomas, ed., *Calendar of State Papers Foreign Series, July 1583-July 1584* (London, 1914), p. 348, Article 415; George Edward Cockayne, *The Complete Peerage*, X (London, 1945), 280.

troubles faced by the other members of his family.

Exactly which members of his family young Paget was trying to comfort, it is not always possible to determine. The "grandame" who received one or more poems each New Year's day (Items 1 and 307, 13, 16, 23, 24, and 27), must have been his paternal grandmother, Lady Ann Paget, widow of William, First Baron Paget. She seems to have headed the family at their West Drayton house after her son, Thomas, had crossed the channel,[1] and William had apparently remained with her since at least the time of his mother's death. His rejoicing in Items 30 and 32 over his grandmother's recovery from an illness on New Year's, 1587, was premature, for Lady Ann died that February and complete dissolution of what was left of the Paget household followed shortly thereafter.

William's aunts are also mentioned frequently in these juvenile verses: in Item 8, the answer to the riddle posed in Item 7, and in four New Year's greetings, Items 11, 25, 26, and 27. The grieving women addressed in Items 15 and 21 may also have been his aunts, but identification is complicated by the possibility that as many as nineteen of William's aunts may have been alive during the 1580's. Since the records I have examined do not mention a single member of Nazareth's family in any way associated with the Pagets at this time, and since William describes the aunt addressed in Item 11 as "the sister to my syre" (line 14), I have assumed that all the ladies in question were relatives on the Paget side of the family. Even so,

---

[1] Cockayne, X, 280.

any or all of Thomas Paget's six sisters could have been addressed in these works, although I have found only two of them who can be definitely connected with the Pagets during these years. First, Sir Henry Lee's wife, Lady Ann Paget Lee, was living with her mother at West Drayton in 1584,[1] and her two epitaphs in Stanford's anthology, Items 18 and 19, are further indications of her prominence in the household. Second, Griselda Paget Waldegrave must have maintained some contact with the family since her husband, Sir William Waldegrave, is named first among the executors of "the late Lo. Paget" in the Privy Council directive of 1587, which ordered him to deliver young Paget into Sir George Carey's custody. The aunts in question, then, were most likely to have been the Ladies Lee and Waldegrave, in the absence of other candidates.

Identification of the unmarried young women addressed in Items 2, 3, 4, 12, and 14 is even less certain. The two sisters who received Item 12 were William's kinswomen, according to line 15, and Items 5 and 6 as well were perhaps intended for his cousins, as Items 17 and 22 certainly were. Paget, with nineteen aunts, had a great many cousins, of course, and only Item 5, written in 1582, offers any real clue toward a specific identification. This poem praises a young woman through the praise of a flower, the marigold; presumably, then, the woman's name was Mary. About 1553, William Forrest had employed exactly the same metaphor to praise Queen Mary in his "New Ballade of the Marigolde," reprinted in 1570 (STC 11186), presumably in tribute to Mary Stuart,

---

[1] E. K. Chambers, Sir Henry Lee (Oxford, 1936), p. 77.

Queen of Scots. Assuming that young Paget was using the same convention, he might have been writing to Ann Lee's daughter, Mary, who died "in flower & prime of all her yeares" according to her mother's epitaph (Item 18: 14), though probably not before 1583.[1]

Griselda Waldegrave's daughter, Ann, and her two step-daughters by marriage to her first husband, Sir Thomas Rivett, may also have been recipients of some of young William's poetry, but again, real evidence is lacking.

Aside from William and Lady Paget, Lady Ann Lee, and the Waldegraves, perhaps, it is impossible to say with whom Stanford was associated during his years with the Pagets. We are on firmer ground, however, in identifying the literary influences at work in the Paget juvenilia, and in determining the importance of these influences as they relate to Stanford's poetic taste. Most of young William's verses are written in the favorite "Drab Age" meters, poulter's and fourteener couplets, and all exemplify the rhetorical principle of copiousness. The series of anaphoras in Items 11:27-34, 13:1-17, and 15:1-16, for instance, allowed young Paget to be "copious" by providing a rhetorical structure upon which he could drape a number of lines of verse with a minimum of strain upon his fledgling powers of invention. Through similar devices in his other poems, William derived maximal opportunities to practice versification in the copious repetition of only a few essential ideas. The line count Stanford usually recorded at the end of each poem his pupil wrote provides further evidence that quantity output was a first principle in Stanford's theory of poetic instruction.

---

[1] Ibid., p. 79.

By 1586, a specific practitioner of the "Drab Age" copious school of poetry emerges as the model for William Paget's works. Items 24-27 show unquestionable dependence on George Turberville's Epitaphes, Epigrams, Songs and Sonets, published in at least two editions, in 1567 and in 1570 (STC 24326, and 24327).[1] Turberville's "Assured Promise of a Constant Louer," which begins, "When Phenix shall haue many Makes,"[2] was closely imitated in poems 24 and 27, both of which adopt the iambic tetrameter couplets of their model and consist chiefly of a similar list of impossible conditions couched in the same "and / when" rhetorical structure used by Turberville.

Paget's examples within this list, furthermore, are in general mere rephrasings, and in one place a word for word copy, of the original; Paget's "when hauk<u>es</u> shall dread the little bird / & men of owles shalbe afeard" (Item 24: 13-14), for example, corresponds to Turberville's "When Hawkes shall dread the sielie Fowle / And men esteeme the nightish Owle," Paget's "when laurell leaves shall loose ther hew / & frend<u>es</u> no where found to be true" (Item 27: 9-10), modeled on Turberville's "When Lawrell leaues shall lose their hue, / And men of Crete be counted true." Similarly, Items 25 and 26 are based on Turberville's "Vow to Serue Faithfully," which begins, "In greene and growing age, in lustie yeeres."[3]

---

[1] Quotations from Turberville follow the edition of 1570, as edited by Alexander Chalmers, <u>The Works of the English Poets</u> (21 vols.; London, 1810), II, 581-652.

[2] Ibid., pp. 618-619.

[3] Ibid.

Item 25 rephrases in order the conditions through which William will be dutiful to his aunt, as Turberville catalogues those through which he will remain constant in love: in good fortune or bad, day or night, in summer or winter, and so forth. Both poems achieve copiousness by repeating one idea with numerous examples. Poem 26 varies the order of the examples somewhat, but follows the model closely enough to substitute "In latter tyme when sylver hear<u>es</u> appear<u>es</u>" (26:2), for "In latter dayes when siluer bush apeers," and "by daye when phe<u>bus</u> glorious beames appear / by night when foggie mist<u>es</u> do clowde the ayr" (26: 13-14), for "By day when Phoebus shewes his princely pride, / By night when golden Starres in skies doe glide."

It is doubtful that Stanford's reliance on Turberville here, or that any works by his pupils, for that matter, tell us very much about Stanford's own poetic tastes between 1582 and 1587; mid-century meters and copiousness served well for instructive purposes, but Stanford apparently did not feel that Turberville's poetry warranted a place in the serious portion of his anthology. Granted, Stanford copied four <u>Paradise of Dainty Devices</u> excerpts (Items 219, 221, 223, and 227), "Drab" poetry little superior to Turberville's, into the "public" section of Dd.5.75; yet Stanford's overall taste in lyric poetry was well above the mid-century standard. For teaching purposes, however, he continued to favor the older tradition, and even toward the end of his life, after long exposure to such "Golden Age" practitioners as Sidney, Spenser, and Breton, saw fit to instruct George Berkeley in the same copious production of poulter's and fourteeners he had taught to Will Paget a quarter century before.

Item 18

Lady Ann Lee, young William Paget's aunt, and third daughter of William, First Baron Paget,[1] was buried in the church at Aylesbury, Buckinghamshire, 31 December, 1590.[2] Her epitaph was inscribed on her monument in 1584, at least six years before her death, a date which agrees with the position of the epitaph in Dd.5.75, between Item 17, a New Year's gift for 1583/84, and Item 21, a gift for 1584/85. The following collation with the Aylesbury monument text follows the transcription in Chambers' Sir Henry Lee, p. 77.

    title] om.

10 her feere a knight wch Henry Lee was cald] A knight her feere Sir Henry Lee he hight

12 Harry; sone by death appald] Henry; slayn by fortvnes spight

13 wch causd her for to mone] cavsed ther par$\bar{e}$ts m$\bar{o}$e

17-24] om.

27 for certes] for svre

"Incisū" in the Latin title Stanford added to the poem suggests that he had access to a copy of the epitaph taken from the monument, or he may have copied it directly himself. To it he added a fifth stanza, ll. 17-20, which he set off with rules when copying the entire poem into his anthology. He then corrected his miscopying of lines 15 and 25, added a stanza in the margin, lines 21-24, and revised lines 10, 12, 13, and 27, to suit his own taste. Since his original readings in the latter instances agree with the text as it appears on the monument, it seems

---

[1] Sir Egerton Brydges, Collins's Peerage of England, V (London, 1812), 185.

[2] Chambers, Sir Henry Lee, p. 77.

unlikely that Stanford wrote the epitaph, in that none of his corrections are found in the final version of Lady Ann's epitaph.

Item 19

This second epitaph on Lady Ann Lee, apparently a unique text, seems also to have been transcribed during 1584. Assuming that "Lilly" in the right margin beside this poem refers to its author, the attribution might support R. W. Bond's belief that John Lyly had written works in prose and verse for Sir Henry Lee.[1] Bond attributes to Lyly the entertainment Lee arranged for Her Majesty in 1592, "Speeches to Queen Elizabeth at Quarrendon: August, 1592," and "Speeches and Verses at the Tilt-Yard, 1590-1600," which includes a piece that Lee himself recited.[2] E. K. Chambers, however, is doubtful of Lyly's authorship, definitely assigning the entertainment of 1592 to Richard Edes, and transferring its presentation to Lee's estate at Woodstock.[3] As for the epitaph, the quality of the verse would certainly seem to argue against John Lyly's responsibility for it.

Item 20

Quite a different version of this poem occurs in five editions of The Book of Hawking and Hunting, popularly known as The Book of St. Albans, supposedly written by Dame Juliana Berners.[4] In each of these

---

[1] R. W. Bond, ed., The Complete Works of John Lyly, I (photographic reproduction, Oxford, 1967), 404.

[2] Ibid., pp. 410-416, 453-470.

[3] Chambers, Sir Henry Lee, p. 145.

[4] STC 3308, 1485, F4^v; 3309, 1496, E2^v; 3310, 1540, h3-3^v; 3311, 1563?, h3-3^v; 3313, 1586, G1; I have not seen STC 3312, printed by

texts, lines 4 and 5 are omitted, while lines 7 and 8 are replaced by such variants as "syded lyke a teme:/ and chynyd like a beme" (edition of 1496, K2^v), or "sided like a Breame,/ and chined like a Beame" (edition of 1586, G2). As with Items 18 and 19, this poem was probably entered in the manuscript sometime during 1584.

Item 28

The distinguished musician Thomas Tallis died 23 November 1585, and was buried in the parish Church of St. Alphege, Greenwich; his epitaph, Item 28, was engraved on a brass plate marking the tomb.[1] The "Decembris Die" following the epitaph in Dd.5.75, along with the position of this poem just after the New Year's verses for 1585/86, suggest that these gifts, Items 24-27, were prepared and copied with

---

William Copland sometime before January, 1561/62, when he was fined for printing "a boke of hawkynge huntinge and fysshinge contrary to the orders of this howse" (Arber, I, 185). Presumably Copland had reprinted an earlier edition of the book, to which he had no license, and thus the grayhound poem was probably little different in his edition from the earlier versions.

The edition of 1486 appeared in facsimile reprint as The Boke of Saint Albans, by Dame Juliana Berners, introd. William Blades (London, 1901). The "St. Alban's" text of the poem is also found in a versified edition of the book, Hawking, Hunting, Fouling, and Fishing (London, 1596), G2 (STC 12412), attributed to William Gryndall.

[1] I have collated Stanford's text with that made by the antiquarian John Strype from the plate in St. Alphege's (John Stowe, A Survey of the Cities of London and Westminster . . . Corrected, Improved, and very much Enlarged . . . by John Strype (2 vols.; London, 1720), II, Book 6, 92. Since "the inscription was renewed by Dean Aldrich" some hundred years after Tallis' death (DNB, XIX, 349), it is impossible to say who is responsible for the error at line 3 and omission in line 5; shortly after Strype copied the epitaph, St. Alphege's was destroyed.

The epitaph has been reprinted from Strype in Charles Burney, A General History of Music From the Earliest Ages to the Present Period, 1789, reprinted with critical and historical notes by Frank Mercer, II (New York, 1935), 68; Dr. William Boyce, Cathedral Music, I (London, 1849), 16; Sir John Hawkins, A General History of the Science and Practice of Music, I (London, 1875), 458; B. C. Buck, et al., eds., Tudor Church Music, VI (Oxford, 1928), xv.

the epitaph during December, 1585. Apparently, then, Stanford had access to the epitaph within a few weeks of Tallis' death, and while it seems unlikely that the brass plate could have been prepared so quickly, Stanford does specify in the title he added to the poem that it was "incisū" on Tallis' tomb. This may indicate that Tallis was as provident in funeral matters as Sir Henry Lee, who had made ready Item 18, his wife's epitaph, a full six years before her death (see the note to Item 18). Perhaps Tallis had arranged the inscription in advance, albeit this would not explain Stanford's last stanza which gives the year of death--unless Stanford himself added these lines, a possibility, since they do not appear in Strype's transcription of the plate.

Aside from Tallis' fame as a musician, Stanford may well have chosen to preserve the epitaph, may even have received a copy of it, as a result of William Byrd's connection with the Pagets. Both Tallis and Byrd were patronized by English Catholics, and both had strong Catholic leanings of their own. The first official notice of Byrd's recusancy occurred 20 August 1585, but as early as 1581 a list of "'Suche as are relievers of papistes and conveyers of money and other things unto them beyondes the Seas'" included "'Mr Byrde,'" who was known to frequent "'Mr Listers his house on against S^t dunstans or at the Ld Padgettes house Draighton.'"[1] It is not surprising that a man of Byrd's convictions and talents found a warm welcome among such ardent Catholics as the Pagets, to whom he was a near neighbor, for his house at Harlington, Middlesex, was scarcely a mile from the Paget manor at West Drayton. Whether or not Tallis was

---

[1] Edmund H. Fellowes, *William Byrd* (London, 1936), pp. 40-41. Fellowes does not hesitate to identify this "Mr Byrde" with the musician.

also a guest of the Pagets', Byrd's close ties with him would sufficiently account for Stanford's interest in the epitaph. Tallis was Byrd's close personal friend as well as teacher and business partner; he was godfather to Byrd's son, Thomas,[1] and named Byrd a co-executor of his will.[2] Of course, there is no evidence that Stanford was actually acquainted with William Byrd, but their mutual connection with the Pagets makes Byrd a possible source at least for this poem.

title] om.

1 Entōmbed] Enterred

2 who long tyme did; bear the bell] for long Tyme; bore the Bell

3 to say yt Thomas Tallis] to shew, was Thomas Gallys

4 modest] honest

5 And servd; chapple wth] he serv'd; Chapp . . . with

6 In tyme of Marie & our gratious] Quene Mary, and Elizabeth our

10 & liking thirtie] ful thre and thirty

13 had lyvd] dyd lyue

Item 29

Louise Osborn attributes this epitaph to John Hoskyns on the authority of Chetham MS 8012, where it stands ninth in a series of eleven epitaphs assigned to him.[3] Four other contemporary sources,

---

[1] Ibid., p. 7

[2] DNB, XIX, 349.

[3] Louise Osborn, The Life, Letters and Writings of John Hoskyns, 1566-1638 (New Haven, 1937), p. 171. Alexander Grosart edited the Chetham MS as The Dr. Farmer Chetham MS., Being a Commonplace Book in the Chetham Library, Manchester, Temp. Elizabeth, James I, and Charles I (Publications of the Chetham Society, Vols. LXXXIX-XC; Manchester, 1873).

however, give no author,[1] while the couplet's position in Dd.5.75 suggests that it was circulating by late 1585, when Hoskyns was a youth of nineteen. The epitaph may still be his, but the Chetham ascription, made in the early seventeenth century, at least twenty years after the Dd.5.75 transcript, is certainly questionable.

The Chetham and Camden texts given in full below indicate only that Dd.5.75 preserves a metrically less perfect and no doubt older version of the poem.

> An Ep: one a man for doyinge nothinge.
> Here lyes the man was borne and cryed
> tould three score yeares, fell sicke and dyed.
> —Chetham 8012

> Here lieth he, who was borne and cried
> Told threescore yeares, fell sick, and died.
> —Camden's Remains (1605)

Items 33-45

These poems were no doubt written by Stanford for the benefit of the "Robin Carey," mentioned in Item 36, later, Sir Robert, eldest son of Sir Edmond Carey, third surviving son of Henry Carey, Lord Hunsdon.[2]

John Hannah likewise followed the Chetham attribution and text in his Poems of Sir Walter Raleigh . . . and Other Courtly Poets (London, 1892), p. 122.

[1] Ashmole MS 38, Sloane MS 1489, Additional MS 15227, and William Camden's Remaines of A Greater Worke, Concerning Britaine (London, 1605), STC 4521, sig. E5^v. The eighteenth century attribution to Ben Jonson in Ben Johnson's Jests: or the Wit's Pocket Companion (6th ed.; London, 1760), is obviously unreliable.

[2] John Gough Nichols, ed., The Herald and Genealogist, VI (London, 1867), 42. "Robin" should not be confused with his famous uncle, Sir Robert Carey, Lord Hunsdon's youngest son, who was serving as Elizabeth's personal ambassador to James VI at the time his namesake was learning the rudiments of English prosody from Stanford (see Sir Robert Carey's The Memoirs of Sir Robert Cary [Edinburgh, 1808]).

Stanford's pupil was baptized 21 March 1582/83, his godfathers being the Lord Hunsdon, his grandfather, Robert, Earl of Leicester, and his godmother, Lady Carey, wife of Sir George Carey.[1] Stanford probably was employed by the Careys at the time young William Paget became the ward of Sir George Carey, 27 February 1586/87,[2] but it seems unlikely that he then began tutoring Lady Carey's four-year-old godson. He may have continued with young Paget until July or November, 1587, on one of which dates William matriculated at Christ Church College, Oxford.[3]

The comparative simplicity of these verses indicates that they were designed for a pupil younger than Paget, who was learning to write lengthy poems in poulter's measure by age nine, while their position in the manuscript establishes their entry after 1 January, 1586/87, the date of Item 30, and before Item 58, the next poem dated by Stanford, New Year's Day, 1595/96.

Item 46

Such examples of the power of time were commonplaces in English poetry of Stanford's age; for further examples in Dd.5.75, see Item 15.

Items 47-54

All seven riddles appeared originally in Part I of Giovanni Francesco Straparola's *Le Piacevoli Notti* (Venice, 1550); Part II was issued in 1553, and the two parts together in 1557.[4] *Le Notti* follows the familiar frame-

---

[1] Nichols, *Herald*, pp. 46-47.

[2] Dasent, *Acts*, XIV, 351-352.

[3] Joseph Foster, *Alumni Oxoniensis*, IV (London, 1892), 1107.

[4] Giovanni Francesco Straparola, *The Nights of Straparola*, trans. W. G. Waters, I (London, 1894), xiii.

work pattern of the Decameron and the Courtier in which a group of ladies and gentlemen assemble to entertain each other with conversation, songs, and storytelling. In this instance, the stories are told on a succession of nights, and each "Favola" is followed by the posing of an "enigme" for the company to solve. Thus, Stanford's titles refer to the tale and the night on which it was given; the ".2. noctis .4." of Item 49, for example, indicates that this riddle was offered on the second night at the end of the fourth story.

The lack of a contemporary English translation of Le Notti, and the answers in French to riddles 47, 49, 50, 51, and 53, suggest that these entries were translated from one of the many French versions of Straparola's work. Part I was first translated into French by Jean Louveau and printed at Lyons in 1560.[1] Pierre de Larivey altered much of Louveau's work, including the enigmas, and added to it his own translation of Part II, published in 1573.[2] A third edition in French was also printed in 1573, followed by editions in 1576, 1577, 1581/82, 1585, 1595, 1596, 1601, 1611, and 1615;[3] yet despite its enormous continental popularity, only a few of the tales were printed in English during the sixteenth century, and the whole work was not translated until 1894 (see p. 245, note 4).

Stanford probably made his own translations of the riddles, for the French poetry of Items 179, 180, and 182 prove that he knew the language, and he was similarly selective in copying only the riddles

---

[1] Ibid.

[2] Ibid.

[3] Giovanni Francesco Straparola, Les Facetieuses Nuits de Straparole Traduites par Jean Louveau et Pierre de Larivey, introd. P. Jannet (Paris, 1857), Bk. I, p. xii.

from among the other poems in Gil Polo's Enamoured Diana, appended to Bartholomew Young's translation of Montemayor's Diana (Items 229-234). Although the 1585 edition of Les Nuits appeared shortly before the probable date that these poems were transcribed in Dd.5.75,[1] this was not the edition used by the translator,[2] for while Stanford's night and fable numbering follows the Italian versions exactly, the 1585 text omits or re-orders Items 50 and 51, and has nothing in prose or verse during the first night which corresponds with Item 54.

Item 55

This genealogical riddle, similar to Items 9 and 10, seems not to match any of the actual relationships between members of the Paget, Carey, or Stanford families.

Item 56

Given Stanford's connections with Lady Carey, and the date of this entry in the manuscript, shortly before Item 58, dated Newyear's, 1595/96, some consideration is due Thomas Nashe's cryptic remark in his dedication to the Terrors of the Night (STC 18379), where praises of young Elizabeth Carey Berkeley overflow into praises of her mother,[3] for whom he claims that "Into the Muses societie her selfe she hath lately adopted, &

---

[1] Since they closely follow the poems written for Robin Carey, they were probably transcribed after 1587 and before 1595/96, the date of Item 58; the period 1591-1592 would perhaps be a safe compromise.

[2] The text of 1585 was reprinted with an introduction by P. Jannet in 1857 (see p. 246, note 3). I have not seen any of the earlier editions.

[3] A genealogical chart of the Carey family appears on p. xiii, note 1.

purchast diuine Petrarch another monument in England."¹ Ernest Strathmann argues that Nashe could not have meant that Lady Carey wrote "The Visions of Petrarch" appended to Spenser's Complaints volume, but was only alluding to the dedication to her of "Muiopotmos."² The "Visions of Bellay" and of Petrarch would have been included with "Muiopotmos" in Elizabeth Carey's presentation copy, with its own title page,³ and Nashe may have chosen to refer to Petrarch as the most distinguished of the poets represented in that portion of the Complaints. Nor does "lately" in Nashe's dedication, published in 1594, necessarily mean that he had in mind some lost work by Lady Carey instead of Complaints, which was on sale by 19 March 1590/91,⁴ for the Terrors of the Night must have been finished by 30 June 1593, the date of its entry in the Stationers' Register.

While Nashe's remark does not seem to affect Spenser's claim to the "Visions," it does not mean either that Elizabeth Spencer Carey, or her daughter, could not have translated the sonnet, Petrarch's "Mille fiate, o dolce mia guerrera" (Rime XXI), which Stanford copied into his anthology. It is entered, after all, in the portion of his collection reserved primarily for works by himself, his pupils, or other members of the household, yet Stanford too could have translated the poem, from a French translation if not from the Italian, and certainly the inverted

---

[1] Ronald B. McKerrow, ed., The Works of Thomas Nashe, reprint ed. F. P. Wilson, I (Oxford, 1958), 342.

[2] Ernest Albert Strathmann, "Lady Carey and Spenser," English Literary History, II (April, 1935), 44.

[3] Alexander C. Judson, The Life of Edmund Spenser (Baltimore, 1945), p. 151.

[4] Harold Stein, Studies in Spenser's Complaints (New York, 1934), p. 10.

syntax of lines 5, 10, and 14 suggest his hand. Stanford's "Place me" sonnets are adaptations of another Petrarchan sonnet, Rime CXLV, though again, their immediate source cannot be determined (see the notes to Items 284-293). A less literal but rather windy contemporary translation of Rime XXI appeared in The Phoenix Nest (1593), ed. Hyder Rollins (Cambridge, Mass., 1931), pp. 93-94.

Item 57

This stanza corresponds to the "Answere" of Item 7:5-10. Stanford seems to have been fond of such genealogical riddles, and had reworked similar ones, Items 9 and 10, in Item 55.

A Prefatory Note to Items 58-93

In the last few folios of the "domestic" section of his anthology, Stanford disrupts the strict chronological sequence of its entries by adding all together a number of items written over a span of several years. After Item 68, Stanford adds twenty-five poems, all New Year's gifts for 1610/11 through 1612/13, except for Item 85, Stanford's praise of Holland's Britannia, and Item 86, best wishes for a pregnant woman, also, apparently, by Stanford. The arrangement of these poems seems to have been by author instead of date, for Items 69-83 are juvenile verses for all three years by George Berkeley, entered on ff. 17^r-18^v, Items 84-86 on f. 19 are Stanford's, 87-91 on ff. 19^v-20^r belong to young Berkeley, and the last two, Items 92 and 93, are signed by Stanford, who must have copied all twenty-five poems at some time after New Year's, 1613.

It is significant that the earliest of George Berkeley's verses transcribed by Stanford are dated, by modern reckoning, 1611 (for the sake of clarity, dates following in this set of notes will be given their new style equivalents). The earliest poems were written when George (born 7 October 1601), was ten, not long after his parents had signed an agreement to retrench their household expenses, since George's father, Thomas Berkeley, "was profuse in expence beyond his ordinary means."[1] As an economy measure, I suspect that the family spent some of their time with Elizabeth Carey Berkeley's mother, Elizabeth Spencer Carey, Lady Hunsdon; on at least one previous occasion, during the fall of 1602, they were staying with her at Blackfriars,[2] and these visits no doubt became more frequent after 1609. Thomas died sometime during 1611, and widowhood may also have led Elizabeth Berkeley to spend more time at her mother's house, where she and her children must have been in contact with Stanford. He probably never entered the service of the Berkeleys', but remained with the Careys when Elizabeth married Thomas Berkeley, 19 February 1596. Smyth of Nibley does not mention Stanford among George Berkeley's tutors, or in any other capacity, and Stanford's New Year's poem to Lady Hunsdon is entered as Item 66 in 1610, a year before any of the poems by her grandson.

From the appearance in young George's poetry of the same images found in the Paget juvenilia and in Stanford's own works (for specific references, see p. 232, note 1), it is plain that Henry again exerted a very considerable influence over his pupil's verses. And Stanford's

---

[1] John Smyth of Nibley, *The Berkeley Manuscripts*, ed. Sir John Maclean (3 vols.; Gloucester, 1883), II, 397. For the relationship between the Carey and Berkeley families, and Stanford's ties with them both, see pp. xiii-xv.

[2] *Ibid.*, p. 321.

own use of the English (Shakespearean) sonnet almost exclusively after
1596 (Item 58), did not prevent him from instructing George in the outdated poulters and fourteeners he had taught to William Paget in the
early '80's.

I have not been able to identify four recipients of George's
New Year's gifts, James Orwell, Item 71 (1612), Ann Fitch, Items 74,
75, and 83 (1611-1613), Mistress Cave, Item 90, and Mistress Powell,
Item 91, beyond the meager facts set down in the poems themselves.
Possibly the Anne Fitch, aged nineteen, who married James Finch, c.
3 February 1620[1] was one of Ann Fitch's "4. Impes," though only "little
mall" is mentioned by name in the New Year's verse (Item 83:3, 7). All
four recipients of George's poems were probably household retainers of
the Careys or of Elizabeth Berkeley.

The gifts George addressed to his mother (Items 78 and 87), his
grandmother, Elizabeth Spencer Carey (Items 69, 76, and 82), and to
his sister, Theophilia (Items 77, 88, and 89), require no further comment. George's maternal grandfather, George Carey, Lord Hunsdon, died
9 November 1603, so that the New Year's gift addressed to his grandfather
in 1611 (Item 79), was intended for Henry, Lord Berkeley, his paternal
grandfather, who died 26 November 1613.

While Sir John Millecent's connections with the Careys and Berkeleys
remain obscure, his existence at least is recorded beyond George's dedication to him of Items 70, 80, and 81. The Millicent family had been
established in Cambridgeshire since at least the reign of Henry VIII.[2]

---

[1] George J. Armytage, ed., Allegations for Marriage Licenses Issued
by the Bishop of London, 1611 to 1828, Part II (Publications of the
Harleian Society, Vol. XXVI; London, 1887), p. 83

[2] Daniel Lysons and Samuel Lysons, Magna Britannia, II (London,
1808), 230.

John Millicent was knighted 20 January 1607, and attended Cambridge University where he took the M.A. in 1614 or 1615.[1] Weldon recalls that early in the reign of King James, Sir Edward Zouch, Sir George Goring and Sir John Finit "were the Cheif and Master Fools" at Court, "but Sir Iohn Millisent, who was never knowne before was commended for notable fooling, and so was he the best extemporary fool of them all."[2] His talents gained him an official post at Court no later than 1630, when John Taylor dedicated "The Fearefull Summer" (in All the Workes of Iohn Taylor the Water Poet, STC 23725), "To the truely Generous and Noble Knight, Sir Iohn Millissent, Serjeant-Porter to the Kings most Excellent Majestie" (p. 55). To judge from the Churchwardens' accounts of St. Mary the Great, Cambridge, Millicent maintained his Cambridgeshire residence, for his yearly donations to the Church are listed in the records extant between 1627 and 1635.[3]

The Margaret Egerton addressed in Items 72 and 73 may be related to Elizabeth's Lord Keeper, Thomas Egerton, Baron Ellesmere, who became associated with the Careys through his marriage in 1600 to Alice, widow of Ferdinando Stanley, Fifth Earl of Derby, and Elizabeth Spencer Carey's sister. However, the only Margaret Egerton I have found who might have been unmarried in 1611, as Item 72 indicates must be the case, is the

---

[1] William A. Shaw, The Knights of England, II (London, 1906), 141; John Venn and J. A. Venn, Alumni Cantabrigiensis, IV (Cambridge, 1924), Part I, p. 188.

[2] Sir Anthony Weldon, The Court and Character of King James (London, 1650), pp. 92-93.

[3] J. E. Foster, ed., Churchwardens' Accounts of St. Mary the Great Cambridge from 1504 to 1635 (Cambridge, 1905), pp. 411-467.

daughter of Sir John Egerton by Margaret, daughter of Sir Rowland Stanley; the connection of this family with Baron Ellesmere or with the Careys is undemonstrable.

It is more likely, I believe, that Margaret Egerton was the daughter of another Blackfriars resident, Stephen Egerton, minister of St. Anne's Church, Blackfriars, from 1598 until his death in 1622.[1] In November of 1596, Egerton, along with Sir George Carey and other prominent persons dwelling in the precinct, petitioned the Privy Council to forbid the opening of Burbage's Blackfriar's playhouse,[2] while Blackfriars leases dated 1609 and 1611 refer to "the Messuage . . . in Which Stephen Egerton Preacher nowe dwelleth."[3] Although I have not found the names of other members of Egerton's family, he was certainly a neighbor to the Careys at the time George wrote these verses for Margaret, and I suspect that she was Egerton's relative if not his daughter.

The twelve year gap between datable entries in this portion of the manuscript, from Item 61 for New Year's, 1598, to Item 66 for New Year's, 1610, admits to several speculative explanations. The intervening poems here, Items 62-65, have all the earmarks of Stanford's muse and may represent continued chronological entry, but, as with the gap between Item 32 (1587), and Item 58 (1596), there is no way to be sure. Possibly, the gout that Stanford complained of in 1613 as disabling "ioyntes and hands" (Item 92:13), had restricted his copying for years before, and

---

[1] Venn and Venn, II, 91.

[2] Irwin Smith, *Shakespeare's Blackfriars Playhouse* (New York, 1964), p. 481.

[3] Albert Feuillerat, ed., *Blackfriars Records*, Part I (The Malone Society Collections, Vol. II; Oxford, 1913), pp. 94, 126.

entry of young George's poems after that date was a special effort called forth by Stanford's pride in teaching such a pupil. It is also possible that Stanford spent several years as rector of Hansworth, in the immediate neighborhood of his eldest brother's residence at Perry Hall, Staffordshire, though there is no further evidence for this beyond mention of a Henry Stanford there in 1604.[1]

Whatever the reason for the lapse in transcription here, Stanford did copy this ambitious number of entries into at least this section of his anthology after New Year's, 1613, and apparently spent at least his last five years in the Carey household, until his death, and burial at St. Anne's, Blackfriars, in 1616. (Individual notes to specific poems follow).

Items 58-61

All four poems appear to be Stanford's own verses, presented with his New Year's gifts during the years 1595/96-1597/98, judging by the dates of Items 58 and 61. These two poems were no doubt written for Elizabeth Carey Berkeley, the middle two probably for her mother, Elizabeth Spencer Carey, George Carey's wife (for these family relationships, see pp. xiii-xv). While either lady could have been intended in the title of Item 58, the mention of "her Impes" (1. 8), argues that Stanford was not writing to Elizabeth Spencer Carey, who had only one "Imp," her daughter, and, being forty-four years old by this time, was not likely to produce more.[2] Stanford's wish would have been appropriate, however, for young Elizabeth, whose marriage to Sir Thomas Berkeley, 19 February 1595/96,

---

[1] Foster, Alumni Oxoniensis, IV, 1407.

[2] Strathmann, p. 34.

was impending. Stanford may have given her The Historie of France, The Foure First Bookes, 1595 (STC 11276), an anonymous translation of L'Histoire de France . . . Depuis l'an 1550 Iusques a Cest Temps (1581), by Lancelot Voisin, Seigneur de la Popellimière.[1] Although the translator does not make specific reference to Popellimière, the source may have been nonetheless well known to the multilingual women of the Carey family, as well as to Stanford.

Presumably, the gift referred to in the following poem, Item 59, was the two volume "second parte of the ffaery Quene conteining the .4. 5. and .6. bookes," licensed by the Stationers' Company to Ponsonby, 20 January 1595/96.[2] If so, it would have been a gift for New Years, 1596/97. The mention in Item 60 of "nouelles" written by a queen, suggests that the gift in this instance was The Queene of Nauarres Tales, Containing, Verie pleasant Discourses of fortunate Louers, 1597 (STC 17323); the translator, who signed his Preface with the initials "A. B.," termed each of the book's seventeen tales a "Nouel." They are taken from the seventy-two short stories which Margaret of Angouleme, wife and Queen of Henry II of Navarre, wrote for her Heptameron, first published in 1558.[3] Assuming that Stanford's gift was the 1597 translation, the occasion must have been New Years, 1597/98.

---

[1] British Museum General Catalogue of Printed Books, Vol. CCL (London, 1964), col. 190.

[2] Arber, III, 57.

[3] Encyclopaedia Britannica, XIV, (Chicago, 1968), 862.

Providing that the books identified here are the right ones, and that their dates of publication are reliable, these four poems were entered chronologically in the manuscript, perhaps on a year-by-year basis: Item 58 for New Year's, 1596, Item 59 for 1597, and 60 and 61 for 1598, by New Style reckoning.

Items 62-65

These four unique poems deal with Classical history or mythology, and were probably composed or translated by Stanford or one of his pupils. As a group, these items seem to represent Stanford's only entries in the "domestic" section of Dd.5.75 between 1598 and 1610, the respective dates of Items 61 and 66.

Items 66-67

Item 67 seems to be a rephrasing in iambic trimeter couplets of Item 66:13-14. The poem is addressed to Elizabeth Spencer Carey, who became Lady Hunsdon 23 July 1596, when her husband succeeded to the title upon the death of his father, Henry Carey, First Lord Hunsdon.[1] Apparently, Stanford presented her with George Chapman's <u>Homer, Prince of Poets: Translated in Twelve Books of his Iliads</u>. This work was entered in the Stationers' Register 14 November 1608 as "<u>Seven Bookes. of Homers Iliades</u>," and must have been in print by New Year's, 1609/10.[2]

---

[1] Cockayne, VI, 627; for some further account of the Carey family, see pp. xiii-xv.

[2] Arber, III, 394; Pollard and Redgrave (<u>STC</u> 13633), estimate the date of publication at 1610.

Item 68

Lines 8-12 of this sonnet adequately describe the contents of Thomas Heywood's Troia Britanica, or, Great Britaines Troy, 1609 (STC 13366), a versified mixture of classical myth, ancient, and contemporary English history, among other things. Stanford apparently presented Lady Hunsdon with a copy as a New Year's gift for 1613, and since the book saw just one edition, it is probable that the booksellers had it in stock then, some four years after its publication.

Items 69-83

For a discussion of these poems and their recipients, see the preliminary note to Items 58-93.

Item 84

Possibly the Faerie Queene referred to here is the edition of 1609 (STC 23083). The recipient of the gift was Elizabeth Spencer Carey, who became Lady Hunsdon 23 July 1596 (for some further account of Lady Hunsdon, see pp. xiii-xv). This poem's specific references to characters and the allegory of Spenser's work show that Stanford was familiar with at least its first three books.

Item 85

Dr. Philemon Holland's translation of Camden's Britannia was first published in 1610 with the title, Britain, or a Chorographicall Description of the Most Flourishing Kingdomes, England, Scotland, and Ireland (STC 4509). The second edition (STC 4510, 1637), included commendatory verses not found in the first, among them a sonnet by Thomas Meriell, M.A., and Item 85, the only known printed composition by "HENRY STANFORD Master of Arts" (π 6).

Holland was definitely connected with the Berkeleys as young George Berkeley's tutor until late December, 1613.[1] Lady Elizabeth Carey Berkeley's patronage of Holland, however, with respect to his translation of the <u>Britannia</u>, has heretofore rested somewhat questionably upon the testimony of Meriell's sonnet. Meriell praises both the translator and "that rare Phoenix cause of this Translation" (¶ 6),[2] while a marginal note identifies the "Phoenix" as Lady Berkeley, "Mother to the now R. H. George Lord Berkley." This claim, considering Stanford's close ties with the Berkeleys, is fully substantiated by his sonnet, which immediately follows Meriell's. Furthermore, Stanford's poem provides contemporary evidence, as Meriell's perhaps does not, for it was probably written a short time after Holland had completed his work, and certainly no later than 1616. Lady Berkeley is assuredly the "learned dame," at whose instance Holland undertook the translation.

How Stanford's poem came into the printer's hands, and why it was chosen for publication in 1637, remain unanswered questions; collation with the printed text shows only that the printer's copy was little different from the Dd.5.75 text:

<u>title</u>: h. st. to D. Hollande<u>s</u> translation of Cambdens Brittain]
      SONNE OF THE TRANSLATOR

8 stretche] reach

---

[1] Smyth, II, 426.

[2] See <u>DNB</u>, IX, 1047. Meriell may be the Thomas Merriall who took his B.A. from St. Catherine's College, Cambridge, in 1606/07, and M.A. from Jesus College, 1610 (Venn and Venn, III, 178). I have not been able to trace his connections either with the Berkeleys and Stanford or with Holland.

12 such; as is] those; which are

] HENRY STANFORD / Master of Arts

The title here is a puzzle, and perhaps "SONNE" is a misprint for "SONNET:." The other verses in commendation of Holland are given such conventional titles as John Davies' "In honour of the Translator" (¶ 6). The publisher could not easily have confused Stanford with Holland's son, Henry, and while Holland also had three daughters, so that son-in-law could have been intended, I have found no evidence that Stanford, who died without issue, ever married.

Item 86

Stanford presumably wrote this poem as he did the two others on this page, Item 84, a 1611 New Year's gift to Elizabeth Spencer Carey, Lady Hunsdon, and Item 85, in praise of Holland's translation of the Britannia (1610?). If Item 86 was written for Lady Elizabeth Carey Berkeley, it may have concerned her last pregnancy, followed by the death of her youngest son, Henry, 4 March 1612;[1] unfortunately, the date of Henry's birth is not given in the records I have seen. If the poem was not written for Elizabeth Carey Berkeley, I can suggest no other definite recipient in the Carey or Berkeley households at this time.

The first four lines of the poem suggest that its author had a very personal interest in this woman, yet the ending is an impersonal and rather inappropriate tag which Stanford had been using for years (cf. Items 1:25-26, 26:27-28, 76:9-10). The "sweete girle" addressed

---

[1] Smyth, II, 399.

in the "Place me" sonnets (Items 284-289, 291-293), provides the only other evidence that Stanford might have carried on an affair in middle age (he was at least in his mid-fifties by 1610), but here again, the effect of the sonnets, if not their intent, is indescribably platonic. Poem 86, in short, admits to no positive identification of its recipient; its author was probably Stanford, its date of composition, between 1610 and 1613.

Items 87-88

For a discussion of these poems and their recipients, see the prefatory note to Items 58-93.

Item 89

A footnote in Chapman's An Epicede or Fvnerall Song: On the most disastrous Death, of the Highborne Prince of Men, Henry Prince of Wales. (STC 4974), tells us that "The Fever the Prince dyed off, is observ'd by our Moderne Phisitions to bee begun in Hungarie."[1] Obviously, George Berkeley had this text before him as he wrote lines 9 and 10 of Item 89.

Chapman's Epicede was entered in the Stationers' Register 11 December 1612,[2] and, because of its timely subject, must have been in print shortly thereafter. Judging by the date of Item 88, New Year's, 1612/13, it would seem that Item 89, "George again to his sister," was written at about the same time. Theophila did, by the way, survive the fever, and was well enough by 12 August 1613 to marry Sir Robert Coke, son of Chief Justice Sir Edward Coke.

---

[1] Phyllis Brooks Bartlett, The Poems of George Chapman (London, 1941), p. 262.

[2] Arber, III, 507.

Items 90-92

For a discussion of these poems and their recipients, see the prefatory note to Items 58-92.

Item 93

The gift on this occasion was probably a copy of Guillaume de Salluste Du Bartas' La Semaine, or La Seconde Semaine, perhaps the edition of his works in English translation which appeared in 1611 (STC 21651). Still, "the education of the said Theophila was both in Court and Country under the sole direction of her mother,"[1] and we may presume that by age seventeen, Theophila was competent in French, and probably Italian as well. Stanford, then, may have given her one of the many French editions of Du Bartas.

Item 94

This unique text is discussed on pp. lxi-lxii.

A Prefatory Note to Items 95-280, 294-306

After Item 94 on f. 20^v are four blank leaves of the "domestic" section of Stanford's anthology, while the "public" section begins with Item 95 on f. 25^r; the entries in the "public" section are uninterrupted through Item 280. Items 281-293 (ff. 51^v-54^v), apparently represent a portion of the manuscript set off for Stanford's own poetry, but the "public" entries filled ff. 25-51^r, and had to be continued on ff. 55-56 (Items 294-306), after by-passing Stanford's own works. For some

---

[1] Smyth, II, 400.

further account of Stanford's division of Dd.5.75 into sections for specific types of entries, see pp. xxxviii-xxxix.

Item 95

At least nine manuscripts contain copies of this popular work by Sir Edward Dyer: Ashmole MS 781, pp. 140-142 (A), <u>The Arundel Harington Manuscript</u> (from the text edited by Ruth Hughey [Columbus, Ohio, 1960]), ff. 106^v-107^r (AH), Rawlinson Poetry MS 85, ff. 109^r-112^v (Fn), Harleian MS 6910, ff. 158^v-159^r (H), Huntington MS 198, Vol. II, ff. 43^r-45^r (Ht), Harleian MS 7392, ff. 12^r-15^r (Kn), Marsh's Library, Dublin, MS 183, ff. 11^v-14^v (M), and Tanner MS 306, ff. 173^r-173^v (T).[1]

Dyer's biographer, Ralph Sargent, suggests that this poem was written while Dyer was out of favor at court between 1572 and 1575 (p. 167), and Stanford's title, "bewayling his exile he singeth thus," would support this assumption. The earliest contemporary reference to the work, however, occurs in John Harington's 1591 translation of the <u>Orlando Furioso</u> (cited by Hughey, II, 207), while the position of this poem in Dd.5.75 offers the first real evidence that it was composed before that date. Item 95, on ff. 25^r-25^v, is Stanford's first entry in the "public" section of his anthology, a section begun no earlier than 1580. Item 110 on f. 27^v,

---

[1] Miss Hughey collates AH with A, Fn, H, Ht, and T, in her edition of AH, II, 202-206, describing the A text as "so illegible that photostats cannot be made from it." Thus, I have supplemented my own collation with this manuscript from microfilm with her readings from it.

Miss Hughey also notes that a seventeenth century printed text, <u>Poems, Written by the Right Honorable William Earl of Pembroke</u> (1660, pp. 29-30), was derived from Ht, and that the poem had been imitated by the Jesuit, Robert Southwell, and by Fulke Greville; she lists the modern reprint by Alexander Grosart (<u>The Writings in Verse and Prose of Sir Edward Dyer</u> [Miscellanies of The Fuller Worthies' Library, Vol. 4; privately printed, 1872], pp. 25-32), and by Ralph Sargent (<u>At the Court of Queen Elizabeth, The Life and Lyrics of Sir Edward Dyer</u> [London, 1935]), as well as discussing Harington's association with Dyer.

was probably copied in 1585, and thus Item 95's transcription may well precede that date. Dyer had almost certainly written the poem, then, by 1585, an earlier date than could be assigned to it heretofore (for a more detailed discussion of the dating of this section of Stanford's anthology, see pp. liii-liv).

Apparently, Sargent and Grosart chose A for their copy texts because it is the longest version, the last couplet of its eighty-two lines appearing nowhere else; yet A is also a very corrupt text, with at least fifteen certain errors plus the wholesale corruption of lines 19 and 49. H has only six demonstrable errors, but omits twenty-six lines, nearly a third of the poem, while Ht omits sixteen lines and has six faulty readings. AH, Kn, and M omit four lines each, but preserve eighty lines of the poem among them, and are definitely wrong in only three, five, and six readings respectively. The eighty line texts, Fn, T, and Dd.5.75, vary in accuracy: Fn is the most corrupt with at least thirteen errors, while T and Dd.5.75 have eight apiece. The preferable copy text, I think, would be AH, with emendations from M and Kn, and addition of the last two lines from A.

There is too little agreement in error among these nine texts to indicate a stemma, although four similarities in the versions of Fn and M suggest some positive relationship here. The readings "last" in Fn and "leste" in M at line 31 ruin both sense and rime, as does "cropen" in M at line 40; Fn wrote "gotte cropen" first, but changed this to the correct reading, "gotten." With "feeleth" for "feels his" in line 76, both texts omit the essential, implied reference of "his" to the "greefe" of line 75, an error shared with the AH and A versions. Finally, only M and Fn conclude with "Miserū est fuisse." They no doubt belong to the same branch of the stemma, although neither could have been copied from the other, for M omits lines 53-56 found in Fn, while Fn contains no less than eleven errors wanting in M.

title] om. Ht T M H A Fn, secendo vinces Kn, A complaynt of one forsaken of his love AH

1 his] is A

2 hope] hope's Ht, feare H; in vayne] is vayne T Kn AH M Fn A, is fallen H; faith] succours H; in skorn] is scornde Ht T Kn Fn A, ys scorne AH M, voyd H

3 haue] hath Ht T Kn M

4 a place] his place *; rew] morne Kn

5 the smallest] his smallest Ht

6 the day...year] the moneth the day the yeere Ht, either day, or moneth, or yeare H; feele] finde A; lightning] happy Ht, lightsome A

7 wth himself] by him selfe M H Fn

8 fear] cheare Ht, fare Kn, hope Fn; whose helpe] whose hurte Ht T AH M H, his hurte Kn, whose hart A

9 w^{ch}] that Ht T A; not] ne Ht Kn, no T AH M H Fn; nor] ne Ht Kn, or AH; lacke] lacks H

10 free] backe Fn; wracke] wrackes H , lacke A

11 Oh] no T; to well] to good Fn; death] grief Kn AH H; the mynd] that kynde Ht

12 w^{ch}] That Ht; alwayes yeldes] brynges allwayes Fn; extremest] extremestes T, thextremest Kn, extreame A; pangues] paines Ht T Kn AH M H Fn, gref A; but] And Ht T M Kn Fn H, yet A; keepes] leves Kn AH H Fn; worst] leste T Kn

13 w^{ch}] that Ht T Kn AH M H A; but] and Kn M, yet T

14 knowledge] succour Fn; help] hope Fn, helpes Ht; dothe] doe Ht

15 whose spirit] his spyrit Kn AH M; a sacrifice] the sacrifice Ht T Kn M A Fn, to sacrifice AH H

16 sorow] sorrowes Ht T M A Fn; may] can Ht T Kn AH M H A Fn

17 my] whose A; fancies] senses H; goe] walke Kn

18 myn] My M Kn, whose A; argumentes are] rusty hope is Kn; as]
like Ht T Kn AH M H Fn; an] a A; whom] that Ht T A Fn, which H M,
whose AH; force] feare T, foes Kn; hath] ys AH

19 my sent] my sence Ht AH M Kn H, whose sense A, sence is Fn,
my sences T; y^e] my Ht Kn AH H Fn, and M, whose A, om. T; passions]
thoughte A; spie] pine M, whose A; thoughtes] thought AH, passions A;
ruins] ruine M

20 famous Carthage] Carthage A; or...towne] & of Troy Ht, or the
townes H, or the famous towne A; w^ch] that Ht T Fn A

21-24] om. H; 21-26] om. Ht

21 myn eyes] my face Kn A; fall] fates Fn; dothe] doe T Fn

22 but] and T Kn AH M; haue] hath T Kn M

23 thoughtes...thoughtes] thought...thought AH; but woundes] but
bluddie woundes T; somtyme] sometymes T Fn; seates] seat T Kn AH M, sate Fn

24 somtyme] Sometymes A Fn; seates] seate T, store Kn AH M; of quiet]
of rest AH; now of all] now, the nourse of all AH

25 is^{was}] was T Kn AH M H Fn

26 I eat] did reape Fn, I ate Kn M A; w^ch] that T Kn AH A Fn;
lyves] loves Kn, lyffe M; doth bring] did bringe AH Kn H M Fn

27 To...Corne] my Corne to nettles now Ht, To nettles now my feelde Fn;
feild] corne Fn

28 eat^{reap} the] reade this AH H Ht, reape the T Kn, reade the M Fn A

29 peace] ioy A, reste T; rest] ioy H, lif T; life] peace T;
w^ch] that Ht T AH M A Kn

30 Cam] Come Kn Fn; my lotte] the lott Ht; my losse] the losse Ht
T AH H, ther losse M; my smart...more] they might stinge mee noe more Ht,
my hurt might be the more H, my smarte myght be the more AH, my smarte
myghte smarte the more Fn A, my smarte may sting the more Kn

31-32] om. H

31 So to] Thus to A; men^{then}] men Ht T Kn AH M, mañ Fn; best] last Fn,
leste M; fares for] frames to Ht T Kn M Fn A, frames for AH

32 o wordes most dear] O Lookes O WORDES Kn, o wordes, o lookes Fn
Ht T AH M; sweet then] deare then Ht T Kn M Fn A, then deere AH;
but] and T

33 standes] stood H A

34 my horrour] Myne horror AH, My sorrowe's Ht, My sorow M; in the
(yea)] on the (yea) Fn, in the yees Ht; hope] hopes Ht; hanges] hangde
AH H, hange Ht; in the noe] one the (noe) Fn

35 no relief] no delight A; would] dothe T, will H M Kn A

36 I fynd to well] to well To well M; somtyme] to well Ht T Kn AH
H Fn, om. M; my] myne T AH

37-40] om. Kn Ht

37 suche is] here A; what pleasure] Ande nothing Fn A, what thing H;
here is] may heare be H

38 ohe] wher T AH Fn M; care & playnt] cares and playntes AH,
playntes & care M, playnte and care Fn, plaintes & cares A, plaintes
and moans H; dothe] may T; to the] in the M

39-40] om. H

39 am] was T A; then] yea AH, and M

40 they that] he that A T; were cam] cam not T AH M Fn A; to my]
neere my AH; of my] lo my T, to my AH M Fn; haue] hath T A Fn, are AH;
gotten] cropen M, ⟨gotte cropen⟩ gotten Fn

41 then] Now Kn A; is]are A; the sawce] the force Kn, thy fauour Ht,
thie sawce AH T, thy souces A, the cause Fn; thie tormentes] thy tirementes
Ht, the sower M

42 what is] where is Ht T Kn AH M H Fn; the cause] the happe Kn,
the sauce M; many thinke] some throw thee Kn A, some have thought T AH M
H Fn, men haue thought Ht; ther death] Have thought their deathe Kn A,
their deathes M, Thy deathe Fn; throughe] for AH Fn; but] most Fn

43 The statly] thie statlie T A; chast disdayn] Cawse disdaynes Kn,
chaste disdaynde M; the secret] thie secret T A; thankfulnes] shamefastnes Fn

44 the grace] Thie grace T; reserued] Preferd Kn, deserude M;
the common] thie coman T; light] lyef Kn; that shines] wch syes T,
which shines H; in worthiness] through worthynes Ht

45 that yt] would yt Kn M H; or...could] I could it well Kn, that
I yt T, or I it might H, or that I could A, or I could it Fn

46 or that] oh that Ht T A, O would H; wrathe] ronges T;
iudgement] Iudgmentes H; did] myght Ht T AH M A Fn

47-50] om. H

47 frail] false Fn Kn; inconstaunt] vnconstant T AH M A; kynd]
sex Ht; o...wemen] oh faith & trust in none Ht, oh safe in trust to no
man T M, And safe in truste to no man Fn A, FYRME IN FAYTHE TO NO MAN Kn,
oh sure in trothe to no man AH

48 be] are Ht; & lo] ON EARTHE Kn, but loe AH

49 hate] blame Kn, had A; but] not Kn; & not] But even Kn, not A;
faultie on] faultie bene A

50 nor] Ne Ht T Kn; rid] put Kn; fro me] the thinge Kn, me of Ht
T M A, me from A; the bond] from me Kn, those bandes T, the bandes Ht M Fn,
the bonds AH; In w^ch] wherin Kn Fn

51 Alone] I love Ht; whose...loue] by Love Whose like Kn, whose
like by loue T Ht H; was...yet] was never sene as yett T; Was neuer
found out yet Fn

52 the prince the poore] The yonge the old Kn H; nor in prince nor
poore A; the yong the old] the ould the yong Ht T, the prince ye poore Kn,
the riche the poore H, nore young nor old A; the fond] nor fond A;
or full] & full Kn H, nor full T A, are full Fn

53-56] om. AH M; 53-60] om. H

53 here] Hirs T Fn; styll...I] muste I styll remayne Kn; by
death...wrong] by wrong by death Ht Fn, My Love, my Deathe Kn; by
shame] my Shame Kn

54 brest] minde A Fn; what] that Ht T Kn A; loue wrought in]
love hath wrought T; her] his Kn

55 wch I haue] That once I Kn T; that I haue Ht Fn, that held hast A

56 so farre] farre of Kn; wch is] that is Ht T Kn A

57 me yet I] Not that I T Kn M Fn, Nor that AH A, I doe not Ht;
y^s] such Ht; professe] possesse Kn

58 as...could] As to betray Kn, As one that would T M, I never will A;
betray suche trothe] suche tickle truthes Kn, betray such truth T, betray
such trust A; to build] As buyldes Kn, to bynde M, And buyld Fn A

59 for] but Ht T AH M Fn, nor A; yt shall never] never shall it Kn,
shall it ever A; faithe bore] word gave Kn T, faith bare Ht AH M, word
bare A

60 word & gift] gyfte and word Kn, word & dede T

61 Sithe then] And since Kn, Sith that T, Sith needes M, But since H;
yt must] my choyse Kn, that it H; be this] is suche Kn, be thus Ht T AH M,
is thus H; & this] The wch Kn, and thus H Fn

62 I yeld] I hould Fn; curse] course Ht T H, cares M; my hard]
myne harde M; fate] happe Kn

63 wood] woodes Ht Kn AH M Fn; becom] remaine A

64 denne] mines Ht; wherin...runne] in wch I rest or run Ht, to
which no light shall com T, wherto noe light shall Come A, WHERE IS NO
LYGHT OF SONNE Kn, in wch I reste or rome AH, In wch Ille rest alone Fn,
wherein I reste & rufie M, wherein I reste & rome H

65 boord] BOWER Kn; feast] MEATE Kn A (not capitalized)

66 wher w^th] On which H; bodie] carcas T Kn AH M H Fn; till...doe]
vntill they T Kn AH Fn, vntill the feede M

67 my...Niobie] MY REST SHALBEE IN MOULDE Kn, of Niobe my wine Ht,
my pillow of Niobe A; a craggie] of craggie Ht T AH M Fn, a cragged H,
THE CRAGGIE Kn

68 the serpentes...harmonie] MY HARMONY THE SERPENTES HYSSE Kn A (not
capitalized), the serpentes hisse myne harmonye AH M; scriching] shreekinge AH,
SCRYKYNGE Kn; clocke] cocke A

69-72] om. H

69 my] Myne T AH M A

70 bookes] BOOKE Kn; spightfull fortunes] fortune spitfull T;
foiles] spoylles Fn; &] or AH; drery] dolefull Ht

71 my walke the pathe] My walkes the parkes Ht, My walkes the paths M
A; of playntes] of playnt T Kn AH A, to playnte Fn; my prospect] the
prospect T

72 wher] with A; Sisiphus...wight] wretched Sysiphe and his ffeers T
AH M Fn, Sisiphus & all his pheres Ht A, SYCYPHO, AND ALL HYS PHEERES Kn;
in endlesse] in all endles A; payn dothe] paines doe Ht Fn, pain doe T,
tormentes Kn M, torment AH, paines to A

73-76] om. Ht

73 And yet althoughe] And thoughe T Kn AH M H A Fn; the poetes] the
fayninge poetes T Kn AH, ye fayned poetes M H, Poets fained A Fn; stile]
still T

74 ruthfull] rufull AH, wofull A; plight] playnte Kn Fn, flyght AH;
my fall] my fate H; &] or AH H; my exile] myne exile Kn M

75 is my greefe] are my greefs AH, is my woe Fn; wherin] In wch M H; sterue] serue H, strive A; &] or AH

76 feeles his] feels it Kn, feele it T, feelethe AH M Fn A; fyndeth H; shall] may Kn; yt least] his least Fn; his compare] he compare Kn H, his compars T, comparinge his A

77 songe] verse Kn H, muse Ht; greivous case] wrathfull state Ht, hevie case T, grievous chaunce Kn, Rufull plight M; is such] was such H

78 thou] that A; lette] lettst Ht, lest A; his name] T; his folie] whose folly Kn, his follyes Fn

79-80] om. Ht H

79 but best] yt better Kn; is the to] is to Kn, yt is to AH, were the to M, it were to thee to Fn, were this to A

80 on thie deathe] on the earthe T Kn AH M, in the world Fn A; may] can Fn A; thie accent] This accent Kn M Fn, this actaon T, the accente AH, the accents A

after 80 in A: And soe an end my tale is tould his life is but disdaind
whose sorrowes present paine him soe, his pleasures
are full faind

] finis q^th Dier T, fynys q^d DYER Kn, Miserū est fuisse M, Miserū est fuisse E. dier Finis Fn

The Sidney Poems: Items 96, 100-103,

106, 107, 194-196, 200, and 237

These eleven substantive texts of Sir Philip Sidney's poems represent three of his works: Items 96, 100-103, 194-196, and 200, correspond to his Old Arcadia poems 51, 62, 41, 42, 48, 35, 62, 3, and 2; Items 106 and 107 are from his "Certain Sonnets" collection (numbers 30 and 3), and Item 237 is the ninth song from Astrophil and Stella.[1]

The position of these poems in Dd.5.75 argues that Stanford copied them on several different occasions over the space of a decade or more.

---

[1] The numbering of Sidney's poems within his works follows Ringler's edition. Item 100 consists of only the first two lines of Old Arcadia poem 62; Item 195 gives the complete text.

Items 96, 100-103, and 106-107, precede the Musica Transalpina lyrics (Items 116-135), which were probably transcribed late in 1588, as well as Item 110 on Dr. Parry, which may have been copied in 1585. Since Sidney apparently completed his Old Arcadia before the end of 1580,[1] these five pieces and the two "Certain Sonnets," were probably entered between 1580 and 1585. Items 194-196, and 200, the four Old Arcadia poems which follow the Marprelate tract (Items 183-187), were more than likely copied between 1590 and 1595, while Item 237, which falls in the sixth gathering of the manuscript, cannot be confidently dated (for the difficulty of dating the entries in gathering six, see pp. xl-xli).

Professor Ringler suggests that Dd.5.75's Old Arcadia texts "were probably copied from another manuscript miscellany descending ultimately from an original with characteristics similar to but not identical with St."[2] St (St. John's College, Cambridge, MS I.7), the most accurate manuscript of the Old Arcadia poems, represents Sidney's own manuscript in its fourth stage of revision.[3] Five of Stanford's eight complete Old Arcadia poems (Items 96, 194-196, and 200), are closer to the St versions than to any other texts, although only Item 200 indicates any definite relationship. In line 11, both texts have "sūnts," an unusual abbreviation for "servants," characteristic of neither Stanford nor the St scribe. Furthermore, Stanford varies only twice from St in Item 200,

---

[1] Ringler, p. 365.

[2] Ibid., p. 554.

[3] Ibid., pp. 529, 380.

for an average rate of one word in fifty-seven, comparable to his proved accuracy as a copyist. Thus, the St and Dd.5.75 versions of this poem may well be related, and it is even possible that Stanford copied this item directly from St.

For the remaining four poems, however, his rate of variation from St averages between one in thirty-three and one in eighteen words, far too divergent to admit direct transcription from St. And Item 195 provides further evidence that it was not copied from St, for after line 33, Stanford omits a line, but leaves space for it, indicating that his copy here was illegible; yet St is perfectly legible at this point. Items 96, and 194-196, then, apparently came to Stanford's hands from a source considerably more corrupt than that of Item 200, though still representing the text in its fourth stage of revision.

Of the three remaining Old Arcadia poems, Item 103, a couplet, is too brief to indicate any textual relationships. The texts of Item 102 in the 1598 Arcadia (98), Additional MS 41204 (Da), and St, are identical with Stanford's, while Item 101 is significantly closer to Da, derived from Sidney's Old Arcadia manuscript in its second state of revision,[1] than to any other text. Stanford was not copying from Da, however, for the rate of variation between them averages one word in thirteen; still, only these texts and that of Rawlinson Poetry MS 85 (Fn), retain "sweete" for "sweetes," and "sowre dothe" for disyllabic "sower" in line 2, and here, Stanford's correction of "thinges" to "dothe," indicates that he reread the line and carefully alligned it with his copy. Insofar as Items 100-103 were entered in sequence, with

---

[1] Ibid., p. 526.

Items 101 and 102 markedly similar to versions in Da, it may be that all four poems derived from a single source representing the Old Arcadia in its second state of revision.

The variations in the accuracy of these texts, their similarities to different revisions of the Old Arcadia, and their different dates of transcription, may indicate that Stanford derived his Old Arcadia poems from three sources: Items 96, 194, 195, and 196, from a manuscript similar to, but less accurate than St, Item 200 from St or a closely related text, and Items 100-103 from a source representing, as does Da, Sidney's second revision of the Old Arcadia.

Although Items 106 and 107, "Certain Sonnets" 30 and 3, are adjacent in Dd.5.75, they cannot have come from Sidney's original to Stanford's hands through the same channels. Both are more similar to 98, Ringler's copy text for the "Certain Sonnets," than to any other source, but while Item 106 varies from 98 by only one word in eighty-three, and is thus accurate enough to derive from the manuscript from which 98 was printed, Item 107 averages one variant per fourteen words from the 98 text, in addition to omitting a line. "Certain Sonnets" 30 and 3 apparently circulated more than any of the other poems in this collection; they occur together in six of the twelve substantive manuscripts, and singly in three others. It is quite possible, then, that Stanford, or an intermediary collector on whom he depended, obtained number 30 little if at all distant from Sidney's original, and number 3 from a more corrupt and widely circulated source.

For Item 237, song nine from Astrophil and Stella, I have nothing to add to Professor Ringler's conclusion that the Dd.5.75 text may derive from X or Y, the two most accurate branches of the Astrophil and Stella stemma, or from Sidney's original. Whatever the relationship, it must be rather distant, for Stanford's text contains about 11 per cent error.[1] (Relevant collations with Stanford's Sidney texts follow):

Item 96: Additional MS 41204, f. 90^v (Da), Rawlinson Poetry MS 85, f. 9 (Fn), St. John's College MS I.7, f. 109^v (St).

1 sweete] faire *; threasures] treasure Fn

2 age his] ages *

3 som ease (sweete sleap)] sweete sleepe some ease *

7 partes] sence Fn

10 fair] rare *

11 such a] so sweet Fn

12 say . . . spright] playe a lovers parte *

13 spirite] spryte Da

    ] Finis S.P.S. Fn

Item 101: Da, f. 82, Fn, f. 21^v, St, f. 96^v.

1 folke] folkes Da St

2 sweete; dothe] sweetes; om. St

4 chaynes] flames Fn; my] his *

5 seeme] be Fn

6 but] than Fn

7 greife tastes] bytter greif taste Da, Bitter greifes taste Fn, bitter greif tastes St; payne is my] my payne is Fn; rest &] om. *

Item 103: Da, f. 89^v, St, f. 107^v (no variants).

1 thou] then Da

---

[1] Ibid., p. 453.

Item 194: Da, f. 77, St, f. 89ᵛ.

3 further] forthe *

6 this] my *

10 fairer] fayrest Da

12 tiest] eyes Da, tyes St

14 do] to in Da, to me St

Item 195: St, ff. 130-132.

3 haires] heare

4 thoughtes] thought

6 no] a

13 the] om.

15 for black] ffor the black

19 then] them

25 quenapple] Quene Apples

between 33 and 34] no talk vntaught can fynd the waye

34 tippes; Iewels; nede] Tipp; Iewell; nedes

41 pearles a] pearle the

45 far . . . stately] ffayer vnder thes dothe stately

50 eyes] eye

59 beares milken] beares the mylken

63 Indians] Indian

81 & . . . soft] but softe and supple

85 thing must] thinges still muste

87 songes] song

90 cliftes] cleaves

93 fancies] fancye

104 therof] There ofte

107 bewties] settes

109 her] his

111 confect<u>es</u>] compfett<u>es</u>

127 conduit like] conduitlik w^t

129 y^t] the

132 had] hath

140 p<u>er</u>fit] praisefull

Item 196: Da, f. 14^v, St, f. 17.

2 no . . . iknow] as no man them may know *

3 shrewdly burdned] shrewly burthened <u>Da</u>

6 a Iuno] as Iuno <u>Da</u>

9 Iacint] hiacinth <u>St</u>

10 eyes] eye <u>Da</u>

11 trappall] craple <u>Da</u>

12 sylver] silu<u>er</u> vre *

13 those] these <u>Da</u>

14 are those] be they *; will] well <u>Da</u>

Item 200: Da, f. 13^v, St, f. 16.

6 myn] my <u>Da</u>

7 but] booth *

8 in] is <u>Da</u>;   I haue] haue I *

9 myn] my <u>Da</u>

14 what] that <u>Da</u>

Item 106: 1598 <u>Arcadia</u>, <u>STC</u> 22541, Ss5 (98).

16 executour] exectour

21 his] which

29 vild] vile

Item 107: 98, Rr3

1 wrong; burnes] wrongs; burneth

2 weepes] weepeth

3 turnes] turneth

9 alonly; takes] a louely; taketh

11 makes] maketh

<u>between</u> 14 <u>and</u> 15] Sea, drown'd in thee of tedious life bereaue me

15 in w^{ch}] wherein

19 earth, tyme] earth, fame, time

20 help<u>es</u>] helpe

21 am I] I am

23 am; theasure] be; treasure

Items 97-98

For a brief discussion of these unique texts, see p. lxi.

Item 99

Judging from its position in the manuscript on f. 26, Stanford no doubt copied this poem before the late '80's, to which period the works on ff. 30-35 can be confidently assigned, and probably before 1585 (for more detailed discussion of the dating of this section of Dd.5.75, see p. xl). The poem does not seem to have been printed, however, until 1600, when Thomas Morley set it to music in his <u>First Book of Airs</u>, a songbook unlisted by the <u>STC</u> and preserved only in the unique copy at the Folger Shakespeare Library.[1] Edmund Fellowes reprinted this songbook in *The English School of Lutenist Song Writers*, XVI (London, 1932) (Mo), where Item 99 appears as song 12 on p. 54. The poem is also reprinted in Fellowes, p. 629.

Another manuscript text of the poem in Harleian 7392, f. 32 (Kn), resembles the Dd.5.75 version through the first six lines, and only this much of Kn has been collated; the remainder of the Harleian poem is so different from Stanford's that collation would be meaningless. Shakespeare's "Well, 'set thee down, sorrow!' for so they say the fool said, and so say I, and I am the fool" (*Love's Labor's Lost*, IV, iii), perhaps refers to these or some other version of this anonymous lyric.

Without more evidence, it would be futile to speculate on the possible relationship between the Kn and Dd.5.75 and Mo texts. Morley's version is inferior to Stanford's, most noticeably in its variant readings at lines 4, 10, and 15, yet far closer to Stanford's throughout than even the first six lines of Kn.

  2 hang down; thie balefull] Enclyne: the Balefull Kn

  3 that . . . world] That careles pleasure may conceave Kn

  4 our] How Kn; lie at little] repose in little Kn, live in quiet Mo

  5 enfold] Vnfould Kn

  7 is] were Mo

  10 do shew] May see Mo

  15 &; sorowes] Then; sorow Mo

  16 substitute And bitter sauce, all of a broken gall. Mo

---

[1]On the likelihood of Morley's association with the Carey family, see the notes to Item 188, and p. xix.

Items 100-103

For a discussion of these works see the prefatory note to Sidney's poems in Dd.5.75, pp. 269-276.

Items 104-105

For similar comparisons of the lover's state to the features of a specific landscape, see poem 22 of Sidney's "Certain Sonnets" collection (Ringler, pp. 149-151). These unique texts are briefly discussed on p. lxi.

Items 106-107

For a discussion of these works see the prefatory note to Sidney's poems in Dd.5.75, pp. 269-276.

Item 108

This unique text appears to be the copy of a presentation inscription in a book given by a suitor to his mistress.

Item 109

Three early ascriptions of this poem to Ralegh certify his authorship beyond reasonable doubt. Puttenham quoted its last two lines in his Arte of English Poesie (1589), describing the verse as "a most excellent dittie written by Sir Walter Raleigh."[1] The text in Harleian MS 7392, ff. 36^v-37 (Kn), an anthology of the 1580's, is assigned to "RA," the usual abbreviation for Ralegh in this manuscript. Stanford's ascription to "W. R." clinches Ralegh's authorship, and at the same

---

[1] Gladys Willcock and Alice Walker, ed., The Arte of English Poesie (London, 1936), p. 201.

time, the position of this poem in Dd.5.75 establishes the earliest demonstrable date of composition for it. Item 109, on f. 27^r, occurs in the manuscript several folios before the Musica Transalpina lyrics (Items 116-137, ff. 30^r-31^v), which were no doubt copied toward the end of 1588; furthermore, "Calling to mind" just precedes the Parry slander (Item 110), which was probably entered in 1585. Thus, Stanford had acquired a copy of this poem no later than 1588, and probably as early as 1585, or even before. In either case, the poem's composition is pushed back a year or so from the Puttenham dating, 1589 (for some further account of the dating of this section of Dd.5.75, see pp. xxxix-xl).

Other attributions of this verse to Ralegh include seventeenth century testimony in Folger MS 1.28, ff. 30-30^v (Fo), entitled "S^r W: R: A Lover to his Mistresse," and signatures in Ashmole MS 781, p. 138 (A), and Stowe MS 932, f. 85^v (S). The text also appears in Rawlinson Poetry MS 31, f. 2 (31), Folger MS 1.112, f. 20 (C), Folger MS 452.4, f. 89^v (F), Rawlinson Poetry MS 85, f. 104^v (Fn), Harleian MS 6910, f. 142^v (H), Rawlinson Poetry MS 153, f. 20 (R), and in the Phoenix Nest, 1593, K4^v (Hyder Rollins, ed. [Cambridge, Mass., 1931], p. 80; PN). Rollins (p. 179), collates the PN text with A, H, Fn, R, the reprint of a manuscript copy in John Hannah's The Poems of Sir Walter Raleigh (London, 1892), pp. 4-5, the version in Cotgrave's Wits Interpreter, 1655, V2-2^v, and texts in Harleian MS 4064, f. 232, and Additional MS 15227, f. 88^v. The PN text was reprinted by Agnes Latham, The Poems of Sir Walter Ralegh (London, 1951), p. 10; Miss Latham lists other texts in Rawlinson Poetry MS 84, f. 58, and Rosenbach MS 192, p. 106.

The trochaic feet which begin lines 1, 3, and 5, promise an interesting metrical experiment in this poem, but the plan, if it was intentional, was abandoned after the first stanza. In spite of Rollins' claim for the overall soundness of the Phoenix Nest texts, and Miss Latham's choice of PN as copy text for the poem in her edition, I think its readings are questionable, if not absolutely wrong, in four places: line 2, "T'entice" is metrically more awkward than "to cause"; "to seeke to leaue" underplays the meaning, which is fully brought out by "for to forsake"; line 5, "to purchase so" does not make sense in context; line 9, the appositive phrase, "my brest the fort of Loue" fails to make "Loue" the conqueror, in harmony with the "warrs" referred to in line 10.

The most reliable texts seem to be Kn and S; Stanford's version is in error at line 13, which in turn produces a second error in line 14 ("excused" for "excuse"). The texts do not appear to be directly related, although four general groupings can be distinguished among them. PN and Fn agree rather closely despite the unusual inaccuracy of the Fn text. Fo and F agree in error at line 4, and definitely occupy the same branch of the stemma with R, and perhaps, 31. A and S form a third set of similar texts not far distant from Kn and Dd.5.75; C and H could be arbitrarily assigned to either of these last two groups.

] title: S^r W: R: A Lover to his Mistresse Fo, A ffancy R

1 myn] my Fn;   eye] eyes 31 R Fo F;   went long] longe went Fn PN

2 to cause] to entyce Fn, T'entice PN;   for . . . forsake] to leue Fn, to seeke to leaue PN;   my brest] his breast H, my pensyue brest Fn

3 pull] pluck Fo S A 31;   yt] them F Fo R 31, him H;   out] out out Fn

4 devise] advise Fo F; lyved] live C; such vnrest] litle ease R, little rest F, this vnrest Fn

5 he] it Fn PN S A Kn, they Fo R F 31, that C; then] for Fn C, againe F H Fo R, to PN; to regayn] purchase so PN, to winne Fo F R, to get H

6 that . . . his] they sayd, they'd seene my F R, it had once seene my Fn, that it had seene my PN H S Kn A C, that they had seene yor 31, that they had seene my Fo; mistres] lovelye 31

7 An other tyme] And then againe A S; I . . . my] my heart I calld to F Fo R, I gan to call to Fn, I likewise call to PN, I called vnto mynde Kn H S A C, ffull sadd, I call'd to 31

8 It . . . wrought] Thinking that hee this woe on mee had brought Fo, Thinkinge to mee that hee this woe had brought F R, My hart was he that all my woe had wrought PN, My hart was he which all this woe had wrought H Kn, It was my hart wch all my woe had wrought C Fn, It was my hart that all this woe had wrought A S

9 for . . . resignd] Because that hee to Love his Forte had resigned Fo, Because that hee to Loue his fort resigned F R H S A C Kn, For it loue my brest had first resygnde Fn, For he my brest the fort of Loue resignde PN, Because hee had his fforce to Love assign'd 31

10 when on] Whereof Fo, when of F R Fn PN; warres] woe Fo, warre F R, thinges 31; fancie] fancies S

11 he] it PN; haue him] him haue Fo F R Fn PN S C R; slayn] torne 31

12 that] But PN; he] it S A; yours] hers Fo F R; forgon . . . clean] forsaken me clean C, mee quite fforlorne 31, forgon my clayme Fo F R

13] substitute: Perceyuinge then, howe that both eyes and harte 31, At length when I perceue both eye and hart A, At length when I perceiu'd both eie and hart PN Kn C S H, At last when I perceiud both eye and hearte Fn, At last when I perceaud myne eyes and hart R, At last when I perceaud my eyes and hart F, At last I perceiv'd both Eies and hart F

14 excused] Excuse F R Fo H S Kn C 31 A, To excuse Fn; as] not F R; guiltles] guiltye F R A; myn] my F R C Kn

15 found] sawe 31; the cause] was causer Fn 31, was cause PN; all] om. Fn 31

16 and told] I tould 31; my . . . will] that I my selfe would kill F Fo R

17 but] yet F Fo R 31 Kn H A S C; saw] found PN

18 loved; loved] love; loves A

] S^r Wa: Raleigh A, Sir Walter Rawlyegh S, FINIS. RA Kn

Item 110

The convicted traitor William Parry was executed 2 March 1584/85, not without considerable official embarrassment at the whole undertaking, for Parry had been in great favor with the Queen for the past year, receiving from her a pension, and through her influence, a seat in Parliament.[1] On March 1, Burghley wrote Walsingham that "It is desirable the fact of Dr. Parry were better published than it seemeth to be by divers busy printers," and again, on March 4, he advises Walsingham of a meeting at his house "to consider as to publication of the truth of Parry's fact."[2] Item 110 may have resulted from these meetings, although the poem does not seem to have been printed until the 1587 edition of Holinshed's Chronicles (STC 13569, sig. 6 S1, p. 1395).

At his trial, Parry claimed that his father belonged to Henry VIII's guard, and that his mother was related to Sir John Conway, but the government's account follows lines 3 and 4 of the poem Stanford copied; Hicks did not find either claim verifiable (p. 343). Parry had gone abroad once before 1577 and again in late 1579 or early 1580, apparently to escape his creditors. In 1580 he was found guilty of attempting to murder one of them, a gentleman of the Inner Temple named Hugh Hare (lines 7-8). Elizabeth, "she that gaue him life," granted a pardon, though if she hanged a "better" in order to do so, he has not been identified (Hicks, p. 346). Parry left for the continent again

---

[1] Leo Hicks, S. J., "The Strange Case of Dr. William Parry," Studies, An Irish Quarterly Review of Letters Philosophy and Science, XXXVII (1948), 354 (referred to hereafter in this note as Hicks).

[2] Lemon, CLXXVII, 229, Article 1; 230, Article 4.

in the summer of 1581, where his activities as a double agent included the sending of numerous intelligence reports to Burghley and Walsingham, reconciliation with the Roman Church, correspondence with the Pope through Cardinal Como, and discussion with Thomas Morgan and Charles Paget on the prospects of assassinating Elizabeth.

In a letter to the Pope dated 1 January 1584, Parry requested plenary indulgence for "'an enterprise which . . . I shall ere long carry through for the public good, the peace of the whole of Christendom, the restauration of England to its ancient obedience to the Apostolic See, and the liberation . . . of the Queen of Scotland'" (Hicks, p. 352). By March, when the promise of indulgence arrived in a letter from Como, Parry had already revealed the "plot" in audience with the Queen, warning her that Morgan, the Jesuits, and Queen Mary were her enemies—hardly revelations to Elizabeth. Nonetheless, she was much taken with his show of loyalty, and Parry's favor lasted until he apparently tried to repeat the trick of involving others in an assassination plot. On three occasions, Parry tried to persuade another government spy, Edward Neville, to kill the Queen, and on 8 February 1584/85, Neville reported him to the authorities. Confession, conviction, and death quickly followed (Hicks, p. 355).

The collation below suggests that Holinshed, the only other known text of the poem, is not the Dd.5.75 source. In addition to omitting the last stanza of the Chronicles text, Stanford varies from it more than once in every thirteen words, a carelessness in transcription roughly four times less accurate than his copying from known sources. The variants in lines 1, 14, 18, and 20 are particularly atypical of

the kind of error Stanford made in copying from identifiable prints
(the accuracy of Stanford's transcriptions is discussed on pp. xxvii-
xxviii). Parry's execution, moreover, was something of a dead issue
by 1587, while a poem on the subject in March of 1585 would have been
ideally suited to the broadside press and manuscript circulation. The
next datable entries in Dd.5.75 are the Musica Transalpina lyrics on
ff. 30^r-31^v (transcribed late in 1588), and Item 110 on f. 27^v does
sufficiently precede them to allow for entry in 1585. In short, there
is some likelihood that Item 110 was taken from a source other than
Holinshed, and at a time closer to the execution than to the issuance
of the Chronicles.

    3 was he] As is

    4 wherbie] Wherefore

    5 w^{th} . . . best] Like a beast/ with inceast

    12 wherfore he sought] wherefore sought

    14 wastnes; basenes] rashnes; bashnes

    18 voyd of] leauing

    20 bold & base] vile and base

       ] after 22: Wherewith strangled/ And then mangled/ Being dead:
                 Poles supporters/ of his quarters/ And his head.

Item 111

For a discussion of this unique text see p. lxii.

Item 112

During the afternoon of 14 March 1575/76, Elizabeth journeyed
to the Upper House of Parliament, and the House of Commons, "having

notice, repaired thither with Robert Bell their speaker."[1] Mr. Speaker then delivered a lengthy oration covering five major topics, most important of which was part three, a humble petition to Elizabeth to marry and establish the succession to the throne. Instead of replying at once, the Queen adjourned the proceedings to the following day, when her Lord Keeper, Sir Nicholas Bacon, responded on her behalf.[2] Included in Bacon's methodical consideration of each section of Bell's speech was this answer to the third point: that "Albeit of her own natural disposition she is not disposed or inclined to Marriage, neither could she ever Marry were she a private Person; yet for your sakes and the benefit of the Realm, she is contented to dispose and incline her self to the satisfaction of your humble Petition."[3]

Afterward, certain bills were presented for royal approval, Elizabeth prorogued this second session of her third Parliament, and it seemed that the day's business was over. But during the confusion of adjournment, the Queen stepped forward to deliver her own speech,[4] a version of which Stanford entered in his anthology.[5] Elizabeth was too conscious of public

---

[1] Sir Simonds D'Ewes, A Compleat Journal of the Votes, Speeches and Debates, Bothe of the House of Lords and House of Commons Throughout the Whole Reign of Queen Elizabeth (London, 1693), p. 232.

[2] J. E. Neale, Elizabeth I And Her Parliaments (2 vols.; London, 1953), I, 361.

[3] D'Ewes, p. 233.

[4] Neale, I, 363.

[5] Although D'Ewes did not find a copy of the speech for his Journal, it apparently saw some manuscript circulation in both the sixteenth and early seventeenth centuries. Neale mentions texts in Additional MSS 32379 and 33271, and others occur in Harleian MSS 787 and 4808, none of which I have seen. Tanner MS 169, ff. 175-176^v (Tn), also preserves

opinion and her own popularity to dismiss with Bacon's speech the important issue of her marriage. Of course, her words promise no specific action, for, disregarding her personal antipathy toward wedlock, she had to retain her marriageability for diplomatic reasons; long years of the dallying courtship with "Monsieur" were still ahead of her. Speaking in 1576, Elizabeth was only stalling for time, but counting on this personal address to be taken by her subjects as a reassuring sign of her concern with the question which haunted England throughout her reign.

Assuming that Item 110 was transcribed shortly after Parry's execution, 2 March 1584/85, and that the entries here follow a chronological order, this speech probably was copied later in 1585 or in 1586, some ten years after its delivery. If it seems odd that the speech was sufficiently interesting to warrant copying in 1585, it is odder still that the Tn text seems to have been written out by Sir Stephen Powle, the compiler of Tanner MS 169, early in the seventeenth century.

Stanford's source for this Item can only be conjectured; it does not seem to have been printed, but at least one manuscript copy was authorized by the Queen and presented to her godson, John Harington (see Park's Nugae Antiquae, I, 127-128). Elizabeth might well have sent copies to two other favorites, Sir Henry Lee, and John Astley, both members of the Third Parliament[1] and men with whom Stanford might have been in contact. Lee, of course, was William Paget's uncle, and Ann

---

a copy. Neale's reprint of the speech (pp. 364-367), is based upon that in Thomas Park's edition of Nugae Antiquae (2 vols.; London, 1804), I, 120-127, but since this text shows no original authority, I have collated Stanford's transcript with the original Nugae Antiquae, I (London, 1769), 149-154 (NA). Item 220, a poetic plea for the Queen's marriage, is further evidence of Stanford's interest in this subject.

[1] Members of Parliament, Part I: Parliaments of England, 1213-1702 (Ordered by the House of Commons to be printed, 1878), pp. 407-408.

Lee's epitaphs (Items 18 and 19), suggest that Stanford did keep in touch with that side of the family. Astley, Master of the Jewel House and a Gentleman of the Queen's Privy Chamber, was brother-in-law to Stanford's twin sister, Margaret, wife of Richard Astley.[1] Whether or not either of these men was Stanford's source, his correction of NA errors at lines 2, 19, 20, 42, and 56, indicates that Harington's copy did not influence the Dd.5.75 text. Rather, the agreement of Tn and Dd.5.75 in the errors of lines 7, 8, and 36-37, point to their relationship on a branch of the stemma separate from Harington's text, as the following collation indicates.

> title] The Queenes Most Excellent Majesties Oration in the Parlament Howse, Martii 15, 1575 NA; Queen Elizabeth, and in a different hand, The Oration the Queenes Matie made in the end of the Parliament the 15th of March .1576. Tn

1 sacred holie] sacred *; word] om. NA; so] om. *; being] be it *

2 precisely] perfitlie NA; shall] that NA; can] shall Tn

3 mistaking] mistake NA; conster] constre and interpret Tn

4 the] om. Tn

5 gift] guiftes Tn; w^{ch}] that *

6 these delightes] such delightes Tn, those delights NA

7 sweetest tongue or] sweetest speache and NA

8 eloquentest speach] eloquentist tongue NA; man were able] man, I were not able NA

9 bent] had Tn; the greatest] yor greatest Tn

10 bate] abate Tn; myn own] my owne NA; this] those NA

---

[1] Sir George John Armytage, ed., Middlesex Pedigrees (Publications of the Harleian Society, Vol, LXV; London, 1914), pp. 68-69; Stanford's ties with Lee and the Astley's are discussed in more detail on p. xvi.

11 hap] happie Tn, happes NA

12 nor] or Tn; own] private *; his eternall] Godds eternall NA

15 favour yet I must] favour, notwithstandinge, (I must needes NA

16 varietie] vanitie NA; ever so] very Tn; to ther] towardes
    their NA; in children] children NA

17 to ther parentes; to an other] towardes their parents;
    towardes an other NA; as y^t thoughe] Allthough for Tn,
    as thoughe NA

17-18 or perhapes/for] or two NA

18 themselves] om. NA

19 worse] worst NA; ther wonted] of wonted Tn

20 still] till NA; amongest my] amonge yow my Tn

21 Can a] I am a NA; wch of] that of Tn

22 few continew] fewe (becawse the greatest parte is often not
    best inclined) continue Tn, few; because the greatest
    parte is not best inclined to continewe NA

    so...wth out] long without Tn

23 or comon] and common Tn; actions] Actes NA

24 & favourably] and soe favou-/rable Tn

25 twere] were *; ingrate] vngrate Tn

26 my happie] me with happie NA

27 count] account NA

28 byde] abide *;

30 would I] it wold, I NA; trow you] om. Tn; raign] rule NA

31 so great] soe manie great Tn; greatest] great NA

32 that] which NA; sought myn ease] sought ease Tn

33 more seming] in seminge Tn, a more seeming NA

34 linke my self] lincke and matche my sealfe Tn, marry and
    knitt my selfe NA; fast] om. NA; frendés on] freinds
    of Tn

36-37 y^t to mannes/outward iudgement] in that, which to mans judgment owtwardlie NA

37 iudgement this] iudgment that this Tn; this] om. NA; thought om. Tn

38 self so simple] selfe to be soe simple NA

39 strengthes] strengthe Tn; these] those NA

40 self] minde Tn; myn assured] my assured NA

41 I procead] I did proceed *

42 yeares...bothe] yeeres continually God hath prospered Tn; you] om. NA

46 since] sithence Tn; these] those NA

47 among] amongest *

48 proue] proves Tn; beside] besides *; rather] soner NA

50 burden] burthen Tn; or mislike] by mislike NA

51-52 best...for] beste (I suppose) both for Tn

52 for you & me were] weare bothe for you and me NA

53 wening] waighing Tn; furdir] further *

54 wit the] Witt, or the Tn; _____ iudgement] sharpest iudgment Tn, strongest iudgment NA; rake] rave NA

55 or take; captiouse] and take; mens captious NA; opleasing] pleasaunt NA; tales hath] tales) itt shall, omits the rest of line 55, lines 56-58, and the first four words of line 59 Tn

56 or would be] and be gladder NA

57 And touching] Nowe, touchinge NA

59 the lord] my L. Keeper NA; must confesse] must needes confesse*

60 so...striue; a pail] to strive soe much: the paile Tn

61 myne arme] my arme *; by, I] by, and I Tn

62 y^t single state to] that poore single State, not to Tn, that poore and single state to NA; match my self] matche with NA

62-63 I con/demne] I doe condemne *

64 but wish y^t] but that I would none Tn; dryven] drawen NA

65 saue] but NA; kepe honest] keepe themsealves in honest Tn; behoufe] behalfe *

65-66 no/waye] nothing Tn

66 difficile] difficulte NA; my private] mee privatelye Tn; private, w^{ch}] privat person, which NA; could not] will not NA

68 m$\bar{y}$ vpper] my vpper NA

69 encombred] combred Tn; I...behoufe] om. NA; behoufe] behalfe Tn

71 properties] propertie Tn; required me wth] had reason to NA

72 whilest] whiles Tn, while NA; prepare] I prepair NA; almightie] om. NA

73 as yf others] And if other Tn; coulde not] wolde not NA

74 counted; Myn experience] accompted; Myne owne experience NA

75 these] those NA; nor] not Tn; furder] further *

76 then...taken] om. Tn; least in] that in NA

77 or begin] or begin-/ning Tn, and beginn NA; & fall] or fall Tn

78 by dispute] to dispute Tn

80 that shall; be at all when] that I shall; be when NA; thinges be] points are NA; beside] besides Tn

80-81 speak/ in] speake of in Tn

81 of my wordes] not my wordes NA

82 to others] om. NA; hath byn] hath not been Tn

85 your securitie; wch yeldeth; more thankes] yowr full securitie; that yeeldeth; moe thanks NA

87 to the] youe vnto the NA

89 floud] pond Tn; to deface & cancell] to cancell and deface NA; these my speaches] my speeches Tn, those speaches NA

Item 113

Besides Dd.5.75, at least ten other manuscript texts of this poem are extant: Folger MS 1.112, ff. 17^V-18 (C), two texts in Egerton MS 2642, the first on ff. 232^V and 236 (Co), the second on ff. 324^V-325, derived from Co but considerably longer than the parent text;[1] Rawlinson Poetry MS 85, f. 104 (Fn), Harleian MS 3787, f. 212^V (H37), Harleian MS 7392, f. 62^V (Kn), Marsh's Library MS 183, f. 22 (M), the Pierpont Morgan folio sheet in the "Rulers of England" Collection, Queen Elizabeth, Vol. I (Pm),[2] and Tanner MS 169, f. 70^V (Tn). I have not seen the Ellesmere MS text mentioned by Herbert Grierson in his edition of the Poems of John Donne, II, (Oxford, 1912), xcix-c, Note 2. H37 is reprinted, inaccurately, in A Catalogue of the Harleian Manuscripts in the British Museum, III (London, 1808), 78.

Dr. Bühler examines the allusions in this poem's imaginary card game and concludes that they must refer to the political situation in France after the death in 1584 of the heir apparent to Henry III, Francis, Duke of Anjou.[3] For the next four years, the other three figures mentioned in the poem opposed each other over the succession to Henry's throne: Henry, Duke of Guise, planned to keep the protestant Henry of Navarre from becoming King of France by crowning a puppet King, the aging Cardinal

---

[1] The metrical irregularities of the additions to the poem show that they were not the work of the original poet, but were probably added by the compiler of Egerton 2642, Robert Comauger.

[2] From the transcription by Curt F. Bühler, "Four Elizabethan Poems," Joseph Quincy Adams Memorial Studies, ed. James G. McManaway, et al. (Washington, D.C., 1948), pp. 700-701. Bühler collates Pm with C and the faulty reprint of H37 in the Harleian Catalogue.

[3] Ibid., p. 704.

of Bourbon, and thus establishing a Guisean dynasty. By the Treaty of Joinville, secretly ratified 31 December 1584, Philip of Spain pledged financial support to this endeavor;[1] lines 11-16, as Bühler notes, seem to refer to this pact.[2] In lines 21-22, furthermore, Bühler argues for an allusion to the summer of 1588, "when Guise was in Paris and Henry III was trying to placate him while attempting to improve his own position," and he concludes from this that "we can, then, with some confidence, date the poem as having been written about 1588."[3]

The allusions in lines 21-22, however, seem hardly specific enough to warrant this date, for Henry does not seem to have "proferd daliaunce" at that time in order to save the Guise's "stake." The Duke of Guise was leading open rebellion against him and was at last murdered by the King's assassins, 24 December 1588. The 1588 dating is further disputed by Co, a text apparently unknown to Bühler, which declares in its title that the poem was "translated oute of frenche into Englyshe Anno domini 1585"; and certainly the position of "The State of France" on f. 29 of Dd.5.75 suggests that it was copied before the summer of 1588. It is preceded by the verses on the traitor William Parry, which must have been entered shortly after his execution, 2 March 1584/85 (see the notes to Item 110), but followed on ff. 30-31ᵛ by the Musica Transalpina lyrics, transcribed no doubt by late 1588 (see the notes to Items 116-137). Item 113, midway between these datable works, was more than likely copied by

---

[1] Martha Walker Freer, Henry III, King of France and Poland (3 vols.; London, 1858), II, 382.

[2] Bühler, p. 704.

[3] Ibid.

Stanford in 1586 or 1587; there is no reason to doubt the Co claim that an English text of the poem was circulating in 1585.

The other claim in Co's title, that "The State of France" was translated from a French original, is also supported by external evidence, for the following work from Harleian MS 7392, f. 60^v, appears to be an unpolished translation of the French version (for the sake of clarity, I have replaced asterisks in the Harleian text with superscript letters and put the corresponding marginal corrections at the bottom of the page).

> Seinge the altrynge facions of our tyme
> Whyche dayly Swaye a new & sodayne chaunge
> [a]One may compare fraunce to a Table where
> 4 mighty gamsters sit playinge at Prymero
> The Kynge on whom the entyre losse [b]should fall
> Sayes passe (if well I may) [c]my game beinge fayre
> Burbon discharginge of his Cardynalls hatte
> Dothe vye the game. not carynge what insues
> Or what [d]good hap hys after carde will brynge.
> Navar he vowes to hazard were it more.
> The Guyse in hope but of a silly flushe
> Sets vp hys rests. and hazardes all their partes.
> But Phyllyppe standyng at hys elbowes ende
> Being hys halfe do secretly loke on or beinge halfe ryche hym
> Lendynge hym (money to dyscharge the game
> In truthe [e]pretendynge to have rest and all.

The rough blank verse here is the natural meter one would fall into in translating a pentameter French poem into English; indeed, this is the only blank verse in Harleian 7392. The marginal revisions also suggest translation, for they seem to be attempts to regularize the meter, and to offer alternate readings which change and clarify the sense. The content too can be reconciled with the popular English version: lines 3 and 4 establish the comparison to primero set forth in lines 1 and 2 of the

---

[a]vnto a table fraunce. we may compare: where at Prymere 4 great gamesters sit. [b]shall [c]although my game be fayre [d]bad [e]or intendyng.

standard text; the King then passes, the Cardinal with his hat, and confident King of Navarre are described, along with the Guise, and Philip standing at his elbow. Guise and the Cardinal appear in reversed order, and the Queen Mother is omitted, yet it is conceivable that the Harleian poem was taken from a French original also translated into Item 113. The appearance of a French poem, comparing French politics of the mid 1580's to a game of primero, would clinch the case for translation, though I have not found such a work.

Although Pm attributes "The State of France" to Ralegh, the testimony of this lone manuscript, as Miss Latham admits, "can show very little authority."[1] If Ralegh were connected with the poem, his name would almost certainly have been affixed to it in one of the other manuscripts, all of which appear to be earlier than Pm, which is assigned by Bühler "to the first decade of the seventeenth century."[2]

]   title: The State of fraunce translated oute of frenche into Englyshe Anno domini 1585 Co, The French Primero Tn, On the State of France under ye Administration of ye Guises by Sr Walter Rawleigh Pm

1 state] estate H37; now it] it now Tn

2 at] of Kn Tn

4 &] the Kn C, Butt Fn; proue] be Kn Tn M H37 C Fn; to] om. Co

6 nedes] not Pm

7 but] yet C; to] vnto Co

8 he] om. Co; of nought streight wayes] Straightwayes of naughte C; wayes] way Kn M H37 Fn Pm Co

---

[1] Latham, p. 172.

[2] Bühler, p. 706.

-295-

9 next] in C

10 no] not doubte Fn

11 fayntly] faintlier Pm; fayntly held the vie] he aloofe dothe lye M Fn; held] holdes C; the vie] his vye Kn

12 & watcht] and sekes M Fn, waitinge C; for to spie] to espye M Fn

13 for to goe out] O to give ov^{er} M, And to geue ouer Fn; out] on C; frendes] ffreend Co; bides] bedes Kn

14 but] for C; make] makes Kn M Fn Pm C

15] om. with a space left for it by Fn and M; all restes] when restes C, all rest Pm; all were] vyes were C

16 whilst] whyle Kn M Fn, then C, whiles Co, and Pm, Till H37; philip] Phillips Tn; wrought] workes Tn, sought H37; that] the M Fn

17 stoode] standes Tn, standeth M Fn C; behind] at M Fn C

18 tought] teached Tn; how] om. Co; to make his] the cardes to M Fn; his] the Kn Co, a C

19-22] om. Kn H37

19 who] that M Fn C Pm, whiche Co; the] their Fn Pm; cardes] wordes Pm

20 sayes] sayed Tn C Co Pm, sayth M Fn; goe] goeth M, goes Fn Co; you] we Tn M Fn Pm, yo^{ur} Co

21-22] om. M Fn

21 He] So Co; proferd] profers Pm

22 to saue] then saues Tn; himself] his owne C; Guises] Giues his Tn, Gwyze his Co

23 we] I M Fn; saw them & ther] saw all their foule Tn, stoode and sawe them and ther M Fn, did see all this C, him at this staie Pm

24 them] him Pm; cam awaye] came o^{ur} way Tn, came my way M, wente away C, came oure way H37, rune our waie Pm

] finis Fn

Dd.5.75 seems to preserve the best text of this rather undistinguished poem; Kn and H37 were probably copied from the same or a nearly derived original and are both very close, excepting the missing stanza, to Stanford's version. M or Fn could have been copied from the other, and either one could be 'Y' in the stemma below:

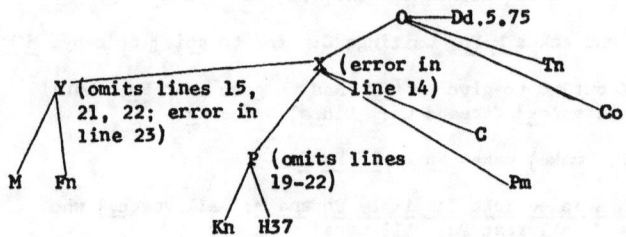

Items 114-115

For a discussion of these unique texts see pp. lx-lxi, lxii.

Items 116-137

All twenty-two poems appear in Nicholas Yonge's <u>Musica Transalpina</u> (<u>STC</u> 26094), printed "by Thomas East, the asigne of William Byrd. 1588." In his dedicatory epistle, Yonge explains that in his attempts to find Italian madrigals which had been translated into English, "I had the hap to find in the hands of some of my good friends, certaine Italian Madrigales translated most of them fiue yeeres agoe by a Gentleman for his priuate delight" (A2). The gentleman, of course, would not hear of publication, so Yonge patiently held onto the songs "till such time as I heard, that the same beeing dispersed into many mens hands, were by some persons altogither vnknowen to the owner, like to be published in Print" (A2), at which time Yonge brought them out himself.

Despite the rather conventional stance of this excuse for publication, some truth may lurk behind it, and the lyrics may indeed have circulated in manuscript. Yet Stanford was almost certainly copying from the Cantus part of the 1588 Musica Transalpina,[1] for the songs numbered there 23, 24, 28, 30, 31, and 32, are given these same numbers in Dd.5.75, while the order of the unnumbered manuscript items also follows, with one exception, their sequence in the Cantus part of the printed text.

Stanford's taste for lyric poetry was no doubt primarily responsible for his transcription of these poems; if William Byrd's connection with the work also influenced his choice,[2] it is surprising that Stanford did not copy song 44, "The fayre yong Virgin," Byrd's sole contribution to the songbook.

Stanford began his transcription with song 25 on signature D1 (Item 116), then turned to the front and copied the first fourteen lyrics in order, Items 117-130. He passed over songs 16 through 20, copied 21, skipped 22, copied 23 and 24, skipped 26 and 27, copied 28, omitted 29, took 30 through 32--and stopped, with twenty-four songs remaining. Collation with the contemporary print reflects a predictable increase in variant readings as Stanford tired of his task and became more selective with those poems he took the trouble to copy.

I have found no contemporary manuscript copies of these poems, though three of them were reprinted in later Elizabethan songbooks. Item 116 appeared in John Bennet's Madrigalls to Foure Voyces, song 3, 1599 (STC 1882), Item 135 in Michael East's Second Set of Madrigals, songs 13 and 14, 1606 (STC 7461), and as songs 9 and 10 in George Kirbye's

---

[1] The Musica Transalpina of 1597 (STC 26095), duplicates none of the lyrics of the 1588 edition.

[2] For the possibility of Stanford's acquaintance with Byrd, see the notes to Item 28.

First Set of English Madrigalls, 1597 (STC 15010). Byrd reprinted Item 137 in his Songs of Sundrie Natures, song 9, 1589 (STC 4256). The full text of the 1588 Musica Transalpina was reprinted by Edward Arber in An English Garner, III (Birmingham, 1880), and more recently by Fellowes, pp. 319-331. Mary Augusta Scott comments on Italian originals of the lyrics in Yonge's collection in her Elizabethan Translations from the Italian (Boston, 1916), pp. 128-129.

Collation of Dd.5.75 with the 1588 Musica Transalpina follows:

Item 116

2 an] a

Item 117

3 sometimes] sometime

7 Loue say] say Loue

Items 118-119 (no variants)

Item 120

3 & craft] and all thy craft

Items 121-124 (no variants)

Item 125

9 he] her

Item 126

5 ioye] Ioye me

Item 127

5 not] nor

Item 128

2 no] none

Items 129-130 (no variants)

Item 131

1 playnt<u>es</u>] plaint

Item 132

2 suche] so

6-7 enrage/ to quiet] enraged still & content to quyet

Items 133-134 (no variants)

Item 135

6 bynding her] bynding my hart with those her

7 my distresses] my long distresses

Item 136

4 to] into

Item 137

4 agaynst agaynst the case] against the cage

5 overflowing] overswelling

The error of inversion in line 7 of Item 117 resulted unquestionably from the repetition of that phrase, as it was meant to be repeated when sung, in the songbook. These repetitions made the <u>Musica Transalpina</u> lyrics rather difficult to copy, yet Stanford changed only twenty-four of the 1,420 words of his source, an average of one variant per fifty-nine words. Since Yonge signed his dedicatory epistle "From London the first of October. 1588" (A2), Stanford could not have transcribed these poems before that date, while the entry of Items 166 and 167 between late 1588 and June, 1589 suggests that he must have copied them within a month or two of their publication (see the notes to Items 166-167).

Items 138-146

The Latin title of Item 146 suggests that this series of unique poems may be translations from a Latin original, but if so, I have not been able to identify the source.

Items 147-164, 168-178

All twenty-nine poems are taken from A Treatise of Moral Philosophy, written in prose and verse by William Baldwin, and first published in 1547, but taken over, enlarged, and revised several times in the next twenty years by Thomas Paulfreyman. This popular book is a relic of the earnest desire for moral improvement which characterized Tudor Englishmen as much as it did their medieval ancestors. Baldwin set forth the humanist belief that the pagan philosophers could be reconciled with, or were even anticipatory of traditional Christian ethics. As such, they were well suited to the sixteenth century interest in conscious moral improvement through any sort of edifying moral instruction. Baldwin's (and Paulfreyman's) precepts, often silly and never profound, nevertheless required at least eighteen editions between their first publication and 1640, a longer and greater contemporary popularity than Euphues, The Faerie Queene, or any of the works of Shakespeare. Verses from the Treatise were also eagerly copied into several manuscript anthologies.[1]

The Scottish collector and scribe, George Bannatyne, copied a total of twenty-four poems from the Treatise, seven of which were also copied into Dd.5.75 (Items 160, 161, 162, 166, 167, 175, and 176). This does

---

[1] Seven such excerpts in common with Dd.5.75 appear in The Bannatyne Manuscript (printed for the Hunterian Club, 4 vols.; Glasgow, 1873-1894); references to this manuscript follow the text and foliation of this edition. A manuscript in the possession of Arthur A. Houghton, Jr., Wye Plantation, Maryland (described by Ringler, pp. 540-541), contains Items 157, 164, 175, and 176, among several folios of extracts from an edition of the Treatise I have not been able to identify. These four versions differ from the Dd.5.75 texts more than any of the prints. Sloane MS 2497 preserves a copy of Item 151 on f. 34, in a series of similar adages not taken from the Treatise.

not of course indicate any relationship between the two manuscripts, but is only a further tribute to the popularity of Baldwin's work. Bannatyne compiled his anthology years before Stanford began his, during "the thre last monethis of this yeir," 1568 (f. 375). Since the poem beginning "In quhat ordor sa evir a manis lyfe is heir led," (f. 15), did not appear before the third revision of the Treatise in 1567 (STC 1259), Bannatyne must have copied from this edition, which was also the first to contain all twenty-nine poems found in Dd.5.75, although seven other editions had reprinted them as well by 1600.

The position of these poems in Dd.5.75 argues that they were transcribed after October, 1588, the earliest date that Stanford could have copied the preceding poems, Items 116-137, from the Musica Transalpina. Stanford then entered Items 138-146 at the top of f. 32^r, and Items 165-167 on f. 32, before deciding to enter the Treatise poems, which fill the bottom part of f. 32^r, but skip 32^v to be continued at the top of 33^r. This does not mean, however, that any great length of time elapsed between the filling of f. 32 and transcription of the Treatise items. Folio 33 had remained blank, but was filled in after the Treatise poems had been copied with the topical epitaph on Leicester (Item 181), and was followed on f. 34 by the Marprelate poems, which were in print by the end of December, 1589.[1] The Treatise items, then, were no doubt transcribed sometime before late December, 1589.

In transcribing these poems, Stanford must have thumbed through the entire book, passing over all the prose to pick out the verse adages,

---

[1] William Pierce, An Historical Introduction to the Marprelate Tracts (London, 1908), p. 231.

and then only the shorter ones; in the cases of Items 172 and 173, indeed, he copied only the last two lines of two four-line poems. Ignoring the pieces he skipped over, the sequence of his entries exactly follows their order in all printed editions, further proof that these Items were copied from a book and not from manuscript. The editions of 1587 (STC 1262), and 1584 (STC 1261), would seem to be the most likely sources of the Dd.5.75 texts, yet collation with all eight editions between 1567 and 1600 is inconclusive.[1] Below, the texts of the 1575, 1579, 1584, 1587, and 1591 editions are compared with Stanford's texts. In only a few instances do the printed readings differ from one another, and these would seem to indicate that the Treatise of 1587 could not have been Stanford's source. His maximum rate of variance from any one of the other texts collated averages one error per fifty-four words.

    Item 147 (no variants)

    Item 148

    1 or vessell] a vessel *

    Item 149

    1 ons instance] one instance 1575 1579 1584

    Item 150

    1 & hundred] An hundreth *

    Item 151

    1 yt is] is the *

---

[1] The work was so popular and went through so many editions that quite possibly others were printed between 1587 and 1591. At least two editions are known which are not recorded by the STC: one, dated 1564, held by the University of Chicago Library, and another, dated 1605, in the Folger Shakespeare Library.

Item 152 (no variants)

Item 153

1 for a woman] for women *

Items 154-157 (no variants)

Item 158

1 knowing] knoweth 1587

Items 159-162 (no variants)

Item 163

1 & lucre] or lucre *

Item 164 (no variants)

Item 168

1 glose to lie] glose and to lye *

2 or] nor 1587

Item 169 (no variants)

Item 170

1 to me by] by means of *

Items 171-172 (no variants)

Item 173

1 wisdom] For wisdom *

2 but written in] but writ in *

Item 174 (no variants)

Item 175

4 is a true] is iudge *

Item 176

2 true daughter] daughter 1587

Items 177-178 (no variants)

Item 165

Stanford must have entered this item in his anthology before 25 September 1593, when Ferdinando Stanley dropped the title, Lord Strange, upon succeeding his father as the Earl of Derby.[1] The poem can be more precisely dated, however, by its position in Dd.5.75, since it follows the Musica Transalpina lyrics (Items 116-137), in print after 1 October 1588, but precedes Items 166 and 167, which must have been entered before June, 1589 (see the notes to these Items). Accordingly, Item 165 was probably entered between October, 1588 and June of 1589.

To the best of my knowledge, this text brings to three the known poems of Ferdinando Stanley. Another work specifically attributed to him was found in a manuscript owned by John Hawkins, who submitted a transcription of the verses to that hodgepodge of ancient documents, The Antiquarian Repertory.[2] In the manuscript, according to Hawkins, the poem is described as a sonnet, but it turns out to be a 140 line pastoral complaint, rather inferior to most of Breton's work in the same line.

Rawlinson Poetry MS 85 preserves a second poem ascribed to "L: Strange," a rather sensuous plea to his mistress, tolerably executed in fourteeners. The Dd.5.75 verse is also better poetry than the pastoral, reminiscent, as is the Rawlinson text, of the love lyrics of Dyer, Gorges,

---

[1] Judson, p. 6.

[2] Francis Grose and Thomas Astle, ed., The Antiquarian Repertory (4 vols.; London, 1807-1809), III, 432-437. I have not been able to trace Hawkins' manuscript. Stanley is also mentioned as a contributor to Bodenham's Garden of the Muses, 1600 (STC 3189), A5, but I have not found excerpts from his three known poems in that work.

or even Sidney. Both poems substantiate Spenser's posthumous praise of Stanley as Amyntas, a shepherd who "could pipe himselfe with passing skill" (<u>Colin Clouts Come Home Againe</u>, 1. 443).

The ascription to Stanley in Dd.5.75 is unquestionably the most reliable of the three in light of his family ties with Stanford's employers, for in 1579, Ferdinando had married Elizabeth Spencer Carey's younger sister, Alice (for some further account of these family ties see p. xix). This connection no doubt explains how Stanford would have had access to the work of a poet whose verses must have seen very little circulation, to judge from their absence in other contemporary anthologies.

Items 166-167

The marginal note beside Item 167 runs so close to the edge of the page that some of the outermost letters are illegible, most importantly those after "m<u>aster</u> h." Stanford's most common signature to his own works in Dd.5.75 is "h. st" (Items 84 and 85; "H. St." for Item 66), and in all probability the letters "st" were intended. Assuming that Stanford wrote Items 166 and 167, he would certainly have had opportunity to deliver them to the Lord Chamberlain, a post held by Henry Carey, Lord Hunsdon, from 1585 until his death in 1596.

As literary types, both works may be classified as rather abbreviated "prophecies of Merlin," in the tradition of those included by Geoffrey of Monmouth in his <u>Historia Regum Britanniae</u>, Book VII. Stanford's purpose here differs from most of his medieval counterparts, and so, his poem lacks the "<u>gotterdammerung</u>-ending," the obscurity, length, and "general pessimism or moral scolding" which J. S. P. Tatlock found typical of the medieval prophecies of Merlin.[1] But Stanford did use, in his forthright tribute to Drake, the equally characteristic devices of animal symbolism, and the "foretelling" of events which had already taken place.

The events in lines 1-10 are too vaguely described to permit identification, for among Drake's exploits, the West Indies voyage of 1585, the raid on Cadiz in 1587, or the defeat of the Armada all could fit the conditions listed here. The last two lines, however, seem to be in specific reference to the ill-fated Lisbon expedition of 1589. On April 18 of that year Drake sailed for Spain with an English Armada carrying some 15,000 soldiers and a commission to enthrone Don Antonio, pretender to the crown of Portugal, if conditions were favorable.[2] Drake was literally honored with a king insofar as Don Antonio accompanied the expedition personally, eager to receive the throne if Drake could seize it for him. But conditions were very unfavorable, and Drake limped back to Plymouth toward the end of June, his mission "widely regarded at home as a disastrous failure."[3]

If these were the specific circumstances Stanford had in mind, the dates of his composition are limited to 19 October 1588, when Queen Elizabeth first indicated that she would commit Drake to such an undertaking,[4] and June of 1589, when he returned to England in disgrace.

---

[1] J. S. P. Tatlock, <u>The Legendary History of Britain</u> (Berkeley, 1950), p. 407.

[2] Julian S. Corbett, <u>Drake and the Tudor Navy</u> (2 vols.; London, 1899), II, 300.

[3] <u>Ibid.</u>, II, 331.

[4] <u>Ibid.</u>, II, 296.

This span of time also agrees well with the position of these works in the manuscript, between the <u>Musica Transalpina</u> poems, published in October, 1588, and the Marprelate tract, which appeared late in 1589.

Items 168-178

For a discussion of these extracts from Baldwin's <u>Treatise of Moral Philosophy</u>, see pp. 300-303.

Items 179-180

I have found no other texts of these anonymous French verses.

Item 181

"Little Robin" no doubt refers to Robert Dudley, Earl of Leicester, who died 4 September 1588. The epitaph reflects Leicester's general lack of popularity, which found its most violent expression in <u>The copie of a Letter Wryten by a Master of Arte of Cambridge</u>, 1584 (<u>STC</u> 19399), better known by its seventeenth century title, <u>Leicester's Commonwealth</u>.

The date of Leicester's death and the position of his epitaph in Dd.5.75 indicate that this item was transcribed while it was still of topical interest. It is preceded by Items 166 and 167, in praise of Drake's Lisbon expedition, which was known for a failure by the end of June, 1589, and is followed by the Marprelate poems (Items 183-187), which seem to have been transcribed by the end of 1589 (see the notes to these Items). Thus, Item 181 was probably entered during the latter half of 1589; since it was unprintable, the private currents of manuscript circulation may well have kept this poem from Stanford's hands until more than a year after Leicester's death.

Item 181 also occurs in Dyce MS 44, f. 71, in the Victoria and Albert Museum, but its position in a section of that manuscript devoted to epitaphs (ff. 59-76), makes dating impossible. Collation of the texts indicates that this poem may have seen considerable manuscript circulation, for the Dyce version is most corrupt and widely divergent from Stanford's text.

1 lies . . . make] lyeth buried

4 neuer . . . for] was borne never to be

5-6] om.

7 his . . . divilishe] One y^t never wanted mischievouse

9-10] reversed

9 care . . . tell] doe not care nor knowe not well

10 Whither . . . to] And whether his soule be in

11 But . . . they] Yet sure I am we

12 lothsomly stancke] stunke while he liv'd

Item 182

Philippe Desportes, author of Item 182, attended the court of Henry of Valois, who was elected King of Poland in 1573, and crowned in Cracow in February, 1574. Henry was as ill-pleased with Poland as Desportes, and rushed home to become Henry III of France on the death of his brother, Charles IX, 30 May 1574.

Desportes added this poem to his Premières Oeuvres of 1576, and it appeared in all later editions.[1] Modern reprints include, Oeuvres

---

[1] Victor E. Graham, ed., Diverses Amours et Autres Oeuvres Meslées (Geneva, 1963), p. 151.

de Philippe Desportes, ed. Alfred Michiels (Paris, 1858), pp. 424-425, and Graham, pp. 151-153.

Below, the Dd.5.75 text is collated with three contemporary prints, Les Premieres Oevvres De Philippes Des Portes, Av Roy De France et de Polongne (Paris, 1581), T10^v-11^r, Les Oevvres De Philippes Des Portes (Lyons, 1583), Aa7^v-8^r, and Les Oevvres De Philippes De Portes (Antwerp, 1591), T2-2^v. The texts of 1581 and 1583 are identical, while 1591 is in error at lines 7 and 29. Stanford's readings are undoubtedly wrong at lines 16, 23, 29, 49, and 51, none of which agree with any of the three printed texts. In light of the great difference between Dd.5.75 and these very homogeneous printed versions, it is possible that Stanford's poem represents manuscript circulation of Desportes' work in England; however, a larger sampling of contemporary prints might reveal texts with greater similarity to Item 182, and I have not found any other manuscript texts of this work. In any case, Stanford assuredly was not copying from any of these three prints.

Since Item 182 follows the tribute to Drake (Items 166-167), which were probably copied during the first six months of 1589, and just precedes Stanford's transcription of the Marprelate tract of late 1589 (Items 183-187), it is likely that this poem was entered in the manuscript during mid or late 1589.

] title: ADIEV A LA POLONGNE *

1 terres] plaines *

2 neiges; glaces] neige; glace *

3 de vn] d'vn *

4 displaire] deplaire *

7 Adieu] dieu 1591 only

8 enclosture] closture *

9 enlaces] entaslez 1583, entassez 1581 1591

   ] between 10 and 11: Vn tel mesnage à l'âge d'or ressemble *

15 ne] n'en *

16 ne] Ny ne *

17 leussay] L'eusse *

22 en; &...terre] à; ou s'endort sur la terre *

23 Mars; revere] vn Mars; renommé *

24 croiseez] creusees *

25 loups] loup *

27 charnus] charnus ny *

28 font] sont 1591 only

29 le] La *

30 bien] mieux *

31 quelle] qu'elle *

34 quelle eut] Qu'elle eust *

40 flamonde] Flamande *

47 quen] qu'en *

49 bient] bien *

50 d avoir] d'auoir *

51 iour...parvienne] iour à l'empire il paruienne *

53 debvoir] le voir *

Items 183-187

These poems comprise a transcription in toto of one of the last Marprelate tracts, Marre Mar-Martin: or, Marre-Martins medling, in a manner misliked (quarto half-sheet, STC 17462). Marre Mar-Martin, written and published anonymously, attacked both sides in the Martinist dispute on grounds that the greatest danger still came from without; that while true Englishmen argued among themselves, "Romishe traitours here are set athryving" (Item 183:11). The response was chiefly modeled, however, on a specific anti-Martinist tract beginning, "I know not why a trueth in rime set out" (Mar-Martine, STC 17461).[1] The poems Stanford copied were apparently in print before the end of December, 1589,[2] a date which agrees with their position in Dd.5.75 following the Musica Transalpina lyrics of late 1588 (Items 116-137), and Items 166 and 167, Stanford's verses on Drake's Lisbon expedition, composed before July, 1589 (see the notes to these items).

If Stanford copied directly from the printed pamphlet, Marre Mar-Martin, he averaged about one error in every nineteen words, more than three times less accurate than his transcriptions of such identifiable texts as the Musica Transalpina poems, the adages from the Treatise of Moral Philosophy (Items 147-164, 168-178), or the Diana riddles (Items 229-234). Stanford may have been working carelessly, even improving his text in Items 184:8, or 185:16, or changing it to suit his own

---

[1] Bond reprints the parts of the Mar-Martine tract which he attributes to Lyly, III, 423-426.

[2] Pierce, p. 231.

beliefs in Item 186:15, yet his correction of a perfectly sound alternate reading in Item 185:5 indicates instead that he was following his source rather closely. Considering both the high rate of error here, and the strict official suppression of the Martinist tracts, it is at least possible, I think, that Stanford was copying from another manuscript or from a lost edition of the pamphlet, whose text was much closer to Dd.5.75 than the surviving print. In either case, the date of transcription cannot be far from late 1589.

Item 183

3 truthles; sith] fruitles; since

9 Bache] The

10 passeth; passeth] passes; passes

11 such traitour] such traitors

12 here are set] now are set

13 Whilst; marring] While; a marring

15 amongest] among

Item 184

5 This] The

6 as thoughe] As if

7 the gaping] that gaping

8 my name is] my name (said he) is

Item 185

3 drew] tript

5 ⟨threw⟩ flang] flang

6 is] was

12 got] gets

13 vppon vppon his] vpon his

15 that] thats

16 latter] the latter

18 their] this

Item 186

2 alas our health] and alas our helth

6 fruict; so be] fruits; be so

9 Christ<u>es</u>] Christ

13 Soveraign] Queene

15 yours ill all] you must spie

Item 187

4 that] which

Item 188

I have found only one other text of this poem, song 11 in Thomas Morley's <u>First Book of Airs</u> (1600; not listed by the <u>STC</u>), reprinted by Fellowes, <u>The English School of Lutenist Song Writers</u>, Vol. XVI, 49. The lyrics from this song book also appear in Fellowes, p. 628. Item 99 was printed as song 12 in this same book, although Stanford seems to have copied his text in the mid '80's, while Item 188, immediately following the Marprelate tract (Items 183-187), was no doubt transcribed after 1589. Regardless of dating, collation of both poems with Morley's texts shows that Stanford could not have been copying from the inferior songbook versions.[1]

---

[1] For an evaluation of the songbook text of Item 99, see the notes to that poem. Morley does correct Item 188 at line 2, but the songbook variants at lines 1, 10, 14, 15, 17, and 18 must be corrupt readings.

It is possible, however, that both Morley and Stanford derived their texts, in one sense, from a common point of origin. Morley had apparently received patronage from Henry Carey, for in dedicating his Canzonets to Five and Six Voices to George Carey in 1597, he recalls "all those sweete and gratious favors which tied me to that deere Lord your father of happie and precious memorie" (p. xv).[1] And Morley seems also to have been well enough acquainted with the Carey household to know that George Carey was "never disfurnished of great choice of good voices, such indeede as are able to grace any mans songes" (p. xv). This association with the family, and the existence of Items 99 and 188 exclusively in Stanford's anthology and Morley's 1600 songbook, support my belief that the Careys' patronage of the arts made their home something of a clearing house for poetry; from this point, it would seem, lyrics were passed on to the songbooks of Morley and Dowland, as well as to Henry Stanford's private collection.[2]

At lines 5, 6, 7, and the second reading of line 9 in the collation below, the songbook readings are not necessarily variants, but record the words obscured by an ink blot in Stanford's text.

1 thie] my

2 must thou; loue as she] Wilt thou; love as well as she?

3 falshod flie; for] falsehood flee; though

---

[1] References to the Canzonets (STC 18126), follow the reprint by Fellowes in The English Madrigal School (Vol. III; London, 1921).

[2] It is perhaps worth noting that song 13 in Morley's First Book of Airs is the first half of Breton's "Fair in a morn," the last eighteen lines of which Stanford transcribed (see the notes to Item 201).

5] The change she finds is

6] Despair, which is my love

7] truth

8 I . . . my] I must not let mine

9 die;   ] be; and

10 yt must] she must

13 doth . . . once] at once do please

14 agrieved; do] agreed; to

15 speake as] spake not

17 that . . . yt] the due to her

18 I; song<u>es</u> for] I'll; song or

19 yf she do; shall] if I find; will

21 this] so

Items 189-190

For a brief analysis of these unique texts, see p. lxiii.

Item 191

The first two lines of this anonymous poem occur in Folger MS 452.4, f. 59^v, an anthology with one other poem in common with Dd.5.75, Sidney's "What tonge can her perfections tell" (Item 195), "copied from 1621 or a later print" of the <u>Arcadia</u>.[1] The fragment of Item 191 collated below must also have been transcribed after 1621, to judge by its position in this seventeenth century collection, while Stanford's text, closely following the Marprelate poems of late 1589 (Items 183-187),

---

[1]Ringler, p. 560.

was probably entered about 1590. The unusual content of this poem will perhaps explain its appeal to an anthologist working some thirty years later.

At first glance, this poem seems to be an ordinary sort of mid-century look at the lover's state: it is alliterative, full of wordplay, couched in fourteener couplets, and rather similar in technique to poems from Tottel's *Miscellany*, or to Items 95 and 216 by Sir Edward Dyer. But the sustained feminine rime here with its propensity for humorous effect, was not common in "Drab Age" poetry, and after the introductory couplet, we find that "syllie Ihon" is too overjoyed to make orthodox use of the mid-century conventions. The alliterative repetitions of lines 3-5 surpass the mid-century extremes, for example. The sun and moon imagery of lines 7-8 is confusing and inappropriate, the wholly conventional simile of line 9 is undercut by the tautological absurdity of line 10, and the hyperbole is just slightly extreme throughout. By overplaying the stock devices, the poet has created a parody of "Drab Age" love lyrics, just as Sidney, by different means, parodied them in his description of "brave Mopsa" (Item 196).

1 had; Ihon] hath; thee

2 his loved] thy sweetest; white as any] whiter then the

The "Gorges Group": Items 192, 193, 199, 204, 205, and 208; A Prefatory Note

Miss Sandison believes that in these six poems "we can almost detect the copyist in the act of culling his entries from Gorges' papers"

(p. xxxvii);[1] yet I doubt that Stanford's texts, aside from Item 199, are directly related to Gorges' own papers, and certainly not to the texts of these poems in his personal collection, Egerton MS 3165. This manuscript, executed for Sir Arthur by two professional scribes, is written in an extremely legible Italic script which would have been easier to read and transcribe than either secretary or black letter print. Accordingly, if Stanford had access to Egerton 3165 or to other copies made by these scribes, we should expect him to average no more than one variant per fifty words (see pp. xxvii-xxviii for evidence of Stanford's scribal accuracy). Item 192, however, varies from Egerton more than once in every nine words; the average rate of variance for Item 204 is one word in thirty-six, for 205, one word in eighteen, and for 208, one in twenty-four. Only Item 199 suggests transcription from the professional Italic hand, for here Stanford makes only one error in a text of 126 words.

For the five poems remaining, there is ample evidence that Stanford did not have access to texts approved by Sir Arthur, and certainly not to the Egerton manuscript. First, Gorges made holograph corrections in his fair copies of Items 204 and 205, none of which appear in Dd.5.75, which preserves the original readings. If Stanford did see the Egerton text, it was definitely before these revisions had been made.

Second, Miss Sandison suggests that the indecipherable mark above Item 208 "may be the transcriber's effort to Copy a $\underline{D}$ such as Gorges

---

[1] All six Egerton 3165 texts are reprinted in Sandison's edition of that manuscript (poems 1, 8, 39, 72, 79, and 98).

used in Egerton" to mark those poems he dedicated to his wife (p. 183). This is certainly a plausible reading of the sign, but in the Egerton manuscript no "D" appears over the poem. Third, Miss Sandison accounts for Item 193's complete dissimilarity from the Egerton text by labeling it "a fumbling experiment all its own" (p. 210). Aside from the fact that a fumbling experiment could hardly be distinguished from the work of a master in a poem of this sort, I do not believe that Stanford would have transformed an entry for his "public" section of Dd.5.75 to this extent. Experiments of his own were reserved for the first twenty-four folios of his anthology, and to ff. 51^V-54; in between, he seems to have copied his texts with considerable fidelity.

Finally, if Stanford at least had access to Gorges' papers, the poems he copied were not arranged in the Egerton manner. Their sequence of entry there is, by Miss Sandison's numbering, 1, 8, 39, 72, 79, and 98; in Dd.5.75, however, they occur in the order, 8, 79, 72, 39, 98, and 1, and not all together at that, but interspersed with a total of thirteen other poems. Thus, the accuracy of the 199 text alone suggests that Stanford did indeed copy it from the work of one of Gorges' professional scribes, or even from Egerton 3165. In the other instances, I think that the texts had gone through one or perhaps several hands before they reached Stanford, and I am unconvinced that Item 193 is at all related to the Egerton text.

Item 192

I know of only one other text of this poem, on f. 6^V of Egerton MS 3165; Miss Sandison collates the Dd.5.75 version on p. 186 in her edition of that manuscript. This is the most corrupt of Stanford's

Gorges poems, averaging one variant per nine words, and demonstrably in error at lines 1, 8, and 15. I think there is little liklihood that Stanford was copying from a text with authorial sanction.

Gorges' claim to this verse rests upon its appearance in Egerton 3165, his personal collection of his own poems. Stanford's copy was probably made during the early 1590's (see p. xl).

    1 were show] weare a shoo

    4 wore] ware

    5 step] stepps

    6 these; fancies] those; fancye

    8 likewise did see] did lyckewise vewe

    9 vew] see

    11 garter] garters

    14 no suche] so much

    15 knowes] knowe

    16 I . . . two] in too collours I the truth

    17 garters] garter

    18 truthe] proofe

Item 193

This poetic novelty enjoyed a seemingly continuous popularity for at least seventy years. It is found in Egerton MS 3165, f. 61 (E), and in Harleian MS 7392, f. 66^v (Kn), while two eight line texts occur in a seventeenth century manuscript, Rawlinson Poetry MS 117, ff. 111, and 118^v (R17). It was printed in William Barley's A new Booke of Tabliture, 1596, A4^v (STC 1433) (B), in Brittons Bowre of

Delights, 1597, F1-1^v (STC 3634) (D), the Phoenix Nest, 1593 (STC 21516, ed. Hyder Rollins, p. 71) (PN), and in the Poetical Rhapsody, 1602 (STC 6373, Hyder Rollins, ed. [2 vols.; Cambridge, Mass., 1931], I, 223; Rollins also collates with the editions of 1608, 1611, and 1621) (PR).

On pp. 174-175 of his edition of PN, Rollins collates the D, B, PR, and R17 texts, along with copies in Additional MS 15227, ff. 84^v-85, Additional MS 22118, f. 34, Wit's Recreations, 1641, T1^v, and John Cotgrave's Wits Interpreter, 1655, G7^v-8. The verse also occurs in Le Prince d'Amour, 1660, pp. 131-132. The PR text was reprinted by Hannah, The Poems of Sir Walter Raleigh, pp. 15-16, and the B text, by Fellowes, p. 350.

I have found no new evidence which might help resolve the question of authorship of this work, now in dispute between Gorges and Ralegh.[1] Below, I collate only the first thirteen lines of Item 193, since thereafter it differs so dramatically from all other texts as to make further collation meaningless. The change from "her" to "your" throughout in B indicates that this alternate pronoun had been introduced aside from the Dd.5.75 text no later than 1596. The versions in R17 also suggest that Stanford's was not a completely isolated text, for its eight lines vary from Item 193 at only five points, while all other texts show in these same eight lines a minimum of seven variants plus three entirely different lines (6-8). It is at least possible that Stanford's unique form of this poem did circulate elsewhere, and

---

[1]The arguments for each are set forth by Sandison, pp. xxxix-xl, and by Latham, p. 160.

I would not be surprised to find such a version in some presently unknown manuscript.

1 your] Her throughout E Kn D PN PR

2 sweete] somth R17

3 moud] bent E Kn D B PN PR; then knit] then hitt E Kn D PN, so hite B, now hitt PR

4 my eyes] myne eye E Kn D PN PR, my eye B R17; myn eares] mine eare E Kn D B PN PR, my eare R17; my] mine D

5 myn eyes myne eares] Myn eye Myne eare E Kn D B PN PR, My Eye, my eare R17; my] mine D

6-8] substitute in Kn, D, and B, collated with E, PN, and PR:

    To Lyke, to Learne, to Love
    Your face, your Tongue, your wytt] her throughout E PN PR
    doth leade, doth teache, doth move

7 dwelles in] Affects R17

9 your] Her throughout E Kn D PR, oh PN

10 light] beares E Kn B PR, line D; substitute With frownes, With checke, With smart, PN

11 blind] bynde Kn D; chain] charm E Kn D B PR; wilte] knitt E, Rule Kn D B PR; substitute Wrong not Vexe not, Wound not PN

12 eyes] eye E Kn D B PR PN

13 eyes] eye E Kn D B PN PR; myne eares] mine eare E Kn D PR PN, My eare B; my] mine D

Items 194-196

For a discussion of these works see the prefatory note to Sidney's poems in Dd.5.75, pp. 269-276.

Item 197

Other manuscript appearances of this sonnet, Spenser's Amoretti VIII, suggest a date of composition well before the appearance of Amoretti

and Epithalamion (Am), in 1595 (STC 23076, sig. A5^v). Harleian MS
7392 (Kn), a collection of the 1580's, contains the first four lines
of the poem on f. 28^v, while Rawlinson Poetry 85 (Fn), dating from the
mid to late '80's, has the complete text on f. 5^v. Stanford apparently
copied the Marprelate poems (Items 183-187), late in 1589, so that
transcription of Item 197, which occurs two folios later in Dd.5.75,
may well have preceded the 1595 printing. A third manuscript text is
preserved in a seventeenth century anthology, Sloane MS 1446, f. 43 (Sl).

The other *Amoretti* sonnets apparently did not see much if any
manuscript circulation, and number VIII is further set apart from them
by its English form, for all the rest are "Spenserean" sonnets, with
their quatrains linked by the rime. Finally, before 1586, Fulke Greville
wrote either the model for this poem or an imitation of it, his *Caelica*
III, first printed in 1630.[1] Presumably, Spenser wrote his version
before his journey to Ireland in 1580, while he was still held "in
some use of familiarity" by Sidney and Dyer, and through them, could
either have seen *Caelica* III or brought his own work to the attention
of Greville, the third important member of Sidney's circle.

The Fn ascription to Dyer may indicate that he was at some point
responsible for the circulation of *Amoretti* VIII in England. At any
rate, Spenser's poem apparently circulated in manuscript during the

---

[1] Martin Peerson set Greville's poem to music as songs 5 and 6
of his 1630 *Mottects or Grave Chamber Musique* (STC 19552); the complete *Caelica* appeared in Greville's posthumous *Certaine Learned and Elegant Workes*, 1633 (STC 12361). Both Geoffrey Bullough, editor of the *Poems and Dramas of Fulke Greville* (2 vols.; Edinburgh, 1938), I, 41, and G. A. Wilke ("The Sequence of the Writings of Fulke Greville, Lord Brooke," SP, LVI [1959], 491), agree that the first seventy-six sonnets of *Caelica* were written before 1586, while William A. Ringler, Jr. ("The Chronology of Spenser's Sonnets" [unpublished paper delivered at the Modern Language Association Annual Meeting in Washington, D. C., 28 December 1956]), suggests that *Caelica* III was probably written between 1582 and 1585.

1580's (and after), and was added to the Amoretti collection by the author, who did not bother to recast its form to match the others.

It is tempting to suppose that Stanford became personally acquainted with Spenser through their mutual connection with the Careys (see p. xviii), and that he received his copy of Amoretti VIII directly from the author; however, an examination of Stanford's text offers no support for this assumption. While Am no doubt represents Spenser's final version of the sonnet, all three complete manuscript texts (Fn, Sl, and Dd.5.75), diverge uniquely from it in seventeen places; indeed, the agreement of Am and Sl at lines 6 ("out," and "base"), 12, and 14, suggests that Sl derived from a version much closer to the printed text than either Fn or Dd.5.75.[1]

    ] title: Sonnet. VIII. Am

    1 More fayr then] More then most Sl Am Kn, O, more than Fn; the] that Sl

    2 the highe creatour] vnto the maker Am Kn

    3 not] no Sl Am Fn; wth whom] in which Am, wherwth Kn; all powers] ye heavens Kn, the fates Fn

    4 to the; nought els] in this; may else Sl

    5 your deer] theire cleere Fn, your cleere Sl, your bright Am

    6 forth] our Sl Am; dartes] darte Fn; bare] base Sl Am, blase Fn; affections wound] affectinge woundes Fn

---

[1] Laurence Cumings ("Spenser's Amoretti VIII: New Manuscript Versions," Studies in English Literature, IV [Winter, 1964], 125-135), suggests that all four manuscript versions represent stages in Spenser's revisions of the poem, Fn being derived from his original version, while Dd.5.75, Sl, and Kn, represent the second, third, and fourth recensions, respectively. Professor Ringler, however ("The Chronology of Spenser's Sonnets"), demonstrates that Spenser was not in the habit of revising his poetry so extensively, and that these different manuscript versions resulted merely from textual deterioration as the poem circulated.

-324-

8 on] ohe Fn; bewtye] beauties Sl

9 you rule] you hold Sl, you frame Am, The mor Fn; you fashion] and fashion Am

10 stay] tie Sl, stop Am; & moue my] and force my Sl, and teach my Am, yet force myne Fn

11 stormes] storme Am Fn; y^t passion] when passions Sl; dothe] doe Sl, did Am Fn

12 looke] power Sl, cause Am, looks Fn; but through] but by Fn; bewties] vertue *

13 Loue is not knowen] Dark is the world Am; loue shineth] light shined Am Fn, light shineth Sl; never] euer Sl

14 blessed . . . w^{ch}] well is he borne, that Am Sl, Thrise happy he that Fn

] finis after line 4 Kn, Finis M.^{er} Dier. Fn

Item 198.

The placing of one half of this work at the bottom of f. 37^v, and the other at the bottom of f. 38, suggests that it was copied after Items 196, 197, 199, and 200, the poems at the tops of these pages. Its position after the Marprelate tract on ff. 34-35 indicates that it was undoubtedly transcribed after 1589 (see the notes to Items 183-187).

Below, Stanford's text is collated with versions in Additional MS 34064, ff. 12-12^v (64), Rawlinson Poetry MS 85, f. 14 (Fn), and Harleian MS 6910, ff. 146^v-147^r (H). The 64 text appears in Alexander Grosart's <u>The Complete Works in Prose and Verse of Nicholas Breton</u> (2 vols.; Edinburgh, 1879), I, 17. Breton's authorship rests solely on the Fn ascription, while the signature in H, "La: R.," no doubt refers to Penelope Devereux, who became Lady Rich in 1581.[1] She is not known to have written poetry, however, and these can hardly be her verses.

---

[1] Ringler, p. 438.

The Dd.5.75 text is little different from 64 and Fn, while H is widely variant from all three. I suspect that Stanford's reading at line 32, "singing," refers correctly to the song which began at line 7; if so, the other texts are in error here, though they do not wholly agree. The only other agreement in error comes at line 18, where 64, H, and Dd.5.75 read "no" for "now," albeit no textual relationship can be established upon such frail evidence. Generally, the 64 text, with only one other probable error, at line 32, is the most accurate. Dd.5.75 is next with four unquestionably incorrect readings (lines 4, 18, 29, and 33), while Fn and H have six errors apiece.

1 sorow] sorows H

2 bleedes] bledd *; eyes] eye H; are] were *

3 heaven] high H, heavnes 64

4 mourn] mourninge *

5 wher] when Fn 64; wth handes] wth her handes H; rufully] wofull *

7 all] now *; leaue of endighting] giue ouer writting H

8 now] all *; gyue over wrighting] leaue of enditing H

11 Cupid now is] Cupid's waxen but H; warling] worldlinge Fn

12 venus] honors *

14 hast thou] Thou haste Fn

15 do] Doth H

16 y^t] as *; shall] should H

17 but; Ioy] And; Loue H

18 no loue] now loue Fn; should leaue me] shall leaue Fn, shall leave me 64, should please me H

19 So] Go H 64; my . . . leaue] then flocke leaue of 64 Fn; go] leaue H

20 now lies] lyes now *

21 while] when Fn 64, whilse H

22 could offend] might offend H

25 Muses] Sorrowes *; all] now H

27 trees now bear] let beare H, trees Beare Fn

29 & loue] let H, And of loue Fn 64; more be] more of Loue be H

31 Therw^th all] And with that H, Wherwithall Fn

32 she] He Fn; her singing] his shininge Fn, her shining H, her shrining 64

33 wher] when *

35 that] all H; sorowes] sorrowe *

36 & poore Coridon then awaked] And then poore Coridon awaked H, And so pore Corridon awaked Fn

] finis La: R. H, Finis Britton. Fn, finis 64

Item 199

(For a general discussion of the Gorges texts in Dd.5.75, see the prefatory note, pp. 316-318). The only other text of this poem is in Gorges' personal manuscript collection, Egerton MS 3165, f. 57 (reprinted by Sandison, pp. 71-72). Stanford's copy differs from this version only at line 9, where Dd.5.75 reads "liked" for "lyqued." This one error in a text of 126 words may well indicate that Stanford did in this case have access to a scribal fair copy in one of the Italian hands of the Egerton manuscript. This is Stanford's most demonstrably accurate job of copying, but then, the Egerton italic is clearer than either secretary or black letter print.

Item 200

For a discussion of this work see the prefatory note to Sidney's poems in Dd.5.75, pp. 269-276.

Item 201

In its complete form, this poem is preceded by eighteen additional lines, beginning, "Fair in a morn (o fairest morn)." The full text is printed in the 1600 edition of England's Helicon, STC 3191, G4-5 (EH),[1] in the edition of 1614 (STC 3192), and in Cotgrave's Wits Interpreter, 1655, H1-1^v. Rawlinson Poetry 85, ff. 1^v-2^r (Fn), and Additional MS 34064, ff. 17^v-18^r (64), preserve manuscript copies of the entire poem.

The two parts of this work no doubt circulated separately as well, for Harleian MS 6910, f. 140^r, Folger MS 2071.7, f. 183^v, and Morley's First Book of Ayres, 1600,[2] give only the first eighteen lines. I have found no print or manuscript besides Dd.5.75 which contains only these last eighteen lines, yet this part must have circulated by itself too, for separation of the nearly independent halves would have come about quite naturally. In 64, for example, there is more than a three line gap between the two parts, so that the poem could easily be mistaken for two works, while Fn labels the last part, "The songe," and begins it on the page following the first part. Thus, it is not surprising that a number of half-texts were copied as the poem circulated.

Nicholas Breton's claim to Item 201, along with the preceding eighteen lines, is almost incontestable; it is supported by appearance

---

[1] I have taken the EH collation from the Helicon reprint edited by Hyder Rollins, p. 34. The edition of 1614 contains no important variants. Rollins also collates Fn, 64, the Harleian and Folger manuscripts, and the Wits Interpreter versions, with reference to a print of the first eight lines from "Smith's" MS, mentioned in Cornhill Magazine, LI (1927), 287. Alexander Grosart printed the EH text in The Complete Works . . . of Nicholas Breton, I, 8.

[2] Not listed by the STC; reprinted by Fellowes, English School of Lutenist Song Writers, XVI, song 13. For Morley's connections with the Careys, and Stanford too, perhaps, see the notes to Items 99 and 188.

of the text in 64, an important collection of Breton's works, by the ascription of Fn, and by the Helicon cancel slip which transfers the authorship from Sidney to Breton. The cancel slip, of course, would have been a bothersome undertaking for the printer, and such a measure may indicate that Breton himself demanded due credit for his verses here.

Stanford probably copied Item 201 in the early 1590's, and certainly after transcription of the Marprelate tract on ff. 34-35 (Items 183-187), which he probably copied late in 1589. Perhaps he obtained a copy of another Breton poem, Item 198, along with 201, using the first to fill in blank spaces on ff. 37^v and 38^r, and entering the second at the top of f. 38^v.

The four texts collated below have so many unique variants that no relationship among them is apparent. The Fn text alone alternates "C" and "P" to the left of the lines, a useful indication of the speakers in this poetic dialogue, Coridon and Phillis. Fn and 64 are the most accurate versions of the poem, while EH is defective in the omission of lines 5 and 6, and errors at lines 11 and 12. Stanford's text, however, is by far the most corrupt. He apparently transcribed a mediocre version of the work in a difficult secretary hand, which led him to mistake "&" for 's' at line 15 ("sheapheard &"), "make" for "walke" at line 14, and "Sphilomita" for an abbreviation of "Sweet Philomel," at line 9.

] title: The songe Fn

1 fayer] Sweete 64 Fn; quene so fair] such a quene *

2 her] the Fn

3 Swete; yet did eye] Faire; eye did yet EH

4 constantest] constant 64, constants EH, truest Fn; faith] harte Fn; kept lames] had lambe 64 Fn, kept flocke EH

5-6] om. EH

5 finest] fairest 64; y^t ever] as euer Fn

6 trewest] constantest Fn

7 only] sweetest EH

8 did keepe the] kept Lambs in EH

9 Sphilomita] sweete Philomen 64, Sweete Philomele Fn EH; breed] birde *; thoughe] yitt 64, but Fn; be he] was he 64, is he Fn

10 did hear] doth here *; thoughe] but Fn; be she] is she Fn

11-12] placed between 14 and 15 EH

11 loues yet] loue, though EH

12 the gardens] and Gardens 64 Fn; sweete; groundes; yet Coridon is] fair; ground; though Coridon be EH

13 soowes] owes *

14 make] walke *; but] yitt 64, though EH; is] be EH

15 since; phillis only] Sith; only Philis Fn; sheaphard & only] shepperds only *

16 her only; a sheaphead] the only; her shepperde *

18 go] no Fn EH; thie] the EH; shalbe] will be 64

] finis 64, Finis. Britton Fn, ascribed to S. Philip Sidney in EH, but corrected to N. Breton with a cancel slip

Item 202

Although Professor Bradner groups this poem among Queen Elizabeth's doubtfull verses, the manuscript attributions argue rather strongly for her authorship.[1] Two of the three earliest texts, Kn and Fn, attribute the poem to Elizabeth, while Stanford's version, copied not long after 1589, to judge by its position in Dd.5.75 after the Marprelate poems (Items 183-187), is anonymous. The C ascription to the "l: of oxford" may be as late as 1610,

---

[1] Leicester Bradner, ed., The Poems of Queen Elizabeth I (Providence, Rhode Island, 1964), p. 7. Bradner, p. 76, collates his copy text, Harleian MS 7392, f. 21^v (Kn), with Folger MS 1.112, f. 7^v (C), Folger MS 2073.4, f. 169 (F1), and Rawlinson Poetry MS 85, f. 1 (Fn). Among other reprints, the poem appears in Hebel and Hudson, p. 54, and Elizabethan Lyrics, ed. Norman Ault (London, 1925), p. 37.

and while the feminine narrator fits in with the Queen's authorship, it is not so appropriate for the Earl.

The content of Item 202 in general describes Elizabeth as she might have portrayed herself during her last round of courtship with Anjou, 1581-1582, when it was vital for her to convince Monsieur of her affection.[1] Indeed, a crossed out but legible title in Fn reads: "Verses made by the queine when she was supposed to be in loue wth mountsyre," and Bradner acknowledges that she was writing poetry during this courtship by assigning to her verses "On Monsieur's Departure" (p. 5).

Bradner's main objection to Elizabeth's authorship here is stylistic: "I do not believe that she could have turned out such a facile piece of ironical wit" (pp. 75-76); yet the "Departure" poem is equally witty and even more felicitously worded, while the irony of Item 202 would not exceed a schoolboy's capacity (i.e. it is ironic that, while I formerly rejected my suitors, now that I am in love, I wish I hadn't).

The most telling argument against Elizabeth's authorship, I think, lies in the implications of the first line, "When I was fair and young and favor graced me," for presumably, the forty-eight year old Queen would not have wished to emphasize her age during the nego-

---

[1] J. B. Black, The Reign of Elizabeth (2nd ed.; Oxford, 1959), pp. 353-355. In 1581-1582, Elizabeth negotiated for a French marriage and a French alliance in order to influence French foreign policy against the increasing power of Spain. "The key to the complicated diplomatic history of the period," according to Black, "is to be found in the marriage negotiations, which assumed an importance out of all proportion to their intrinsic worth" (p. 354).

tiations of 1581-1582. Still, the rest of the poem fits her needs on that occasion very well, and I think it is quite possible that Elizabeth wrote the poem and allowed it to circulate in her name at the time of Anjou's last visit to England.

While Fn, Kn, and C are quite similar texts, and Kn and C nearly identical, the versions in Dd.5.75 and Fl are widely divergent from all three and from each other.

   ] title: Another Fl (referring to the title of the preceding poem in the manuscript, A Song)

1 & favour] then favour Kn C, then beauty Fl

2 sought] woed Fl; vnto] om. *

   ] between 2 and 3: fa-la &c Fl

3 said to] answerde Kn C Fn

   ] after 4, the Fl text concludes with:

      When rip yeares grew on & beauty gann to fade
      To them I made my mone whome I before denyed   fa la la &c
      But then they answered me as I did them before   Goe goe &c
      And scorne your freinds noe more   fa la la &c

   ] between 4 and 5 (text of Kn collated with C and Fn):

      How many wepinge eyes, I made to pyne in woe] wth woe Fn

      How many syghyng hartes I have not skyll to shoe] no skyll Fn

      But I the prowder grew, and still thys spake therfore] Yet I Fn; thus spake C

      Go, go, go seeke some other wher importune me no more

5 but there] Then spake Kn C Fn; fair] brave C; braue] proude Fn

6 said . . . art] Saying, yow daynty Dame, for y^t yow be Kn C, And sayde: fyne Dame since that you be Fn

-332-

 7 wound . . . therfore] pull yowr plumes, as yow shall say no more <u>Kn</u>, pull plums as you shall say no more <u>C</u>, plucke your plumes, that you shall say no more <u>Fn</u>

 9 but . . . my] A sone as he had sayd such change grew in <u>Kn</u>, As sone as he had sayd such care grew in <u>C</u>, When he had spake these wordes such change grew in my brest <u>Fn</u>

 10 the . . . not] That neyther night nor day I could take any rest <u>Kn</u> <u>C</u>, That neyther nyghte nor day since that, I coulde tak my rest <u>Fn</u>

 11 for . . . sore] Wherfore I did <u>Kn</u> <u>C</u>, Than loe I did <u>Fn</u>

 ] FINIS. ELY <u>Kn</u>, 1: of oxforde <u>C</u>, Finis. Elysabethe regina <u>Fn</u>

Item 203

For a brief analysis of this unique text, see p. lxi.

Item 204

(For a general discussion of the Gorges texts in Dd.5.75, see the prefatory note, pp. 316-318). At line 22, Sir Arthur Gorges changed "cares" to "wounds" in his personal manuscript copy of this poem in Egerton MS 3165, ff. 33^V-34^V (reprinted by Sandison, pp. 45-47). Stanford's maintenance of the original reading proves that he was copying the unrevised text, and I have not included this variant in determining his rate of divergence from the Egerton text, one word in thirty-six. Aside from Item 199, this is the least corrupt of the Dd.5.75 poems in common with the Egerton manuscript, and yet, not really accurate enough to suggest that Stanford was copying from that source.

 12 greif] griefs

 17 yee] yow

 19 happ] hope; hope] happ

 22 cares y^t doth] ⟨cares⟩ wounds that doothe

24 loued] loueth

25 so] to

27 thus don] This sayde; on] to

Item 205

(For a general discussion of the Gorges texts in Dd.5.75, see the prefatory note, pp. 316-318). The readings of E (Egerton MS 3165, ff. 101^v-104^v), at lines 5, 51, 57, 61, 63, 104, and in the lines substituted for lines 41-44, represent Gorges' holograph revisions. Stanford copied from an unrevised text, however, for he includes all the lined out readings of E and lacks the four line substitution. The first forty-eight lines of the poem occur in Additional MS 15117, ff. 10^v-11 (A17), which gives all of the E revisions to that point: the correction at line 5, and a version of the four line insert in addition to lines 41-44.[1] PR, the Poetical Rhapsody text of 1602 (with applicable variants from the editions of 1608, 1611, and 1621, as cited by Rollins),[2] prints Gorges' correction at line 104, but lacks the other revisions, and may well have arrived at this one independently. While PR agrees in error with Dd.5.75 at lines 38 and 40, this does not seem to indicate any direct relationship between the texts, since PR avoids Stanford's errors at lines 19, 22, 35, and 67, and Stanford does not follow the PR errors at lines 21 and 91.

The following collation shows that Dd.5.75's copy is closest to the unrevised version of the poem in the Egerton manuscript. PR is also derived

---

[1]Lines 1-4 and 21-24, written in a secretary hand, are set to music in A17, while the rest of the poem is entered in an Italian hand at the bottom of the page and on f. 11^r.

[2]Rollins reproduces the text of 1602, I, 45-49, and collates A17 with it, II, 112.

ultimately from this earlier text, while A17 is closest to the revised form of E.

 title] An Ecloge betwen a Shephearde and a Heardman E, II Eglogve. Shepheard. Heardman PR, a dialogue A17

 ] between the title and line 1: S E

1 wth me] by mee PR

4 the frō] the hoate *

5 made] framde E A17; somers] Summer PR

6 for . . . of] of . . . for A17; phoebus] Summer PR

8 the] thes E

9 for daphne ever] Where gentle Daphnee PR

10 flowring] flowry PR A17

14 would her garlandes] should her Garland PR

17 yet thoughe that] But, whereas PR; bear] bears A17

18 favours] favour *

19 sheapheard] shepher A17; loved] loueth *

20 these] those E PR

21 now] om. PR

22 loue lodged] loue ys lodgd *; so] to A17

23 of] on PR; flocke] flockes E

25 besot] befill A17

27 beyond] aboue PR

32 sheapheardes] shephearde E A17

33 is coid] becoyd PR

35 favous scorn] fauoure scornes *

36 of] By PR

37 I . . . now] Wherefore I warne thee to PR

38 our] my PR; walk] wake E A17

39 louely] lowly PR

40 mate] make E A17

] In E, four lines in the top right margin were meant to replace lines 41-44:

And though ye muske & ambar fyne
  So ladylyke they cannot gett
yet wyll they weare ye sweete woodbyne
  the prymerose and ye vyolet

41 nor . . . pearles] no pearles nor Gold PR A17, nor Pearles nor golde E

42 nor] No PR

] between 44 and 45 in A17:

wher is noe muske nor amber fyne to please the dayntie nose
but wher is worne the sweet woodbynd the violet and the rose

44 that vailes] Which vaile PR

45 turtlels] Lasses PR; byn] bee A17

] after 48, finis A17

49 liest] raueste E, rau'st PR

51 great] hyghe E

53 for . . . Ile] the truth that I PR, for trothe that I the tell E

57 for . . . bookes] And dooth for proofe olde tales E

58 that] how E

61 beloued] esteemd E

62 sheapheard] Shepheards PR

63 proued] deemd E

65 we] I PR

66 these] those E PR

67 our courages] My courage PR, Our curadge E

68 happes] happ E

70 nor bear] And beare PR

73 others thoughtes] other thought PR, other thoughts E

74 eyes] Eye E PR

75 passions] passion E PR

79 fier] fevar E PR

80 faith] faith's PR

84 t'endure] endure E PR

86 fancies breed] fancye breeds E PR

91 & till] And whilst PR; thie] this E

93 haples] wretched PR; flocke] flocks E

94 these proud desires] This proude desire E PR

95 wretched plight] woefull state PR

97 even] e'en PR (euen in the editions of 1611 and 1621)

100 thirsting] thirsty PR

102 whilst] where PR

104 loue] see E PR

105 for thoughe] Although PR; deserved] deserueth E

107 hap] happs E PR; marke] marks E, meanes PR

114 might do] would do PR

115 delay] allay PR

119 loose] breake PR

120 paines] paine PR

125 Adieu good heardman] Then Heard-man, farewel PR, Adyeue good heardgrome E

] between 126 and 127: H E

127 might] mought E; these] thy E PR

] Ignoto PR (om. from editions of 1608, 1611, and 1621)

Items 206-207

For a brief analysis of these unique texts, see pp. lxii-lxiii.

Item 208

(For a general discussion of the Gorges texts in Dd.5.75, see the prefatory note, pp. 316-318). This is undoubtedly the work of Sir Arthur Gorges,[1] and one of his most widely circulated poems, albeit it does not seem to have circulated in his name. Besides the text in his own manuscript, Egerton 3165, ff. 2-2^v (reprinted by Sandison, pp. 3-4) (E), the verse also occurs in Rawlinson Poetry MS 85, ff. 17^v-18 (Fn), in Harleian MS 7392, ff. 63^v-64 (Kn), and in the Phoenix Nest, 1593, L4-4^v (from Rollins' edition, pp. 79-80) (PN). Although Stanford's version is closer to E than any of the others, his rate of variance is one word in twenty-four, and he is undoubtedly in error at lines 12, 23, 27, 35, and 42. Again, it is unlikely that Stanford was working from E or from copy strikingly similar to it.

2 the] my Fn PN

3 landés] land Fn Kn PN

4 savour . . . delight] glimmer wth the lighte Fn Kn

6 but] and *; augment] augments PN

7 medowes] meades are Fn Kn PN

8 clothed treen] clothed the treene E, cloth'd the treene PN, clad the treene Fn Kn

9 fethers new] silver notes Kn

10 whom] when PN; wrong] loue Fn

11 attyre] Attyres PN

12 leaues] leafe *; amiddest the] amydste his E, amidd his Fn PN, amiddes the Kn

13 And . . . we] Eache man maye Fn, And as yew Kn PN

---

[1] For the arguments favoring Gorges' claim see Sandison, p. xxxviii, and William Ringler, "Poems Attributed to Sir Philip Sidney," Studies in Philology, XLVII (1950), 126-151.

14 this; bud] his; buds Fn Kn PN

16 this] the Fn Kn PN

17 colour doth] colours doe Fn Kn PN

20 to raunge] abroad to Fn Kn PN

21 in . . . place] Among the buddes Fn, Amonges the buds Kn, Amongst the buds PN; wher] when PN, of Kn; bewtie springes] Bewties springe Kn

22 ever] only *

23 even as] Lyke to Kn Fn, As doth PN; the] a E; that] thats *

24] substitute: And mourns when all his fellows singes Fn, And mournes when all his ffellowes singe Kn, And mourns when all hir neighbours sings PN

25 all men are] al men els are E, every man is Fn Kn PN

27 place] walke *

29 her] his Kn

31 do I] I do Fn Kn PN

32 woes my ioyes] Ioyes my woes Kn

34 pleasures] pleasure Fn

35 hap] hate PN; doth] om. *; shew] say Fn Kn PN; but] is Fn Kn PN

41 haue . . . w^{th}] thence trace from Fn, hence trace from Kn

42 better] better reste *

] Finis Fn, FYNYS S. P. Sidney Kn

Item 209

This anonymous verse was first printed as song 6 in John Dowland's First Booke of Songes or Ayres, 1597, C2^v, STC 7091 (Do). Reprints of the lyrics from this songbook appear in Arber's An English Garner, IV, 37-38, and in Fellowes, p. 457.[1] I have found only one other manuscript

---

[1] Fellowes' Notes to the song (p. 737), mention the occurence of

text, on ff. 9^v-10 of Dyce MS 44 (Dy), in the Victoria and Albert Museum.
This collection, also known as the Todd Manuscript, is partially described
by Joan Grundy, who used the Constable sonnets on ff. 12-43 as copy text
for her edition of that poet's works.[1]

The wording of all three texts is surprisingly similar, although the
ordering of the lines is different in each. Breaking down the poem into
seven stanzas of four lines each, the order of these stanzas would be, for
Dd.5.75, 1-7, for Do, 1,3,2,3,5,4,6,7, and for Dy, 1,2,5,4,6,7,3. If stanza
three is considered to be the chorus, however, the differences in arrangement of the stanzas are not so striking: the songbook text repeats the chorus
only after the first two stanzas, while Dy leaves it to the very end, and
both reverse the order of stanzas 4 and 5 (lines 13-16, and 17-20). Whatever the arrangement of the chorus, Stanford's order of stanzas 4 and 5
seems preferable. In this way, stanzas 5 and 6 fall together as they should,
for both open with similar clauses, "deere frō the when I am gon," and "dere
yf I do not return," which do not properly balance each other if there is
an intervening stanza. Stanford's arrangement, furthermore, best develops
the increasing seriousness of the parting: in stanza 4, the poet vows his
love can only be stopped by death, in 5, he swears that their parting will
deprive him of all happiness, and in 6, that "loue & I shall die togither"

---

lines 1 and 2 in Marston's Eastward Ho, III, ii, but the text bears no relation to Do or the manuscript versions ("Now, O now, I must depart/ Parting
though it absence moue"). The same note refers to quotation of line 9 in
John Forbes' Songs and Fancies to Thre, Foure, or Five Partes (Aberdene,
1662), song 47, recorded by Cyrus Lawrence Day and Eleanore Boswell Murrie,
English Song-Books, 1651-1702 (London, 1940), first line number 2405, p. 300.

[1]Joan Grundy, ed., The Poems of Henry Constable (Liverpool, 1960),
pp. 84-86.

if he does not return. Stanza differences are ignored in the following
collation, which silently alligns the Do and Dy versions with the Dd.5.75
text:

    3 ioy] joyes <u>Dy</u>

    4 loye] Joyes <u>Dy</u>

    5 while] Whiles <u>Dy</u>

    6 when] wheer <u>Dy</u>

    12 she] thow <u>Dy</u>

    13 Absent . . . her] And although youre *

    15 doth] do <u>Do</u>

    17 frō . . . I] when I from thee *

    18 gon all] Gone are *

    19 loued] loue <u>Dy</u>

    23 me . . . absent] my absence never *

    25 I . . . althoughe] we must though now *

    26 frō] wth *

    27 die] lie <u>Do</u>

    28 both] hath <u>Dy</u>; died] dieth <u>Do</u>

<u>Dy</u> and <u>Do</u> are very similar in their readings as well as in their
ordering of the stanzas, while Stanford's text is clearly divergent. Dy,
the most accurate version, omits the songbook error at line 27, and Stanford's
at line 18, and probably, 23.

    As with the lyrics from Morley's <u>First Book of Airs</u> (Items 99 and
188), Item 209 has "household" connections. Dowland was foremost among
the musicians patronized by the Careys, and indeed, his <u>First Book of Songs
or Airs</u>, containing Item 209, was dedicated to Sir George Carey, with due
homage to his wife, Elizabeth: "Neither in these your honours praises may

I let passe the dutifull remembrance of your vertuous Lady my honourable mistris, whose singular graces towards me haue added spirit to my vnfortunate labours" (* 2). Dowland may have introduced the song and its lyrics at the Careys before he published it, or perhaps he came across the poem there and set it to music afterward. In any event, it would seem that poems which found their way into Stanford's anthology and the songbooks of Dowland and Morley, probably had a common point of origin in the Carey household.

Items 210-211

Both of these lyrics are unique texts and rather similar in technique and development; for a brief analysis of Item 211, see p. lxii.

A Prefatory Note to Items 212-234

The period from about 1585 to 1590 is represented in Dd.5.75 by the manifestly chronological sequence of entries on ff. 25-40 (gatherings four and five), a sequence apparently broken by these poems of the sixth gathering, ff. 41-46. At any rate, the content of these works and dates of other texts in print argues against transcription of Items 212-234 after 1590.

The slanders of Edward Bashe and Mary, Queen of Scots (Items 212-214), must have been composed before their deaths in 1587, and certainly Item 220, a plea to Queen Elizabeth to marry and establish the succession to the throne, was written before 1587. The only other known text of Item 215 was printed in 1580, that of Item 217 only in the editions of Tottel's <u>Miscellany</u> between the second, in 1557, and the last, in 1587. Item 219 appears in all editions of the <u>Paradise of Dainty Devices</u> (1576-1606), but collation shows that Stanford's text is most closely related to the three editions between 1578 and 1585, while the only other text of Item 227 appears in the 1576 edition. Item 221 is made up from two <u>Paradise</u> poems, and Item 223 is also found in every edition of that anthology. Interspersed with these printed texts are two poems which apparently circulated only in manuscript (Items 216 and 222), and five probably unique poems (Items 218, 220, 224, 225, and 226). But just as the pattern of a late 1570's to mid 1580's grouping begins to form, we are confronted with Items 228-234, transcribed undoubtedly in 1599, yet preceded on f. 46 by the <u>Paradise</u> poem found only in the edition of 1576.

Collation, furthermore, does not suggest that Stanford was copying from any of the known printed texts, although his transcriptions from the <u>Musica Transalpina</u> (Items 116-137), from the Treatise of <u>Moral Philosophy</u> (Items 147-164, 168-178), and from Yong's translation of Montemayor's <u>Diana</u> (Items 229-234), prove that he was not above copying from printed books. When he did so, however, he copied the items in sequence, and averaged no more than one variant per fifty-four words, while divergence from even the closest of the printed texts listed above ranges between one error in ten words to one in twenty-six, only half as accurate at the best as his transcriptions from identifiable sources.

If we assume, nonetheless, that Stanford was working from an edition of the <u>Paradise</u>, how are we to explain the scattered arrangement of the poems (Items 219, 221, 223, and 227), which could not have resulted from an attempt either to save space while the pages were blank or to fill in blank spaces later. On the other hand, all five <u>Paradise</u> texts represented here are found in the same general area of that collection (Rollins' numbers 67, 68, 71, 72, and 95), and amateur experimentation could account for the splicing of Paradise poems 71 and 95 to form Item 221.[1] Thus, these four Items must bear some relation to the Paradise texts, although their random entry in the manuscript and variation from all of the prints argue against direct copying.[2]

I can suggest three possible explanations, none of them entirely satisfactory, which might account for so much contradictory data. First, Stanford may have organized this portion of his anthology in commonplace fashion. Items 212-214 were entered together as libels, while Items 215-234 were taken from works printed between 1576 and 1599. Commonplace organization, however, does not explain the non-sequential entry of the Paradise poems, nor the absence of printed texts for Items 216, 218, 220, 222, 224-226, and 228.

Second, the entire gathering may be out of place. Item 227, after-all, comprises only the last two stanzas of a three stanza poem in the Paradise, and Stanford's numbering of his stanzas, "2" and "3.," probably indicates that he had copied the whole poem and that some disruption of the manuscript resulted in the loss of one or more folios here. If so, gathering six may have originally preceded the fourth and fifth gatherings, with their sequence of entries between 1585 and 1590, though such dislocation does not explain why Stanford left two-thirds of f. 46^r blank, nor why he decided to fill it in at least a decade later, in 1599, with Items 228-234.

---

[1] Hyder Rollins, ed., The Paradise of Dainty Devices (Cambridge, Massachusetts, 1927). In the notes and collations following, references to the Paradise are to the text and list of variant readings in Rollins' reprint.

[2] Rollins concluded that "X," the lost edition of 1577, "was almost certainly identical with the edition of 1578" (p. xiv), would therefore not have contained Item 227, and cannot explain the apparent derivation of Item 227 from the 1576 Paradise, and Item 219 only from some later edition.

Finally, this series of poems could represent chronological entry and still occupy a gathering in its original place in the manuscript, for Items 212-227 could all have been circulating in manuscript, as 212-214, 216, 221 and 222 certainly were. Stanford carefully numbered the stanzas of poems 215-227, a practice he followed nowhere else, and one which is found in none of the printed texts. Possibly, he was following a single manuscript collection of these poems which numbered the stanzas in the same way. Such a collection would explain the jumbled order of the Paradise texts, the apparent representation of at least two editions of that anthology, and the considerable variation of Stanford's texts from any of the printed versions. Gathering six, then, could represent Stanford's transcriptions in chronological sequence between 1590 and 1599, although the occasional nature of the two libels and of Item 220 argues against this. In short, the evidence will not support any of these three explanations satisfactorily, and while I believe that the third one is the most likely, position of texts in Dd.5.75 after f. 40 cannot alone establish the date of transcription.

Items 212-213

For a discussion of the literary influences at work in this libel and identification of the allusions to its subject, Edward Bashe (died 20 May 1587), see Ruth Hughey's notes to poems 182-183 in her edition of The Arundel Harington Manuscript, II, 293-301. The libel pokes much fun at Bashe's humble origins, and it would seem that he fell victim to this attack largely because his service to the crown as surveyor of victuals for the navy produced a steady increase in his worldly fortunes; as Stanford had recorded in Item 146, "a Lewder wretche ther lyves not vnder skye, then clown y^t climes fro base estate to hie."

On 24 July 1586, Bashe declared in a letter to Walsingham that he had served as victualler of the navy a total of forty years, under the father, brother and sister of the present Queen.[1] His major rewards for that service began, apparently, with the grant of a coat of arms in 1550 (Hughey, II, 300). He was summoned to Queen Elizabeth's first two Parliaments (1559 and 1563-1567), and was sufficiently in favor at Court, at least in 1577/78, to exchange New Year's gifts with the Queen.[2] In 1585, Bashe reported to the Privy Council concerning a suspected recusant in his neighborhood, and, in his official capacity as sheriff of Hertfordshire, was himself reported in that same year by one Robert Snagge, "for certain disorders committed towards him and others, his clients."[3]

Preferment was certainly not the whole story for Bashe, who must have worked hard for his gains during the great era of the expanding Tudor navy. Judging from the frequent occurrence in the State Papers of his complaints to Burghley, Bashe faced the chronic problem that plagued so many of Elizabeth's administrators, the performance of his duties without an adequate budget. And his requests for more money do not necessarily mean that Bashe siphoned off large sums for his private use, since his widow, Jane, petitioned after his death for reimbursement of funds her husband had taken from his own pocket for victualing of the navy.[4]

Although Miss Hughey identifies the young wife referred to in the libel (lines 123-127), with Bashe's third wife, "the daughter of one

---

[1] Lemon, CXCI, 341, Article 28.

[2] Return. Members of Parliament, Part I, pp. 400, 404; John Nichols, The Progresses, and Public Processions of Queen Elizabeth, I (London, 1788), 88.

[3] Lemon, CLXXXIV, 299, Article 41; CLXXVII, 230, Articles 5-6.

[4] Ibid., CCV, 441, Article 66.

Baker" (II, 300), it seems more likely that his widow, Jane, was intended.
Lines 136-138 mention the birth of a son to Bashe, and according to the
1634 Visitation of Hertfordshire,[1] Jane, the daughter of Sir Ralph Sadler,
was the only wife to bear him sons. If so, the composition of the libel
can be assigned with some probability to the mid or late '70's, if we
assume that Bashe's second grant of arms, in 1572, resulted from his marriage into the prosperous Sadler family. The birth of his sons, Ralph, and
William, presumably followed that marriage, and the libel must have followed
one of these births. The later limit of composition, of course, would be
20 May 1587, the date of Bashe's death.

Other copies of the libel are found in Additional MS 34064, ff. 36-40 (64), apparently entered during the early 1590's, and in Lansdowne MS
740, ff. 87-91 (L), copied in the early seventeenth century. From her
collation of the Arundel Harington text, ff. 137-139 (AH) with L and the
Rawlinson Poetry MS 85 version, ff. 66-72 (Fn), Miss Hughey concluded that
AH and L must have been derived from the same source (II, 293). Collation
of the Dd.5.75 and 64 variants, which Miss Hughey had not seen, does not
reveal further textual relationships. Since all four texts omit lines
found in all the others, none could be the immediate source for any of the
others, barring individual scribal additions. In general, 64 falls in with
AH and L against Fn and Dd.5.75, but there is not sufficient or consistent
agreement in error on which to base a definite stemma.

Samuel Tannenbaum mentions a sixth copy of this poem in a Rosenbach
MS ("Unfamiliar Versions of Some Elizabethan Poems," PMLA, XLV [1930],
821), but I have not seen this manuscript, nor had Miss Hughey.

---

[1]Walter C. Metcalfe, ed., The Visitations of Hertfordshire . . . in
1572 . . . and . . . 1634 (Harleian Society Publications, Vol. XXII; London,
1886), pp. 125-126.

]title: The Coppie of a Libell. Written against Bashe AH, Bash. L,
The lybell Fn, A spightfull lybell entered by yᵉ parties whome it
concerned, into yᵉ records of Chancerie 64

3 on] a 64, out L;   now] newes 64

4 &] But 64; me whie or] I know not AH L; how] whose? 64

5 witte is] witts are *

6 bourd] play 64

9 is] tis 64; rime] rye 64

10 is large] is verie large 64

11 bound] tyed AH L; by] to 64

12 spavavade] Spa, noe vade 64

14 gennette] Iennes 64

15 witte is] witts are L

17 & thoughe he] Perhapps you Fn

18 yet] butt Fn; of]to 64

19 Let...sure] Though he be rough 64

20 rune] ryme *

21 would] will AH L 64; wᶜʰ] what Fn

22 for] or AH L 64; all] it AH

23 It] Thys Fn

26 butcherlye] Butcherlike AH L 64

27 this] thy Fn; squier] exquire 64

28 Hartford] Harford *

29 beefe] beefes 64, Beeues Fn; named] made Fn

31 Count] Countie AH L 64, And Coutye Fn; of...degree] else
calves-head, this is hee 64

32] om. *

33 & viconte] Vice-count of 64; Neatestongues] Neates tongue Fn; this...he] that is he Fn, of like degree 64

36 doe] trye Fn

38 birth & Countrie] name of great AH L, birth and countryes Fn; crown] good 64, renown AH L Fn

between 38 and 39: Because he came of noble bloode 64

39 this...born] Borne he was Fn

between 39 and 40 : A place too good for such a clowne 64

40 perhaps] Perchance 64; as] for 64 Fn

42] om. AH L; of truth] Of y^t truth 64; that his] y^t was his 64, it was his Fn; mercerie] misterie 64 Fn

43] om. AH L

44 as] And 64

45 father wont] father was wont 64

46 wandring] wandring here 64; both...nere] thorough here & there AH L

47 many a] sundrie AH L

48 take the] seeke the AH L, seeke his 64; vantage] fortune AH L: of his] by good 64

50 and 51 reversed Fn

50 In] Att Fn; Beuer] Bevis 64; by] in AH L Fn; vale] dalle Fn

54 let...passe] thense he gott 64; hap] looks Fn, lulke 64, lucke AH L

55 that] a Fn

56 and 57 om. 64

56 thence] whence L; skapt] came AH L

57 after] for him Fn

58 & then] From thence 64, but so AH L; he came] hee went AH L, he coms 64

59 sondry] manie 64; clyming] climings 64, clyme Fn

60 of] in AH L 64

61] substitute: (To make good all his trecherie) 64

62 & Brothels] brothells Fn, and scoulers 64

63 Cutthroate merchantes] With cut-throates, Cut-purses 64, cutthroats in chaunters AH L, Cutt throttes, theeues Fn; &] om. L

64]substitute: powlers, takers, and purvaiers 64; couriers] convayers AH L Fn

65] om. AH L Fn; substitute: Brokers, coiners, and convaiers 64

66] om. 64; pollers] Privie AH L

67] om. 64

after 67 in AH L Fn; after 65 in 64: of euerye wicked fashione
And all abhominatione } wth all abhomination AH L

68 at lengthe] in fewe yeares Fn 64, at the last AH L; suche] so much L

69 wth] by AH L 64; Cuckoldes] cuckould Fn

70 as] That *; now] more 64; gan]began Fn

71 was] twas AH L

between 71 and 72 (AH collated with L):

    & on ye ground he might not tred] mought not
    for Ioulting of his heavie head
    well let it bee, as be it might.
    This scabbed squyre this donghill knight] Scabby squier
    gan now on Cockhorse for to ride] one Horsback
    along the street in pompe & pride

between 71 and 72 in 64:

    And on the ground he might not tread
    For ioltinge of his heavie-head,
    Or else for feare to sweate so faste,
    That all his grease should melt at last.
    And so this filthie stinkinge fatt,
    Thus gott wth spoile of this or that,

>   should melt like snow against ye sunn,
>   For he that thus his goodes had woone
>   Was euer more affraide to leese
>   And to be pluct vppon his knees
>   Well; lett it be, as be it might.
>   This lowsie esquire, this dung-hill knight,
>   Gan nowe on hors-backe for to ryde
>   Alonge ye streetes, through pompe & pryde

   72 yet] but AH L 64

   75 could] would 64; such] his AH L 64

   76 once was] was once L Fn

   77 squire] Synior AH L, esquire 64

   78 his; at] The; of AH L; Stansted] stand-steed 64

   79 &] Thatt Fn; now must they] they muste now Fn, then must they AH L

   81 fowle] great AH L

   82 will they] this will 64, shall his AH L, will this Fn; last] lengthe Fn

   83 for thoughe] Although 64; mast] Mas^er AH Fn, this L; did] do Fn, hath 64; skape] scapt 64

   84 & now be] & be as AH L, and is as 64; or] and 64

   85 yet] But Fn; yf you] he shall 64; lines 164-260 follow 85 in 64

   86 cope] coate Fn

   between 86 and 87 in 64: the strongest part of Base-son rope

   87 ther] Then *; of his] of this AH; this must hitte] this needs must hitt AH L, this muste needs hitt Fn, this needes must chaunce 64

   between 87 and 88 in 64: (els I mistake my part ith' daunce)

   88 will] shall 64, must AH L

   89 raptor] rapto AH L; alter habebit] alter hanc habebit 64

   92] om. AH L; this] that Fn, it 64

   93 knaves _____] knaves life *; scarse] skant AH, not worth Fn L; the] om. AH L

94 would would] I could AH L, I woulde Fn, 64

95 he vsed] he hath vsed Fn 64, he hath spent AH L

96 vnder] in the AH L 64

97 stocke] stake Fn

98 no] for AH L

between 99 and 100: were she sore, or were she sownd AH L,
Was she whole or was she sounde Fn, yea were she poxt, or were she
sounde 64

99 harlot] strumpett AH L

100 durst] would AH L; barrell] bellie 64

101 brothers] brother L

102 Syr] then AH L 64; say] said 64

103 y^t] this Fn; amongest] among AH L

104 vox populi] Vix populi 64

105-108] om. AH L

105 yea] Well 64

107 him] his Fn

108 since] if 64; the colt could] he could not Fn, the colt would 64

109 god knoweth] Alas AH L; knoweth...he] knowes he might full
little 64

110 plucke] pull AH L; his] one of his 64; own] om. Fn 64

111 wth] Even wth 64; a] suche a Fn AH L

112 be] were AH L 64

113 of an] one in Fn; thanckfull] shame-facet 64

114] substitute Surelie he should take the pain AH; Surelie he
would take the paine L; do well] well do Fn, have done 64; these] the 64

115 to send] And sent 64

116 or els]] so AH L; to lend] to let AH L, have lent 64;
som] haue AH L

117 ther] trwe Fn, good 64

118 he once might] he then might AH L, he myghte once Fn, that he might 64

119] om. 64

120 I] he 64

121 and 122 reversed 64

121 that] For 64

122 he...abrode] abroad he needs not for AH, abroad he need not for L, rome] come 64

124 s^r; he bought] om. ; he hath bought AH L

125 long] sore AH L

126 nor] And 64; was]is Fn

127 nor...mans] But this was scant an honest 64

128 but sure; yt pincht her] And that; doth greive at 64

129 wherof] of wch AH L, Wherfore 64

130 for trulie] although & AH L, Or surely 64

131 could] would 64; assure] wish 64, afforde Fn

133 toothsom] proper AH L; neate] sweet *

134 Neatstongues] Neatstongue Fn

135 alas] om. Fn

136 as] om. Fn; heare] heard 64; she...men] whie of late I haue heard AH L

137 delyuered] she was delivered AH L; this] but this 64

138 knaues] knave AH Fn

139 wotte you what] what of that? 64 Fn

140 how; the] but; om. Fn

142 both] om. AH L

143 that] there AH L 64; a] hir Fn

145 might] would AH L 64; to marie] to haue marid AH L

146 so double] t'haue done some good AH L, so to doe a good 64, to to do double Fn; deedes] deede 64

147 carue] help AH L, serve Fn 64; nedes] neede Fn 64

148 next] then AH L 64

149 poundes & pence] pence and powndes Fn 64

150 but] surely 64; synce I haue] sith that now I haue AH L; this gear] om. AH L 64

151 assay] assaylle Fn

153 he] it AH L 64

154 a] to a Fn

155 well doth] doth well Fn

156 thoughe yt be] which is as AH L, shall se'et 64

157 yet...playnly] then out of doubt he AH L, yet certainlie he 64

158 loueth] loves *

between lines 158 and 159 (text of AH, variant of L in right margin):

or if a man the truth should tell
ffirst if his bodie were set vpright
& his necke were cut of quite
a man y^t had good list to shite] lust
might sitt at ease vpon his necke
& down his throate ⟨abo⟩ wthout all checke
The durt would fall in to his gutts
& then it might be tried by cutts
whether the durt that down did fall
or y^t wch was there first of all
be putrified best of twayne
this is a question that is plaine

between lines 158 and 159 (text of 64, variants of Fn in right margin):

For drink he will, till bellie swell,   ] om.
And if a man the truth should wright] But if; shoude tell
First if his head were cutt off quyte
And then his bodie sett vpright
A man y^t hath good list to shite] had; luste to 77382
May sitt at ease vppon his necke] Maghte make his neycke a double 32827
And downe his throate wth shitten check] That downe; by gobbs and flakes
The dirt would droppe into his guttes] myghte dropp

And then it must be tried by cuttes] But than it mighte be
Whether the durt y^t downe doth fall] the dongue
Or that which were ther first of all] was there
Be putrified work, or noe, of twaine] puryfyed beste of the twayne
It is a question verie plaine] This is a questione that is playne

  159 A question also haue I] or if it bee as I haue AH L, An other question haue I herde Fn, Another question eake I heard 64

  160 fewtered] feltred AH L, fethered 64

  161 were] bee AH L 64; to serue] om. AH L

  162 for] else 64; masker wth a] master on a AH, Masker one his L

  163 & then this] Another AH L, and eake this 64

  after 163: whether his bodie beinge clad with frise 64

  lines 263-286 follow 163 in 64

  165 all for ale] all of drincke AH L, out wth ale 64; ought for] ought of AH L, out with 64

  166] om. Fn; and] or AH L

  167 &] om. L; trothe] truthe Fn

  168 again] om. AH L; will] there be y^t AH L; put this] make a AH L, moue this Fn, put in 64

  169 whither; turkey coloured] As; whether; colored Turkeyee Fn

  171 deale] dally *

  172 I doe know &] this I boldlie AH L, I perceue and Fn 64

  174 made] And AH L; of] in AH L 64

  176 he] she Fn

  177 paddocke] Mattocke AH Fn L, Mathoote 64; he] she Fn

  178] om. Fn; stinkes] skinks AH

  180 worthie to] worthie for to 64

  181 Chancellours] councellers AH L Fn; child] daughter *; doth] om. AH L

  182 yes trulie &] yes indeed & AH L, yea surlye and Fn, yes certainly, for 64

  183 nose wth tongue] with tongue & mouth AH L, with tonge, wth nose 64, wth nose, with tongue Fn

185 I] it AH L

186-187 between 189 and 190 in 64

186 he goeth] & hee goes *

187 rowling] roylynge Fn; as] like *

188 seate] set *

189 & he sittes] hee rydeth AH L 64; demie] deniee AH

190 or] S^r Fn; I not] I need not Fn, I do not AH L

191 a toad vppon] like a toade on AH L

192 and] but AH L 64; for yt is] and so tis AH L, for so tis Fn 64

193 &...west] And lett his face hange East, or West AH L 64

194 vppon] and on AH L, Then on 64; shoulders] shouldure Fn; wilbe fixed] wilbe spred AH L, shall be spredd Fn, may well be spied 64

195 a] the AH L 64; the] a AH Fn 64

197 forgotten] forgot it AH L Fn, forgotten it 64

199 thicke] faire AH L; full &] full AH L, fowle and Fn, full of 64

200 som] & AH L; other] others AH 64; yt is so] that itt is 64; so fyne] om. Fn

201 and 202 follow 203 in AH L

201 like to] much like 64, like the AH; taber] taster *

202 and 203 om. 64

202 som] And some Fn; by] to AH L; a] om. Fn; takes most] haue great AH L, take moste Fn

203 &] om. AH L; likest to] tis like vnto AH, it's like vnto L, lykewyse to Fn

204 &...rightly] but this I dare be bold to AH L, But if y^t I shall plainely 64, But if that I shall rightlye Fn

205 yt is a] Tis like a 64

206 prate; Clatter] eate; chatter 64

208 rayle] cogg AH L

209 sneke] squeak 64, speake Fn

between 209 and 210 (text of AH L, variants of 64 in right margin):

    To speake like a Prelate] talk like
    To thinke like a Pilate] meane like

210 letter] letters Fn

211 checke] tawnt AH L 64; y^e] his *; better] betters Fn

212 into] vnto Fn 64, to AH L

213 fowler] falser AH L Fn; tongue can no man] knave you cannot Fn, ⟨ ⟩e you cannot 64

214 synce] sith *

215] om. 64

216 me thinkes] I thinke AH L 64

217 &; he giues] om.; doth hee beare 64

218 from] out of 64

219 beares] geues Fn

221 for] but AH L 64; Heraultes] herraulde Fn; did] might 64

222 his; at] the; of AH L; Stansted] Stand steed 64, sansted Fn

223 &] they AH L 64; playnly] om. AH L 64; might] did 64 Fn; perceaue] perceiue and guesse AH L 64

224 would haue] must needes haue AH L 64, would needs haue Fn

225] om. Fn; they...be] bicause he was so trimly AH L

between lines 225 and 226 in AH, L, and 64:

    Clarentieux, knew it verie well
    for as I heard some herald tell AH] And as...Harrolds L

    Clarentins ment it verie well
    For as I heard the Heraldes tell 64

226 they then] He hath 64, they haue AH L Fn; appointed] assigned AH L

227 a] the Fn

228 yt] he 64 Fn

229 the] his AH L Fn

230 men] om. L 64 Fn, do AH

231 now tell me] But sir AH L

233 yet...beast] nor Bashe him self y^t beast at least AH L, And yet the beast himself att least 64, Ye Bashe him selfe the beast at leaste Fn

234 could...this] did ever know the AH L; espie] spie 64 Fn

235 tooke] takes AH L

236 now sure] Forsooth AH L 64; myne] my Fn

237 ye herauldes] the Herrald AH L, They 64; vsed him] handled him most 64

238 yet] And yet 64; is alwayes] had bene AH L; is the 64

239 among] amongste 64 Fn

240 of] for Fn

241 herald] herralds AH

242 but yf] except AH L; I should for] I would of AH L, they would of 64

243 a] the 64

244 these; then should he] what; he then should AH L

245 par] deleted by scribe AH; panche] pate 64; durtie] wth durt AH L, first dirt 64, durte Fn

246 his] the 64; cheiffe] neck AH L

247 three] two AH L 64; stynt strife] stint all strife AH L, stynte ye stryfe Fn

248 cheuron like] Chevin like AH L, chevorne, not 64

249 like] with 64

250 broidred] imbroydered AH, imbrothered L, bordered Fn

253 might] should AH L 64; his] the AH L

254 that] the 64 Fn

255-264] om. AH L

255 a] om. Fn

256 least yf] For if 64

257 straine] break 64; the halter; his stresse] his haulter; the stress Fn

258 this] The 64

259 & on] Or in Fn; this may] there might 64, this myghte Fn

260 a...of] The Butt-end of a shepheardes 64

261 yet] it Fn

263 mantled] Mangled Fn, Mantles 64; mangie...w^{th}] or mangie he lived in 64

264 thus] Thys Fn; beare; my devise] fare; mine advice 64

265 as] And AH 64 L; he should] I would 64

266 oues boues] Oves et boues et *; pecora] vniuersa pecora Fn

267 for] om. AH L; so he will] so shall AH, soe he shall L, a knave he will 64, a kn: he shall Fn

268 mast] mass Fn 64; mast Bashe I] for sooth to AH L

269 me...I] I think tis time to AH, I thinke it's time to L, I thinke it time to 64; I bid adieu] to bydd you adewe Fn

270 stable] scabby AH L, scabbed 64 Fn; squire] esquire 64

271 but; before] and; or ere AH L

272 thing] one thing *; to...nedes] to yow I must AH L, I to yow must 64, to you must I Fn

for 274-275 substitute: Attend to me, mark well my worde
                       I am not in yor debte a tourde   64

274 on] a AH L

275 no not] Not to AH L Fn

276 not] what AH L, om. 64; yes] ys AH; sure] surlye Fn

277] om. 64; I...yt] I thinke I vs'd not y^t word yet AH L

278 see] loe AH L 64; how...sone] how soone one maie AH, how one may soone L

for 279 substitute: well then sith I such curtsie vse AH] curtesie L

279 whie] Well 64

280 tell; might] know; would 64; like] please Fn

282 deuils] deuyll Fn

283-284 follow 279 in AH L

283 take...to] and freelie giue yow leaue to AH L, Take euen which turde you lyst to Fn, I give you leave more for to 64

284 & so] And se Fn, Then ser 64, then see AH L; you] y^t yow AH L

285 vse yt] take all AH L, take it 64; as a] as your Fn, of yor 64

286 turd] A tourde Fn; thers] there AH L Fn, soe 64

   ] Finis AH Fn, TEΛO 64

      Item 213 (om. 64; precedes Item 212 in Fn)

   ] libell against Bashe: to the Reader: Fn, Lenuoy L

1 you] all L; my rime] this ryme AH L

2 take] count Fn

3.] om. AH L; thoughe] Allthough Fn

between 3 and 4: In playne termes of knauerye Fn

4 for therin] for why AH L, for this Fn; surely...I] I orderly haue AH L

5 keepe] obserue Fn

6 tought me] taught it mee AH

7 a] this AH L; pretie] noblle Fn

8 would] should AH L

9 not like] vnlyke Fn

10 &] Wherfore Fn, so AH L; haue writ] haue rym'd AH L, wryte Fn

13 be] are L

14 Il...writ I] yf ill favordly rym'd I AH L, Ill vauored if I wrytten Fn

15 whie] om. AH L

16 Brauishe] knavishe AH L Fn

17 &] Butt Fn

      ] Finis AH L

Item 214

This indecent slander follows Mary Stuart's career to her arrival in England, 16 May 1568, or perhaps to her stricter confinement after exposure of the Ridolfi Plot in 1571. The personal nature of the attack, the charges that lechery and atheism led Mary to such crimes as incest with her uncle, the Cardinal of Lorraine, and complicity in Darnley's murder, is characteristic of anti-Marian propaganda during her first few years in England.[1] Lack of reference to Mary's involvement in the later plots on Queen Elizabeth's life also argues for a relatively early date of composition, perhaps during the 1570's.

I have found only one other text of this poem, in Harleian MS 7371, f. 132^v, which must have been copied after Mary's execution, 8 February 1587, unless its title recording that date was added after transcription of the poem. Without evidence of this, it would seem that this verse was circulating after 1587, when Scottish and continental objection may have revived this outdated defense of her execution.

The words "Dutam patricij Buocsargensis" in Stanford's title may refer to the author of the poem, though I cannot relate them to a specific person. George Buchanan, Mary's most voluminous detractor, may have been intended, although this is not the usual Latin form of his name, nor did Buchanan use Latin Skeltonics in his anti-Marian works.

The Harleian text collated below is shorter than the Dd.5.75 version, and has been crossed out with several slanting lines, though all its readings are legible. It bears no demonstrable relation to Stanford's text.

---

[1] James Emerson Phillips, *Images of A Queen* (Berkeley, 1964), p. 83. Phillips does not refer to this particular slander of Queen Mary.

title] substitute detruncat apd foderinghay in com Northt. .8. febr. 1587

2 vndiq;] maxime

5 quae] Que

6 mersos] mechos

7 vinoq;] vinaq;

8 futuis] intus; gota] rota

10 magis] mage

14 temeras; bina] temerans; trua

20 procax] praxq;

21-23] follow lines 24-27

22 pudorem &; aperisti] om.; aperuisti

23 seram tuae cistae] ceram tue ciste

24 praeter] precor

28-38] om.

39 no me] Non me

41 &]huic

42 iugulase] iugulasi

44 duxisti] duxisse

47 & crudeli] O crudeli

50 nes; telae] vos; teli

51 feli] fele

52 plus ferrea] mage feri

55 At] Ac

56 moecho] mechus

57-58] om.

63 & hæc] hec et

64 vsq;] atq;

66 Antagonista] Antigonista

67-68] om.

71 predicta] predcā

72 misera; es prorsus] om.; prorsus es tu

78 merita . . . icta] merito vt faxis fore retro

83 &] om.

87 tibi] ibi

88 quod] quia; chari] rari

92 imperitare] imperitari

93 clare] clari

94 anticipare] anticipari

96 aūūcula] in cute

99-100] om.

101 fortuna bella] fortune vota

102 væ] vel

Item 215

John Lyly, among others, specifically warned against the evils of foreign travel, a popular topic of Elizabethan debate, through Euphues' advice to Ephoebus,[1] while a poem added to the Paradise of Dainty Devices in 1585 offers a good example of the counter-argument (Rollins' number 123). Item 215 is Thomas Churchyard's attack on foreign travel and related evils, printed in A Pleasaunte Laborinth Called Churchyeardes Chance, 1580, K2ᵛ-K3 (STC 5250). Stanford's rate of divergence from this text, not

---

[1]Bond, I, 283-284.

counting the lines he omitted, is about one word in twelve.

    ] <u>title</u>: Of wandryng and gaddynd abroad.

3 feede] please

4 carrieth] carries

    ] <u>after</u> 4: What seest thou foole in princely hauls, that maie
a poore man eas,
Whose state is toste with tennis balls, and turns
with winde & seas

6 greates] furthest

8 those that sore haue; are] those are gone that; and

9 the; vnknowen] thy; uncouth

11 heaped; hast] heape; hath

13 braines; muche] braine; but

14 then; paines] Thus; paine

15 then hart] the harte

    ] <u>after</u> 15: A triumphe but a pagent seems, when paste is all the sho,
All other thyngs that man estemes, man lothes at length
also

17 trusse . . . toyes] take vp thy trusse

18 els] here

Item 216

Of the manuscript sources I have checked, all fifty-four lines of this poem occur only in Dd.5.75 and in Harleian MS 6910, ff. 149^v-150^r (H). Ralph Sargent bases his text of the poem on sources which omit lines 47-52, Rawlinson Poetry MS 85, ff. 6^r-6^v (Fn), collated with Folger MS 1.112, ff. 6^r-6^v (C).[1] Harleian MS 7392, ff. 23^v-24^r (Kn), also contains the

---

[1]Sargent, pp. 180-181, 205.

shorter text, while Sir John Harington quoted its last two lines in his translation of Ariosto's Orlando Furioso, 1591, L4^V (STC 746):

> He that hath plast his heart on hie,
> Must not lament althoughe he die.

The four ascriptions to Dyer (C, Fn, H, and Kn), and the marginal note to Harington's excerpt, "Master Edward Dier a Somersetshire man," establish his authorship without much question, and certainly the wordplay which complicates this examination of the lover's state is typical of Dyer's work. The stemma below explains the relationship between the texts if we assume that Stanford's version of line 19 represents Dyer's final intent. If the other version of this line, found in each of the other texts, was the final choice, then H would be taken directly from the author's original, while line 19 was changed to the Dd.5.75 reading either by Stanford or by an intermediate source between Dd.5.75 and the original. In either case, it is from H and Dd.5.75 that Dyer's original should be reconstructed; the abbreviated texts, C, Fn, and Kn, are similarly inaccurate and offer few if any preferable readings. Harington's two lines suggest that his copy of the poem may have diverged widely from all five of the other texts, and I have thus placed his version, speculatively, on a separate branch of the stemma.

5 wishe] woulde Fn C Kn; yt were] it not C; should] woulde *

7 would god] I woulde *; knew] to knowe Fn; meane] meanes C

8 meane] meanes C; knew] soughte *

9 my] not C; fancie] fancies H

10 these] suche Fn C Kn, those H; thoughtes . . . ensew] ioyes as loue hath wroughte Fn, Ioyes wch love hathe wroughte C Kn, thoughtes that Loue hath wrought H

11 only to] But now H; to] my *; least of all] lefte at all C Kn, leaste at all H

12 we know the] to knowe a Fn C Kn, is knowne the H

13 that] whiche Fn C

14 thou . . . semely] semelye thou doste Fn

15 twise] Thrise *; for thie hartes] man, if thy Fn, man for thy C Kn

16 ioyn] winne Fn C Kn

17 is] to Fn

18 hap] helpe Kn; acquite yt] acquiet Fn Kn, nor quiet H, make quiet C

19 my . . . life] The budds of hope are staruede Fn C Kn, The Birds of hope are staru'd H

20 my sore] his foe Fn C Kn, my feare H

21 fate] state *; hap; did] hope; shoulde Fn C Kn

22 hap] hope H

23 diamant] diamond Fn C Kn, diamondes H

24 or] O H; wth . . . fret] in goulde Ifrett Fn C, wth Gould yfrette Kn

25 behold] For loe Fn C Kn

26 baiting] beatinge *

27 at my] on my H; heele] feet*

29 wing . . . doth] wings to mounte alofte make Fn C Kn, wings to get to gate do hast H

31 Suche; plight] This; state Fn C Kn; this] thus *

32 we] Theye *

33 youthe] boye Fn

34 teache] learne Fn

35 poynt] course H; so neare] agaynste Fn

36 blames . . . sea] drownde in seas Fn C Kn, blam'd the sea H; name] wracke H; hath] that Fn C Kn, had H

39 who lyue in] pore mann, on Fn C Kn, that liue on H

40 deathes] cares H; pangues] paynes Fn Kn, paine C, griefs H; spend] sende Fn

41 loue . . . playnt] greife, now hope, now loue Fn, griefe now plaint now loue C H Kn

42 sorow] sorrowes H; short] small C

43 scarre & fellon] pheere and fellour Fn, feare and fellow C H Kn; my] thy *

46 gripe doth] gryphes do Fn C, Grypes do Kn; tire &] daylye Fn, allway H, gnawe and C Kn

47-52] om., Fn C Kn

47 whie] loe H

48 the thing that] That wch the H

50 vild; would] vile; may H

51 faltes] fates H

52 worke the same] do worke their shame H

53 who . . . advanced] But he that lyfts Fn, but he y^t _____ C, But he that vauntes Kn; on] to Fn C, om., Kn

] Finis Master Dier Fn, finis H, dyer C, FYNIS DY. Kn

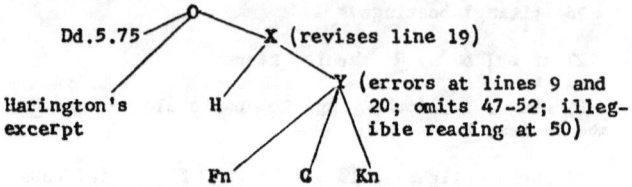

Item 217

This anonymous work first appeared in the second edition of Tottel's Songs and Sonnets, printed in the summer of 1557 (STC 13861; Rollins' number 310). All later editions correct "bodies" (line 28), to "bodie," in agreement with Stanford's reading, but otherwise follow the second edition with which I have collated Item 217 from Rollins' reprint.[1] The rate of variation

---

[1]Hyder Rollins, ed., Tottel's Miscellany (2 vols.; Cambridge, Massachusetts, 1966), I, 258.

between these two texts averages about one word in eleven.

Apparently, the marginal note, "the dolefull bell y^t systers larūs ringes," was meant as a title for this poem. If this is Stanford's addition, he may have entered this work as a memorial on the death of one of his own sisters, for the loved one whose death the poet is mourning could fittingly represent one of them--he had five, including a twin sister, Margaret. Unfortunately, I do not know when any of Stanford's sisters died, so that the speculation is still of no help in dating the transcription of this poem.

title] The louer lamenteth that he would forget loue, and can not.

3 this] the

5 more] mo

8 that rageth] Which raigneth

10 had] hath

12 w^{ch}] That

16 on fire] a fire

18 seeking] To seke

22 wth y^e] of the

23 wethered rotten] rotten withered

26 slake / shake] slake

27 extreme . . . draweth] cold then straineth

28 body quake] bodies shake

31 she] her

35 that] Yet

37 an] One

Item 218

For a brief analysis of this unique text, see p. lxi.

Item 219

W. H. (William Hunnis), is credited with this poem (Rollins' numbers 72 and 109), in every edition of the <u>Paradise of Dainty Devices</u> in which it appears (1576-1606; leaf missing from the first of the 1596 editions). Beginning with the edition of 1578, two lines attributed to Richard Edwards are added to the end of the poem, but Stanford's text has only the first twelve lines, omitting even Hunnis' final tag, "Fie, fie, vpon suche trecherie." The Dd.5.75 version is collated below with the first edition of the <u>Paradise</u>, 1576 (76), and with the second, 1578 (78). The latter introduces the significant readings at lines 3 and 10 which agree with Item 219 and which are also found in the 1580 and 1585 editions of the <u>Paradise</u>; thus, Stanford's text is slightly closer to these three editions than to the first. The rate of divergence, in any case, is about one word in ten.

title] The fruites of fained frendes *

1 chance] happ *; sirenes] Cirēs <u>78</u>

2 myne eyes] my eares *

3 voyce] noise <u>76</u>; great] sure *; was] is <u>78</u>

5 fortune; doth not] Treasure; doe not *

6 as...but] doe seme as frends and †

9 can; that<u>es</u>] gan; thus*

10 fauell] flatterer <u>76</u>; mightest] might *

12 yet; pretendst; art] Whiche; pretends; are *

] <u>after</u> 12: Fie, fie, vpon suche trechery. *

            Finis. W. H. <u>76</u>, W. H. <u>78</u>

Item 220

For a brief discussion of this unique text, see p. lxiii.

Item 221

This is a composite work, with its first stanza corresponding to the first six lines of poem 71 in the Paradise of Dainty Devices, and its last two stanzas to lines 7-18 of Paradise poem 95, beginning, "The bitter sweate that straines my yelded harte." Both poems appear in all editions, number 71 ascribed throughout to Lord Vaux, number 95, to Jasper Heywood.

The full text of Paradise poem 71 is found in Harleian MS 6910, f. 168^v (H), a collection with five other poems in common with Dd.5.75 (see p. xlvii); below, I collate the stanza of Item 221 which both manuscripts share. Another complete text of poem 71 was set to music in William Barley's New Book of Tabliture, 1597 (STC 1433). Later reprints include Alexander Grosart's Miscellanies of the Fuller Worthies' Library (4 vols.; privately printed, 1872-1876), IV, 371-372; Hebel and Hudson, p. 40; Fellowes, p. 352.

Paradise poem 95 appears in the Gorgeous Gallery of Gallant Inventions, 1578 (G), ed. Hyder Rollins (London, 1926), p. 72, and I have collated the Dd.5.75 text with the version of G in Rollins' reprint. The relevant stanzas of Paradise poems 71 and 95 are collated only with the edition of 1576 (76), the closest of all to Stanford's version, except that all editions after the fifth (published c. 1590), agree with the Dd.5.75 reading, "knowes," at line 6. For the Paradise texts, and for H, the average rate of variation from Item 221 is about one word in fourteen, while G varies by about one word in sixteen.

title] No pleasure without some paine 76

1 yt; quight] the; awaie 76 H

2 somtymes] sometyme 76 H

3 yt] the H

6 knowes] knoweth 76

7 that] which G; goodly] golden 76 G

8 alwayes] alwaie 76

9 mazed] mated 76, matched G; suit] sutes 76 G

11 betwene] betwixt G

12 trouble] troubles 76

14 ye] their G

16 paines] panges G

17 hap; none] hope; no 76

Item 222

Other texts of this poem occur in the Arundel Harington MS, ff. 167-167{v} (AH), and Harleian MS 7392, ff. 49{v}-50 (Kn), where it is attributed to Queen Elizabeth. The original signature in Kn, however, seems to have been, "FINIS I.M," although the initials have been crossed out by a hand other than the one which transcribed the poem, and the word "Regina," added. Bradner included this work among Elizabeth's doubtful poems, but noted that despite the Haringtons' close connections with the Queen, it is entered anonymously in their collection.[1] The evidence is very much against Elizabeth's authorship.

---

[1]Bradner, pp. 76-77; Bradner's text on pp. 8-9 is based on Dd.5.75. He collates all three manuscripts on p. 77, but since our findings vary, I have included my own collation below. Miss Hughey did not know of the Dd.5.75 and Kn texts at the time she published her edition of AH.

Although none of the texts are clearly descended from one of the other two, Dd.5.75 and AH are quite close in their readings, while Kn presents a divergent text.

    4 be] ar Kn

    10 how] Her AH

    13 earthly] youthly *, in the margin, full Kn

    14 rot] rotton *

    15 that] the Kn

    16 forgot] forgotten *

    17 men] new AH, all Kn

    18 lust desires] youth requiers Kn

    20 reckles] retcheles *; requires] desires Kn

    21 wch delightes] such desire Kn

    22 folie] follow Kn

    25 from] for AH; pleasures] pleasure Kn

    27 life] place Kn

    28 wherto] wherein AH

    29 or] nor Kn

    30 ne] nor *; yet] all Kn

    31 gan] can *; youthfull] willfull Kn

    32 cam] comes AH, com Kn; stealing] creping Kn

    33 the] These Kn

    34 do pleasure] did pleasure AH, delighted Kn

    35 my] myne AH; yeares] yeres, corrected in the margin, age Kn

    36 follie] follies *

    37 the] these Kn

    38 fond] vaine Kn

41 prooffes / pro̱cesse worn] processe worne A̲H̲, pro̱fes am warnd,
    corrected in the margin to, worne K̲n̲

42 am] And K̲n̲

43 might . . . byn] ought to be K̲n̲

45 by w^ch] wch by K̲n̲; proofe] will A̲H̲, word̲e̲s K̲n̲

] ffinis A̲H̲, FINIS ⟨I. M⟩ Regina K̲n̲

Item 223

Rollins believes that William Hunnis wrote this poem, which is attributed to "M. B." in the first edition of the <u>Paradise of Dainty Devices</u>, (1576), but to Hunnis in all later editions (Rollins' notes, p. 233). Stanford's text averages one variant per eighteen words from its closest <u>Paradise</u> text, the edition of 1576, collated below.

] <u>title</u>: He assureth his constancie.

2 my . . . fill] to fill my penne

3 but] With

4 euen . . . virtues] for your great vertues

7 lent her] ledd his

11 of tree] the tree

13 thou] then

16 euen for] For an

Items 224-226

For a brief discussion and classification of these unique texts, see p. lxi.

Item 227

These two stanzas comprise the last two stanzas of a poem appearing only in the first edition of the Paradise of Dainty Devices, 1576 (Rollins' number 68), where it is ascribed to Richard Hill. Item 227 is entered at the top of f. 46^r, and since its stanzas are numbered "2" and "3.," it is possible that Stanford did originally transcribe the entire poem and that a folio, or more, is missing before 46. This transcription is closer to the Paradise than any of the other three works from that anthology (Items 219, 221 and 223), averaging one variant per twenty-six words, still only one half as accurate as Stanford's copying from known sources. The error at line 5 strongly suggests manuscript transmission in that the spelling of "sothe" with a long 's' and descender to form the 'o' could easily be mistaken in secretary hand for "fle," although more than one such example would be needed to make manuscript transmission a probability.

1 but] by
5 fleashe] sothe
10 that lyued; none] But liued; no
] Richard Hill

Item 228

While the preceding seventeen poems, Items 212-227, cannot be confidently dated (see pp. 341-344), Item 228, entitled, "to ye Q. by ye players 1598," was unquestionably copied into Dd.5.75 shortly after 18 February 1598/99 (for further discussion of this poem, see p. lxiii).

Items 229-234

The only known edition of The Diana of George of Montemayor, Translated out of Spanish into English by Bartholomew Yong, was entered in the Stationers' Register 9 September 1598, and printed in that same year, according to its title page (STC 18044). Of all the poetry in this volume, Stanford entered in his anthology only the six verse riddles from Book V of the "Enamoured Diana, made by Gaspar Gil Polo," which Yong appended to his translation of Montemayor's Diana (Rr 5-6^v, pp. 477-480). Item 228, "to ye Q. by ye players 1598," was no doubt transcribed after 18 February 1598/99 (see p. lxiii), and the Diana riddles which follow must have been copied afterward, as indicated both by their position and the use in Items 229-234 of a different or newly sharpened quill. Probably then, Yong's Diana came out toward the end of 1598, and Stanford copied these six riddles from it shortly after Shrovetide, 1598/99.

In transcribing this 435 word text, Stanford made only five errors, counting the alternate readings of Item 229:2 as one, an average of one substantive error per eighty-seven words of text.

Item 229

  mi ⟨ght⟩
2 could] might

Item 230

5 herbers] herbes it

Item 231

7 she is] She's

Items 232-233 (no variants)

Item 234
  doth
3 that] that

9 breathes] breath

Items 235-236

The lover's paradoxical sufferings enumerated in Item 236 were commonplaces of Elizabethan poetry; Item 101 provides another example in Dd.5.75 of their sustained treatment. Item 236 appears to be a unique text, as is Item 235, which is discussed briefly on p. lxii.

Item 237

For discussion of this work, song IX from Sidney's Astrophil and Stella, see the prefatory note to Sidney's poems in Dd.5.75, pp. 269-276.

Items 238-251

For a brief discussion of these unique poems, see p. lx.

Items 252-280

For a discussion of these riddles and epigrams, see pp. lix-lx.

Items 281-283

For notes to these hymns, apparently written by Stanford himself, and discussion of this section of the manuscript, see pp. xlii, xxxviii-xxxix.

Items 284-293

(On the possibility that these poems were entered in a section of Dd.5.75 reserved by Stanford for his own works, see pp. xxxviii-xxxix).

From its position at the very bottom of the page, it would seem that Item 290, a couplet in praise of George Berkeley, was copied some time after the nine sonnets which fill folios 53-54. It could not have been written before George's birth in 1601, and probably 1607 to 1613 would be the reasonable limits of composition, while George was old enough to understand the verse, but not too old to be offended by it.

I have found no other texts of the sonnets, which Stanford almost certainly wrote, though for what purpose or to whom I cannot imagine. The "sweete girle" referred to in the last line of Item 292 suggests a courtship, although it seems incredible that a man who had read and transcribed love poems by Sidney, Spenser, or even Dyer, could have conducted his wooing with these cold and tedious exercises. Their pedantry suggests, indeed, that these are the strictly platonic works of the household tutor, innocently addressed, say, to young Theophila Berkeley (born 1596), recipient of a 1613 New Year's gift from Stanford (Item 93), or to one of the other ladies of the house (see pp. xiii-xx for further information about the Berkeley and Carey households). The date of composition of these sonnets may be roughly fixed between the mid-nineties, when Stanford seems to have begun writing sonnets, and his death in 1616.

The idea behind such sonnets as these originated with Petrarch, or perhaps even with Horace.[1] Petrarch's Rime 145, beginning, "Pommi ove 'l sole occide i fiori e l'erba," appeared in Tottel's Miscellany in an English translation by Henry Howard, Earl of Surrey (Rollins' number 12), and in a different, anonymous translation in the Phoenix Nest, 1593 (sig-

---

[1] Rollins, Tottel's Miscellany, II, 140.

nature M1^v). None of Stanford's versions could be considered translations of Petrarch's sonnet, yet they may be indebted to the Italian original, and not to any of the English translations, since Stanford alone translates "Pommi" as "Place me" (the others begin, "Set me"). Item 56, a very literal translation of Petrarch's <u>Rime</u> 21, is further evidence of Stanford's exposure to the works of that poet.

I have found no specific source from which Stanford might have drawn the geographical allusions for his "sonnet sequence"; perhaps there was none, and he simply relied throughout upon general knowledge. The result, at any rate, richly deserves the criticism George Puttenham levelled at Surrey's lone version of the sonnet, that "All . . . might haue bene said in these two verses. Set me wheresoeuer ye vvill, / I am and vvilbe yours still."[1]

Items 294-296

Stanford copied Item 293 on f. 54^r; f. 54^v is blank, while the numbered series of riddles and epigrams beginning with Item 252 and discontinued at Item 280, appears to be resumed on f. 55^r with Item 294. For further discussion of these texts, see pp. lix-lx.

Item 297

An expanded, prose version of this poem appeared as Riddle 21 in the earliest known edition of <u>A Help to Discourse</u>, 1619, K7^v-8^r (<u>STC</u> 1547). The text is widely divergent from Stanford's, but short enough to be given entire:

---

[1] Willcock and Walker, p. 223.

> A man and no man, seeing and not seeing in the
> light and not in the light, with a stone and no
> stone, strooke a bird and no bird, sitting and
> not sitting, vppon a tree and no tree.

The resolution, "Androgins the Euenuch in the twylight strooke a Bat, with a pumice stone, setting vpon a mustard tree," fits all but the "fleing not flying" of the Dd.5.75 version.

The <u>Help to Discourse</u>, compiled by W. B. (William Basse?), was a popular collection of anecdotes, riddles, and epigrams which saw thirteen editions by 1638; I have seen only the 1619 text, which also contains a version of Item 322.

Items 298-306

For a discussion of these riddles and epigrams, a continuation in numbered series of Items 252-280, and 294-297, see pp. lix-lx.

Items 307-308

These poems were written by young William Paget as New Year's gifts for 1581/82. The leaf they appear on, f. 57, originally preceded f. 1, but was at some time inserted between the present ff. 56 and 58. For more detailed analysis, see pp. 231-232.

Items 309-317

Folios 58-62^r are blank, and may represent the unfilled section of his anthology which Stanford devoted to his own poetry, represented now by Items 281-293. These nine Biblical riddles on f. 62^v seem to be unique texts which begin Stanford's <u>enfer</u>, a section of trivial and risque works which extends through f. 63. For further comment, see pp. xxxviii-xxxix.

Items 318-320

These riddles and axioms seem to be unique texts. For discussion of this portion of Stanford's anthology, see pp. xxxviii-xxxix.

Item 321

A manuscript version of this riddle in Rawlinson Poetry MS 212, f. 101^v, bears no apparent relation to Stanford's text, but may indicate that the other works on this page, f. 63^r, did circulate in manuscript.

] title: Aenigma in Acu

1 wonde &] wonder

2 therof is] of it tis

4 mouthe . . . by] Shee had no mouth but in

5 an] a

6 100 . . . clothes] And shee as oft her cloaths did cast

7 daunct] plaid

8 skipping] Leaping

9 question] counsell

10 yt was] Either

Item 322

Other versions of this riddle occur in Sloane MS 1446, f. 37 (S1), a text of the first four lines only, in Rawlinson Poetry MS 172, f. 9^v (Ra), and in A Help to Discourse (STC 1547), 1619, K3^v, Riddle 8 (HD).[1]

---

[1] A version of Item 297 appeared as Riddle 21 in the Help to Discourse, a popular collection of anecdotes, riddles, and epigrams which saw thirteen editions by 1638. The text of 1619 is the earliest known edition and the only one I have seen.

The texts of Ra and HD are nearly identical, while S1 and Dd.5.75 differ from them both and from each other:

    ] title: A Riddle S1 Ra

    1 A certain] There was a *; bespake] beespoke S1

    2 owner] maker S1

    3-4] reversed in Ra and HD

    3 bespake yt] bought it Ra HD

    4 &] om. *

    5 had yt did] hath it doth Ra HD

    6 whither] Whether Ra HD; had] hath Ra HD; yt] the thing Ra;
        yea] I HD, om. Ra

    resolution: a dead mans coffen] A Coffin S1, A Coffin bought by
            another for a dead man HD

Items 323-338

These riddles and adages seem to be unique texts; for further discussion of this section of Stanford's anthology, see pp. xxxviii-xxxix.

Item 339

The text of this couplet in Harleian MS 7392, f. 41, has been crossed out, though it is still perfectly legible; Stanford apparently felt no compunction about copying the verse, but added it to f. 63, a leaf devoted to similarly risque materials. Neither source gives any indication of authorship, while the occurrence of this work in the Harleian anthology, a product of the 1580's, merely suggests that it was composed and circulating in manuscript before 1590.

    1 mens hartes] men

    2 so wemen; hot] Even so they; om.

APPENDIXES

APPENDIX I
INDEX OF FIRST LINES

First Line (Prose works are indicated by italics)	Item Number
A certain man bespake a thing	322
A Crabtre face the felow had	62
A Diamond is a good fair stone	268
A fiershovell doth	38
A foole or a phisition I know not whither	255
A freind did to Erasmus write	272
A frend is not knowen but in necessitie	174
A gloue I do present	2
A goodlie thing in vs ther lies	49
A Grayhound must be hedded like a snake	20
A haples man of late whom loue had plunged in feares	204
A Lewder wretche ther lyves not vnder skye	146
A little map may represent	14
A man, not a man seing not seing	297
A newyeares gift receaue thrice honourd dame	68
A nice wife & a backe dore	152
A paper I do send as Herault of my hart	17
A pastie of red dere cold	318
A restless life by losse of that I loue	165
A sillie fowle was Barbarossa	254
A syllie Ihon surprisd with Ioy	191

First Line	Item Number
A table for a chamber is nedefull	42
A thatcht howse & a showre of raine	265
A vico'nt came vp to this towne	253
A wretch I lyue yet haue the world at will	236
Adeiu poloign adeiu terres desertes	182
Aetos is a cruel bloudie king	276
Alas when shall I ioy	217
Almes distributed vnto the indigent	177
Althoughe for a while thie vice thou maye hyde	176
Althoughe thou art not sprong	4
<u>An ignorant is worse then an affectionate iudge</u>	299
And hundred tongues and mouthes as many	150
<u>And when I haue beheld the market</u>	296
Are dreames but toyes to tosse in idle brayn	207
Are woemen craftie are they so?	252
As gallant as you see this youth	238
As in the night we see the sparkes revived	122
As long as a tonne or vessell may last	148
As newyeares gift this booke I send	39
As the diall hand tells ore	228
As wemen haue faces to set mens hartes on fire	339
At supper three companions sate	48
Backe bent smocke rent	332
Be merie and glad honest and virtuous	162
Because the nightes are long	60

First Line	Item Number
Behold a ladie fair al couered in her hair	270
Better yt is for a man to be mute	178
By fortunes good fortune who commeth in favour	155
By newyeres gift to seperate	12
By on thing somme men famous are	64
By ordring the tongue is a triall most true	154
By threatninges or by flatterie	140
Calamus pontificis men say it growes in Rome	279
Calisto was taken vp to heauen	277
Calling to mynd myn eye went long about	109
Cardanus & Pontanus bothe	259
Com gentle heardman sit with me	205
Com sorow com sitte down and mourn with me	99
Commaund a child to eat a pear	138
Content is turnd to malcontent I see	190
Couldst thou not frier Bacon	278
Cut with a < > com hunt	334
Deere mother I you wishe a merry yeare	78
Deere nephew pallas put not on thie dismall armour	63
Dere sister I this newyeares tyde	88
<u>Do I see godes most sacred holie word</u>	112
Draco maximus & fidelis	166
Draw home betyme ere youth take leaue	215
Enclosd betwene two walles	53
Entombed her doth lie a worthie wight	28

First Line	Item Number
Fayr Courteous Dame I the besech	7
Fair in a morn (see, Fayer philis)	
Fayer philis is the sheapheardes quene	201
False loue now shoote and spare not	120
Farewell since I must want of force	218
For covetous people to die yt is best	151
For newyeares guift accept this little booke	93
For serpentes never so deadly do sting	172
For to vnfold these riddles darke	8
From what part of the heaven	129
Goe booke as token to my mistris	58
Go my flock go get you hence	237
God send you all content & to bring forth a boy	86
Good fortune makes good bloud	300
Great wealth great health & holie mynd	239
Hard is the choise where the best is to bad	251
Hauing no other gift right noble dame	84
He brake vp howse put mise to grasse	144
He hath much nede of god his blessing	336
He is nether rich happie nor wise	157
He is not wise which knowing he must hence	158
He that at ons instance an other will defame	149
He that his mirthe hathe lost	95
He that of all men wilbe a correctour	171
He that to wrathe and anger is thrall	161

First Line	Item Number
He which of heavenly father was before	282
He worthiest is who all thinges knowes	245
Her face, her tongue, her wit (see, Your face)	
Here lies he who was born, & cried	29
Here lies interred to make wormes meate	181
Here lies the man (see, Here lies he)	
Holbourn is quasi holie bourn	294
How can that tree but wast & wither quight	221
How can you make a thing of weight	263
How durst a seelie painter vndertake	199
How is my sonne whose beames are shining bright	102
I alwayes would yet haue no will	98
I am a thing both fair and smooth	50
I am ashamed my name to tell	47
I haue a hole aboue my knee	330
I haue a thing & roughe yt is	331
I haue a thing yt standethe stiffe	327
I know not how yt comes to passe	212
I know not whie a fruictles ryme in print	183
I muse what iealousie did the moue	203
I pray the booke when I am gon	108
I saw a hill vppon a day	230
I saw a spider draw her thred	210
I saw a wonder wondrous was the sight	321
I saw my ladie weeping and loue did languish	132
I saw of late a lady were show	192

First Line	Item Number
I would yt were not as yt is	216
Yf all be true that lawyers say	187
Yf Davus do but talke amisse	142
Yf farting be naught els	269
Yf Momus wish had taken place	308
Yf passing by this place thou doe desire	18
Yf so thou wilt be wise	249
Yf that a beard doth make men wise	241
Yf that in virtue thou take any paynes	164
Imitating sir Iohn that was beyond sea born	298
In absence cheif to rest	337
In choise of frendes what chance had I	219
In everie place I fynd my greife and anguish	130
In every place of old and yong	54
In greene & childish aege in lustie yeares	26
In morning rising thinke thou hast	246
In sign of this new year and myndfull mynd	45
In sign that phebus now	11
In sign that thou art fair	59
<u>In the 7th yeare of this quenes raign</u>	267
<u>In the yeare of our lord twice fiftie</u>	271
In tyme the vnruly steere is made to draw	15
In vain he seekes for bewtie that excelleth	123
In yong & tender aege in youthfull yeares	25
In stede of gift a stammering verse I send	69
It was my chance of late to see	324

First Line	Item Number
Yt were better for a woman to be barreyn	153
Ioy so delights my hart	119
Ladie that hand of plentie	126
Ladie your looke so gentle	128
Laertes sonne what so I say	141
Laeticia afficior mihi ter gratissima mater	30
Last newyeares day I wish'd the well	80
Last newyeares day my rugged rime	71
Let all reioce & sing for birth of Iesus Christ	281
Let your many officers your tongue well advise	262
Like as from heaven the dew full softly showring	133
Like those sicke folke in whom straunge humours flow	101
Liquide and watrie pearles loue wept	136
Loe here in signe of seruice which is due	61
Locke vp sweete liddes the threasures of my hart	96
Long tyme mans becke for to obey	46
Ludi magister qui quicquid per egisset in nates	335
Mack Mackrell in may & Iune	256
Mary Bloomer hath the properties of an honest wife	261
Maximus olim Ille orientis qui iure certo	31
Me thinkes that bewtie hath but small avail	247
Myn Alderleivest lady deere	16
More fayr then most fair full of the lyving fyre	197
More than most fair (see, More fayr then)	
Most louing mother this new year	87

First Line	Item Number
My Caue I wishe the this new yeare	90
My deerest dame this history I send	92
My Egerton receaue my verse	73
My Egerton this paper I you send	72
My fitche I the salute	83
My fitche I wishe the store of heauenly grace	74
My Grandame dere I do reioice	32
My Iohn I would thou shouldest me gyue	52
My knight as many happie happes I wishe	70
My loue is pure & true, I never lerned to flatter	1
My masters you that read my rime	213
My Nan althoughe I haue scarse tyme	75
My Powel I this newyeares tyde	91
My wife like Nioba is turnd to stone	309
Nature a niggard of her giftes hath shewed herself	320
Nature hath shewed her self to me vnkynd	319
Nere to a sheapheard did a damsell sit	229
Nethor life nor death affordes ease	94
No faith nor frend nor suertie vnder sonne	114
No miracle no oracle no beaste no birde no man	273
Now leaue & let me rest, dame pleasure be content	222
Now o now I nedes must part	209
O Greife yf yet my greif be not beleved	121
O lord< > Let heaven & earth reioice	283
O Maria scota meretrix	214

First Line	Item Number
Of bodylie imprisonmentes sicknes is the cheif	159
Of fairest mother more then fairest child	189
Of force I must prayse her I like her so well	111
Olympus head is raised aboue the reache of wynd	105
On whitson even last at night	184
On brother by my fathers side, I haue	9
On lyving with two dead hath made on lyue	51
Pastereau ie vous aime bien	180
Permission pages let a gibbihorse passe	303
Place me in England scotland or hibernia	293
Place me in Europe Afric Asia	292
Place me in Iapan Zeilan Barbarie	289
Place me ithe town which ay enquird for newse	287
Place me i the town which name toke from hartes horn	284
Place me ithe town which was the ey of Greece	286
Place me on Tuarus Athos Carpathus	291
Place me where I did sleape 300 yeares	288
Place me where pawle shooke viper from his hand	285
Plucke vp your heart leaue all to me	139
Prayer to god is the only mean	160
Right dreadfull is the talke what thing & pain is hell	226
Ring out your belles let mourning shewes be spred	106
Robyn Hoode in grenewood stode (prose after the first two lines)	274
Shad shad an other cries	257

First Line	Item Number
She that doth go to euerie faire	211
She that was thought so full with widsom fraught	275
Shew me a horse of such a kynd	233
Syr Ihon hunt, cut my punt	338
Sir Iohn I the salute, & wishe the this new yeare	81
Syr on is my brother by my fathers syde	10
Sith that the sonne his yearly course hath brought	23
Sitting late with sorow sleping	198
Sleepe Sleepe myn only Iuel	134
So fair a creature never I, with eyes of myne	6
So gratious is thie sweete self	116
Sound out my voice with pleasaunt tunes	135
Sweete Cosin though I want som gift	22
Sweete gloue the witnes of my secret blisse	194
Sweete loue when hope was flowring	125
Sweet Phyllis is (see, Fayer philis)	
Sweete roote saye thou the roote of my desire	103
Sweete sister you are riche in golden giftes	89
Sybyllas tyme I wishe you sister deere	77
Tell me good sirs what bird is yt that flies	234
Tell me what ladie by 2 lordes	316
Tell me what maister he may be	232
Tell wher yt was the cat would see	315
The bitter sweet that strains (see, How can that tree)	
The doues shall leaue to haunt the stately towres	76
The earth no worse a monster bredes	21

First Line	Item Number
The face they say a picture is	3
The fair Diana never more revived	118
The faithfull drake most great of might	167
The feoffees were but vlpian	305
The fier to see my wrong for anger burnes	107
The first is my vncle of my fathers side	57
The frendes whom profit and lucre encrease	163
The gentle season of the year	208
The glore great of blisfull fate	225
The goodwife hathe in store	326
The goodwife went to the market	325
<u>The horrour that all or most men find</u>	295
The marigold all flowers doth passe	5
The more that a man hath of abundaunce	156
The nightingale so pleasent and so gay	137
The noblest clown did wed	310
The palme ere yt by force doth faynt	97
The roister weares not alwayes plumes	143
The sainct I serue (see, Thus while I helde the Ele)	
The state of fraunce as now yt standes	113
The tyme is ronne about & Phebus golden sphere	307
The valiantst prancke is not to hack & kill	302
The Virtuous lady Lee Sir Henry Lee his wife	19
Then comes a third blest might she be	258
Ther is a thing as I suppose	333

First Line	Item Number
Ther is a thing is granted free	280
Ther is no good for to be don	145
Ther is somtyme a serpent to be sene	266
Ther was a ladie leaned her back to a wall	328
These that be certain signes of my tormenting	117
They that describe the world thre famous lakes do note	104
Theues came to my house & wrapt me all in woe	323
This a. b. c. you do read	33
This bed may well be cald	36
This booke good matter doth in yt contain	40
This brushe dothe serue to kepe our garmentes net	44
This chimney to this chamber is	35
This fauour streight was tane away	65
This glasse the outward shapes	37
This globe to vs you see	34
This rushe I take in hand	41
This window dothe to vs the north directly show	43
Thou lookest in glasse to see thie self	243
Thou nedest not greatly recke my frend	248
Three thinges are in the world which more the vemin vile offend [sic]	244
Thrice honourd dame yf I a gift estem'd	66
Thrice honourd lord the prop & cheifest stay	79
Thrice Phebus in the Goate hath taken vp his Inn	82
Thus while I held the eele but by the tayle	227
Thie glasse deceaves the gellia	242

First Line	Item Number
To beastes much hurt hapneth	170
To fayn to flatter to glose to lie	168
To homer once this bone a sawcie seaman gaue	304
To pray I will not cease	67
To purchase peace at those fayre eyes of thyne	56
To strike an other yf that thou pretend	169
To two freindes every day	260
Transformed in shew but more transformed in mynd	200
Two bookes vppon a table lay	185
Two stones hathe yt or els yt is wrong	329
vraiement vous estes importun	179
<u>Ware & wades mill are worth all london.</u>	306
We of these .2. children are the 2. mothers	55
Weried with thoughtes of troubled anguishe	115
What bird is that so light	231
What Cambden wrote for proffit & delight	85
What yf thie mystresse now will needs vnconstant be	188
What length of verse can serue braue mopsas good to show	196
What meanethe loue to nest him	124
What pilot ever with his ship did sail	311
What Pilot ever with his ship throughe deepest seas	317
What sonnes? what fathers? sonnes and fathers fighting?	186
What thing a man in tender age hath most in vre	147
What tongue can her perfections tell (first two lines only)	100

First Line	Item Number
What tongue can her perfections tell (complete text)	195
What woer ever bare the bell	313
What ever yt chaunce the of any to hear	175
When I was a little swain	206
When I was fayr and yong and favour graced me	202
When men to catche the fleting fish, shall angle in the ayre	13
When on their helmes captaines did horsetailes weare	301
When pallas lost the price & Iuno toke offence	224
When shall I cease lamenting	131
When turtle shall forsake his make	27
When turtle shall haue many a make	24
Where will wantes wit welth worketh woe	250
Whiles depe conceipt renowned quene	220
Whilst nature doubted which to make	290
Who ever did most of on kin from libick land convay	314
Who spares to toyle & spares not how to spend	240
Who will ascend to heaven and ther obtain me	127
Whose deathe bemond before he died	312
Whie dothe the syluer smithe like a sot	264
William Parrie was ap Harrie by his name	110
Wisdom in bookes with the booke will rotte	173
With painted speache I list not proue my conning	223
You loue you say & loue for loue you craue	235
Your face your tongue your witte	193

APPENDIX II

INDEX OF AUTHORS

Author and Item (An asterisk indicates that the Item is ascribed to the author in Dd.5.75).

Baldwin, William (or, Thomas Paulfreyman), 147-164, 168-178

Berkeley, George, thirteenth Baron Berkeley, 69-80*, 81, 82-83*, 87-90*, 91

Berners, Dame Juliana, 20 (?)

Breton, Nicholas, 198 (?), 201

Churchyard, Thomas, 215

Derby (see Stanley)

Desportes, Philippe, 182

Dyer, Sir Edward, 95, 216

Elizabeth I, Queen of England, 112*, 202 (?), 222 (?)

Gil Polo, Gaspar (translated by Bartholomew Yong), 229-234

Gorges, Sir Arthur, 192, 193 (?), 199, 204, 205, 208

Heywood, Jasper, 221 (the last twelve lines only)

Hill, Richard, 227 (?)

Hoskyns, John, 29 (?)

Hunnis, William, 219, 223 (?)

Paulfreyman, Thomas (see Baldwin)

Paget, William, fourth Baron Paget, 1*, 2-17, 21-22, 23*, 24-27, 30-31*, 32, 307*, 308

Petrarch, Francis (an anonymous English translation of _Rime_ 21), 56*

Ralegh, Sir Walter, 109*, 113 (?), 193 (?)

Author and Item

Sidney, Sir Philip, 96, 100-103, 106-107, 194-196, 200, 237

Spenser, Edmund, 197

Stanford, Henry, 33-46, 58-61, 66*, 67-68, 84-85*, 92-93*, 166-167, 281-289 (?), 291-293 (?)

Stanley, Ferdinando, fifth Earl of Derby, 165*

Straparola, Francesco (Riddles Englished from a French translation), 47-54

Vaux, Thomas, second Baron Vaux, 221 (first six lines only)

Yong, Bartholomew (see Gil Polo)

SELECTED BIBLIOGRAPHY

Historical and Biographical

Arber, Edward, ed. A Transcript of the Registers of the Company of Stationers of London. 5 vols. London, 1875-1894.

Armytage, Sir George John, ed. Allegations for Marriage Licenses Issued by the Bishop of London, 1611 to 1828, Part II. Publications of the Harleian Society, Vol. XXVI. London, 1887.

_____, ed. Middlesex Pedigrees. Publications of the Harleian Society, Vol. LXV. London, 1914.

Black, J. B. The Reign of Elizabeth. 2nd ed. Oxford, 1959.

Calendar of Salisbury Manuscripts, Part III. London, 1889.

Carey, Sir Robert. Memoirs of Sir Robert Cary. Edinburgh, 1808.

Cass, Frederick Charles. "Notes on the Church and Parish of Monken Hadley." Transactions of the London and Middlesex Archaeological Society, Vol. IV. London, 1875.

Chambers, E. K. The Elizabethan Stage. 4 vols. Oxford, 1923.

_____. Sir Henry Lee. Oxford, 1936.

Cockayne, George Edward. The Complete Peerage. 14 vols. London, 1910-1959.

Corbett, Julian S. Drake and the Tudor Navy. 2 vols. London, 1899.

Dasent, John Roche, ed. Acts of the Privy Council of England. New Series, 32 vols. London, 1890-1907.

D'Ewes, Sir Simonds. A Compleat Journal of the Votes, Speeches and Debates, Bothe of the House of Lords and House of Commons Throughout the Whole Reign of Queen Elizabeth. London, 1693.

Encyclopaedia Britannica. 24 vols. Chicago, 1968.

Fellowes, Edmund H. William Byrd. London, 1936.

Feuillerat, Albert, ed. Blackfriars Records, Part I. The Malone Society Collections, Vol. II. Oxford, 1913.

Foss, Edward. Biographia Iuridica, A Biographical Dictionary of the Judges of England. Boston, 1870.

Foster, Joseph. Alumni Oxoniensis. 4 vols. London, 1891-1892.

_____, ed. Churchwardens' Accounts of St. Mary the Great Cambridge from 1504 to 1635. Cambridge, 1905.

Freer, Martha Walker. Henry III, King of France and Poland. 3 vols. London, 1858.

Gillow, Joseph. A Literary and Biographical History . . . of the English Catholics. 5 vols. London, n.d.

Hicks, Leo. "The Strange Case of Dr. William Parry." Studies, An Irish Quarterly Review of Letters Philosophy and Science, XXXVII (1948), 343-362.

Judson, Alexander C. The Life of Edmund Spenser. Baltimore, 1945.

Lemon, Robert, ed. Calendar of State Papers, Domestic Series, Elizabeth, 1581-1590. London, 1865.

Lomas, Sophie Crawford, ed. Calendar of State Papers Foreign Series, July 1583-July 1584. London, 1914.

Lysons, Daniel, and Lysons, Samuel. Magna Britannia. 3 vols. London, 1808.

Members of Parliament, Part I: Parliaments of England, 1213-1702. Ordered by the House of Commons to be printed. n.p., 1878.

Metcalfe, Walter C., ed. The Visitations of Hertfordshire . . . in 1572 . . . and . . . 1634. Publications of the Harleian Society, Vol. XXII. London, 1886.

Neale, J. E. Elizabeth I and her Parliaments. 2 vols. London, 1953.

Nichols, John Gough, ed. The Herald and Genealogist. 7 vols. London, 1861-1868.

_____. The Progresses, and Public Processions of Queen Elizabeth. 3 vols. London, 1788.

Phillips, James Emerson. Images of A Queen. Berkeley, 1964.

Pierce, William, An Historical Introduction to the Marprelate Tracts. London, 1908.

Shaw, William A. The Knights of England. 2 vols. London, 1906.

Smith, Irwin. Shakespeare's Blackfriars Playhouse. New York, 1964.

Smyth, John, of Nibley. The Berkeley Manuscripts. Edited by Sir John Maclean. 3 vols. Gloucester, 1883.

Stein, Harold. Studies in Spenser's Complaints. New York, 1934.

Stephen, Leslie, and Lee, Sir Sidney. Dictionary of National Biography. 63 vols. London, 1885-1900.

Stokes, E., ed. Index of Wills Proved in the Prerogative Court of Canterbury. The Index Library, Vol. V. London, 1912.

Strathmann, Ernest Albert. "Lady Carey and Spenser." English Literary History, II (April, 1935), 34-47.

Strype, John. A Survey of the Cities of London and Westminster . . . Corrected, Improved, and very much Enlarged . . . by John Strype. 2 vols. London, 1720.

_____. Annals of the Reformation. 4 vols. London, 1820-1840.

Venn, John, and Venn, J. A. Alumni Cantabrigienses. 4 vols. Cambridge, 1922-1924.

Weldon, Sir Anthony. The Court and Character of King James. London, 1650.

Williams, Franklin B., Jr. Index of Dedications and Commendatory Verses in English Books Before 1641. London, 1962.

Williams, Sarah, ed. Letters Written by John Chamberlain During the Reign of Elizabeth. Camden Society Publications, Vol. XIX. London, 1861.

Literary

A Catalogue of the Harleian Manuscripts in the British Museum. 4 vols. London, 1808-1812.

A Catalogue of the Manuscripts Preserved in the Library of the University of Cambridge. 5 vols. Cambridge, 1856-1867.

Arber, Edward. An English Garner. 8 vols. Birmingham, 1877-1896.

Ault, Norman, ed. Elizabethan Lyrics. London, 1925.

Baldwin, William. A Treatise of Moral Philosophy. 8 editions, 1567-1600, STC 1259-1265.

Barley, William. A New Booke of Tabliture. 1596. STC 1433.

Bartlett, Phyllis Brooks. The Poems of George Chapman. New York, 1941.

Basse, William (?). A Help to Discourse. 1619. STC 1547.

Ben Johnson's Jests: or the Wit's Pocket Companion. 6th ed. London, 1760.

Bennet, John. Madrigalls to Foure Voyces. 1599. STC 1882.

Berners, Dame Juliana (?). The Book of Hawking and Hunting. 1485-1586. STC 3308-3313.

_____. The Boke of Saint Albans, by Dame Juliana Berners. Facsimile reprint with an introduction by William Blades. London, 1901.

Bodenham, John. Belvedere, or the Garden of the Muses. 1600. STC 3189.

Bond, R. Warwick, ed. The Complete Works of John Lyly. 3 vols. Oxford, 1902.

Bond, William H. "The Cornwallis-Lysons Manuscript and the Poems of John Bentley." Joseph Quincy Adams Memorial Studies. Edited by James G. McManaway, et al. Washington, D. C., 1948.

Boyce, Dr. William. Cathedral Music. 3 vols. London, 1849.

Bradner, Leicester, ed. The Poems of Queen Elizabeth I. Providence, Rhode Island, 1964.

Breton, Nicholas. Brittons bowre of delights. 1597. STC 3634.

British Museum General Catalogue of Printed Books. 263 vols. London, 1957-1966.

Buck, B. C., et al., ed. Tudor Church Music. 10 vols. Oxford, 1922-1929.

Buck, P. M., Jr. "Add. MS. 34064 and Spenser's Ruins of Time and Mother Hubberd's Tale." Modern Language Notes, XXII (1907), 41-46.

Bühler, Curt F. "Four Elizabethan Poems." Joseph Quincy Adams Memorial Studies. Edited by James G. McManaway, et al. Washington, D. C., 1948.

Bullough, Geoffrey, ed. The Poems and Dramas of Fulke Greville. 2 vols. Edinburgh, 1938.

Burney, Charles. A General History of Music From the Earliest Ages to the Present Period, 1789. Reprinted with critical and historical notes by Frank Mercer. 4 vols. New York, 1935.

Byrd, William. Songs of Sundrie Natures. 1589. STC 4256.

Camden, William. Britain, or a Chorographicall Description of the Most Flourishing Kingdomes, England, Scotland, and Ireland. Translated by Philemon Holland. 1610. STC 4509.

_____. Britain, or a Chorographicall Description of the Most Flourishing Kingdomes, England, Scotland, and Ireland. Translated by Philemon Holland. 1637. STC 4510.

_____. Remaines of A Greater Worke, Concerning Britaine. 1605. STC 4521.

Castiglione, Baldesar. The Book of the Courtier. Translated by Charles S. Singleton. Anchor Books. New York, 1959.

Chalmers, Alexander. The Works of the English Poets. 21 vols. London, 1810.

Chapman, George. An Epicede or Fvnerall Song: On the most disastrous Death, of the Highborne Prince of Men, Henry Prince of Wales. 1612. STC 4974.

_____. Homer, Prince of Poets: Translated in Twelve Books of his Iliads. 1610. STC 13633.

Churchyard, Thomas. A Pleasaunte Laborinth Called Churchyeardes Chance. 1580. STC 5250.

_____. Churchyard's Challenge. 1593. STC 5220.

_____. Pleasant Discourse of Court and Wars. 1596. STC 5249.

Cummings, Laurence. "John Finet's Miscellany." Unpublished Ph.D. dissertation, Washington University, 1960.

_____. "Spenser's Amoretti VIII: New Manuscript Versions." Studies in English Literature, IV (Winter, 1964), 125-135.

Day, Cyrus Lawrence, and Murrie, Eleanore Boswell. English Song-Books, 1651-1702. London, 1940.

Desportes, Philippe. Diverses Amours et Autres Oeuvres Meslées. Edited by Victor E. Graham. Geneva, 1963.

_____. Les Oevvres De Philippes Des Portes. Lyons, 1583.

_____. Les Oevvres De Philippes De Portes. Antwerp, 1591.

_____. Les Premieres Oevvres De Philippes Des Portes, Av Roy De France et de Polongne. Paris, 1581.

_____. Oeuvres de Philippe Desportes. Edited by Alfred Michiels. Paris, 1858.

Dodge, R. E. Neil, ed. The Complete Poetical Works of Spenser. Cambridge, 1908.

Dowland, John. First Booke of Songes or Ayres. 1597. STC 7091.

East, Michael. Second Set of Madrigals. 1606. STC 7461.

Fellowes, Edmund H. English Madrigal Verse. 3rd ed. Revised and enlarged by Frederick W. Sternfeld and David Greer. Oxford, 1967.

Forrest, William. New Ballade of the Marigolde. 1570. STC 11186.

Grierson, Herbert, ed. The Poems of John Donne. 2 vols. Oxford, 1912.

Grosart, Alexander, ed. The Complete Works in Prose and Verse of Nicholas Breton. 2 vols. Edinburgh, 1879.

_____. The Dr. Farmer Chetham MS., Being a Commonplace Book in the Chetham Library, Manchester, Temp. Elizabeth, James I, and Charles I. Publications of the Chetham Society, Vols. LXXXIX-XC. Manchester, 1873.

_____. Miscellanies of The Fuller Worthies' Library. 4 vols. Privately printed, 1872-1876.

Grose, Francis, and Astle, Thomas. The Antiquarian Repertory. 4 vols. London, 1807-1809.

Grundy, Joan, ed. The Poems of Henry Constable. Liverpool, 1960.

Gryndall, William. Hawking, Hunting, Fouling, and Fishing. 1596. STC 12412.

Hannah, John, ed. The Poems of Sir Walter Raleigh. London, 1892.

Harbage, Alfred. Annals of English Drama. Revised by S. Schoenbaum. Philadelphia, 1964.

Harington, Sir John. Orlando Furioso in English Heroical Verse. 1591. STC 746.

Hawkins, Sir John. A General History of the Science and Practice of Music. 5 vols. London, 1776.

Hebel, J. William, and Hudson, Hoyt H., eds. Poetry of the English Renaissance. New York, 1929.

Heywood, Thomas. Troia Britanica, or, Great Britaines Troy. 1609. STC 13366.

Holinshed, Raphael. The first and second volumes of Chronicles. 1587. STC 13569.

Hughey, Ruth, ed. The Arundel Harington Manuscript of Tudor Poetry. 2 vols. Columbus, 1960.

Kirbye, George. First Set of English Madrigalls. 1597. STC 15010.

Latham, Agnes M. C., ed. The Poems of Sir Walter Ralegh. The Muses Library. London, 1951.

McKerrow, Ronald B. An Introduction to Bibliography for Literary Students. Oxford, 1927.

_____, ed. The Works of Thomas Nashe. 5 vols. Reprinted with corrections and supplementary notes by F. P. Wilson. Oxford, 1958.

Marre Mar-Martin: or, Marre-Martins medling, in a manner misliked. 1589. STC 17462.

Montemayor, Jorge de. Diana. Translated by Bartholomew Yong. 1598. STC 18044.

Morley, Thomas. Canzonets to Five and Six Voices. 1597. STC 18126. Reprinted by Edmund H. Fellowes, The English Madrigal School, Vol. III. London, 1921.

_____. First Book of Airs. 1600. Not listed by the STC. Reprinted by Edmund H. Fellowes, The English School of Lutenist Song Writers, Vol. XVI. London, 1932.

Nashe, Thomas. Christ's Tears over Jerusalem. 1593. STC 18366.

_____. Mar-Martine. 1589. STC 17461.

_____. The Terrors of the Night. 1594. STC 18379.

Navarre, Margaret of Angoulême, Queen of. The Queene of Nauarres Tales. Containing, Verie pleasant Discourses of fortunate Louers. 1597. STC 17323.

Osborn, Louise. The Life, Letters and Writings of John Hoskyns, 1566-1638. New Haven, 1937.

Park, Thomas, ed. Nugae Antiquae. 2 vols. London, 1804.

Parsons, Robert. The copie of a Letter Wryten by a Master of Arte of Cambridge. 1584. STC 19399.

Peacham, Henry. The Compleat Gentleman. 1625. STC 19502a.

Peerson, Martin. Mottects or Grave Chamber Musique. 1630. STC 19552.

Pollard, A. W., et al. A Short-Title Catalogue of Books Printed in England, Scotland, and Ireland. London, 1926.

Popellimière, Lancelot Voisin, Seigneur de la. The Historie of France, The Foure First Bookes. Translated anonymously. 1595. STC 11276.

Puttenham, George. The Arte of English Poesie. 1589. STC 20519. Edited by Gladys Willcock and Alice Walker. London, 1936.

Ringler, William A., Jr. "Poems Attributed to Sir Philip Sidney." Studies in Philology, XLVII (1950), 126-151.

_____, ed. The Poems of Sir Philip Sidney. Oxford, 1962.

Robertson, Jean, ed. Nicholas Breton: Poems not Hietherto Reprinted. Liverpool, 1952.

Rollins, Hyder E., ed. A Gorgeous Gallery of Gallant Inventions. Cambridge, Mass., 1926.

_____, ed. A Handful of Pleasant Delights. Dover Books. New York, 1965.

_____, ed. A Poetical Rhapsody. 2 vols. Cambridge, Mass., 1931-1932.

_____, ed. England's Helicon. 2 vols. Cambridge, Mass., 1935.

_____, ed. The Paradise of Dainty Devices. Cambridge, Mass., 1927.

_____, ed. The Phoenix Nest. Cambridge, Mass., 1931.

_____, ed. Tottel's Miscellany. Revised edition. Cambridge, Mass., 1966.

Saluste du Bartas, Guillaume de. Bartas: his deuine weekes and workes. Translated by John Sylvester. 1611. STC 21651.

Sandison, Helen Estabrook, ed. The Poems of Sir Arthur Gorges. Oxford, 1953.

Sargent, Ralph. At the Court of Queen Elizabeth, The Life and Lyrics of Sir Edward Dyer. London, 1935.

Scott, Mary Augusta. Elizabethan Translations from the Italian. Boston, 1916.

Spenser, Edmund. Amoretti and Epithalamion. 1595. STC 23076.

_____. Colin Clouts Come Home Againe. 1595. STC 23077.

_____. The Faerie Queene. 1609. STC 23083.

Straparola, Giovanni Francesco. Les Facetieuses Nuits de Straparole Traduites par Jean Louveau et Pierre de Larivey. Introduction by P. Jannet. Paris, 1857.

_____. Le Piacevoli Notti. Venice, 1550.

_____. The Nights of Straparola. Translated by W. G. Waters. London, 1894.

Tannenbaum, Samuel. "Unfamiliar Versions of Some Elizabethan Poems." PMLA, XLV (1930), 809-821.

Tatlock, J. S. P. The Legendary History of Britain. Berkeley, 1950.

Taylor, John. All the Workes of Iohn Taylor the Water Poet. 1630. STC 23725.

The Bannatyne Manuscript. Printed for the Hunterian Club. 4 vols. Glasgow, 1873-1894.

Warner, William. Albion's England. 1597. STC 25082.

Wilke, G. A. "The Sequence of the Writings of Fulke Greville, Lord Brooke." Studies in Philology, LVI (1959), 489-503.

Yonge, Nicholas. Musica Transalpina. 1588. STC 26094.

_____. Musica Transalpina. 1597. STC 26095

For Product Safety Concerns and Information please contact our EU representative GPSR@taylorandfrancis.com
Taylor & Francis Verlag GmbH, Kaufingerstraße 24, 80331 München, Germany

www.ingramcontent.com/pod-product-compliance
Lightning Source LLC
Chambersburg PA
CBHW071232300426
44116CB00008B/1010